Sound Mind Investing

Dear Valued Reader:

I hope this book has been helpful to you! If so, I believe you'd be interested in knowing about my "Sound Mind Investing" newsletter and website. Launched in 1990, it has grown to become America's best-selling investment resource written from a biblical perspective. It takes you out into the marketplace and helps you implement the investment philosophy and strategies explained in this book, and much more. It offers:

- Biblical goal-setting. Our Four Levels format, based on the priorities taught in Scripture as laid out in this book, helps you do "first things first." In every monthly issue, you get help in four areas.

- In Strengthening Your Foundation (the Level 1 column), you'll receive tips on how to: apply strategies for getting debt-free, make wise purchasing decisions, build savings, choose appropriate insurance protection, navigate marital financial issues, and many more.

- In Developing Your Investing Plan (Level 2), we focus on topics that help you implement an investment strategy that takes into account your personal goals, attitude toward risk-taking, and current season of life. We explain investing essentials, discuss SMI's core investing strategies, and help you decide which is best for your situation.

- In Broadening Your Portfolio (Level 3), you'll learn about a wider range of investment securities and markets. By further diversifying your holdings, you can create a more efficient, less volatile portfolio.

- In Looking Toward Retirement (Level 4), we talk about issues of increasing importance as you move through your 50s, 60s, and beyond. We'll address topics such as reducing your investment risk, generating income from your portfolio, Social Security strategies, long-term health care, advanced giving strategies, and estate planning.

- SMI Investing Strategies. Powerful, yet easy-to-use strategies that can be incorporated into the long-term investing plan this SMI Handbook is helping you create. You'll gain access to the core strategies described in this book (see chapters 14, 17, and 18), as well as several optional advanced strategies.

- Instructive feature articles. Each month, our cover article will give you a detailed look at a particular economic, investing, or biblical issue. As you grow in your understanding of investing principles, you'll be better equipped to take charge of your financial life and reach your long-term goals.

In my newsletter, I make very few assumptions about your level of understanding of economic and investing matters. That means using everyday, plain-English language (rather than industry jargon) to teach and instruct you.

To learn more about "Sound Mind Investing," visit our website at www.soundmindinvesting.com and check out our subscription options.

For less than the cost of a daily cup of coffee, I'll lead you through the financial maze and show you how to make consistently sound, biblically consistent investing decisions.

I hope to hear from you soon!

Cordially,

Austin

If you're looking for a trustworthy guide through the financial maze, consider what these respected leaders have said about Austin Pryor and *The Sound Mind Investing Handbook.*

"*The Sound Mind Investing Handbook* is an inviting, step-by-step primer for anyone who finds the subject intimidating. Austin's 30 years of experience in the field make him a knowledgeable guide, yet he writes in an easy-to-understand manner that will appeal to those just starting out. And best of all, it's Biblically-based, equipping readers to 'have more so they can give more.' *The Sound Mind Investing Handbook* will help Christians build eternal portfolios."

Howard Dayton
Co-founder with Larry Burkett / Crown Financial Ministries

"I have had the privilege of knowing Austin Pryor since the beginning of my Christian life. There are few that I have as much respect for and confidence in than Austin. His counsel in the investment area has proven to be extraordinarily wise and discerning over a long time period. I can recommend *The Sound Mind Investing Handbook* without hesitation as a 'must read' for anyone interested in investing in very uncertain economic times. I consider it a privilege to be able to make this recommendation."

Ron Blue
Founding Partner / Ronald Blue & Co.

"When I wrote *The Glorious Journey,* I had to include a quote by Austin Pryor in my book. Here is a man of great insight who has the ability to make difficult subjects easy to comprehend. It is obvious that *The Sound Mind Investing Handbook* combines biblical wisdom with very practical and understandable application. Anyone would profit from reading this book."

Dr. Charles F. Stanley
Senior Pastor / First Baptist Church of Atlanta

"As a communicator, I'm always on the lookout for resources that speak clearly and knowledgeably. Austin Pryor does exactly that in *The Sound Mind Investing Handbook*. It is thorough, easy-to-understand, and grounded in 40 years of successful investing experience. The *Handbook* is a valuable sources of practical guidance for anyone who wants their financial decisions to line up with biblical principles. Austin and *Sound Mind Investing* get my highest recommendation."

Josh McDowell
Josh McDowell Ministry / Author of More Than a Carpenter

"If you're looking for an attractive easy-to-follow investment guide written in plain English, look no further. Austin Pryor writes without vested interests in any specific plan or fund. This means greater candor and objectivity. I'm frankly skeptical of a lot of stuff coming out of the financial realm with its short-term 'for this life only' perspective. Austin is a man with a larger and better perspective."

Randy Alcorn
Director of Eternal Perspective Ministries / Author of Money, Possessions & Eternity

"In the same way that I am no economist, I'm not exactly an investment wizard either. That's why I am a huge fan of Austin Pryor, author of *The Sound Mind Investing Handbook*. I suggest you get a copy and read it straight through. It's not at all difficult, but the knowledge you will gain will give you tremendous confidence. Everything I know about investing I learned from Austin Pryor."

Mary Hunt
Founder and Editor / Debt-Proof Living

"Here's my checklist for what makes a great financial resource — consistent with God's word, an easy-to-understand writing style, practical lessons that are relevant to my situation, and specific advice on investing for retirement. Fortunately, Austin Pryor has covered all these bases with his *Sound Mind Investing Handbook* and other financial resources. He has taught me so many scriptural stewardship lessons that I'd overlooked before. I heartily recommend Austin's counsel."

Dave Stone
Senior Pastor / Southeast Christian Church / Louisville, Kentucky

A road map that includes what you

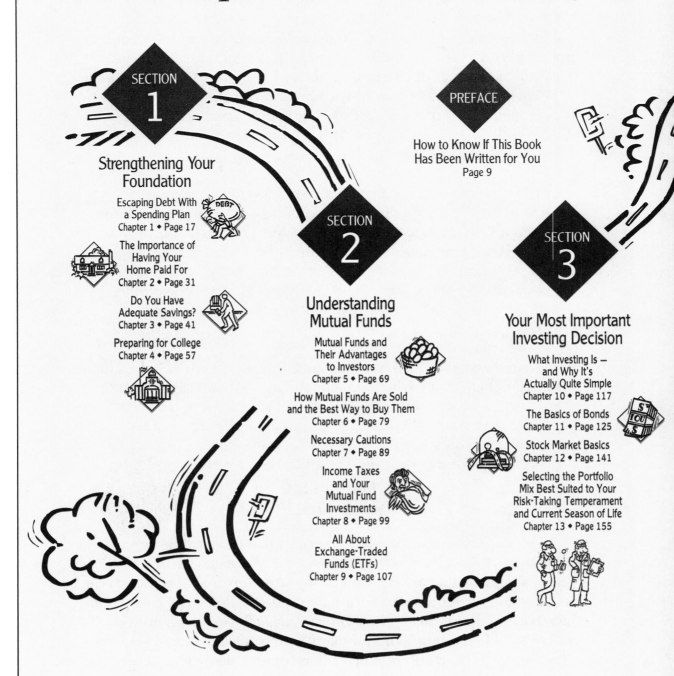

need to know and where to find it

About the Authors

Austin Pryor co-founded his investment management firm in 1978 where he saw his average client account return 25.5% annually during its first five years of operations, good enough to be rated among the top 5% of investment advisers nationwide. You can read about his years as a money manager in chapters 12 and 28.

In 1990, he launched *Sound Mind Investing*, a financial newsletter targeted to the Christian community. It has grown to become America's best-selling investment resource written from a biblical perspective.

Austin was a regular guest on Larry Burkett's *Money Matters* program from 1992-2007. He has been a featured speaker at various mayor and governor prayer breakfasts, and at various functions of the Christian Business Men's Committee, Christian Women's Clubs, and The Jesus Film Project.

Mark Biller is the Executive Editor of the *Sound Mind Investing* newsletter and website, where he has worked closely with Austin since January 2000. Mark helped create and establish SMI's online membership outreach, which has attracted over 10,000 monthly subscribers since its inception.

Along with Austin, Mark has played a key role in creating, refining, and implementing several of SMI's popular strategies, including the Fund Upgrading and Dynamic Asset Allocation strategies discussed in this book. Mark also serves as the Senior Portfolio Manager of the three Sound Mind Investing mutual funds that employ these strategies.

Mark's writings on a broad range of financial and investment topics have been featured in a variety of national print and electronic media. He frequently appears as a financial commentator for various national and local radio programs, including the popular *MoneyWise* program with Howard Dayton and Steve Moore of Compass—finances God's way.™

The

SOUND MIND INVESTING

SIXTH EDITION ✳ REVISED AND EXPANDED

HANDBOOK

A step-by-step guide to managing your money from a biblical perspective

AUSTIN PRYOR

WITH MARK BILLER

ISBN 978-0-8024-1215-7

Library of Congress Cataloging in Publication Data

1 3 5 7 9 10 8 6 4 2

Printed in the United States of America

How to Know
If This Book Has
Been Written for You

"C'mon, Herb. We've got to go.
Are you going to buy the book or not?"

The foundation of every successful investment program begins with a clear understanding of one's motivation: "What's my purpose in investing?"

For the Christian, the answer is two-fold: (1) to provide financially for the needs of your household, and (2) to increase your assets in order to serve God more fully. This book was written to help you do both.

If you're like most Americans these days, you look with bewilderment at the flood of investment opportunities passing before you. You're encouraged not only to invest in mutual funds and trade stocks, but also to buy commodities, stock and index options, plus other complicated securities. Some financial gurus even suggest investing with money borrowed against the equity in your home.

During the past 30 years, the variety of financial opportunities available to the average investor multiplied greatly. For most people, it's too much of a good thing—this "option glut" often serves to paralyze them. Many of the alternatives seem quite complicated. Strategies that used to occupy only the wealthy now appear to be urged on everyone. Even everyday financial decisions that should be routine now seem to require as much research and planning as a a high-level corporate takeover!

Finding your way isn't made any easier by the investment industry.

To a large degree, any intimidation felt by the average investor is the result of the way the industry conducts itself. For one thing, investment "experts" make your task of learning more difficult because everything they say sounds so complicated. They create the impression that investing is very hard, and that it might be best if it were not entrusted to amateurs (like you).

And then there's the matter of the industry's preoccupation with making forecasts. It's one thing to help investors make more informed decisions by giving out economic data, corporate profiles, historical trends, and the like. But to use that information as the basis for market predictions is quite another. The fact is that nobody knows for sure what's coming next year, next month, next week, or even tomorrow. Forecasts from the brokerage community and investment media, at best, are conflicting and confusing. At their worst, they're totally misleading and eventually will prove extremely expensive to any investor who takes them seriously.

Most people have only vague notions as to what their long-term investment goals are. As a result, they move through life as responders...

...deciding on a case-by-case basis whether to say yes to the various investment opportunities that randomly come to their attention. Their thinking is short-term. Depending on their mood that day, or the advice of a friend

---

Sidebar:

Why does this book already have yellow highlighting in it? Because I went through and highlighted the points that I especially wanted to impress upon you or bring to your attention. It's another of the ways I've tried to make the book user-friendly and visually interesting.

(Underlining added for emphasis in all verses.)

For God has not given us a spirit of fear, but of power and of love and of a sound mind.
2 Timothy 1:7
(NKJV)

If any of you lacks wisdom, he should ask God, who gives generously to all without finding fault, and it will be given to him. But when he asks, he must believe and not doubt . . .
James 1:5–6

who's in on a "good thing," or even how persuasive a salesperson is, they make a decision whether to invest. Often, they give little thought as to exactly where that particular investment fits in fulfilling their long-term goals.

Responders feel a need to "do something" when a major news story hits. Because they're not quite sure where *they're* going, they tend to watch the crowd to see where *it's* going. They begin listening for the hot tips, taking the gurus seriously, and putting too many eggs in the same basket. They might realize they're going somewhat out of bounds, but they're looking for that extra edge. The problem is they're drinking from "broken cisterns," to use a biblical phrase. The crowd and the experts don't know what's coming next any more than they do!

The plans of the diligent lead to profit as surely as haste leads to poverty.
Proverbs 21:5

Suppose one of you wants to build a tower. Will he not first sit down and estimate the cost to see if he has enough money to complete it? For if he lays the foundation and is not able to finish it, everyone who sees it will ridicule him, saying, "This fellow began to build and was not able to finish."
Luke 14:28–30

To find peace of mind in your investment decisions, you need to become *an initiator* rather than *a responder*.

Initiators have a concrete game plan in mind. They have made the effort to develop a strategy that specifically takes into account their long-term financial goals as well as their own personal investment temperament. It is shaped around what they hope to accomplish in the future, and it fits who they are "inside." In this book, I'll help you develop such a plan.

Make it your goal to become an initiator! Be like a shopper at the food market who buys only those ingredients needed to prepare a specific recipe. Before she goes to the supermarket, Cindy knows what she's looking for. When confronted with special promotions for products that aren't on her shopping list, she passes them by. Cindy won't spend time considering whether to buy them *because her shopping is purposeful.* Similarly, before you begin to invest, put together a long-term strategy that takes into account the risk of loss you can comfortably carry—both financially *and* emotionally—and let it guide your decision-making.

If you're ready to spend a little time learning a few basics, you can be of good cheer!

This book is written with your needs in mind to equip you to have the confidence to take charge of your financial life—to become an initiator. I plan to help you do this in five ways.

THE
"COMPLETE GUIDE"
APPROACH TO
TEACHING

THE
"ONLY WHAT YOU NEED TO KNOW"
APPROACH TO TEACHING
USED IN THIS BOOK

The Daredevil

"There's a lot of money to be made by people who aren't afraid to go for it! I may be overly optimistic (and a tad impulsive), but I don't usually worry about my investment decisions once they're made."

The Researcher

"I don't believe in investing in something just because everyone else is doing it. Once I make a decision, I have a lot of confidence in it, even if other investors around me are changing their minds."

The Explorer

"To be successful in investing, you've got to keep in step with the latest trends. I'm open to new investment opportunities with potentially large returns even if they are a little more risky."

The Preserver

"You can't be too careful when it comes to investing your money. I am much more interested in minimizing my chances for losses than I am in taking greater risks to earn possibly higher returns."

❶ **I'm going to teach you only what you** *need to know*, **not all that there** *is to know.* (That should be pretty good news, right there!) I don't take the "complete guide" approach. Instead, I assume that you just want the essentials for now. And put that way, there really isn't all that much for you to learn. Just as you can throw a wall switch and enjoy the benefits of electricity without understanding how it all works, so it is with mutual funds. I will cover just enough information here to teach you to "throw the switch" that will enable you to establish a practical (and relatively easy to supervise) long-term investment strategy.

❷ I'm going to give you a framework for setting priorities on how to spend (or invest) your monthly surplus. It's based on working your way progressively toward financial security. If you have consumer debt outstanding or lack a sufficient contingency fund, I believe it's best to apply your surplus in those areas. However, that doesn't mean you are free from making important investment decisions in connection with stock, bond, and money market securities. If you have an IRA, you have a responsibility to manage it. Or perhaps you have a pension plan at work, such as a SEP-IRA or 401(k), where you are allowed to make decisions as to how your account is invested. Perhaps you've purchased a variable annuity, which offers you similar choices. These retirement investments represent money that was set aside in the past, and although you may not be adding to them at present, you still must decide how best to invest the money that's already there. To one degree or another, you will do a better job of making these decisions if you have a basic understanding of the investment markets. Even if you're still working on getting debt-free, you can use this time productively to build your understanding of investing principles. Then, when you have larger amounts to manage in the future, you won't need a crash course—your knowledge and confidence levels will be up to the task!

❸ **I'm going to introduce you to four basic investment temperaments—four approaches to risk-taking.** They're represented by the cartoon images you see on the left. In chapter 13, I'll lead you through a process of discovering which of the four is most appropriate for your basic emotional makeup and financial situation. Once you learn this, you'll have a yardstick for measuring risk that will be helpful to you for years to come.

❹ **I'm going to teach you in a user-friendly way.** The lessons are worded in everyday "plain-English" language, and come in small, easy-to-digest portions. Also, I've put lots of time into making the layout and design of these pages as clear, interesting, and easy-to-follow as possible (as I hope you're beginning to notice by now).

❺ I'm going to base all of the above on the time-tested principles taught in Holy Scripture. *"There is nothing new under the sun"* (Ecclesiastes 1:9), so you shouldn't be surprised to learn that the underlying values and priorities that shape the very practical strategies taught in this book are merely the outworkings of concepts taught in God's Word for centuries. Investing in the 21st century, we may be tempted to think we've grown too sophisticated for biblical lessons. However, current census and economic statistics reveal that our need for biblical truth is more serious than perhaps we realize! Individually, and as a nation, we have built our financial houses on the sand, and we are reaping the consequences. We dare not ignore God's wisdom any longer.

I have devised this book to serve as a tool to help you follow through and build on the biblical principles that Ron Blue, Howard Dayton, the late Larry Burkett, and others . . .

. . . have written about so well. Where they have tended to stay with general principles, I want to take you the next step—showing you how to apply those principles in specific ways out in the financial marketplace. I've often used the analogy of learning how to "dress for success." Books that teach fashion concepts (including information about fabrics, color coordination, fit, and style) help build an understanding of the basics. But you still need to get in your car, drive to the local mall, and purchase your wardrobe.

I think of myself as the person who goes with you, helps you pick the clothes out, watches you try them on, and offers you opinions on whether the style, color, and fit is a good one for *you*. I also know a few things about the reputations of various stores and clothing manufacturers, and steer you away from the bad ones.

To avoid information overload, you need to develop a sense of proportion. Everything doesn't have to be learned immediately or done yesterday. There's no such thing as "wealth without risk," so accept that you'll make a few mistakes along the way. But that's OK. You'll do fine over the long haul if you follow the basics, exercise self-discipline, and stay the course.

Before you begin your stock and bond market investing, however, you need to achieve a certain level of financial fitness. It's like those exhortations . . .

. . . to see your doctor for a physical exam before launching out on a new exercise program. Think of it as practicing financial aerobics. Now, I know working out isn't any fun. Personally, I am very sporadic in getting to my workouts. Driving to the fitness center just seems too time consuming. Not to mention that I'm lazy.

Web Sidebars
Financial information is constantly changing, and while the principles taught in this book won't change, the details will. For current articles and links to updated information, visit our web site at www.soundmindinvesting.com.

My workout schedule tends to go something like this. I work out faithfully for three months, starting in early March, to get ready to go out in public in my beachwear. Then, it's off to the beach where I have a great time with family and friends. Upon my return, I carefully avoid the fitness center until the following March. During those recurring nine-month periods of well-deserved rest from exercising, I have made a discovery. It's tedious, hard work to get in shape, but it's remarkably easy to get out! All you have to do is… nothing. Just relax. Stop investing time in it. It's amazing how quickly you can get out of shape. I wish it weren't like that, but it is. Being in shape, it turns out, has a very short shelf life.

We all would like to have great health and physical fitness, but only the people with self-discipline achieve such goals. Other areas of life are the same way. Invest time, commitment, and sacrifice in your marriage or dating relationship, and it grows stronger by the month. Replace that with neglect and making decisions just to please yourself, and the relationship weakens. The same is true of your career and a host of life's other activities—including your financial affairs. They also need time, commitment, and sacrifice in order to be healthy and grow. Are you in shape financially?

If you're not, I'm writing this book with the assumption that you're serious about making progress. At the very least, you've got good intentions. I'm hoping that this book will help those good intentions lead to determined action. Now, let's get started with your financial fitness tests to see just what kind of shape you're in! ◆

SECTION

1

Strengthening Your Foundation

By wisdom a house is built,
and through understanding it is established.
Proverbs 24:3

The wicked borrows and does not pay back...
Psalm 37:21

"It's from the credit card company.
Says it's our final notice."

Escaping Debt With a Spending Plan

I. **Before you begin investing your surplus funds in the markets, you should pay off any outstanding consumer-type debts.**

A. For purposes of this book, consumer debt includes credit-card debt, local charge accounts, auto loans, home-equity loans, and even student loans. First mortgage loans on one's home will be covered separately in the next chapter.

B. Aside from the *practical* advantages of getting debt-free—such as less financial stress and savings on interest expense—there are *biblical* ones as well.

C. Having a thoughtful and workable plan for getting debt-free is a sign of maturity.

II. **A winning financial strategy begins with a monthly surplus. And making sure you have a monthly surplus begins with a workable budget or spending plan. A good plan can help you:**

A. Apply your current income more strategically, as you manage spending decisions more proactively and steadily eliminate your debt;

B. Reach financial goals that would otherwise be unattainable while also equipping you to withstand economic downturns;

C. Increase your giving to the Lord and His work;

D. Stay motivated by giving you a sense of accomplishment as you measure your progress;

E. Wipe out your debt as quickly as possible.

III. **Are you using your credit cards or are they using you?**

A. Many people are carrying high levels of credit card debt—and are paying for it.

B. Consumers continue to use and abuse credit cards for various reasons.

C. If you decide to use credit cards, follow the four "rules of the road."

D. This chapter offers a plan for digging your way out, and staying out, of debt.

The <u>wicked borrow and do not repay</u>, but the righteous give generously.

Psalm 37:21

<u>Give everyone what you owe him</u>: If you owe taxes, pay taxes; <u>if revenue, then revenue</u>; if respect, then respect; if honor, then honor. <u>Let no debt remain outstanding</u>, except the continuing debt to love one another, for he who loves his fellowman has fulfilled the law.

Romans 13:7–8

We begin our journey toward financial security and peace of mind by making it a priority to . . .

. . . pay off those credit cards, car loans, and other short-term debts. That's right, the first financial fitness test you need to pass is the "debt" test. Webster's defines debt as anything you're "bound to pay or perform; the state of owing something." Using that definition, few Americans are free of debt.

Why place an emphasis on getting debt-free as the first step toward a sound *investing* strategy? Because it's unwise to take on the risks that come with investing unless you have staying power. That means you don't want to be in a position where circumstances unrelated to your investment strategy force you to sell your holdings and use the money elsewhere, such as for interest and debt payments. Also, for Christians, debts are moral as well as legal obligations. They must be honorably met no matter the circumstances.

Have you ever wished you could "begin again" financially?

I once heard a sermon in which a noted pastor read a poem called "The Land of Beginning Again." The pastor then presented the claims of Christ, explaining that He is *King* in the Land of Beginning Again! Each of us has experienced his share of errors, failures, and missed opportunities. We all have things we would do differently if given a second chance. What wonderful news to know that, in Christ, the slate is wiped clean and we do have the opportunity of beginning again.

In a similar fashion, many who have become weighed down by debt wish they could get free. They have learned that the satisfaction that comes with spending is brief indeed when compared to the pressure of making monthly payments that may go on for years. For some, the situation seems hopeless. You may sometimes feel this way yourself.

If so, take heart! You can make great strides over the next year, but it will require planning, discipline, sacrifice, and singleness of purpose.

Without singleness of purpose and specific goals, we can become like the person described in Scripture as double-minded. *"That man should not think he will receive anything from the Lord; he is a double-minded man, unstable in all he does"* (James 1:7-8). So let me encourage you to engage in a meaningful goal-setting exercise as you work to get debt-free. Here are suggestions for effective goal-setting in any area of life; adapt them to your financial situation.

• **Set goals that are consistent with God's Word.** Many successful people have accomplished much, yet remain unhappy. Having singleness of purpose toward the wrong goals only leads to wrong results. Examine your motivations, as well as your actions, in the light of God's wisdom.

"I wish that there were some wonderful place
Called the Land
of Beginning Again
Where all our mistakes
and all our heartaches
And all of our selfish grief
Could be dropped like
a shabby old coat by the door
And never be put on again...
'The Land of Beginning Again'
by Louise Fletcher

• **Ask God for His guidance.** This is not the same as having scripturally sound goals. This has more to do with having the wisdom needed to set the right personal priorities. God promises to guide us if we're willing to submit to Him. It's not: "Show me Your will, Lord, so I can decide if I'm willing." Rather, it's: "Before You even reveal Your will to me, Lord, the answer is yes."

• **If you are married, set goals together.** If two have become "one flesh," how critical that they have a singleness of purpose in their commitment toward common goals. Few areas will so quickly affect a couple's relationship as a financial plan that limits their spending freedom because it brings mutually conflicting goals into the open. If you can't reach a meeting of the minds on what your priorities should be, perhaps the marriage relationship itself needs some work.

• **Put your goals in writing, signing your name and date.** This act helps cement in your thinking that you really have made a firm commitment of your will to achieving your goals. It is also helpful to have your goals posted where you will see them daily as additional motivation to stay the course when the inevitable temptations to compromise arise.

Aside from the practical reasons for getting out of debt—namely, less financial stress and huge savings on interest expense—there are biblical reasons as well. Here are three that are compelling:

• **To be obedient.** *"Give everyone what you owe him: If you owe taxes, pay taxes; if revenue, then revenue; if respect, then respect; if honor, then honor. Let no debt remain outstanding, except the continuing debt to love one another, for he who loves his fellowman has fulfilled the law"* (Romans 13:7-8). When God's Word tells us to pay our debts, that instruction should be just as binding on the conscience of the follower of Christ as is biblical teaching about loving others, avoiding sin, preserving our marriage, and a host of other moral guidelines that we take seriously.

• **To maintain your integrity.** *"The wicked borrow and do not repay, but the righteous give generously"* (Psalm 37:21). Many Americans look at bankruptcy as a "fix" for their debt problems. In the 12-month period ending in March 2013, more than 1.1 million U.S. households filed for bankruptcy protection. Obviously, many people are faced with debt that they believe to be unconquerable. However, bankruptcy can never be more than a temporary solution for the Christian. When we borrow, we are making a vow to repay under the agreed-upon conditions of the loan. Unless the lender releases us, we are obligated to pay the debt back. In some forms of bankruptcy, the courts establish a repayment plan based on the amount of debt that you can afford to pay and directs the creditors to operate within this plan. These arrangements, rather than help you avoid responsibility for your debts, make it possible for you to honor your vow and maintain your integrity and witness to the faithfulness of Christ.

• **To preserve your allegiance to Christ alone.** *"The rich rule over the poor, and the borrower is servant to the lender"* (Proverbs 22:7). To be in subjection to those from whom we borrow makes it impossible to serve Christ with our undivided energies. Is it possible that we may have missed exciting and rewarding opportunities for serving Him because we weren't available? Those who love Christ want to be available to be used by Him in His kingdom work, but how can He use us in a new vocation or field of ministry when our debt obligations make it impossible to say "Yes!" to the call? We want to conduct our lives so that, to the greatest extent possible, we're free to serve Christ.

The problem we face in attempting to get completely debt-free is that we are our own worst enemies.

Most debt problems result from an excess of spending, not a lack of income. It's not hard to spend money. With a little practice, most of us get really good at it. Advertisers show us things that (they say) will make our lives more fun, exciting, and fulfilling. And if our eyes are bigger than our wallets, lenders shower us with credit cards and encourage us to pamper ourselves. It may be expensive, but after all "we're worth it." For the most part, we're all prone to being tempted by the neat stuff we see around us.

If you've made more than your share of past mistakes, it's never too late to correct poor spending habits! The solution is deceptively simple: You need a plan:

- to keep you on course;
- to remind you where you want to go and help you get there;
- to assure that you spend less than you earn;
- to help you live out your priorities.

Then you'll have a *monthly surplus* that can be applied to gradually eliminating your debts. Let's discuss cash flow plans and how to put one together that fits your situation. but first, a little motivation.

So you want to be be a millionaire? Okay, here's what you do.

Starting when you're 30 (starting earlier would even be better!), save $475 a month. Invest it in a tax-deferred account, such as an IRA, and earn an average return of 7% per year. When you reach your full retirement age at 67, voilà, you'll have a million bucks!

Of course, how much that will buy when you reach retirement is another story. Assuming 3% inflation, $1 million will be worth less than one-half as much as it is today. I throw that in only to impress you with the fact that, while $475 is a nice starting point, you'll probably want to set aside much more.

For now, however, the question is this: Do you *have* an extra $475 each month? Or let me put it this way: If your family were a business, would you be showing a profit of at least $475 a month? After all the income is counted and all the bills are paid, is there money left over? There better be, because that monthly surplus is the key to building your financial security.

If you're not sure you even have a monthly surplus (let alone how much it is), then you have got two choices. One, you can continue your "easy come, easy go" approach, spending your money according to your moods and whims of the day. That's a fun way to go through life—until you begin drowning in debt. Meanwhile, you're robbing yourself of the opportunity to move toward financial stability and security. By the time you come to your senses, it could be extremely difficult to redeem the situation.

Or, two, you can buckle down and develop a plan to guide your spending decisions. In other words, act like a grown up. Sure, creating and living by a budget takes time. But if you're tempted to skip this section, you do so at your peril. For 99.9% of us, having a plan is absolutely essential to progressing financially. It certainly was for my family (more on that shortly). A winning and gratifying financial strategy begins with your monthly surplus. And making sure you have a monthly surplus begins with a workable budget and—there's no sense kidding ourselves—a healthy dose of self-discipline. A good plan can help you:

Planning Tools
A good introductory look at some of the popular online tools is available to visitors at www.soundmindinvesting.com in an article "Taking Your Household Budget Online."

- Apply your current income more strategically as you reduce or eliminate unneeded or impulsive spending.

- Improve communication with your spouse as you set priorities.

- Steadily eliminate your debt.

- Withstand economic downturns.

- Increase your giving to the Lord and His work.

- Stay motivated by giving you a sense of accomplishment as you measure your progress.

- Reach financial goals that would otherwise be unattainable.

- Invest for the long-term with regularity.

Excellent resources are available that will guide you through the process of putting together a workable spending plan (see sidebar). They generally follow an allocation-type strategy in which all your expenditures are categorized and spending boundaries are assigned to each category. Your spending is monitored weekly (or monthly) to make sure you're staying within the amounts allotted.

My wife Susie and I have used this kind of rigorous approach to control our spending . . .

. . . and it worked well. Here were our "keys to success."

1. Be truthful in your communication. I keep track of the money in our family, and I was the first to realize we were facing a serious financial challenge (see chapter 28 for background). Susie knew that we were experiencing financial difficulties, but she didn't know just how difficult it had become to balance our income and outgo. Even though some of the events that had caused the problem were beyond my control, I felt like a failure in my role as the financial provider in the family. I hated the idea of telling her our situation, but knew it would take both our best efforts to deal with it responsibly.

2. Be thorough in your preparations. As I began working on our cash flow plan, I listed not only every category of spending I could think of, but also every anticipated item within each category. For example, I didn't just put down $500 for family birthdays—I listed each person on the gift list and how much we typically spent on that person. (The more categories you have, the better idea you'll have of where all the money's going and, consequently, the more ideas you'll get on where you can save.) Furthermore, I didn't just put down round numbers that "seemed right." I used my cancelled checks, Visa bills, and old tax returns to see what I'd actually spent in the past.

3. Be willing to change your lifestyle. All of my work simply gave us a picture of where our money had gone in the past. Now it was time to go over the spending categories and discuss what we could do to lower (or temporarily eliminate) the spending in each one. Savings are possible in almost every category if you're willing to make changes in your lifestyle and shopping habits.

4. Be consistent in monitoring your spending. My goal was to account for 100% of our spending—an almost impossible task, as I was to find out! It's amazing how much money is spent a few dollars here and a few dollars there. This was more of a burden on Susie than on me. (In most families, wives handle the majority of the routine spending.) We decided to use old reliable—the envelope system—to help us stay within our budget. Here's how we did it.

Each week, we would put enough cash for that week's expenses in a small envelope that Susie would carry in her purse. If she went to the grocery store and spent $48.24, she'd write "Groceries $48.24" on the front of the envelope at the time she withdrew the money. Ditto the drug store, gas station, school lunch money . . . whatever. There were two advantages to doing it this way. First, she was reminded to keep track of her spending because she was pulling the cash from the actual envelope. Second, she could pace herself as the week went along and she saw her cash begin to dwindle. At the end of the week, she'd give me the old dog-eared envelope so I could track everything on a computer worksheet. Any unspent money was transferred to a new envelope and the process would start over.

An area of confusion for many couples is how to handle the spending that occurs periodically rather than weekly. The way that worked best for us was to divide those items into two groups. I took responsibility for the expenses that were somewhat automatic with respect to the amount and date due—for

Helpful Resources

The trendiness of frugal living has given rise to several helpful newsletters on how to live well on less money. One of the best known is *Debt-Proof Living*. With wit and humor, editor Mary Hunt makes saving money almost a pleasant experience. The design is great, and the content is even better. Mary has gained national recognition by appearing on such programs as "The Today Show" and "Focus on the Family." There's a wealth of money-saving information and encouragement in this website. Go to www.debtproofliving.com. The cost is only $3.99 for a monthly membership, and you can cancel at any time. If you prefer, annual memberships are available for $29.

example, monthly mortgage, life insurance premiums, utilities, and tuition payments. These were typically paid by check. Susie took those categories where purchasing decisions were involved—birthdays, clothing, household items and repairs—and we set aside an amount in an envelope for each one. These were handled like the weekly envelope system except she typically didn't need to carry these particular envelopes with her every time she went out.

5. Be disciplined in staying within your agreed upon limits. The reason you need to closely monitor your spending is so you will know if you're on target or whether mid-course adjustments are needed. This gives you a certain degree of flexibility. If you go over in one area, you'll need to cut back in another. For example, an unexpected dental bill of $200 may have to come out of your "recreation" envelope if the "medical" envelope is already empty. Or, you might prefer to take $20 out of 10 different envelopes to spread the shortfall around and lessen the impact on any one category.

6. Be mutually supportive. Susie was great! She wasn't critical or complaining in any way. In fact, she continually reminded me that God was our source of supply, and we would just need to do the best we could while waiting on Him to send a solution. Her positive attitude was a tremendous encouragement to me as we "tightened our belt." It was key to have her cooperation. If you and your spouse aren't of one mind as to the importance of developing and living out this kind of lifestyle, conflicts will arise frequently.

The point of all this feverish effort is to make sure you have a monthly surplus. Assuming you're successful in that regard what's the best use for it? I encourage you to *initially* use your monthly surplus toward accomplishing the crucial (and God-given) goal of getting out of debt. Once that's done, all the money that was previously going toward monthly debt payments can then be profitably redirected to an investment portfolio (more on that later).

Here is a tried-and-true seven-step formula for using your monthly surplus to wipe out your debt in the fastest possible time.

1. Stop adding to your debt. Today. No exceptions, no excuses. Obviously, you can't get *out of* debt if you keep going *into* debt. This is fundamental. The remaining steps will not work if you fail here.

2. List all your debts—credit cards, personal loans, college loans, car loans, home equity loans, and house mortgage—in order according to the amount you owe. Include your minimum monthly payment. I also like to show the interest rate, but that's strictly for informational purposes; it has no bearing on the order in which you will pay off the debts. We target the smallest debt first because it has a motivational benefit. When you see progress being made, you're encouraged to continue being faithful to the program.

(Many people elect not to include their mortgage on the list because they don't feel it's realistic to expect to pay it off early. We'll look at that decision in chapter 2. For now, I want to include it so I can show the impact it would have.)

3. Ask for a better rate. If you have a solid history of paying your bills on time, call the customer-service number listed on the statements of any of your credit cards that are charging especially high interest rates. Ask the person to look up your account. Once they have it on their screen say, "I believe I've been a good customer and I'd like to keep my account with you, but many of your competitors are charging lower rates. Would you be willing to lower your rate?" If they turn you down, ask to speak to a supervisor and repeat what you said to the first person. What's the worst that can happen? They might say no. Then again, they might say yes. And a lower rate will greatly speed up the process of getting out of debt.

4. Determine your payments. If you take on no new debt and dutifully pay the minimum due each month, then that minimum required amount will actually decline a little bit each month. It isn't the kindness of the credit card company; it's math. The minimum due is based on a percentage of your balance, so if the balance goes down a little each month so, too, will the minimum required payment. However, paying only this declining minimum payment is what keeps you in debt for approximately… forever! So, take note of your *first* month's required payment and pay *at least* that amount each month

5. Pay more than the amounts you initially planned. If you really want to jump start the process, look for ways to tighten your belt a little more (or bring in some extra income) so you can increase this number. This should be possible because the minimums set by the credit card companies are abnormally low. Most credit cards require only 2%-3% of your total balance as a minimum monthly payment. *They don't want you to pay off your balance quickly*—the longer it takes, the more they'll make on your interest payments.

6. Target your smallest debt first, applying any extra monthly surplus you come up with toward that debt. When that debt is paid off, take the money you had been paying on it and add it to the amount you're paying on your second smallest debt. This technique is called the "debt snowball," because the continual rolling over of your monthly payments toward each succeeding debt grows in a powerful way, just like rolling over layers of snow can quickly build a large snowball.

7. Persist, persist, persist. For motivation, use an online calculator to prepare a time line that shows how long it will take you to get debt-free. Reflect on how much money you'll be saving on interest costs by speeding up the process.

To see a debt snowball in action, look at the sidebar on the right where we will track the experience of Tom and Linda, a young couple with a typical variety of debts. Table A shows their situation when they begin. They have consumer loans totaling $22,334 plus a remaining balance of $125,893 on a house mortgage they took out two years ago. Their minimum monthly payments total $1,374. Since these are already factored into their budget, their monthly surplus isn't needed to make those payments. They decide to use $100 of their monthly surplus for their debt elimination strategy. This brings their total monthly payments to $1,474. This is the amount they will pay each month until their creditors are all paid.

Tom and Linda begin their program by first targeting the Visa debt because it's the smallest. They add the $100 to the $25 minimum payment they had been making and begin sending in $125 each month. Table B shows the results after seven months. Most of their debt balances have fallen rather slowly due to their making only the minimum payments required, but the Visa debt has disappeared entirely. Now they have $125 a month available they no longer need to send to Visa. Resisting the urge to spend this new "found" money, they begin paying it toward their Discover card bill, the next debt on their list. They had previously been paying $42 a month; now they can send in $167.

At the 15-month mark, the Discover bill is history, and they move on to the MasterCard debt. Adding the $167 they had been paying to Discover to the $83 going to MasterCard allows them to up their monthly payment to $250. Since the MasterCard balance at that point is only $529, it doesn't take long to eliminate that debt. In the 19th month, they're able to increase the monthly student loan payment to a hefty $482 ($232 previously plus $250 from the retired MasterCard debt). It's paid off in another 11 months.

With the student loan being paid off by the 30th month, they take that $482 and add it to the $294 a month going toward the car loan. The new amount is more than enough to pay off the balance of the car loan in only two more months. In just 32 months, then, Tom and Linda paid off over $22,000 in debts, and saved themselves thousands of dollars in interest charges to boot.

Plus, they now have an extra $776 a month in their monthly surplus. They've had to sacrifice to stay on course (which involved living within their budget and not adding any new debt), and you can't blame them if they want to celebrate a bit by using that $776 for lifestyle treats they've been denying themselves. Or they might take just part of it for enlarging their budget a bit, and put the rest toward a long-term investing strategy.

But, just for the sake of argument, let's say they decide to keep rolling their debt snowball and go after the house mortgage. Originally a

TOM AND LINDA'S DEBT SNOWBALL STRATEGY

Table A: At the Outset

Debt Item	Balance Due	Fixed Payment	Interest Rate
Visa	$ 826	$ 125	2.9%
Discover	1,412	42	16.9%
MasterCard	1,786	83	15.9%
Student Loan	8,628	232	7.0%
Car Loan	9,682	294	4.0%
House	125,893	698	5.0%
Total	$148,227	$1,474	

Table B: After 7 Months

Discover	$ 1,240	$ 167	16.9%
MasterCard	1,354	83	15.9%
Student Loan	7,334	232	7.0%
Car Loan	7,831	294	4.0%
House	124,664	698	5.0%
Total	$142,423	$1,474	

Table C: After 15 Months

MasterCard	$ 792	$ 250	15.9%
Student Loan	5,789	232	7.0%
Car Loan	5,663	294	4.0%
House	123,214	698	5.0%
Total	$135,458	$1,474	

Table D: After 19 Months

Student Loan	$ 4,804	$ 482	7.0%
Car Loan	4,557	294	4.0%
House	122,471	698	5.0%
Total	$131,832	$1,474	

Table E: After 30 Months

Car Loan	$1,100	$ 776	4.0%
House	120,363	$698	5.0%
Total	$120,467	$1,474	

Table F: After 32 Months

House	$ 119,522	$ 1,474	5.0%

30-year, $130,000 loan, there's still 25+ years to go. How long would you guess it would take to retire the remaining $119,522 if they paid an *extra* $776 a month toward their principal each month? Just a little over eight years! Not only would they then own their house free and clear, but they'd save more than $64,000 in interest payments by paying off their mortgage 17 years early!

Now, let's turn to the challenging task of managing our credit and using credit cards wisely.

According to recent estimates based on Federal Reserve data...

...almost one-half of U.S. households have at least some credit-card debt. Of those that do, the average balance is around $15,000. Of course, some use credit cards for convenience and pay the balance in full every month. For others, though, too much credit-card use leads to an ever-growing credit-card debt.

Most of us are aware of the pitfalls of credit cards, so why do we continue to use them?

• **Convinced by convenience.** Simply put, they're easy. And you can use them almost everywhere. Why mess with carrying cash or writing all of those checks? Just pull out that handy, little card and you're on your way. And how about the luxury of pay-at-the-pump gasoline? Enough said.

• **Just no other way around it.** Sometimes it's hard to get what you want any other way. From buying online to reserving a hotel room, credit cards seem to be the new necessity.

• **Seeking rewards.** From frequent-flyer miles to insurance and extended warranties, we love the perks. We figure, we're going to spend the money anyway, so why not get something for it?

• **Keeping up with the Joneses.** We see something we want but don't want to wait until we can pay for it outright. We work hard and feel like "we deserve it."

• **Emerging emergencies.** Like a comforting security blanket, that extra credit card is always there—just in case.

• **Perishing for lack of knowledge.** By focusing on the monthly minimum rather than the total cost, some of us justify credit purchases by rationalizing that we can afford the minimum credit card payment. This leads to our first lesson in negative compounding interest. By then, it's often too late and we're overwhelmed by the deep, dark hole of credit card debt.

Fortunately, there's a better way.

If you're going to use credit cards, here are four "rules of the road."

1. Use credit cards only for pre-planned, budgeted items. If you have $50

A Credit Card Vocabulary

Before we go any further, let's review some basic credit card lingo.

• Annual Fee
Flat fee some credit cards charge you each year for having their credit card.

• Transaction Fees
Fees for cash advances, late payments, going over your credit limit, etc. Some credit cards even charge an inactivity fee if you don't use your card.

• Finance Charges
Interest costs and all related transaction costs.

• Annual Percentage Rate (APR)
Interest rate measuring your credit cost as a yearly rate.

• Periodic Rate
Interest rate applied to your outstanding account balance when calculating your current finance charge.

• Grace Period
The number of days you're allowed to pay off your balance before the credit card company starts charging you interest. Once a balance goes unpaid in any month, the grace period is lost until the balance is once again paid down to zero. Typically this means that new charges on that card begin incurring interest costs the day the purchase is made.

budgeted for clothing this month, you can charge $50 worth of clothing.

2. Record your credit-card purchases as if you paid cash. Electronic budget tools such as Mint.com will do this for you. But if you use a paper and pencil budget, record your credit-card spending when you make each purchase. If you charged $50 worth of clothing purchases today, write it down today. It counts against this month's clothing budget.

3. Always pay your entire balance in full each month.

4. If you can't follow rules 1-3, don't use credit cards!

To understand what lenders take into consideration when deciding whether to extend credit, you need to know a few basics about credit scores.

Your credit score matters greatly in determining if you will qualify for a mortgage and how much you'll pay.

FICO credit scores range from 300-850, with the lowest loan rates going to those with the highest scores. (FICO stands for Fair Isaac Corporation, the company that created the credit score.) To obtain the best rate on a mortgage, you'll need a score in the mid 700s or higher.

If you think your score may be on the low side, it's worth paying to find out before applying for a mortgage. (As maddening as it may be, your credit *report* is free, but not your *score*.)

You have three credit scores, one from each of the three credit reporting bureaus. At www.myfico.com, you can purchase your scores from two of the three—TransUnion and Equifax—for $19.95 each. The third bureau, Experian, does not sell its score. (Also go to www.annualcreditreport.com where you can get your free credit *reports* from all three of the bureaus.)

The two credit scores you buy should be within about 50 points of each other. If not, something may have been misreported to one of the bureaus, so go over your credit reports with a fine-tooth comb.

If your scores are lower than you think they should be, look for indications that you have paid your bills late. If so, and if you know that information is incorrect, contact the creditors in question and ask them to change how that information was reported to the bureaus. Next, look at your credit utilization. That's the percentage of available credit you use. The best scores go to those who use 10% or less per line of credit and across all lines of credit. If yours is much higher than that, start using less. For example, if you have a credit card with a $10,000 limit, spend no more than $1,000 per month on that card. (Of course, pay your bill in full each month).

If you and your spouse apply for a mortgage together, all six of your scores will be reviewed (each of you has three). Lenders typically choose the lower

Recommended Resource

If you follow all the steps in this chapter and still can't make even the minimum payments on your debts, it may be time to get in touch with a credit-counseling agency. Here's some good advice on how to do that from financial teacher Matt Bell:

Among other services, these agencies offer debt management plans (DMP), in which they negotiate with creditors on your behalf, usually lowering the monthly payments and often stopping additional late and over-limit fees. You send the credit-counseling agency one check each month, which the office will divide among your creditors. When you begin working with a credit-counseling office, many collection activities will stop.

There are thousands of such offices around the country. Be careful in choosing one, however, as a number of unscrupulous players have entered the field. Find a local office associated with the National Foundation for Credit Counseling (NFCC). Founded in 1951, the NFCC is the oldest and largest network of community-based, nonprofit credit-counseling agencies in the nation.

All NFCC counselors are certified credit counselors, and all of the agencies are accredited by an independent third party. You can search for an office near you on the NFCC website at www.DebtAdvice.org or by calling 800-388-2227.

(next page)

of both of your middle scores.

If you are applying for a mortgage that will require only one income (more on this wise decision later) and the person whose income you will use has a score in the mid 700s or higher, you don't need to worry about the other person's score, at least not for the purpose of applying for a mortgage. It is fine to apply in only one spouse's name. In most cases, though, it's best to *title* the house in both spouses' names.

To save on interest costs, many play the "transfer game."

You've probably heard about this—transferring an existing balance to a new card in order to get a lower introductory interest rate. Some people shuffle their balances from one card to another when the introductory period expires. By doing this, all of their payment goes toward reducing the debt's principal, rather than paying interest. Since this reduces their profitability, credit card companies are making the process more expensive. Many are now charging "transfer fees" or treating transfers like cash advances.

Financial author Matt Bell, in his book *Money Strategies for Tough Times*, suggests a cautious approach to employing a transfer strategy, and offers a few shopping tips:

Whenever I teach workshops about getting out of debt, someone always asks about the wisdom of transferring their high-interest credit card balances to a new card offering a low or even 0 percent interest rate. This sounds like a smart idea, but watch out. It comes with numerous hidden snares. Keep in mind that making this transfer won't necessarily change the amount you have to pay each month, unless the new card bases its minimum-required payment on a lower percentage of the balance than your current card.

When considering a balance transfer, here's what to look for in the fine print:

• ***Is there a transaction fee?*** *Some cards charge a fee based on a percentage of the transferred balance.*

• ***How long will the 0 percent rate be in effect?*** *Some cards offer the rate for only a short "introductory period."*

• ***What money does the low rate pertain to?*** *With some cards, it applies only to the transferred balance. The card company may then require you to make a minimum number of purchases with your card each month, with those purchases subject to a higher interest rate. Any payments you make each month will not apply to those new charges until you finish paying off the transferred balance. Unless you pay off the entire transferred balance and your new charges, you'll rack up interest charges.*

• ***What happens if you don't follow all the rules?*** *If you make one late* *payment or exceed your credit limit one time, will the company raise your rate to its standard rate or higher?*

One other factor to consider is the potential impact on your credit score, that three-digit number that affects everything from your ability to get a job to how much you pay for insurance. Opening any new account gives you access to more credit, which can lower your score. Also, make sure your debt-to-available-credit ratio does not get too high. A good rule of thumb is to keep that ratio at 10 percent or below (this advice even pertains to people who pay their balance in full each month), so know what your credit limit will be on the new card and see what percentage of that limit your transferred balance will constitute.

Once you are well on your way to escaping the credit-card pit, a few additional steps remain.

• **Close old accounts.** As you pay off and transfer balances, close unnecessary accounts immediately. Your total available credit line will be analyzed to determine your credit risk to a given credit card company (which in turn affects the interest rate they're willing to give you). There's a possible exception, however. If you've always been prompt in your payments and have a good standing with a credit card you've used for a long time, that can improve your credit score — you may not wish to close such accounts.

• **Take advantage of online payment convenience.** To avoid late payments, you may want to try paying your bill online as soon as you receive it. Most banks allow you to specify when the payment will be posted (that is, charged) to your account. This allows you to handle the paperwork on the bill immediately (so you don't forget), but set the payment due date, which may be weeks away, in the future.

• **Beware cash advances.** Most cards charge a cash advance fee of 2% or more of the advance amount. They may throw in a flat dollar amount as well, as in 2%/$10. This means the fee will be the *greater* of 2% or $10. If you pay $10 to get a $200 advance, that's a 5% fee. And that's just for handing over the money. In addition, upon taking the advance, interest begins to accrue immediately at a rate that is typically *higher* than your regular interest rate. Lastly, any payments you make will be *applied to the lower interest balances first!*

• **Stay on top of things.** Credit card companies can change their terms by written notice, so pay attention to everything they send you. They may decide to increase your interest rate because they determine your risk has increased. Watch out — increasing your credit limits or making late payments (to them or any other creditor) may qualify you for a rate hike! Make sure to check your credit report annually.

Once you find a local office accredited by the NFCC, go a step further and check with the Better Business Bureau via its website (www.bbb.org) to see if any unresolved complaints have been filed against the office. If you can't find a credit-counseling office near you or prefer not to visit the office in person, check for one that offers its services online or over the phone.

Once you select an office, get all fee information up front and in writing. Typical debt management plan fees include a one-time setup fee of about $50 and monthly fees of $35. If your finances are really tight, you may be eligible to work with an agency at no cost because one of the NFCC's standards for membership is a willingness to work with people regardless of their ability to pay.

One sign that you're talking with the wrong agency is if they require much higher fees. Another warning sign is if the agency tries to put you into a "debt management plan" (DMP) without first looking for other solutions to your situation, such as helping you find ways to lower your expenses or increase your income. According to Gail Cunningham, spokesperson for the NFCC, "If we've pared the budget, explored income options, and there still isn't enough money to service living expenses and debt obligations, then we'll consider a DMP as one of the resolution options."

A debt management plan can be used with only certain unsecured debts, such as credit card and medical debt. Student loans cannot be renegotiated through credit-counseling offices. Whether tax debt can go through a DMP depends on where you live. At the least, a credit-counseling office can provide guidance about tax debt. You will have to keep making your mortgage and vehicle payments separately. However, the NFCC also has a large number of certified housing counselors who can help you with foreclosure-prevention assistance.

— From "Money Strategies for Tough Times" by Matt Bell

• **Celebrate as you go!** You're following a long, hard road, so it's important to celebrate when you've reached certain milestones, such as paying off an account or reaching the halfway point. Be creative — get the family together for a bill burning or bake a cake!

**As we wrap up our discussion of credit cards,
take a moment to consider why you use credit cards.**

Determine how the use of credit cards affects your ability to stay on your budget, and by extension, your ability to reach your goals. Identifying any unhealthy tendencies is the first step towards overcoming them. Ask the Lord to show you practical ways to improve in your handling of credit.

One *alternative* to credit cards — that sacrifices little of their convenience — is using debit cards. These cards are a hybrid of credit cards and checks. You use them like credit cards, but the funds are automatically withdrawn from your checking or savings account, as they would be if you'd written a check. By treating these plastic purchases like a check, you save yourself the end of the month trauma of discovering long-forgotten charges on your credit card statement.

Since debit cards access your money directly (and immediately), you may be in for some headaches if your card number is stolen and you don't realize it quickly. Until the problem is resolved, you may have bounced checks and corresponding fees. Fortunately, your debit card theft-liability protection is similar to that of a credit card. For more information, visit the "consumer protection" section of the Federal Trade Commission web site at www.ftc.gov. ◆

Credit Counseling
One of the most well known credit counseling organizations is The National Foundation for Consumer Credit. The Atlanta office of the Consumer Credit Counseling Service is a member. Visit them at www.cccsatl.org.

CHAPTER PREVIEW

The Importance of Having Your Home Paid For

I. **If you can't afford to make extra principal payments on your home mortgage and at the same time put money into a retirement plan, which should have the priority?**

    A. As we see by following the experiences of Rob and Mort, contributing to the retirement plan is more profitable from an economic viewpoint. Ultimately, it's a decision based on your personal convictions with respect to debt.

    B. It's generally not advisable to cash in one's retirement plan in order to retire a mortgage.

II. **As a general rule, surplus funds are better used for paying off the mortgage on your home than they are for other investing because:**

    A. You could lose your home if the investments don't work out as planned, possibly leaving you more in debt than ever.

    B. You could lose your home if your present level of income falls due to being disabled or laid off, general economic recession, or childbearing.

    C. My recommendation is that you *not* consider taxable investments before paying off your mortgage unless the three listed conditions are met.

III. **Home equity loans are dangerous because you can lose your house for nonpayment. Such loans should have the top priority for repayment, even ahead of other consumer debt.**

IV. **The parable of two families: the LiveHighs and the ThinkSmarts.**

    A. In identical financial situations, the LiveHighs choose to finance their higher standard of living by taking a 30-year mortgage when buying their home; the ThinkSmarts elect a 15-year mortgage on a less expensive (but functionally similar) home.

    B. After 15 years, the ThinkSmarts paid their mortgage in full and began redirecting their monthly mortgage payments into their retirement investment account. You'll likely be greatly surprised at how much more the ThinkSmarts have in their retirement account after 30 years than the LiveHighs have.

"If we can't afford to make extra principal payments on our home mortgage and at the same time put money into our retirement plan, which should have the priority?" . . .

. . . is a question I receive quite often. Unfortunately, there's no one-size-fits-all answer—your age, your tax bracket, what you would do with the tax savings from your mortgage interest, how long you expect to live in your home, and your general attitude toward being debt-free all play significant roles.

Let's say that two readers of this book who have different goals are each wrestling with this question. Rob is leery about the long-term health of Social Security and wants to begin building his retirement funds immediately. Mort thinks being in debt is more of a concern and plans to use any monthly surplus to make additional principal payments on his mortgage.

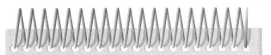

ROB EMPHASIZES SAVING FOR RETIREMENT

At End of Year	Balance Due on Mortgage	Value of 401(k) Account	Tax Savings Mortgage Interest	Tax Savings 401(k) Contributions
1	$133,047	$5,495	$1,697	$1,649
2	125,810	11,198	1,609	1,609
3	118,279	17,115	1,518	1,568
4	110,441	23,255	1,422	1,525
5	102,283	29,626	1,323	1,481
6	93,793	36,236	1,220	1,435
7	84,957	43,092	1,113	1,387
8	75,761	50,205	1,002	1,336
9	66,191	57,582	885	1,284
10	56,231	65,233	765	1,230
11	45,864	73,168	639	1,173
12	35,076	81,396	508	1,115
13	23,848	89,928	372	1,053
14	12,162	98,774	230	990
15	0	107,945	82	923
Summary	$0	$107,945	$14,384	$19,759

For comparison purposes, let's make their two situations identical: They both have new $140,000, 15-year 4% fixed-rate mortgages; both can set aside $1,200 out of each month's paycheck (their monthly mortgage payment is $1,036, leaving them each an extra $164 for payment of the principal *or* investment in a retirement account); both are in the 31% tax bracket (25% federal plus 6% state), and both have the opportunity to contribute to a retirement plan at work that will earn 6%, which is 2% more than their mortgages are costing them.

When they make their first month's mortgage payment, $467 of it is tax deductible as interest expense. This will lower each of their taxes by $145 a month (31% of $467). What they do with that $145 savings can make a big difference.

Let's assume that both Rob and Mort would like to get their hands on that savings sooner rather than later. They would get it back when they filed their income tax returns anyway, but why wait? So, they both change the withholding instructions they give their employers so that about $145 less is withheld for income taxes each month. By adding that amount to the extra $164 left from their monthly surplus, they each now have an extra $309 to work with. Rob contributes his $309 into his company's 401(k) plan while Mort takes his $309 and makes an extra principal payment on his mortgage.

Now here's where it can really get confusing. To construct an accurate picture, we have to recognize that Rob gets a *second* tax deduction—this time for putting money into the retirement plan. Rob's $309 contribution is worth another $96 tax savings, which he could then also put into his 401(k). But then that $96 contribution would save him an additional $30 in taxes, which he could also put into his 401(k). But then that $30 . . . well, you get the idea. If Rob took maximum advantage of this, he could ultimately put $448 into his company retirement plan that first month (his $164 monthly surplus plus the tax savings of $145 for mortgage interest plus another $139 in tax savings for contributing to the company 401(k)).

Assume that both men are able to take the maximum advantage of the available tax savings as the years pass. Mort pays down as much extra on his mortgage each month as he can and pays it off completely in a little over 11 years. At that point, he shifts all the money he formerly put toward his mortgage each month into his retirement plan. He also adjusts his withholdings to take maximum advantage of the tax savings his contributions create.

At the end of 15 years, their experiences can be summarized this way. Both men had the same out-of-pocket expenditures—$1,200 per month over 15 years, totaling $216,000. In return, they both accomplished paying their $140,000 mortgage loans in full and were able to invest for retirement. It's interesting to note that, although they proceeded according to different time tables, Rob and Mort ultimately saved an equal amount ($34,144) on their taxes. This was due to each of them always taking full advantage of the tax-deductibility of mortgage interest and 401(k) contributions with their surplus dollars.

The important difference in their financial situations after 15 years is found in the value of their retirement accounts. Rob's 401(k) grew to $107,945 and Mort's to $85,780. Although they had both saved the same amount in taxes which could then be invested for retirement, Rob's savings were "front-loaded." That meant he could put them to work in his 401(k) earlier than Mort could. In this way, Rob was able to take greater advantage of the tax-deferred compounding of profits. *The difference in his 401(k) would have been even greater if Rob's employer contributed matching funds.* Mort's retirement account later came on strong, but Rob's head start was too great.

Should you follow Rob's example? Perhaps, but not necessarily. To make it work, you've got to be able to aggressively use *all* of the tax savings, and more important, you need 15 years of relative stability in your job, the economy, and the tax code. That seems to be asking a lot from the next decade.

MORT EMPHASIZES PAYING OFF HIS MORTGAGE

At End of Year	Balance Due on Mortgage	Value of 401(k) Account	Tax Savings Mortgage Interest	Tax Savings 401(k) Contributions
1	$129,330	$0	$1,676	$0
2	118,361	0	1,542	0
3	107,086	0	1,404	0
4	95,496	0	1,262	0
5	83,581	0	1,117	0
6	71,334	0	967	0
7	58,744	0	813	0
8	45,803	0	655	0
9	32,500	0	493	0
10	18,824	0	326	0
11	4,767	0	154	0
12	0	14,230	14	4,313
13	0	36,668	0	6,470
14	0	60,489	0	6,470
15	0	85,780	0	6,470
Summary	$0	$85,780	$10,422	$23,722

The advantages of following Mort's approach are: It more quickly provides the security of debt-free home ownership, which will better enable you to weather any economic storms; in case of an emergency, the wealth in your home is more accessible than assets tied up in a retirement plan; and while Rob's return in the 401(k) could fall or (even turn negative), Mort's interest savings on his mortgage is guaranteed.

It's one thing to temporarily lower or eliminate putting money into a retirement plan in order to work on a debt-reduction plan; it's another altogether to close out your retirement plan.

Questions such as, "Should I cash in my pension plan in order to pay off my mortgage?" or, "Should I close my IRA and take the proceeds to pay off my consumer/car loans?" involve much more serious decisions than the example we just discussed.

Recommended Resource
The Banker's Secret
by Marc Eisenson

If you have a mortgage, this could be one of the most important books you'll ever buy! Eisenson has a simple premise: Prepayments on your loan prove that there is no reason to keep your family enslaved in debt for thirty years while you pay the bank back three to four times the mortgage money you borrowed. "In fact, the only difficult thing about pre-paying is understanding how such a good idea could have been kept a 'banker's secret' for so long." Highly recommended! (See excerpt on page 39.)

The steps, once taken, are irreversible. You can't change your mind later. So it's important to understand and weigh all the factors. Be sure you understand the tax consequences of prematurely withdrawing money from a tax-deferred plan. Let's say you cash in $10,000 before age 59½ (or 55 in some plans). First, the IRS hits you with a 10% penalty. That leaves $9,000. Next there are the ordinary federal income taxes. Assuming you're in the 25% marginal bracket, there goes another $2,500 (the penalty isn't deductible). So you only have $6,500 of your original $10,000 left to apply against your debts. Then there is the opportunity cost of not having the $10,000 compounding tax deferred for years into the future. So, it's a pretty costly decision from a tax standpoint.

To look at it from a strict planning point of view, I asked Jim Shoemaker—a certified financial planner and the president of his own financial planning firm in Memphis, Tennessee—what advice he would give in such a situation:

To a large degree, it depends on the person's age and whether they are currently managing their debt successfully. By "managing" I mean they are making consistent progress month by month and can see the day coming when they will be debt-free, even if it's a few years off. The 40-45 year age range is roughly the dividing point—getting one's debt under control before the end of this five year period is critically important.

If a person is 40 or younger and is currently managing their debt, I would advise they leave their retirement funds alone. However, if they are heavily debt-ridden (for example, $25,000-$35,000 in debt with an income of $35,000-$50,000 and no realistic options of getting the debts paid), I would say to go ahead and get the debt under control even though there is a heavy penalty and tax bite. Now, I'm not talking about home mortgages here, just consumer-type debts and home equity loans. If a person is over 45 and has still not overcome their debt, it becomes very difficult to effectively deal with debt as well as retirement. It's a difficult decision, but I would be hesitant to eliminate one's retirement fund because, at that late date, time is no longer on their side.

Don't be too quick to give up on the idea of making short-term lifestyle adjustments that would result in a greater monthly surplus. Examine all of your budget items closely — are there ways to lower them further? Or, are there assets you could sell (a second car, bicycles, boats, guns, an extra computer, etc.) and apply toward your debt retirement? Most families can raise an extra $100-$200 a month if they're willing to put up with some belt-tightening.

Up to this point, we've been looking at the merits of paying down your mortgage versus investing in or maintaining your retirement plan. Now let's look at a similar question that involves investing outside a tax-deferred account.

In the earlier analysis, powerful tax incentives worked in favor of Rob's strategy of investing versus Mort's strategy of paying down his mortgage. And as I pointed out, if Rob's employer was matching his 401(k) contributions, the case would have been even more compelling. However, these advantages are missing when we talk about investing in regular brokerage accounts.

In those situations, I believe most families are better served if any surplus funds are initially used to pay down the house mortgage rather than used for investing. First, as we've already discussed, investments don't always pan out as hoped. You might be left with more debt than ever — and possibly even lose your house! Second, you probably are assuming that your income will continue at its present level or higher. But what if you are disabled, or laid off, or unexpected developments harm your business? Be careful about presuming on the future. And third, your patience will eventually be rewarded. The guaranteed interest savings from a faster pay-down will free up other funds that can be used for future investing (as we saw with Tom and Linda in chapter one).

I would recommend that you *not* consider other taxable investments (as opposed to paying down your house mortgage) unless these conditions are met:

❶ Both spouses are in *complete* agreement that the investment should have the top priority;

❷ The remaining unpaid balance on your mortgage is less than 75% of the current value of your house (for example, your house would sell for around $160,000 and you owe less than $120,000 on your mortgage); and

❸ The investment will provide a return that is *virtually certain* to be greater than the interest rate on your mortgage.

If these three criteria are present, using your surplus income for investing rather than paying extra on your mortgage could be considered a reasonable and prudent decision. (This assumes you already have an adequate contingency fund in place — see chapter three.) I want to make clear, however, that what we are talking about here applies only to first mortgages.

Is It A Matter of Conviction?

Naturally, the intensity of one's beliefs about the importance of being free of debt should play a major role in balancing the various pros and cons. Financial planner Steve Humphrey, former director of counseling at Crown Financial Ministries, has this to say:

"For some who are carrying large sums of consumer debt (not mortgage debt) and have convictions about the importance of being debt-free, it might be the best thing for them to cash in a retirement plan. Eliminating the debt burden gives them a fresh start. From that point, they can begin to address other goals, such as retirement planning and mortgage reduction. The most important thing is that people need to have clearly stated goals that are based on their Christian convictions rather than on income tax considerations."

Do not boast about tomorrow, for you do not know what a day may bring forth.
Proverbs 27:1

A stingy man is eager to get rich and is unaware that poverty awaits him.
Proverbs 28:22

"Home equity loans" are another story altogether. Americans used to take out second mortgages as a last resort. Now . . .

. . . many consider them a sign of savvy tax planning. Why the change in our thinking? Aside from the obvious fact that our entire society has become increasingly addicted to debt, we should understand the major roles played by the federal government and our friendly bankers. First, Congress got the ball rolling when it passed tax legislation that eliminated the income tax deduction for consumer interest payments unless they were made on a home mortgage. Then, lenders made it easy for us by offering low teaser rates and often waiving closing costs and other fees. Toss in the fact that, with interest rates so low, the cost of borrowing is less than it has been for quite a while. Now homeowners are using these loans to pay for everything from vacations to college tuition to new cars. Everybody seems happy, so what's the problem?

I don't like these loans for the same reasons that banks love them. First, home-equity loans greatly increase the amount of money banks can safely lend to you (and therefore the amount of interest they receive). Most Americans don't need more credit and more debt. Second, if anything goes wrong with your loan, the bank is protected and can always foreclose on the house. It's one thing when getting laid off or having unexpected medical expenses shoots a hole in your monthly budget and your new car is repossessed. It's quite another when they come for your house!

There are other concerns as well. Some lenders have let homeowners borrow up to 100% (and more!) of their equity—where would you ever get the money to pay off such a large loan? Years of building equity through your monthly payments can be completely erased by one problem loan. Especially beware of loans that allow you to pay interest-only during the term of your loan and then call for immediate payment of the full principal. Finally, if the loan has a variable rate, check the periodic cap (the limit on interest rate changes at one time) and lifetime cap (the limit on interest rate changes throughout the loan term). Such "caps" can vary widely. All in all, home equity loans are a threat to your financial safety, and their payment in full should be a priority.

Refinancing your mortgage to take advantage of lower interest rates— and/or shorten your payment schedule to a 15-year maturity—can result in significant savings on interest expense.

Refinancing your mortgage involves paying your existing mortgage off early by taking out a newer loan at a lower rate. The key statistic in deciding whether to refinance is learning how far down the road you "break even." Here's what you do. First, understand what "points" are (see next page). Next, shop for the best deal and learn (1) what your total closing costs will be (excluding any prepayments for insurance, taxes, or interest) and (2) what your new monthly "prin-

Mortgage Rates
The www.bankrate.com site has links to where the best current mortgage rates can be found.

cipal and interest" (P&I) payment will be. Next, subtract the amount of your new P&I payment from your old one. The difference is how much you'll save each month. Finally, divide this monthly savings into your closing costs. This tells you how many months before the refinancing pays for itself (tax considerations aside). That's your break-even point; after that, you're saving every month.

Here's an example: If your new monthly payment would be $140 less than your current one, and if your total closing costs (including one point) were $2,800, then it would take 20 months' worth of savings to pay your expenses (2800 divided by 140). After that, you'd be ahead an extra $140 each month.

It can get confusing trying to compare different proposals, so here's a handy way to convert points into a percentage rate: treat each point as if it added ¼ of 1% to your loan rate. Example: a 6% rate with one point is roughly the same as a 6¼% rate with no points.

Once you know the break-even point for each loan you've been quoted, the main consideration is how long you expect to be in your present home. If you don't think you'll be there long enough to reach the break-even point, forget it. If you think you'll be there past break-even and decide to go ahead, you still have to decide whether to take a loan that features a lower rate but more points, or a higher rate with fewer points. The general rule is that the shorter the time past break-even that you expect to live there, the more you should lean toward the lower transaction costs. That means a shorter stay equals fewer points with a higher rate; a longer stay equals more points but a lower rate.

> ## MORTGAGE "POINTS"
>
> A typical mortgage loan, in addition to the interest rate you pay, carries one "point." A point is equal to 1% of the loan amount and is charged by the lender to cover the up-front costs of originating the loan. Credit reports, appraisals, title insurance, and the legal fees for preparing and recording documents are additional expenses. Points are subtracted from your proceeds at the time of your loan closing.
>
> For example: If your new mortgage is for $120,000 and you are charged one point, then you really only receive credit for $118,800 at the loan closing ($120,000 times 1% equals $1,200 in points paid).

To keep things simple, some lenders offer a "no points or closing costs" option where they let you skip the points and closing costs entirely . . .

. . . in exchange for a higher interest rate. Then it becomes simply a matter of comparing the interest rate they quote you with the rate you're paying now. For example, if you're currently paying 5.0% but can get a "no points or closing costs" rate of 4.5%, you're guaranteed to save. In fact, there's no reason you wouldn't want to refinance multiple times over the years when the advantages are this clear cut. Sure, there's some paperwork involved, but there's probably nothing else you can do that will pay you (in saved interest) such a high hourly rate for your time! I'd consider refinancing whenever you can save at least one-quarter of a percent on a "no points or closing costs" basis. Depending on the overall level of rates, you'll save $6,000–$7,000 in interest over 30 years on a $100,000 mortgage for *every* one-quarter percent reduction in your rate. However, the shorter the remaining term of your mortgage, the less you will save. With under 10 years remaining on a mortgage, it is unlikely that refinancing will result in much savings.

Here are some other shopping tips that can help you save money. First, look into getting a 15-year mortgage rather than a 30-year one. The monthly payment will be higher, but the interest rate is lower. The savings in interest is dramatic! Second, if you refinance and end up with a lower monthly payment than you're now making, the temptation will be to take the savings and spend it elsewhere. Don't do it! Instead, send in the same amount using two checks. One check will be for the new monthly payment; the other can be applied to pre-paying principal and hastening the day when you own your home free and clear. Many lenders allow you to accomplish this using a single check, but either way be sure to include a note explaining that the extra payment is to be applied to the principal balance. Other points to keep in mind:

• You can refinance with the original lender or go to a new one.

• Find out when the rate on your loan will be "locked in" (permanently set). Is it when you apply? When the loan is closed? Many borrowers have been hurt when interest rates rose after the original proposal was made but before the lender locked in the rate.

• Get a commitment in writing of the exact terms of the mortgage being offered and how long the offer is good for. It should include the circumstances under which the lender would be allowed to back out (for example, in case of a dispute over the appraised value of your home).

• Check with your loan officer or processor to find out when the appraisal and credit agency reports are due back. Call on the expected dates to see if everything checks out.

Before leaving this topic, let us salute the money-saving virtues of 15-year mortgages. Consider the saga of the LiveHighs and the ThinkSmarts.

Two business partners named LiveHigh and ThinkSmart had a lot in common. Each owned half of the business, and they paid themselves equal salaries. Both were married, and had two kids each. Both LiveHigh and ThinkSmart spent several years saving for a down payment on a house, and each had accumulated $30,000. Finally, the moment they'd worked so hard for arrived: the day they went looking for that first new house for their families.

Each had budgeted for monthly principal and interest payments of around $1,200. With this in mind, LiveHigh knew just the house he wanted—it had an extra large corner lot and a nicely finished basement. He figured that with interest rates down now, he could pick up a 30-year, 4.9% mortgage that, along with his down payment, would enable him to afford the $256,000 price he was able to negotiate

ThinkSmart, more of a bargain hunter, went looking in a somewhat less upscale neighborhood. He found a slightly older house in excellent condition that was very similar in size to the one LiveHigh was buying. The lot was smaller, but so was the price. The $192,000 cost was appealing because it meant his $1,200 monthly payment would fit just right with a 15-year, 4.0% mortgage. He put down his $30,000 and signed on the dotted line.

A SOUND MIND BRIEFING

Big Savings Through Mortgage Pre-payments

by Marc Eisenson

When you take out a loan, you agree to pay back the amount borrowed plus interest. That's fair. But you've probably never realized just how much interest can be. For example, on a $130,000, 30-year mortgage, written at 6.0% interest, the total payback will be over $280,500. That's more than $150,500 in interest charges on a $130,000 loan. More than what was borrowed! Shocking, isn't it?

Well, take heart. Making small, frequent pre-payments with pocket change—that money most of us would never invest, or miss— will save a substantial portion of the more than $150,500 in interest that this $130,000 loan would normally incur. Pre-payments are not additional costs. They are simply small amounts paid sooner.

Every month, or whenever you are expected to make a payment to your lender (for convenience we'll assume all borrowers are homeowners and all lenders are banks), the bank's computer calculates the amount of interest you owe for having used its money during the previous month, and subtracts that interest from the amount of the check you send in. What's left is credited toward the outstanding balance of your loan.

To make it easy to keep track of how much interest you are being charged and how much of each payment is being credited toward the principal of your loan, it is necessary to use an appropriate pre-payment schedule. These computer printed charts, often referred to as amortization schedules, separate out the interest and principal components of each monthly payment, along with the balance remaining after each payment has been made.

Shown above is a pre-payment schedule showing the payments during various time periods for our sample loan. When each payment is made, the balance of the loan gets reduced by the amount of the principal portion only, not by the amount of the total monthly payment. If the sample loan shown were your mortgage, you would be expected to pay $779.42 every month for thirty years. You could not pay less, or skip any payments without risking a foreclosure. But, you could pay more.

For illustrative purposes, let's assume that you are about to mail in mortgage payment #1. If you add $130.07 (principal payment

MORTGAGE SCHEDULE

Amortization based on 30 year,
$130,000 loan at 6% interest.
Monthly payment of $779.42

Payment Number	Interest Portion	Principal Portion	Balance Remaining
1	$ 650.00	$ 129.42	$ 129,870.58
2	649.35	130.07	129,740.51
3	648.70	130.72	129,609.80
120	545.13	234.29	108,790.73
121	543.95	235.47	108,555.27
122	542.78	236.64	108,318.62

#2) to the $779.42 which is due every month, and mail in a single check for $909.49, the bank will properly credit your pre-payment of $130.07 and you won't have to make interest payment #2. You will never pay that $649.35!

Next month, when you mail in your check for $779.42, it will be credited as if it were payment #3, since the principal portion of payment #2 will have already been credited, and the interest payment which the bank's computer will show as due, is the interest amount shown for payment #3. Now for the bonus: Not only will that $130.07 save you $649.35, but it will also reduce the term of your loan by one month. That's pre-paying in a nutshell. The only place where you can earn more just as safely with such tiny investments is by pre-paying on your credit cards.

You can begin pre-paying at any time; however, the sooner you begin, the greater your savings will be. That's because interest payments are higher and principal payments are lowest at the inception of the loan. Later on, the savings will still be substantial, although smaller. Let's look at a portion of the schedule of our sample mortgage ten years down the road. We'll assume that no pre-payments have been made. Assume an additional principal payment of $236.64 is mailed in with payment #121 (for a total of $779.42 + $236.64 = $1016.06). You will save $542.78 (interest payment #122) and retire the loan one month earlier. The following month's payment would be #123, not payment #122.

Note that even after 120 monthly payments of $779.42 each have been made, totaling $93,530.40 (120 x $779.42), the balance on this loan has only been reduced by $21,209.27 ($130,000 less $108,790.73). The remaining $72,321.13 ($93,530.40 paid less the $21,209.27) all would have gone toward interest—that's more than half of what was borrowed in the first place!

If pre-paying seems like a good idea to you, get a pre-payment schedule for your loan and begin! No matter what type of loan you have, whether it's a fixed rate, adjustable, or bi-weekly, the more you pre-pay and the sooner you begin, the more you will save!

Amortization Calculator

If locking in the higher payments of a 15-year loan is too scary, consider prepaying your 30-year loan. The net effect can be the same as a 15-year loan, without the obligation of higher payments.

One of the best ways to prepay (see previous page) involves using a loan amortization schedule. To create one for your loan, see the Mortgage Calculator at www.bankrate.com.

But godliness with contentment is great gain. For we brought nothing into the world, and we can take nothing out of it.
1 Timothy 6:6–7

With saving for their down payments out of the way, the partners each began investing $300 per month into their new retirement accounts. As time passed, the business grew slowly but steadily. We pick up our story 15 years later as ThinkSmart is writing the check for his final mortgage payment. What a great feeling! He and his wife decide to go out for the evening to celebrate. They talk about how much fun it would be to "trade up" to a newer home, but agree they don't want to get back into mortgage debt again. Instead, they decide to increase the amount they put into their retirement account. Every month they deposit the $1,200 that formerly went to the mortgage company.

We can fast-forward 15 more years to the end of our story. Mr. and Mrs. LiveHigh are happy. After 30 years, they have written their final mortgage check. As they think of the future, they agree: "With this taken care of at last, it's time to begin putting more money into our retirement account."

Meanwhile, ThinkSmart and his wife are also thinking of the future. Their quarterly statement came today, and the current balance in their investment account is quite impressive! As they look through some travel brochures, they agree: "With this much in savings, it's time to begin enjoying some of the fruits of our labor."

Assuming that both families earned 6% on their retirement investments over the years, how much more do the ThinkSmarts have than the LiveHighs?

First, let me point out the *reason* the ThinkSmarts have more: they were willing to accept a lifestyle with comfortable, but more modest, amenities. Although the houses themselves were similar in size and functionaility, the LiveHighs were unwilling to do their home shopping in older, less upscale neighborhoods. For most couples who have debt problems, their difficulties began when they obligated themselves to a larger mortgage payment than was reasonable given their income.

This is especially true if they relied on two incomes when computing their ability to comfortably make long-term monthly mortgage payments. In that event, if either income is interrupted for any reason—the economy, corporate strategic planning, technical obsolescence, disability, or childbearing— they automatically have a financial problem on their hands.

Now, here are the numbers reflecting the surprisingly high costs of the LiveHighs' lifestyle. After 30 years of paying on their mortgage and contributing to retirement, the LiveHighs have $302,800 in their retirement account. Meanwhile the ThinkSmarts, after paying off a smaller mortage in only 15 years, have $653,600 in their retirement account. Thus, they have $350,800 more, more than twice as much. The status and comforts of their "nicer" home ended up costing the LiveHighs far more than they could have ever imagined! ◆

◇
3
◇

CHAPTER PREVIEW

Do You Have
Adequate Savings?

I. **Before risking your money in the stock and bond markets, you should have an adequate contingency fund set aside in a separate savings account.**

  A. It serves as a contingency fund for dealing with the unexpected. Financial planners frequently recommend six months' living expenses as an adequate size. You'll want to invest your contingency fund in an account that is immediately accessible and provides complete safety.

  B. Second, your savings reserve can be used as an accumulation fund where you save for major expenditures that are not provided for in your monthly budget. Typically, an accumulation fund allows you to have a longer time frame in mind (say, a year or more before you'll need to withdraw the money). In that event, you can improve your returns by looking at a different set of investment options.

II. **We review four safe havens suitable for investing your emergency fund savings.**

  A. Bank savings accounts offer convenience and federal insurance.

  B. Credit unions often offer better rates and service than banks. They also can offer federal insurance.

  C. Money-market mutual funds are not federally insured but are virtually as safe as FDIC-insured accounts.

  D. U.S. Treasury bills offer the greatest degree of safety and liquidity, but are not convenient to purchase nor are their returns as high as other alternatives.

III. **We also look at three ways to invest your accumulation fund.**

  A. Bank certificates of deposit offer safety and reasonable returns but lack some flexibility due to the early withdrawal penalties. You should be willing to shop nationwide if you want the best rates.

  B. If you won't need to cash in for two to three years, short-term bond funds offer the potential for better returns at a slight increase in volatility.

  C. If you won't need to cash in for three or more years, another option is a mortgage-backed bond fund. Ginnie Maes offer attractive yields and pay monthly dividends which you would reinvest in more shares.

**Even if you have not completely reached your goal
of becoming debt-free, it's still a good idea to begin setting
aside some money for emergencies or large purchases.**

Although it is economically sensible to first pay off debts that are carrying
high interest charges, don't use every spare penny for that purpose. Everyone
needs a savings reserve for two reasons.

First, it is a contingency fund for dealing with the unexpected. Perhaps
you will have unanticipated medical or auto repair expenses. Or, it might be
a case of a temporary layoff at work or a disabling injury. If you don't have
a "cushion" to fall back on, you'll eventually wind up back in debt because
of the unhappy financial surprises that come everyone's way occasionally.
By having this money set aside and readily available, you can "borrow" from
yourself rather than from family members or your bank.

How large should your contingency fund be? Many financial planners
recommend having from three to six months' living expenses set aside. The
amount is up to you, but I think living expenses for at least three months
would be a minimum. You'll want to invest your contingency fund in an
account that is immediately accessible and provides complete safety. Shortly,
we'll go shopping for just such investments.

Second, your savings reserve can be used as an accumulation fund where
you save for major expenditures that are not provided for in your monthly
budget. Such items might include replacing your old car, buying some new
furniture as the family grows, or funding that home remodeling project you've
been looking forward to. Typically, an accumulation fund allows you to have
a longer time frame in mind (say, a year or more before you'll need to withdraw the money) than is the case with your contingency fund. Liquidity is
not quite as important. In that event, you can improve your returns by looking at a different set of investment options. We'll do that later in this chapter.

To be sure you save, pay yourself first.

When one of my teenage sons came to me for help in getting his finances
organized, the first thing I did was get him set up on a pay-as-you-go basis
using the "envelope" system that I mentioned in chapter 1. That's where you
cash your paycheck(s) and divide your income into several envelopes, one
for each of your major spending areas. When the money in a particular envelope is gone, that means no more spending in that area until the next payday.

Modern technology has enabled us to improve on this approach—now we
use the "Ziploc™ bag system" so all the loose change doesn't fall out!—but there's
one thing technology can't do: restrain us from overspending. That part still requires self-discipline, sacrifice, and a long-term perspective. Arriving at financial
independence is very satisfying, but the journey can be tough along the way.

Here's the process my son used as he worked on building his savings. *After* setting aside his tithe and taxes, what was left was his spendable income. This was the "pie" that he proceeded to "cut" several ways. The *first* piece of 10% went into his contingency fund account. Then, the remainder of his spendable income went into bags for his current bills, debt repayment, and monthly living expenses.

His contingency fund came in handy twice during his first few months using the system—to pay for emergency brake and transmission repairs. The money in the savings account was used up, and he had to begin building it anew. But having it on hand prevented him from going back into debt to pay for those items. That's why it makes sense to set aside some savings in a contingency fund.

Automation beats procrastination.

When it comes to saving, despite your best intentions, it's easy to rationalize putting it off until the next paycheck. So it often helps to have some of your money put aside *automatically* before you have the opportunity to spend it. I suggest you sign up to have part of your paycheck (you decide how much) automatically deposited into your savings account at your credit union or bank. It's easy, convenient, and offers some useful discipline. Plus, your savings are insured and available for withdrawal without penalty whenever you wish.

Consider a strategy of saving 5%–10% of your gross income when you're in your 20s. Initially, this will go toward building your contingency fund. Once that's in place, your savings can be used for a down payment on a house and other large purchases. Then, move up to 10%–15% in your 30s and 40s. Usually at this age, the primary use of savings is to invest for retirement. In your 50s, as home-buying and child-rearing costs are tapering off, you might be able to boost your savings rate to the 15%–20% area in final preparation for your approaching retirement years.

The unrelenting power of compound interest is one of your greatest investing weapons.

Consider this updated version of the saga of Jack and Jill. Jack started a paper route when he was eight years old and managed to save $1,200 per year. He deposited it in an IRA investment account that earned 8% interest. Jack continued this pattern through high school and "retired" from the paper-delivery business at the ripe old age of 18. All told, he saved $13,200 during that time. He left his savings to compound until he reached 65 and *never added another dollar* during the entire intervening 47 years.

Jill didn't have a paper route, but waited until her post-college days to start her savings. At age 26, she was sufficiently settled to put $3,000 into her IRA retirement fund. This she continued to do *every year for 40 years*. She also

How Much Does
Impulse Buying Reduce
Your Savings?
You have to begin looking on
impulse purchases as one of
your most formidable foes in
the battle to save more.

Impulse purchases usually
violate the following rules for
wise shopping: shopping
around for the best buys,
keeping tight control on the
use of your credit card, buying
only what you really need,
buying what's practical, and
checking carefully for quality.

Here are some suggestions
for using an "impulse list" to
guide your spending:

• Never buy anything
unless you have budgeted for
it. Instead, write it down on
your impulse list.

• Get at least three
prices for the same item
from different sources.

• Wait at least ten
days to buy it.

• Never have more
than one item on your list.

The only way to conquer the
impulse is self-discipline.
Without discipline, no budget
will help. "For a man is a slave
to whatever has mastered
him" (2 Peter 2:19b).

earned an 8% compounded return on her savings. Now, the question is which fund was larger at age 65 — Jack's IRA into which he put $13,200 or Jill's into which she put $120,000?

Surprisingly, Jack is the winner. His IRA has grown to $894,000, an amount equal to *about 68 times* more than what he put in as a child. Jill did almost as well with hers, which grew to $878,000. But Jack's earlier start, even with much smaller amounts and deposits for far fewer years, was too much to overcome thanks to the tremendous power of compounding. The moral is: invest early and often — even small amounts can make a big difference!

Making the sacrifices necessary to get debt-free and save for future needs is not a lot of fun. But laying this foundation is vitally important and, if you'll commit yourself, it can be done. So, be diligent and be prayerful.

God's provisions include our physical needs as well as our spiritual ones. God's provisions are unmerited; we've done nothing to deserve them. God's provisions often come after we wait in expectant obedience. God's provisions are generous and overflowing. And over all of this is Christ's complete sufficiency regardless of the circumstances. Pastor Ron Dunn once illustrated the truth of Christ's sufficiency this way:

He said to John on the island of Patmos: "I'm the beginning and the end. I'm the Alpha and the Omega." He was saying: "I'm the A and the Z." He's the whole alphabet. Isn't that amazing? I just bought a set of the Encyclopedia Britannica, and you know, I made a discovery the other day. I think I'm going to read through the whole encyclopedia and see if this is really true, but I believe they wrote that entire encyclopedia with only twenty-six letters. Boy, that's something, isn't it? Now my little nine year old girl has a book "See Dick Run," and I can imagine that they wrote that with twenty-six letters, but to come to the Encyclopedia Britannica or to any book you want to write, and to say I wrote this with just twenty-six letters, I tell you that's amazing to me. You don't need to go outside the alphabet to write anything! And I'll tell you something else — you never need to go outside of Jesus for anything that you need. He's the Alpha and the Omega. He's all that you need.

I know that sometimes the effort to be a responsible steward can be tiring. Whether it's giving faithfully, getting debt-free, saving for the future, making prudent investing decisions, or planning for retirement, it usually includes a sacrifice of time and material comforts. Let me encourage you to continue trusting Him to provide all that you need to be obedient and victorious in these areas.

God encourages us in His Word to pray expectantly. *"This is the confidence we have in approaching God: that if we ask anything according to his will, he hears us. And if we know that he hears us — whatever we ask — we know that we have what we asked of him"* (1 John 5:14-15).

Now it's time to consider some of the primary ways you can invest that emergency fund you're going to be building.

Your emergency fund is not a part of your long-term portfolio and should be handled differently than your other investments. You should look for a "parking place" for your money that is absolutely safe and can be easily converted to cash without early withdrawal penalties. The interest rate earned is a lesser consideration than assured immediate availability. We'll look at four safe havens that are suitable for this purpose, starting with your local bank.

There are many different ways you can save at your local bank, but you need to know that the sweetest deals these days are found online.

Sure, if you want convenient locations and tellers who know your name, there's no substitute for a local bank. But if you want to earn the best possible return, the offerings at local banks typically don't compare with their online competitors.

More than 65% of consumers currently use online banking, a huge increase from the roughly 5% using it at the turn of the century. Initially, this surge in demand came from younger people, specifically Generation X (whose ages now range from roughly 30 to 50), led the way in online banking use. As this group entered the work force, they brought their computer savvy with them into everyday life.

But more than anything, the increasing availability along with advances in technology played the major role. Broadband Internet connections are now the norm. Not surprisingly, people with "fast access" to the Internet are twice as likely as others to use online banking. And the explosion of smartphones (and now tablets) has made it easy to bank online anytime, anywhere.

Online banks (also sometimes called "Internet-only" or "Web-only" banks) tend to offer significantly better rates on every type of savings instrument — and you don't have to give up the security of FDIC insurance. The higher rates are the result of lower expenses, since online banks don't have to maintain lots of "brick-and-mortar" branch offices. Knowing that most consumers are reluctant to stop banking locally, online banks make it easy to set up a savings account that links electronically to a local-bank checking account. Transfers from local checking to online savings are as simple as a few mouse clicks.

In any event — online or local — here's a guide to the most common types of accounts being offered.

• **Regular Savings:** These accounts typically offer the lowest rate but have low minimum requirements. They may pay interest either from the day of deposit or, in some cases, the first of the following month. The only reason to have such an account is if you can't meet the minimums required for the better-paying types of accounts. (All the rates mentioned in this section are from

---

Change A Habit.
Boost Your Savings.

I am going to point out something about your spending that you may never have thought of (and may not be able to get out of your mind once I put it there). Have you ever stopped to consider what the "future value" of the money you spent today could have amounted to?

That is, if you'd saved it rather than spent it, what would it be worth as you neared retirement, say in twenty years?

For example, let's say you spend $7 each workday for lunch on the job. What if you decided to fast once a week and save that $7 rather than spend it? You continue to do this once a week for twenty years. Invest it at 6% and it would grow to . . . (drum roll) . . . $14,061!

Surprised?
I thought so.

Now, start applying that same logic to other adjustments you can make in your lifestyle. What if you could save $20 a week in gas and parking if you were to carpool or take the bus? You might be more inclined to endure the extra hassle when you realized you were going to have an extra $40,176 waiting for you down the road.

And if you buy cigarettes at a pack-a-day rate, that's $56,246 up in smoke. Well, you get the idea.

Think about it.

mid-2013, a time when interest rates were at very low levels.) Savers could earn 0.75% or more by putting their savings in an online-bank account. This was a meager payout to be sure, but nevertheless compared well to the 0.25% average rates at local banks.

• **Money-Market Accounts (MMAs).** These accounts typically pay higher rates than regular savings, but require larger minimum deposits. The minimum account is usually $1,000, and there is a service charge ($5 or $10) if the balance falls below it. Check-writing privileges are available, but only for a few checks per month. Local banks are paying 0.25%-0.40% on MMAs, depending on the size of the deposit. Online banks, in contrast, are offering MMA rates in the 0.60%-to-1.00% range. (Don't confuse money-market *accounts* with money-market *funds*. MMFs are mutual funds, not bank instruments. An advantage of bank MMAs is that they are guaranteed by the FDIC up to $250,000.)

• **Certificates of Deposit (CDs).** As with other bank offerings, you are lending money to your bank for a fixed rate of interest. Unlike the others, however, you agree not to withdraw your money for a set period of time. If you take it out early, you forfeit a large part of the interest you would have earned. In return, banks typically pay a higher rate on CDs than they do on MMAs. We'll discuss bank CDs in more detail later in the chapter.

Credit unions are another option. They're to banks what generic drugs are to name brand prescriptions . . .

. . . excellent substitutes that typically give you good value for your money and are just as safe. Credit unions are not-for-profit financial services "cooperative" organizations. That means they are owned and operated by their members, such as employees of certain companies or employees and alumni of particular universities. Today, more than 7,000 credit unions are in operation in the U.S., serving more than 93 million members. They excel in two key areas: rates and customer service.

 Rates. Because of their unique structure, credit unions tend to operate conservatively. (They largely avoided the sub-prime mess that entangled so many big banks a few years ago.) Being not-for-profit organizations means credit unions typically (but not always) are able to pay higher interest rates on savings accounts than banks do, while charging lower rates on loans. One consideration: Many credit unions do not pay interest based on *average* monthly balance but on *lowest* monthly balance. Such a policy is designed to discourage withdrawals, so if your plan is to draw on your savings regularly, a money-market account (see above) may be preferable.

Service. In surveys, credit unions typically score high marks for customer service (after all, they are owned by their members!). But lack of convenience can be a downside, since most credit unions have

---

Things You Should Know About FDIC Insurance

The $250,000 insurance limit applies per person and not per account. This means that all checking accounts, savings accounts, certificates of deposit, and business accounts (if run as sole proprietorships) combined at any one bank is limited to $250,000 of protection.

The $250,000 limit includes any interest you might have coming. For example, if you had $248,000 in CDs which earned $8,000 in interest before the failure, your total recovery would be limited to $250,000 and you would lose $6,000 of the interest.

Not All Banks Carry FDIC Insurance Protection

Many rely on state-sponsored programs instead. Unfortunately, state deposit insurance has proven unreliable in many instances. Here are two precautions you can take. One, immediately move any deposits you have in an institution that carries only state deposit insurance to one protected by FDIC insurance. And two, never exceed the $250,000 limit at any one institution.

fewer branches and ATMs than banks. So it's worthing finding out if a particular credit union belongs to the Co-Op Network, which gives members access to more than 30,000 no-fee ATMs across North America. Many credit unions offer discounts on automobile and life insurance. That can be a strong plus.

 **Safety.** Approximately 98% of credit unions are protected by a federal agency that insures their deposits just like the FDIC does for banks. (Don't settle for state-sponsored or private deposit insurance—many have had problems in the past.) However, the rules governing which kinds of accounts are insured and for how much can be confusing. To be absolutely sure you're fully covered, request the booklet *Your Insured Funds* from your credit union. Have an officer go through it with you and explain which sections apply to your account. The booklet is also available from the National Credit Union Administration at their web site (www.ncua.gov) or by calling 703-518-6300.

Eligibility. Most credit unions are sponsored by employers or trade and community associations, and they limit membership to employees or those with geographical proximity. However, there are some that cater to the investing public at large, so it's worth calling the Credit Union National Association (800-358-5710), or going online to visit their website (www.creditunion.coop), to see if there is one in your area that you could join.

Now, let's turn to a third safe haven for your emergency savings— money-market mutual funds. What is a money-market fund, anyway?

When you open a savings account or buy a CD at your bank (that is, lend them your money), your bank turns around and lends your money to others at a higher rate than it's paying to you. Obviously, the less it pays you on your savings, the more profit it makes. The problem with this arrangement is that you and your bank are financial adversaries.

Fortunately, there are other borrowers, the "big time" players, who would like you to lend to them *and will typically pay you more interest than your bank will*. These organizations include the federal government, big corporations, and even other banks. However, to do business with them readily, you need a go-between. That's where a special type of mutual fund comes in, one that specializes strictly in the short-term lending of money in the financial markets. Hence, its name: money-market fund.

Your money-market fund is on *your* side; it will try to get you the best rates it can, while still not taking undue risks. You give the fund your money; the fund gives you one of its shares for every $1 you put in. It takes your money and lends it out to the big time players, often getting a rate of interest higher than your bank will pay you over the same time period. (This has not always been the case during the extremely low interest-rate environment during 2008-2013.) The value of each money-market fund share doesn't fluctuate; it is kept at a constant $1—the same amount you paid for each share.

As the fund earns interest from its investments, it "pays" you your portion by crediting you with more shares. You earn interest, that is, receive more shares, every single day. The longer you leave your money in, the more shares you'll have. In this way, you

WOULD TAX-FREE MONEY MARKET FUNDS GIVE YOU A BETTER RETURN?

Tax-free money funds invest solely in the IOUs of state and local governments which will mature sometime within the next year. These bonds were originally issued in order to raise money for the construction of public projects like roads, schools, and hospitals, and now the time is close at hand when they will be repaid in full. They are called municipal bonds (or "munis") because of the governmental units which issue them.

By law, the interest earned on such bonds is exempt from federal income taxes. Because of the value of these tax benefits to investors, issuers of tax-free bonds can borrow money at lower interest rates than those paid by other borrowers. Even though their yields are lower, you might be better off investing in tax-free money funds. Here's how to find out—use the formula explained in the example below to convert the yield of any tax-free fund to its *equivalent before-tax yield*. Then you can compare apples with apples. All you need to know is your "marginal" tax rate. At present, the federal tax law provides for seven basic tax rates (which start at 10% and can rise as high as 39.6%—see page 137). How high up the tax ladder does your income take you? That's your marginal rate.

If the Vanguard taxable MMF is yielding 3.46% and Vanguard's tax-free fund is yielding 2.39%, who would benefit from using their tax-free fund?

<u>For a 28% Marginal Tax Bracket Investor</u>
1 minus .28 = .72
2.39% divided by .72 = equivalent to a 3.31% pre-tax rate
Conclusion: Not as good as the 3.46% Vanguard taxable yield

<u>For a 33% Marginal Tax Bracket Investor</u>
1 minus .33 = .67
2.39% divided by .67 = equivalent to a 3.56% pre-tax rate
Conclusion: Better than the 3.46% Vanguard taxable yield

Thus, the tax-free fund would be a better deal for savers in the 33% tax-bracket (or higher) but not those in the 28% bracket (or lower). This will not always be the case. Money fund yields can change quickly, so it pays to run the numbers regularly.

Tax-free money funds offer the same liquidity and other advantages as their taxable counterparts, but there are a few additional considerations that make their risk slightly higher. For one, there is a default risk on muni securities where there is virtually no such risk for other money market securities like Treasuries and bank CDs. Another is that, due to the limited number of muni securities available at any one time, tax-free money funds have occasionally had to extend their average maturities or lower their quality standards in order to acquire the dollar amounts needed.

Having said this, however, the increased level of risk is relatively small due to the diversification you get when buying shares in a large money fund portfolio.

are assured of getting all of your money back, *whenever* you want it, plus all the interest you've earned in the meantime.

Newcomers to money-market mutual funds often hesitate to use them because they don't carry FDIC protection. This caution is unnecessary. Thanks to the short-term nature of their portfolios (average maturity of all their holdings cannot exceed 60 days) as well as Securities and Exchange Commission (SEC) regulations governing quality that were further tightened in 2010, money-market mutual funds are essentially as safe as insured bank accounts.

Opening a money-market fund account is similar to opening a checking account—a few forms to sign and you're on your way.

There are three different kinds of money-market funds.

❶ Those that lend money to businesses and bank. These are the most common ones. I'll refer to these as corporate money-market funds because they invest primarily in bank certificates of deposit and commercial paper. This kind pays the highest yield to investors and is the most popular.

❷ Those that lend money only to the federal government and its agencies. These are for people who want added safety. However, given the excellent track record of the corporate kind (in more than 30 years, only one corporate retail fund has ever lost value and that was limited to just three cents on the dollar), it's debatable whether the added caution of sticking strictly with Uncle Sam's securities is worth the slight reduction in yield.

❸ Those that invest only in tax-free municipal bonds that are very close to maturity. For people who are in high tax brackets, the income from these money funds is free from federal income taxes. And if you invest in a single-state tax-free fund for your state of residence, your income is exempt from state income taxes as well. However, their yields are typically the lowest of the three.

To intelligently shop for a good money-market fund, you need to understand the way yields are listed in the paper.

Barron's, a weekly newspaper published by Dow Jones, is a great source of data for savers, and a lot of the content is free online. At barrons.com/listings, you'll find alphabetized links to hundreds of taxable and tax-free money funds.

Since most of the major money-market mutual funds offer similar services and portfolio risk, the decision as to which to buy usually rests on where the best returns are to be found. In researching this information in *Barron's,* you will see different yields listed for each fund.

The first percentage listed is usually called the "7-Day Average (or Current) Yield." This reflects the annualized equivalent of what the fund earned for its shareholders over the past week. The limitation of this measure is that it ignores the long-term benefits of daily compounding. So, to more accurately reflect the actual results from investing in a money fund over time, another yield is shown. This percentage is called the "7-Day Compounded (or Effective) Yield." This is what an investor would actually earn over a one-year period at the current rate.

The rate of interest you earn changes a little bit every day because the funds have such short average portfolio maturities. This simply means that their "loans" are extremely short-term—measured in days. Almost every week, at least one of these loans is repaid to the fund. The fund must then take this money and lend it out all over again at a new rate. This constant process of re-lending the money in the pool causes money-market fund yields to change rather quickly. That means the numbers published are slightly dated, but are sufficiently accurate for comparison purposes.

We can't leave this subject of "parking places" for your emergency fund without looking at our fourth safe haven—U.S. Treasury bills.

When the government issues bonds that have very short maturities, they are called Treasury "bills" (or "T-bills" for short). T-bills are initially sold to investors in three-month, six-month, nine-month, and one-year maturities. The minimum denomination is $100. You can buy newly issued T-Bills directly from the Treasury Department, or from a Federal Reserve branch, a local bank, or a broker. You can also buy them *after* they've been issued (in what's called the "secondary" market). When you buy your T-bills in the secondary market, you are buying them from another investor who wishes to sell. Your broker serves as the intermediary. Regardless of how you buy them, you can always sell them before maturity through your bank or broker without an interest-rate penalty (although there is a transaction cost).

The greatest advantage of T-bills is their safety and liquidity. Also, the interest earned on T-bills, as with all Treasuries, is exempt from state and local—but not federal—income taxes. The disadvantage is that you can't lock in long-term yields

Should you buy T-bills directly from the U.S. Treasury or invest in them via a Treasury-only money fund?

Do you want the highest possible yields, or are you willing to sacrifice a little interest in return for convenience? The *easiest way* to buy T-bills is through a money-market fund that specializes in investing only in very short-term securities of the U.S. government. T-bills can also be purchased at your broker or local bank for a fee (usually one-half to one percent). However, this convenience comes at a cost—the fund operating expenses and bank fees reduce your net return.

You can *avoid fees and realize better returns* by skipping the middleman and dealing directly with the government. This can be done by opening your own "Treasury Direct" account. Treasury Direct is web-based system that allows investors to buy federal government securities, including Treasury bills ("T-bills"), electronically. All securities are held online (you won't be issued a paper certificate or paper account statement). For more information, go to www.treasurydirect.gov.

due to their short-term nature.

There is one aspect to T-bills that often confuses the new investor: they are sold in "discount" form. That simply means you buy them at less than their face value, and when they mature you get the full face value. The difference between what you pay and what you get back at maturity is your "interest."

For example, assume you bought a one-year $10,000 T-bill at a 4.00% discount. That means you paid $9,600 ($10,000 face value less the 4% discount of $400). You hold it for one year, during which time you receive no interest. After the year is up, you receive the full $10,000 face value. This means you earned interest of $400. Now, here's the tricky part. Even though your discount was only 4.00%, your actual rate of return was 4.17% (the $400 return you received divided by the $9,600 you actually invested).

We've reviewed four safe havens — banks, credit unions, money-market funds, and T-bills — for the storage of your *emergency* fund.

Now, it's time to go shopping for the best places to invest *your accumulation fund,* that part of your savings reserve where you're saving for major expenditures that are not provided for in your monthly budget. An accumulation fund allows you to have a longer time frame in mind (say, a year or more before you'll need the money). In that event, you can improve your returns by looking at a different set of investment options.

Let's begin with an investment you're probably already familiar with — certificates of deposit (CDs) at your local bank or credit union. As with other bank offerings, you are lending money to your bank for a fixed rate of interest. Unlike the others, however, you agree not to withdraw your money for a set period of time (the "term" of the CD) anywhere from one month to as long as five years. The longer you commit to leaving your money, the higher interest rate the bank will usually pay you. If you take it out early, however, you forfeit a large part of the interest you would have earned.

When investing in a certificate of deposit, your decision is guided by your interest rate expectations. For example, you would not want to invest in a two-

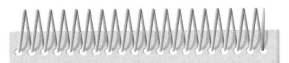

SHOPPING FOR CDS LONG DISTANCE

As you phone around or surf the Web for the best deals in bank CDs, here are some questions to ask.

❑ Are my deposits here insured by the FDIC?

❑ What is the stated rate of interest (the rate before compounding)?

❑ What is the "annual effective yield" (the return after compounding)?

❑ If I don't keep a certain minimum amount on deposit, or if I close my account within a certain period of time, will I be charged a fee?

❑ Will I earn interest from the day of deposit without a hold being placed on my check?

❑ What penalty do you charge for early withdrawal on CDs?

❑ When my CD matures, how much time do I have before you automatically roll it over into a new CD?

❑ Will you notify me first?

year CD now (that is, tie your money up for two years) if you knew that rates would be rising through the coming year. In that event, you'd invest instead in a three-month CD. When it matured in ninety days, you could then reinvest the proceeds in another three-month CD at the new, higher rate. This is called keeping your maturities "short." Conversely, if you had a reasonable certainty that rates would fall over the next twelve months, you would feel free to lock-in today's higher rates by investing in a two-year CD. This is called "extending" your maturities.

The difficulty, of course, lies in knowing what rates will do over the coming year. This dilemma is known as the "interest rate" risk. As I'll explain in chapter 11 ("The Basics of Bonds"), even investing professionals who specialize in studying the economy have poor records of predicting the direction of interest rates. So, should you prepare for rising rates, falling rates, or both?

What you should do depends on your personal goals and needs. If your accumulation fund needs can be met by locking in for a longer term and earning the higher return, then that's probably the thing to do. You trade off the possible opportunity of making a little more in return for the knowledge that the present deal will *assure* that you reach your goal (which is, after all, the primary objective).

Another way to decide is to ask yourself: Which scenario would frustrate me the most—missing the opportunity to lock in a satisfactory rate, or missing the opportunity to make a little more?

If you still can't decide, I would suggest taking the short-term CD. This will give you another chance to make the decision in a few months when either (1) your own circumstances are more clear, or (2) the trend in interest rates seems more settled.

One popular strategy for dealing with interest-rate risk is to build a "savings ladder."

Assuming you find current interest rates generally satisfactory, you might desire to lock them in for the next few years. That's where a strategy of building a "ladder" of staggered maturities can help boost your returns while surrendering only a portion of your liquidity.

Say you have $5,000 to invest. Tell your bank that you want to divide it evenly among CDs with the following maturities (yields are hypothetical and may be higher or lower when you read this): 6 months (0.75%), 1 year (1.0%), 18 months (1.25%), 2 years (1.5%), and 30 months (2.0%). Each six months when your $1,000 CD comes due, reinvest the proceeds in a new 30-month CD. Eventually, you'll have all your savings earning interest at the higher-paying 30-month CD rate, yet one-fifth of your savings will reach maturity (and be available to you) every six months. You'll still have some flexibility.

Wire Transfers are a very quick way to move your money between banks. Your funds travel through the Federal Reserve bank wire system (it generally takes a few hours) and, if done early enough in the day, the receiving bank will give you credit for your money the same day you send it. Check with your bank to find out how early in the day they need to receive your instructions and what they charge for this service.

Best CD Yields To locate banks with the top CD yields at present, go to www.bankrate.com.

A SAVINGS LADDER OF CDs

Until Maturity	Interest Rate	6Mos Interest On $1,000
6 Months	0.75%	$3.75
12 Months	1.00%	$5.00
18 Months	1.25%	$6.25
24 Months	1.50%	$7.50
30 Months	2.00%	$10.00

Average 1.30% Return
During First 6 Months

Many investors buy CDs from their local bank without shopping around. This can be a costly mistake. Why limit yourself to your local market if the banks there are not offering CDs that are competitive with insured CDs available outside your area? Bankrate.com is a good source for this kind of information. Just click on the "CDs" tab at the top and you can search for high-yielding CDs by length of term (6 months, 12 months, 18 months, etc.). Once you do a search, you'll see the annual percentage rate (APR), the minimum deposit required, and a link to the issuing bank.

When shopping for CDs long distance, be sure to verify that you will earn interest from the day of deposit without a "hold" being placed on your check (see the notepad on page 50 for a list of other questions you may want to ask). Obtain a pre-assigned account number, and write it on your check along with the inscription "For Deposit Only." Send a cover letter with instructions as well as your daytime phone number.

The remaining investment options we'll look at in this chapter have something in common—they're all bond-oriented mutual funds.

Before going further, however, I need to make sure you understand a little about bonds and how they work in relation to changes in interest rates. We'll get into this in more detail later, so if you find this primer too brief just move on over to chapter 11 ("The Basics of Bonds") for a fuller explanation.

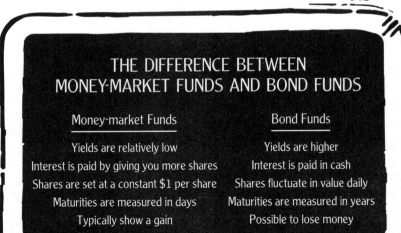

THE DIFFERENCE BETWEEN
MONEY-MARKET FUNDS AND BOND FUNDS

Money-market Funds	Bond Funds
Yields are relatively low	Yields are higher
Interest is paid by giving you more shares	Interest is paid in cash
Shares are set at a constant $1 per share	Shares fluctuate in value daily
Maturities are measured in days	Maturities are measured in years
Typically show a gain	Possible to lose money

Bonds are like IOUs. They are a promise to repay the amount borrowed at a specified time in the future (called the "maturity date"). Bond funds diversify among a great many individual bond issues, each of which has its own maturity date. Learning the "average" maturity for all the bonds in a portfolio tells you a lot about the risk of investing in that fund.

Now, for purposes of this chapter, here are the most important things you need to know about bond funds: (1) The value of a bond fund moves up or down a little each day the markets are open, depending on changes in the level of expectations for interest rates. (2) When interest rates go *up*, bond values go *down*. (3) When interest rates go *down*, bond values go *up*. (4) The *longer the average maturity* of the bonds in the portfolio, *the more it will go up or down* in value. (5) The *shorter the average maturity* of the bonds in the portfolio, *the less it will go up or down* in value.

To better control your risk, you'll want to match your expected holding period (how long you will stay invested in a bond fund before selling your shares) with bond funds of particular maturities. That is the process we'll be looking at during the rest of this chapter.

The first bond category we'll look at is the *ultra* short-term bond group. But we won't look for long.

Bond funds in the ultra short-term category fell from grace during the mortgage subprime crisis of 2007-2008. They previously had such low volatility that many, including yours truly, considered them reasonable substitutes for money-market funds in certain situations. The portfolios of these funds cover a wide range of bonds, including Treasuries, mortgage-backed, and various grades of corporates. The theory is that, under *most* market conditions, the diversification combined with very short maturities would more than compensate for any quality concessions. If all went well, shareholders would receive returns that were superior to money funds while taking little additional risk.

And they delivered on that promise for many years—until 2007, when the bottom began to fall out. The first shoe to drop was the ultra-short fund run by the well-regarded Fidelity organization—it lost 5.1% in value that year. For an investment that was sold as a reasonable alternative to a money-market fund, this was a stunning development.

But the drama was just beginning. In the first quarter of 2008 alone, the Schwab YieldPlus Fund lost an incredible 19.8%, ushering in a flood of redemptions (and lawsuits!) from horrified shareholders. This forced the fund managers to sell securities at deep discounts, leading to further losses, which led to further redemptions, and so on. Other ultra-short funds also suffered significant losses; several liquidated and returned their remaining assets to the shareholders. All in all, it was an astounding display which, by and large, shocked Wall Street.

The loss of credibility by the surviving funds in this category will make it difficult for the group to return to respectability. Having broken faith with shareholders who were told the funds were reasonably safe, it will be a long time before investors will be willing to trust those risk/reward promises again.

If you won't need to cash in for two to three years, you can consider stepping up from money-market funds to short-term bond funds.

The table on the next page shows the annualized performance of the Vanguard Prime Money-Market Fund (a perennial leader) as well as Fidelity Cash Reserves, (another popular fund) over the past 15 two-year periods. For comparison, I also show the results of a short-term bond fund at each of those organizationss. If you study the numbers, you'll find that the short-term bond funds have a performance edge, both in the magnitude of their returns as well as the consistency in which they outperformed their money-fund rivals.

At the bottom of the table, I've listed the average result, the best result, and the worst result of 169 two-year holding periods between 1997 and 2012. For greater accuracy, these numbers were calculated using "rolling" periods. Market results are usually stated in terms of calendar years. For instance, you might look at the performance numbers of the Vanguard Short-Term Investment Grade fund and conclude that the worst two-year results during the period shown occurred during 2007-08 when the annualized return was only 0.4%. But investors don't buy bond funds only at the beginning of the year, so that number is somewhat misleading as to the potential risk. That's where the use of "rolling" periods can be helpful. Here's how I ran the calculations.

	Vanguard Prime Money Mkt	Fidelity Cash Reserves	Vanguard Short-Int Invest Grade	Fidelity Short-Term Bond
1997-1998	5.4%	5.3%	6.8%	6.2%
1998-1999	5.2%	5.1%	4.9%	4.7%
1999-2000	5.6%	5.6%	5.7%	5.6%
2000-2001	5.2%	5.1%	8.1%	7.7%
2001-2002	2.9%	2.9%	6.7%	7.2%
2002-2003	1.3%	1.3%	4.7%	5.1%
2003-2004	1.0%	1.0%	3.2%	2.7%
2004-2005	2.1%	2.0%	2.2%	2.0%
2005-2006	3.9%	3.9%	3.6%	3.4%
2006-2007	5.0%	4.9%	5.4%	3.1%
2007-2008	3.9%	3.9%	0.4%	−1.1%
2008-2009	1.7%	1.7%	4.2%	1.7%
2009-2010	0.3%	0.3%	9.5%	5.6%
2010-2011	0.1%	0.1%	3.6%	2.8%
2011-2012	0.1%	0.1%	3.2%	2.1%
Avg 24 Mos	2.9%	2.9%	4.8%	3.9%
Best 24 Mos	5.8%	5.7%	10.3%	8.4%
Worst 24 Mos	0.1%	0.1%	−0.1%	−1.4%

TWO-YEAR COMPARISONS MONEY MARKET FUNDS VS. SHORT-TERM BOND FUNDS

After looking at the results from buying on January 1, 1997, and holding for 24 months, I then "rolled" to the next month to see what happened if the fund had been purchased on February 1, 1997 and held for 24 months. Then I moved to March 1 and did the same thing. And so on. Continuing in this way, I computed the results for a total of 169 different 24-month holding periods. This is in contrast to 15 such periods when only calendar years are considered. Using this more exhaustive process provides a better picture of the degree of volatility and level of returns that can be expected from an investment. In the example above, I found that the worst-case two-year performance for the Vanguard fund was actually a small annualized loss of −0.1% (December 1, 2006–November 30, 2008). You'll find that number at the bottom of the table.

Okay, so much for the methodology. What did we learn? We learned that over two-year holding periods, odds favor getting a better result from a top-performing short-term bond fund than from a money fund, even an excellent one such as Vanguard Prime. The average result and best-case result clearly favored the short-term funds. The worst-case results tilted only slightly in the favor of the money funds. If you performed the same study for *three-year periods*, even the worst-case results favor the short-term bond funds.

Why are the short-term funds better for longer holding periods? Reason number one: Bonds with longer maturities (quality considerations being equal) typically pay higher yields. Then why not always buy bonds with longer maturities? Because of reason number two: When interest rates go *up*, bond values go *down*, and the *longer the average maturity* of the bonds in the portfolio, *the more it will go down* in value. So when you extend your maturities, you should expect some occasional setbacks as interest rates fluctuate. Over the course of several months or even a year, you can lose money in a short-term bond fund. But if you hold on for two years, you usually make back the first year's losses (if any) and then some—at least this has been the experience of bond funds since the late 1970s.

To be sure, the data are not conclusive. Occasionally you would have been better off with Vanguard Prime. The historical pattern shows you what the tendencies are, but that's no guarantee they'll hold up during the specific period you invest. In sum, if you want to take the more conservative route, go with a money fund. If you're willing to take a little extra risk in search for a better return *and are committed to at least a two-year holding period,* the short-term bond funds are certainly worth a look.

If you won't need to cash in for three or more years, a mortgage-backed bond fund is another good option.

You may think your local lender keeps your mortgage payment, but guess again. Most likely the ultimate recipients are shareholders in a special kind of bond fund. Because they invest in fixed-rate mortgages which meet the standards of the Government National Mortgage Association (GNMA), such funds are often called Ginnie Mae funds. Here's how a typical mortgage investing cycle affects the Ginnie Mae investor.

• Let's say your neighbor Jim takes out an FHA or VA insured mortgage. The local bank or savings and loan that made the loan doesn't keep it on its books. Instead, it's combined with others that have similar terms (say 30-year loans with an 5.5% rate). When the bank has at least $1 million of these loans, it sells them as a package to big institutional investors. In this way, it makes a quick, small profit and has its money back to go out and make more loans.

• The buyers take the package to the Government National Mortgage Association to be sure it meets certain standards. Then, it is assigned a pool number to show that the timely payment of the interest and principal on every mortgage in the package is guaranteed by the "full faith and credit" of the U.S. government.

• A mortgage-oriented bond fund, such as Vanguard's GNMA fund, buys the pool of mortgages and is thereafter entitled to have the monthly mortgage payments—minus a small servicing and insurance charge—"passed through" to it from the original lenders (the local banks and mortgage companies) who are receiving the homeowners' monthly checks. And what does Vanguard do with the money when they get it? They pay the interest portion out to their shareholders every month and reinvest the principal portion in more pool certificates. If you're a shareholder in the Vanguard fund, you'd end up with a portion of Jim's monthly mortgage payment (which would be taxed to you as ordinary income).

The reward from investing in Ginnie Maes is they offer higher returns than are usually available with short-term bond funds. The table on the left is similar to the one on page 54, but this time we're comparing short-term bonds funds—the winners over money-market funds for holding periods of two years or longer—with Ginnie Mae mortgage bond funds. We're looking at the performance results over the past 15 *three-year* holding periods.

You can see that, since 1996, the *average* 36-month return from Vanguard's GNMA fund was 6.1%, comfortably ahead of the 4.9% turned in by Vanguard's short-term bond fund. The same relative superiority is seen when comparing the two Fidelity funds.

The biggest drawback of Ginnie Maes is that if interest rates *fall*, homeowners in the pool will take out new lower-rate mortgages and pay off their old high-rate mortgages. Then, instead of receiving interest from a pool of higher-yielding mortgages for years to come, the fund gets its money back sooner and must reinvest it. Of course, by this time rates have fallen and yields are much less attractive. Bummer. This dilemma is called the "prepayment risk." On the other hand, if rates *rise*, the fund is left with a pool of mortgages that pay a below-market rate, and fund shares will fall in value to compensate (just like other bond funds do).

Because safety is vital for the money stored in your accumulation fund, any risk of loss is cause for concern. It means you have to look at worst-case scenarios. The worst return for the Vanguard GNMA fund during any 36-month period between 1996-2012 was a gain of 2.3%. Holding a GNMA fund for at least three years goes a long way to offsetting the risk of loss. When you stretch your time horizon out that far, you can see in the table that the GNMA bond funds have offered the better combination of risk and reward—their average returns have been better, best-case returns higher, and even its worst-case results (bottom row) still outperformed the short-term bond fund options. For savers who won't be needing their accumulation fund for several years and are comfortable with a degree of volatility, Ginnie Maes are worth considering. ◆

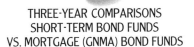

THREE-YEAR COMPARISONS
SHORT-TERM BOND FUNDS
VS. MORTGAGE (GNMA) BOND FUNDS

	Vanguard Short-Term Invest Grade	Fidelity Short-Term Bond	Vanguard GNMA Fund	Fidelity GNMA Fund
1996-1998	6.1%	5.7%	7.3%	6.6%
1997-1999	5.6%	5.2%	5.7%	5.4%
1998-2000	6.0%	5.7%	6.3%	6.1%
1999-2001	6.5%	6.2%	6.6%	6.3%
2000-2002	7.2%	7.4%	9.6%	8.9%
2001-2003	5.8%	5.9%	6.7%	6.0%
2002-2004	3.8%	4.0%	5.4%	5.0%
2003-2005	2.8%	2.5%	3.3%	3.0%
2004-2006	3.1%	2.9%	3.9%	3.7%
2005-2007	4.3%	2.8%	4.9%	4.5%
2006-2008	1.9%	0.8%	6.2%	6.0%
2007-2009	4.8%	1.7%	6.5%	6.9%
2008-2010	4.6%	2.4%	6.5%	7.0%
2009-2011	6.9%	4.3%	6.6%	7.3%
2010-2012	3.9%	2.6%	5.6%	5.9%
Avg 36 Mos	4.9%	3.9%	6.1%	5.9%
Best 36 Mos	7.8%	7.8%	10.0%	9.3%
Worst 36 Mos	1.7%	0.7%	2.3%	2.3%

Preparing for College

I. **Planning for college is a subject of almost universal concern, but won't be overwhelming if you (1) start early enough, and (2) let your children know that paying for college is their responsibility as well as yours.**

II. **When investing your college fund, you have to make two key decisions.**

   A. The first is: *What kind of account* do you want to set up? The type of account you select will determine two things — who owns the account, and what the tax liability will be for any profits. Popular options include:

   1. State-sponsored prepaid tuition plans;

   2. Coverdell Education Savings Accounts;

   3. Roth IRAs.

   4. Section 529 plans (state-sponsored college savings plans);

   B. The second key decision is *how to invest* the money you put into that account. Investments often recommended when planning for college include:

   1. Insurance policies and annuities. These traditionally have been sold as education funding vehicles.

   2. Fixed-income investments. Often utilized for college planning are certificates of deposit, Series EE bonds, and zero coupon bonds.

   3. No-load stock mutual funds. They're simple to invest in and the return, historically, has exceeded the rate of inflation and the rate of rising college tuition costs.

III. **Section 529 plans have become the savings vehicle of choice for many parents and grandparents. In them, your money is invested in a diversified portfolio of stocks and fixed income securities.**

   A. Shop around. The key factors are the quality of the investment managers, number of asset allocation choices, and the level of management fees.

   B. Look closely at your asset-allocation options. Portfolios start out being aggressive when the child is a toddler but can be automatically changed in the direction of less risk as the years pass. Make sure the allocation options fit your desires as to how aggressive you wish to be.

   C. Consider the fees. They can vary by more than 1% annually, and make a big difference over many years.

Important Reminder
The material in this chapter is current as of late-2013, however future tinkering with these college saving laws would not be a surprise. You should check current regulations before beginning a college savings program.

Investing for a college education may be one of the most written about subjects on the planet.

Generally speaking, married couples have kids. And all parents, almost from day one, worry about paying for their child's college education. It's a subject of almost universal concern.

Since 2000, as measured in contrast with the consumer price index, college costs have grown 3-3½ times faster than inflation. Estimates of $85,000-$170,000 are tossed out as the total cost (tuition, fees, room, board) of getting one child through a good school (state-run schools are the cheapest; private schools are the most expensive). Some people may be able to pay such amounts, but most can't—and you don't have to. Here are some practical tips for tackling what can easily be the single largest expense item of your life.

Get started now.

On the investing side, you want to start early because the amount of time you have available to let the principle of compound interest work for you makes a huge difference in your eventual investment results.

The "College Cost Calculator" dramatically illustrates the importance of getting an early start. For example, if you have 14 years before your youngster goes off to college, you need to set aside $401 per month in order to build a college fund of $114,587. That $114,587 is expected to represent about 70% of the amount that will be needed to pay for four years of college at an in-state public school.

On the other hand, if you get off to a late start, your opportunity for compounding is diminished. If, for example, you have just six years remaining until college arrives for your youngster, you'll need to invest $934 every month in order to accumulate the roughly $83,728 you'll need for your 70% share.

Of course, as with any set of projections, there are several assumptions built in that will ultimately miss the mark. Still, projections are useful for illustrating the need to get started. The earlier you begin, the more risk you can take. This means selecting an aggressive portfolio that is 100% stocks and adding short-term bonds or money-markets as you get closer to the time when you'll need the money. The state-sponsored 529 plans we'll talk about later can automate this process for you.

COLLEGE COST CALCULATOR

Years Until College	Monthly Investment Per $1,000	Expected 4 Year Cost After Aid	Monthly Investment Needed
3	$24.90	$74,434	$1,853
4	18.01	77,411	1,394
5	13.89	80,508	1,118
6	11.15	83,728	934
7	9.21	87,077	802
8	7.76	90,560	703
9	6.64	94,182	625
10	5.75	97,950	563
11	5.02	101,868	511
12	4.43	105,943	469
13	3.93	110,180	433
14	3.50	114,587	401
15	3.14	119,171	374
16	2.82	123,938	350
17	2.55	128,895	329
18	2.31	134,051	310

Footnotes: The second column shows the amount of investment needed each month in order to accumulate $1,000 over the period of time shown assuming an annual return of 7% net after taxes. Example: A monthly investment of $13.89 will grow to $1,000 over five years. The source for expected four-year college costs (tuition, fees, books, room and board, transportation, and other) is The College Board's estimate of the national average cost for living on campus at a four-year in-state public school. The third column shows the four-year net cost assuming total costs increase at the rate of 5% per year and that financial aid will cover 30% of the total cost. The final column shows the amount needed to fund that portion of the expected four-year cost which is not covered by financial aid. Example: For a child who will be entering college in six years, a regular monthly investment of $934 earning 7% tax-free would grow to approximately $83,728 during that time. Private colleges (not shown) cost two-to-three times as much as public ones.

Let your kids know that paying for college is their responsibility as well as yours.

It's no longer assumed that parents pay the full costs of their children's college education. According figures from the College Board, parents and students now combine to pay, on average, about 68% of the overall sticker price (tuition, fees, room, board) at public institutions, and about 60% of those same costs at private institutions. The rest (i.e., 32% of the cost at state-run schools, 40%at private colleges) is covered by various kinds of financial aid, either from a school itself or from the taxpayers. (Note: The SMI "College Cost Calculator" assumes a more-conservative 30% level of financial aid.) Of course, getting the highest possible level of assistance requires that parents and students understand the ins and outs of financial aid.

Spending for college is no different than any other purchasing decision. Some of us cannot afford the most expensive car in the showroom and some of us cannot afford to foot the bill for an expensive college education. Let your children know how much you will try to contribute toward their college education. If they can find a school for that amount of money, great. If not, it's up to their savings, summer jobs, scholarships, financial aid, and student loans to make up the difference.

To get them started thinking along these lines, it helps to open a college savings account when they're very young. Some families are able to begin when the child is born with cash gifts received from grandparents. It doesn't have to be a large amount, but opening the account early makes a statement that this is an important expense that must be planned for. Over the years, the account can be added to with checks received for birthdays, earnings from yard work, baby-sitting, etc.

When it comes to investing your college fund, you have two key decisions to make. The first one is what kind of account . . .

. . . do you want to set up? This is a separate issue from how you should invest the money you put into the account (which we'll get to shortly). The investment account is set up to serve as a repository for the securities you invest in. The type of account you select primarily determines two things—who owns the account, and what the tax liability will be for any profits.

The natural inclination of most parents is to retain ownership of the savings being set aside. Not only are many parents reluctant to simply turn property over to an immature or spendthrift child, there's also the desire to have the flexibility to use it for something else if an unexpected need arises. A drawback, however, is that the college funds are vulnerable to creditors. If the investments are owned in your name and you are successfully sued for any reason, the courts can reach the assets to satisfy any claims against you. This is of more practical importance to professionals such as doctors and accountants.

The college savings landscape is dramatically different today than 15-20 years

For Updated Information
The tax code related to college saving has been changing rapidly. For the latest information, visit the "College" section of the SMI web site at www.soundmindinvesting.com.

go. Back then, the most popular vehicles were EE savings bonds, UGMA custodial accounts, and state-sponsored prepaid tuition plans. The savings bonds offered tax advantages but were an inferior investment product. The UGMA accounts offered the opposite—better investing options but potential tax drawbacks. Changes to the tax laws in 1997 and 2001 eliminated these tradeoffs for most college savers, allowing them to now invest on a tax-free basis without having to settle for either inferior investment products or giving up control of the money invested. As a result, EE bonds and UGMA accounts have fallen dramatically out of favor, and it's the rare family that should consider using them at this point.

- **State-sponsored prepaid tuition plans.** These plans (not all available in all states) promise that your investment *today* will cover tuition at certain schools in the state *no matter what the sticker price at the time your child enrolls.* Consider recent examples from Florida's Prepaid College Plan: For the 2012-2013 enrollment period, a lump sum payment of $49,719 for a child in the third grade would cover all of the child's future tuition and fees for four years at a state university—guaranteed.

Less-expensive options are available too, such as the "2+2 Florida Plan": two years at a state-run college plus two years at a state university. For this plan, the lump cost for a third grader (as of early 2013) was $33,590. Cheaper still is the "4-Year Florida College Plan" (all four years at a "public postsecondary educational institution in the Florida College System"). The 2013 lump sum cost for a third grader: $17,283.

Of course, most people don't have enough cash to make a one-time lump sum payment into a prepaid plan. So states offer the option of making monthly payments over a defined period. (Florida, for example, offers two monthly payment plans of differing lengths.)

Prepaid plans were once highly popoular, but they have fallen on hard times in recent years. The financial upheaval that began in 2008 led to sharply lower investment returns for state plans, even as the projected costs of a college education continued to rise. As a result, the financial projections on which prepaid tuition plans were based turned out to be unrealistic.

WHICH KIND OF ACCOUNT IS BEST FOR YOUR FAMILY?

	Coverdell Education Savings Account	State-sponsored Section 529 Plan
Who will own the assets in this kind of account?	Usually the parent or legal guardian, but can be student-owned.	The donor who sets up the account.
Who can set up such an account?	Single tax filers with incomes up to $110K; joint filers with incomes up to $220K.	Anyone.
How much can you put in each year?	Up to $2000 per child under age 18. Less is allowed for incomes above $95K (single) and $190K (joint).	Varies by state. Gift-tax laws may apply.
How are the earnings taxed?	Earnings grow and distributions are made free of federal income taxes provided the assets are eventually used for qualified college-related expenses (or qualified K-12 expenses). State income tax treatment varies.	Earnings grow and distributions are made free of federal income taxes provided the assets are eventually used for qualified college-related expenses. State income tax treatment varies.
How must the money be spent?	Must be used for specified college-related expenses before the student reaches 30. Can be used by other family member.	Must be used for specified college-related expenses at participating institutions in the U.S.
What is the penalty for not following through and using the funds as you originally planned?	If funds are not used as required, income taxes are generally due on the total assets as well as a 10% penalty on the earnings.	If funds are not used as required, income taxes plus a 10% penalty are due on the earnings (unless student receives scholarship, dies, or becomes disabled).

So some states stopped accepting new participants in their prepaid plans, or have made the pricing options less attractive. As a result, fewer parents have access to a compelling prepaid tuition plan. Even so, such plans offer an essentially *no-risk* alternative to paying for a college education. However, as with most no-risk investments, the internal rate of return typically isn't that great. In addition, there are some limits on how flexible these plans are, so be sure to find out ahead of time what the implications are if Junior decides to break a five-generation tradition and forsake Home State U. (gasp!) in favor of its arch rival in the next state.

Unless the guarantee aspect of the prepaid plans is very important to you, I suggest that you instead look to the newer college planning options—Coverdell Education Savings Accounts, Roth IRAs (surprise!) and Section 529 plans. They provide superior tax advantages and planning flexibility. Let's take a quick look at the pros and cons of each of these kinds of accounts.

• **Coverdell Education Savings Account (ESA).** Created in 1997 as Education IRAs, and improved dramatically in 2001, Coverdell ESAs are a compelling savings vehicle for parents who meet the contribution limits. Parents filing jointly with adjusted gross income below $190,000 may contribute up to $2,000 per child, per year, to a Coverdell ESA (the contribution limit is reduced for those with incomes between $190,000 and $220,000). Coverdell contributions are not tax-deductible, but all earnings grow tax-deferred, to be distributed tax-*free* if used to pay the beneficiary's college expenses. $2,000 per year may not seem like much, but it adds up if you start early. Contributing $2,000 per year for 18 years with an earnings rate of 8% would accumulate to more than $70,000.

While Coverdell ESAs and Section 529 plans both offer the prospect of potentially tax-free earnings, only Coverdells and Roth IRAs offer the flexibility to choose the specific investments you desire. Section 529 plans don't, as we'll see shortly. This is a big advantage to using a Coverdell or Roth IRA for those who want to direct their own investment program, either on their own or by following model portfolios such as those offered in the *Sound Mind Investing* monthly newsletter. (Most fund companies or brokerages can set up a Coverdell ESA and/or a Roth IRA for you, allowing you access to their full range of investment products.) In addition, the favored tax treatment of Coverdell earnings extends, for now, to cover elementary and secondary school expenses. The list of qualified expenses is lengthy, and includes both obvious items like tuition and books, as well as non-obvious items like uniforms, transportation, even computers and Internet access for the family during the years the beneficiary is in school.

• **Roth IRAs.** Although Roth IRAs are designed for retirement (we'll look at them in detail in chapter 21), they can be surprisingly useful for college planning as well. While you won't get tax-free treatment on *earnings* saved in a Roth (if used for college), you can withdraw your *contributions* for college expenses without tax or penalty. Ideally, you'll leave any earnings in the Roth for your retirement while withdrawing the principal to pay college bills. In addition, if junior doesn't go to college, gets a scholarship, or whatever, there's no need to move your savings around to a different type of account if it's already in a Roth IRA. It's already in the most tax-advantaged spot for your retirement savings. This can be a big benefit, since the annual Roth contribution limits would likely keep you from being able to transfer large sums from a college-specific account into a Roth

Investing in A College Saving Account

The leading no-load fund companies offer college investing programs that are easy to establish and monitor, including 529-plan, Coverdell, and UGMA accounts.

Many offer online calculators that will help you estimate educational expenses and establish a strategy for meeting those needs. They'll waive their usual minimums if an automatic monthly investment of $50-$100 is chosen (electing this option is a great way to exercise self-discipline).

This strategy of investing the same dollar amount every month, regardless of market conditions, is called dollar-cost-averaging (DCA). It's a popular way to invest in no-load growth mutual funds.

DCA mechanically guides your investing so you acquire more shares when they are more attractively priced. You don't have to worry about timing. (I'll discuss DCA in detail in chapter 15.) Plus, it allows you to begin with small amounts. This helps you to begin sooner rather than later so you can take greater advantage of the principle of compound interest.

down the road. And if you're fortunate enough to be making big bucks by the time the kids go to college, you can pay some college bills out of current income and keep more of your Roth IRA intact (since you may no longer be eligible to make new contributions to a Roth due to your high income).

With the 2013 annual limit for Roth IRAs at $5,500 ($6,500 if you're 50 or older), a married couple would be able to save a full $11,000 (or $13,000) per year in Roth IRAs. Many families with kids aren't going to be able to save more than that anyway, and if they can, Coverdell accounts and 529 plans are available as supplements.

Unfortunately, there is a potential downside to using a Roth IRA to save for college, and that has to do with how IRAs are treated in the financial aid formulas. These formulas consider family income as well as assets. A parent's IRA isn't counted as an *asset* in the formulas, but withdrawals from IRAs often are counted as *income*. In other words, withdrawals from a Roth to pay college expenses are likely to bump up current income in the formulas, potentially decreasing your aid eligibility. Coverdell ESAs and Section 529 plans get the opposite treatment—they count (relatively lightly) against you as parental assets, but withdrawals normally don't count against you as income. As a result, if you think you're likely to qualify for financial aid, saving for college via a Coverdell ESA or Section 529 plan may be a better choice than doing so via a Roth.

The tradeoff is that a primary reason to consider a Roth for college savings in the first place is that bumps in the financial road do happen sometimes. If it comes down to an either/or situation, it's more important that you have a reasonable level of retirement savings than a large college savings fund. Remember, no one will lend you money for retirement; however, they will lend your child money for college.

• **Section 529 plans.** These plans have become the savings vehicle of choice for many parents and grandparents. A 529 plan offers the same potential tax-free savings for college as a Coverdell ESA. Most 529 plans are run by individual states, the majority of which make their plans available to any U.S. resident (rather than just residents of their state). This means a great variety of plans are available to today's college saver. Students are not required to attend college in the state where their 529 plan money is invested either; they can use the assets at any accredited post-secondary institution in the U.S.

Unlike Coverdell accounts and Roth IRAs, there are no annual income limitations for 529 plan contributors, making 529s the natural choice for high-income college savers. In addition, while Coverdell ESAs limit annual contributions to $2,000 per beneficiary and Roth IRAs have a current per-contributor cap of $5,500 ($6,500 if 50 or older), with a 529 plan an individual can contribute up to $14,000 per year to a single beneficiary (that limit being the maximum annual gift tax exclusion). There's even a way to boost this already

---

Series EE Savings Bonds

These bonds, issued by the U.S. government, earn a fixed rate of return. EE bonds purchased electronically (www.savingsbonds.gov) are sold at face value (minimum $25).

Some of the advantages of Series EE bonds include:

• Safety
They're backed by the full faith and credit of the U.S. government.

• Tax advantages
The interest is exempt from state and local taxes, and the federal taxes aren't payable until you cash them in.

• Saving for college
If you buy them and later cash them in to pay for college tuition, you may owe no taxes on the interest you earned. They carry a federal tax exclusion which, for families meeting certain income limits and other conditions, makes the interest tax-free.

• Discipline
They are most commonly purchased through payroll deduction savings plans, so you can impose discipline on yourself by automating your savings.

On the other hand, Series EE bonds have some serious drawbacks:

(continued >)

high limit: a contribution of up to $70,000 can be made up front, then treated as five consecutive annual contributions for gift tax purposes. Given that these limits are per contributor, a *couple* could effectively give double these amounts to a single beneficiary. For most, this means 529 plans offer them the ability to save as much as they can without worrying about any restrictions.

Don't be discouraged if you don't happen to have $13,000 laying around to fund a 529 plan with. Even small amounts invested regularly over an extended period of time can grow surprisingly large. For example, if you can save $100 per month for 18 years and the plan averages returns of 8% per year, you'll end up with $48,000. That may not cover all of Junior's college expenses, but it'll sure put a big dent in them.

A final advantage of 529 plans is that the contributor retains control and ownership of the account. This is important on several levels. For starters, it means that the contributor can pull money out of the account at any time and for any purpose, although taxes and a 10% penalty will result from unqualified distributions. It also allows for a great deal of flexibility in changing the beneficiary from one child (or grandchild) to another. And perhaps most importantly, it ensures that a child who decides not to go to college doesn't wind up with an unintended financial windfall. A 529 plan may not only be a valuable vehicle to help you provide for the costs of a college education, but also to protect your children from receiving a large sum of money that they aren't spiritually and socially equipped to handle yet.

While there are many benefits of 529 plans, there are also some flaws. Savers using 529 plans are limited to a relatively small range of investment options selected by the state. This is a significant downside for those who want to manage their own portfolios, a group which includes many *Sound Mind Investing* newsletter subscribers. Also, many 529 plans are broker-sold which results in paying a sales load that greatly reduces the 529 plan advantages. While overall expenses continue to fall, there are still some plans with outrageously high expenses (1.5% and up). High expenses in a 529 plan— where you don't have the advantage of being able to upgrade between funds— can be the kiss of death.

Now for the second key decision. After selecting the kind of account you want to set up, it's time to decide . . .

. . . how you should invest the money you put into that account. Let's look at the various types of investments often recommended as good ways to invest the money set aside when planning for college.

• **Insurance policies and annuities.** Insurance policies and annuities traditionally have been sold as education-funding vehicles. However, with the advent of the many tax-advantaged accounts discussed in this chapter, life insurance and annuities are not, in my view, an efficient education funding solution.

(continued)

• <u>Relatively low return</u>
The return on Series EE bonds rise and fall along with the yields on five-year Treasuries. Since U.S. government securities are considered to be among the safest of investments, the returns they offer are among the lowest.

• <u>Limitations on tax exclusion</u>
The tax exclusion starts to phase out when the family's adjusted gross income, modified to include Social Security and other retirement income, exceeds $100,650— or $67,100 for single filers— (indexed for inflation). The income test is applied when you cash them in, not when you buy them. If your income outpaces inflation over years of saving and investing, you could end up going over the income limit and facing an unexpected tax bill.

• <u>Limitations on college expenditures</u>
To be tax-free, the interest proceeds can be used only for tuition and related expenses (e.g., books and lab fees). This excludes using them for room and board, two of the major cost components. As a result, scholarships and grants that lower these expenses can reduce or eliminate the tax-free nature of your bonds' interest. Also, should your child decide to skip college, the interest is fully subject to federal taxes.

• **Fixed-income investments.** Generally, fixed-income investments take a principal sum that is on deposit, pay a fixed rate of interest, and if held to maturity, avoid any risk of loss of principal. Fixed income investments often utilized for college planning include certificates of deposit, Series EE bonds, zero coupon bonds, and a relatively new types of bond—Treasury Inflation Protected Securities (see page 160). Their primary advantage is the safety of principal they offer, but their obvious drawback is they limit your upside growth. Generally, fixed-income investments should be used only if you (1) cannot stand any stock market risk, or (2) have a child who is almost college age and wish to guarantee the safety of your principal for the next year or two until it will be needed for college expenses.

• **No-load stock mutual funds.** This is my favorite investment vehicle for the average family. Why? Because, they're simple to invest in and the return on no-load stock funds historically has exceeded the rate of inflation and the rate of rising college tuition costs. You don't have to be an investment expert to know that those invested in the stock market have received historically high returns in recent decades. Investing $100 per month in a stock fund for 18 years at an annual rate of return of 8% yields a college savings fund of $48,000. That same $100 per month invested in a fixed-income investment yielding 4% would equal less than $32,000. (Both examples assume taxes are deferred.) Over the long haul, it pays to take a little risk.

This brings us back to Section 529 plans.

In 529 plans, your money is invested in a diversified portfolio of stocks and fixed income securities. While many plans allow you to pick an investment track—conservative, moderate, and aggressive for example—beyond that, there used to be no way to change the investment allocation of your account. You see, it's the nature of these plans that, even though it's your money going into the plan, you forfeit the right to make investment decisions. That's the tradeoff that gives these plans their tax-advantages. Most 529 plans are managed by mutual fund companies and offer a limited range of investment options. Usually, one or more age-based portfolios are available that invest mostly in stock funds when the child is young, and automatically shift to safer, interest-earning investments like bonds and money-market funds as the child gets closer to college age. In that respect, they're an easy auto-pilot way to save for many investors. But there's a huge variation in how aggressive various states are in their allocations. For example, even in the aggressive track, an 11-year old in New York's plan is only 50% in stocks. Many would argue that isn't enough.

Thankfully, many plans are adding features that allow some fine-tuning. In addition to age-based portfolios, "static" portfolio options are now quite common. These allow the investor to select a specific mix of stock and fixed-income investments that will *remain constant unless the investor initiates a change*. It's not unusual to find states offering multiple static choices, such as Nebraska's 529 plan, which offers three static portfolios in addition to their four age-based options. The static portfolios range from

80% in stocks to a very conservative 75% allocation to bonds, fixed-income investments and cash equivalents. The Nebraska plan also allows 529 investors to choose from among various index funds (see chapter 14 for more on index funds).

So, while you forfeit the right to pick and choose the *exact* investments you want in a 529 plan, you can still exercise a significant amount of control over how the assets are invested by utilizing the ever-expanding array of choices within these plans. For example, the New York plan offers six Vanguard stock index funds, plus a bond index fund, among its 13 individual portfolio choices. Account holders can own up to five of these options in one account and can specify what percentage (minimum 5%) they want allocated to each fund. When you consider that you can change investment options as often as once every 12 months within most plans, and can redirect new contributions at any time, you can see there's quite a bit of flexibility allowed. You also have the ability to roll your account from one state's plan to a different one with better investment choices. This can be done only once in any 12-month period, but aside from that it's a simple process.

Congress put the states in charge of 529 plans, and each one is doing its own thing—creating different rules for who can participate, how much can be put in, how the money will be invested, and so on. The fact that there are so many plans to choose from creates a lot of confusion for parents—but that's certainly better than being saddled with a one-size-fits-all plan. Here are my suggestions as to which factors are most important.

• **Shop around, but check your own state's plan first.** Look beyond your state's borders. Most plans offer state tax deductions for contributions made by their residents, and this often convinces parents to look no further. After all, a 5%-9% state tax deduction on every dollar you contribute ought to get your attention. But be aware that other factors, such as the quality of the investment managers, number and type of asset allocation choices, and the level of management fees, can outweigh the value of a state tax deduction. Check www.savingforcollege.com for an overview of your plan as well as ratings of other plans open to non-residents.

• **Look closely at your asset-allocation options.** Your most important decision is the allocation between stocks and bonds in the account. Many of the age-based portfolios are quite conservative, moving into bonds in large doses at an early age. At the opposite end of the risk spectrum, you can take a more aggressive posture by using the static portfolio options to stay 100% in stocks from birth to graduation. The right balance is somewhere between those extremes. While you don't want to be in bonds too early, it is appropriate for the allocation to get more conservative as college age approaches. This helps assure that the account won't suffer a significant loss just as your student enters college. Make sure the allocation options fit with your desires as to how aggressive you wish to be. One simple approach for those using static portfolios is to invest 100% in stocks until college is five years away, then shift 20% of the account into bonds each year until college arrives.

• **Consider the fees.** Just as with a mutual fund, there are ongoing operating expenses charged to your account. These fees can vary by more than 1% annually, making a big difference over many years.

• **Favor plans with low-cost index fund choices.** I firmly believe that it's possible to beat the market's returns if you're able to rotate between top-performing funds as we do in our SMI newsletter's Fund Upgrading strategy (see chapter 17). However, in a 529 plan, you don't have the flexibility to Upgrade like that. The next best thing, then, is to use index funds. As I'll explain in chapter 14, index funds are a type of mutual fund designed simply to match the market's overall performance. Study after study has shown that index funds will typically beat the majority of actively-managed funds over time, in large part due to their lower expenses. As a result, our advice in picking a 529 plan is to find one with good index fund choices. More and more states are catching on to the virtues of having low-cost index funds in their plans, so it's increasingly likely your state will offer index funds among their investment options.

We've covered a lot of ground in this chapter . . .

. . . and much of it may be new to you. The decisions you make here involve trade-offs between control, flexibility, and tax advantages. Only you can decide which features are of greatest importance to your family.

At this point, Section 529 plans offer the "cleanest" and simplest path to saving for college. They were designed specifically for this goal, and Congress has now removed the uncertainty regarding their future tax status. Assuming you pick a 529 plan that features a solid lineup of low-cost index fund investment choices, the only significant drawback is that you're "settling" for an indexing strategy, as opposed to being able to follow a potentially more profitable Upgrading path within a Roth or Coverdell.

For those who do want to chart their own investment course, fully funding a Roth IRA every year as a joint retirement/college savings account is a good option to consider. However, as college costs continue to escalate, the financial aid implications make it reasonable to question if the average family will come out ahead investing in a Roth vs. indexing in a 529 plan. Unfortunately, there's no easy answer to that as future returns are unknown and many schools use their own financial-aid formulas anyway.

Coverdell accounts fill in this gap nicely, although their $2,000 annual contribution limit makes them less attractive for savers who have the ability to set aside larger sums.

As we have seen, Roth IRAs, Coverdell ESAs and 529 plans all offer pros and cons. Don't spend so much of your time trying to figure out the *very* best option that you postpone making a decision. Any combination of these three choices is better than waiting. Review the options, pray for wisdom and discernment, and get started! Contributing early and often is the best way to win the college savings race. ◆

Understanding
Mutual Funds

Divide your portion to seven, or even to eight, for you
do not know what misfortune may occur on the earth.

Ecclesiastes 11:2

"Let's try it one more time. The stock fund managed by Fulcher apparently owns all
the shares of Biller's growth fund, which is fully invested in the Omnium stock fund,
which seems to have put all its money into the Fulcher fund..."

5

Mutual Funds and Their Advantages to Investors

I. **For most investors, mutual funds represent the best way to assemble a well-balanced, diversified portfolio of securities.**

   A. A mutual fund is simply a big pool of money formed when thousands of small investors team up to gain advantages that are normally available only to wealthy investors.

   B. The money in the pool is managed by a hired professional who is paid based upon the size of the pool and, in some cases, on his/her performance results.

   C. The money in the pool must be invested according to the "ground rules" drawn up when the pool was first formed. Most mutual funds limit their investments to particular kinds of stocks or bonds that are the specialty of the professional managing the pool.

II. **Mutual funds can make your investing easier and safer. In this chapter, 20 advantages of mutual fund ownership are listed and explained. Among them:**

   A. Mutual funds reduce risk by providing extensive diversification. This means their price movements are less volatile and more predictable than are individual stocks.

   B. Funds keep commission costs low.

   C. They provide experienced, full-time professional management that gives your holdings individual attention on a daily basis.

   D. The past performance of mutual funds is a matter of public record.

   E. Funds allow you to efficiently reinvest your dividends.

   F. Mutual fund companies offer many convenient services, such as automatic investing and withdrawal plans, check-writing privileges, handling all the paperwork, creating reports for tax purposes, and providing safekeeping of your money.

   G. Funds can be used for your IRA and other retirement plans.

   H. Mutual funds allow you to sell your shares and leave the pool at any time.

Investment Company
is the technical name
for a mutual fund.

A Mutual Fund
combines money from many
investors into one larger pool of
money, and invests the pool in
stocks, bonds, and other
securities consistent with its
area of specialization. For this
service, the company typically
charges an annualized
management fee that
approximates 1.5% of the value
of the investment.

Portfolio
is a collection of securities
held for investment.

Net Asset Value
is the market value of a single
mutual-fund share.

Security
is a financial instrument that is
bought and sold by the
investing public. The majority
are stocks, bonds, mutual
funds, options, and ownership
participations in limited
partnerships. All publicly traded
securities are subject to the
regulation of the Securities and
Exchange Commission.

**Securities and Exchange
Commission (SEC)**
is an agency in Washington that
regulates the securities
industry. SEC rules govern the
way investments are sold, the
brokerage firms that sell them,
what can be charged for selling
them, what information must be
disclosed to investors before
they invest, and much more.
The SEC is charged with looking
after the general welfare of the
investing public. All mutual
funds come under SEC
supervision.

Abraham Lincoln received an invitation to deliver a college commencement address. The exact date had not yet been set . . .

. . . and he was asked how much advance notice he would need. He reportedly said that depended on how long they wished him to speak: "If you want me to speak for 15 minutes, I'll need three weeks' notice. If it's for an hour, I'll only need three days' notice. And if you'll let me speak all day, I can start right now!"

The point behind his humorous answer is that it takes a great deal of preparation time to be economical in one's presentation while still covering all the essentials. I thought of Lincoln as I was reviewing all the books in my investment library that were written solely on the subject of mutual funds. I've collected 14 different ones over the years; they average more than 264 pages each! Can I hope to teach you more about mutual funds than is already covered in those 14 books? Probably not, especially when you consider that they run collectively to more than 3,700 pages!

I'm going to do something that may be even more valuable to you—teach you a lot *less*. I'm going to mercifully leave out . . .

. . . a lot of material that is best reserved for a more in-depth study, and focus only on the things you need to know about mutual funds to benefit from them. And put that way, there really isn't all that much for you to learn. This section of the book will serve as a primer, and a primer teaches only the basics.

One last word before we begin. The fund industry has experienced explosive growth over the past 20 years. The sheer number and types of different funds (more than 8,000 at last count) is overwhelming. As a result, I find that many people feel a little confused, if not intimidated, by the whole topic. Of course, it can be scary tackling a new subject, especially one that can so dramatically affect one's financial future. If you feel the same way, take heart! I've written this book especially for you. Ready? Let's get started!

The easiest way to understand a mutual fund is to think of it as a big pool of money.

The *Barron's Dictionary of Finance and Investment Terms* defines a mutual fund as a "fund operated by an investment company that raises money from shareholders and invests it in a variety of securities." My plain-English definition is that it's (1) a big pool of money (2) collected from lots of individual investors (3) that is managed by a full-time professional investment manager (4) who invests it according to specific guidelines. When you put money in a mutual fund, you are pooling your money with other investors to gain advantages normally available only to the wealthiest investors. You are transformed from a small investor into part owner of a multimillion-dollar portfolio!

What do you get in return for your investment dollars? You receive shares that represent your ownership in part of the pool. The value of the shares is calculated anew at the end of every day the financial markets are open. Here's how it's done. First, you take the day's closing market value of all the investments in the fund's pool. To that number, you add the amount of cash on hand that isn't invested for the time being (most funds keep 3%–5% of their holdings in cash for day-to-day transactions). That gives you the up-to-the-minute value of all the pool's holdings. Next, you need to subtract any amounts the pool owes (such as management fees that are due to the portfolio manager but haven't yet been paid). This gives the net value of the assets in the pool. Finally, you divide the net value by the total shares in the pool to determine what each individual share is worth. This is called the *net asset value* per share and is the price at which all shares in the fund will be bought or sold for that day. It is also the number that is reported in the financial section of the newspaper and on financial websites the next morning.

What kinds of securities do mutual funds invest in? That depends on the ground rules . . .

. . . set up when the pool was first formed. Every mutual fund is free to make its own ground rules. The rules are explained in a booklet called the *prospectus* that every mutual fund must provide to investors — that is where you learn what types of securities the fund is allowed to invest in.

As we learn about mutual funds, I'll be using examples that might give you the mistaken impression that they invest only in stocks. This is most assuredly not the case. Mutual funds invest in just about every type of security around — corporate, government, and tax-free bonds, federally-backed mortgages, money-market instruments such as bank CDs, commercial paper, and U.S. Treasury bills to name a few. For the average person, mutual funds are the best way to assemble a well-balanced, diversified portfolio containing many different kinds of securities. But to simplify things, I'll primarily use stock-oriented mutual funds when I'm explaining how funds work.

HOW THE XYZ MUTUAL FUND CALCULATES ITS DAILY CLOSING PRICE

List of Investments	Closing Price	Shares Owned	Market Value
3M	$105.95	8,300	$879,385
Alcoa	8.39	6,400	53,696
American Express	65.22	9,700	632,634
AT&T	37.76	7,500	283,200
Bank of America	12.25	6,400	78,400
Boeing	87.21	3,000	261,630
Caterpillar	85.90	7,200	618,480
Chevron	118.64	8,800	1,044,032
Cisco	20.97	4,400	92,268
Coca-Cola	53.98	3,800	205,124
Disney	59.14	14,200	839,788
DuPont	49.23	3,500	172,305
ExxonMobil	88.77	6,000	532,620
General Electric	23.06	4,600	106,076
Hewlett-Packard	22.22	8,400	186,648
Home Depot	71.20	2,900	206,480
IBM	209.22	9,300	1,945,746
Intel Corp	21.75	8,700	189,225
Johnson & Johnson	81.52	6,200	505,424
J. P. Morgan Chase	48.68	7,700	374,836
McDonald's	101.06	9,500	960,070
Merck	45.51	11,400	518,814
Microsoft	29.61	5,700	168,777
Pfizer	29.11	8,000	232,880
Proctor & Gamble	66.26	5,100	337,926
Traveleres Companies	85.27	4,800	409,296
United Technologies	94.45	6,800	624,260
UnitedHealth Group	62.18	3,900	242,502
Verizon	49.36	7,400	365,264
Wal-Mart Stores	78.12	9,500	742,140

Market Value of Investments	$ 13,827,926
Plus: Cash on Hand	+ 465,619
Less: Expenses Payable	–16,744
= Net Value of Pool Assets	$ 14,276,801
Divide By: Number of Shares	524,388
= Net Asset Value Per Share	$ 27.23

A mutual fund usually will limit its investments to a particular kind of security. For example, assume you want to invest only in quality "blue-chip" stocks that pay good dividends. As it turns out, quite a few mutual funds have rules that permit them to invest *only* in such stocks. No small-company stocks, stock options, long- or short-term bonds, precious metals, or anything else. By limiting their permissible investments, mutual funds allow you to pool your money together with that of thousands of other investors who wish to invest in similar securities.

Mutual funds are almost certain to play an important role in your financial future because they offer many benefits that will make your investing program easier and safer. Here are 20 major advantages.

Advantage #1: Mutual funds can reduce the anxiety of investing.

Most investors live with a certain amount of anxiety and fear about their investments. This is because they feel they lack one or more of the following essentials: (1) market knowledge, (2) investing experience, (3) self-discipline, (4) a proven game plan, or (5) time. As a result, they often invest on impulse or emotion. Mutual funds can go a long way toward relieving the burdens associated with investing.

Advantage #2: Fund shares can be purchased in such small amounts that it makes it easy to get started.

If you have been putting off starting your investing program because you don't know which stocks to invest in and you can't afford a personal investment consultant to tell you, mutual funds will get you on your way. It doesn't require large sums of money to invest in mutual funds. Most fund organizations have minimum amounts needed to open an account, which usually run from $1,000 to $3,000. And if that's too much, most funds have dramatically lower minimums for IRAs and "automatic deposit accounts" where you agree to make regular monthly deposits to build your account.

Advantage #3: Mutual fund accounts can also be added to whenever you want—often or seldom—in small amounts.

After meeting the initial minimum (if any) to open your account, you can add just about any amount you want. To make your purchase work out evenly, fund companies will sell you fractional shares. For example, if you invest $100 in a fund selling at $7.42 a share, the fund organization will credit your account with 13.477 shares ($100.00 divided by $7.42 = 13.477).

Advantage #4: Mutual funds reduce risk through diversification.

Stock funds typically hold from 50 to 500 stocks in their portfolios (the average is around 200). They do this so that any loss caused by the unexpected collapse of any one stock will have only a minimal effect on the pool as a whole. Without the availability of mutual funds, the investor with just $3,000 to invest would likely put it all in just one or two stocks (a risky way to go). By using a mutual fund, that same $3,000 can make the investor a part owner in a large, professionally researched and managed portfolio of stocks.

Advantage #5: Mutual funds' price movements are far more predictable than those of individual stocks.

Their extensive diversification, coupled with outstanding stock selection, makes it highly unlikely that the overall market will move up without carrying almost all stock mutual funds up with it. For example, on February 1, 2013, when the Dow jumped 150 points, more than 95% of stock mutual funds were up for the day. Yet, of the more than 3,000 individual stocks that traded on the New York Stock Exchange, only 74% ended the day with a gain. One in four stocks ended the day unchanged or actually fell in price.

Advantage #6: Mutual funds' past performance is a matter of public record.

Advisory services, financial planners, and stockbrokers may have records of past performance, but how

> ### "DIVERSIFICATION"
> The spreading of investment risk by putting one's assets into many different kinds of investments.
>
> Mutual funds usually are regarded as relatively low in risk because they are so widely diversified. While some holdings are moving up in value, others are standing still or moving down. So, the price changes cancel each other out somewhat. The effect of this is to increase the price stability of the overall portfolio. Thus, while an investor is unlikely to score a huge gain in any one year via mutual funds, he or she is also unlikely to incur a huge loss. For the average investor, this relative price stability is one of the primary advantages of investing in mutual funds.

public are they? And how were they calculated? Did they include every recommendation made for every account? Mutual funds have *fully disclosed* performance histories, computed according to set standards. With a little research, you can learn exactly how various mutual funds have fared in relation to inflation or other investment alternatives.

Advantage #7: Mutual funds provide full-time professional management.

Highly trained investment specialists are hired to make the decisions as to which stocks to buy. The person with the ultimate decision-making authority is called the portfolio manager. The manager possesses expertise in many financial areas, and likely has learned—through experience—to avoid the common mistakes of the amateur investor. Most important, the manager is expected to have the self-discipline necessary to doggedly stick with the mutual fund's strategy even when events move against him for a time.

Open-End Funds
sell as many shares as necessary to satisfy investor interest. You can buy and sell shares directly through the fund organization. They are the most common kind.

Closed-End Funds
have only a limited number of shares available. To buy and sell, you go through a stockbroker and transact with other investors just as you do when dealing in stocks.

Bull Market
is a market with rising prices of sufficient duration to indicate an upward trend.

Bear Market
is a market with falling prices of sufficient duration to indicate a downward trend.

Advantage #8: Mutual funds allow you to efficiently reinvest your dividends.

If you were to spread $5,000 among five different stocks, your quarterly dividend checks might amount to $10 from each one. It's not possible to use such a small amount to buy more shares without paying very high relative commissions. Your mutual fund, however, will gladly reinvest any size dividends for you *automatically*. This can add significantly to your profits over several years.

Advantage #9: Mutual funds offer automatic withdrawal plans.

Most funds let you sell shares automatically in an amount and frequency of your choosing. This pre-planned selling enables the fund to mail you a check for a specified amount monthly or quarterly. This allows investors in stock funds that pay little or no dividends to still receive periodic cash flow.

Advantage #10: Mutual funds provide you with individual attention.

It has been estimated that the average broker needs 400 accounts to make a living. How does he spread his time among those accounts? The common-sense way would be to start with the largest accounts and work his way down. Where would that leave your small (relatively) $3,000 account? But in a mutual fund, the smallest member of the pool gets exactly the same attention as the largest because everybody is in it together.

Advantage #11: Mutual funds can be used for your IRA and other retirement plans.

Mutual funds offer accounts that can be used for IRAs, Keoghs, and 401(k) plans. They're especially useful for rollovers. (This is when you take a lump-sum payment from an employer's pension plan because of your retirement or termination of employment and must deposit it into an IRA investment plan account within 60 days.) The new IRA rollover account can be opened at a bank, mutual fund, or brokerage house, and the money then invested in stocks, bonds, or money-market securities. These rollover accounts make it possible for you to transfer your pension benefits to an account under your control while protecting their tax-deferred status. Rollovers are also useful for combining several small IRAs into one large one.

Advantage #12: Mutual funds allow you to sell part or all of your shares at any time and get your money quickly.

By regulation, all open-end mutual funds must redeem (buy back) their shares at their net asset value whenever you wish. It's usually as simple as a toll-free phone call or a visit to your broker's website. Of course, the amount you get back will be more or less than you initially put in, depending on how well the stocks in the portfolio have done during the time you were a part owner of the pool.

Advantage #13: Mutual funds enable you to instantly reduce the risk in your portfolio with just a phone call.

Most large fund organizations (usually referred to as "families") allow investors to switch from one of their funds to another via a phone call or over the Web and at no cost. One practical use of this feature is that it makes it easy to reallocate your capital between funds that invest in different types of asset classes (large-company growth, large-company value, small-company growth, small-company value, foreign stocks, and fixed-income securities) as your goals and market expectations evolve.

Prospectus
is a formal written offer to sell a security. Mutual fund companies provide them free to investors. They explain the fund's investment objectives, its performance history, the fees the company will charge, the special services they offer, and a financial statement. Basically, a prospectus explains the ground rules under which a mutual fund operates.

Advantage #14: Mutual funds pay minimum commissions when buying and selling for the pool.

Funds buy stocks in such large quantities that they always qualify for the lowest brokerage commissions available. An average purchase of stock can easily cost the small investor 1%-2% in commissions to buy and sell (depending on broker, dollar size of order, and number of shares). On the other hand, the cost is a mere fraction of 1% on a large purchase like $100,000. Many investors would show gains rather than losses if they could save almost 2% on every trade! The mutual-fund pool enjoys the savings from these massive volume discounts, enhancing the profitability of the pool. Eventually, then, part of that savings is yours. These commission savings, however, should not be confused with the annual operating expenses which every shareholder pays (see page 83).

A GLIMPSE INTO A MUTUAL FUND PORTFOLIO

Mutual funds report to their shareholders each quarter, providing market commentary, performance data, and a list of the fund's current holdings.

Note that this growth fund is reporting that only about 94% of its portfolio is invested in stocks at the time of this report. Most funds, even those dedicated to investing in stocks, will keep a small percentage of their holdings in cash and Treasury bills to use for future purchases as well as to pay shareholders who wish to sell their fund shares on any given day.

COMMON STOCKS (94.3%)

Consumer Discretionary	Number of shares	Current market value
McDonald's Corp	9,142,779	$809,410
Walt Disney Co.	16,080,251	779,892
Amazon.com Inc.	3,242,569	740,441
Home Depot Inc.	13,770,774	729,713
Starbucks Corp.	6,823,744	363,842
Time Warner Inc.	8,635,756	332,477
Ford Motor Co.	34,333,762	329,261
Group Total		**$4,085,036**
Energy		
Exxon Mobile Corp.	42,070,199	$3,599,947
Chevron Corp.	17,752,080	1,872,844
Halliburton Co.	8,303,601	235,739
Marathon Oil Corp.	6,345,100	162,244
Group Total		**$5,870,774**
Health Care		
Johnson & Johnson	24,708,208	$1,669,286
Pfizer	67,368,435	1,549,474
Merck & Co. Inc.	27,363,924	1,142,444
Abbott Laboratories	14,155,220	912,587
Group Total		**$5,273,791**

Number of shares

Current market value in thousands of dollars (thus, this would read as $729,713 thousand, or a little more than $729 million)

Advantage #15: Mutual funds provide a safe place for your investment money.

Mutual funds are required to hire an independent bank or trust company to hold and account for all the cash and securities in the pool. This custodian has a legally binding responsibility to protect the interests of every shareholder. No mutual-fund shareholder has ever lost money due to a mutual-fund bankruptcy.

Advantage #16: Mutual funds handle your paperwork for you.

Capital gains and losses from the sale of stocks, as well as dividend and interest-income earnings, are summarized in a report for each shareholder at the end of the year (for tax purposes). Funds also manage the day-to-day chores such as dealing with transfer agents, handling stock certificates, reviewing brokerage confirmations, and more.

Advantage #17: Mutual funds can be borrowed against in case of an emergency.

Although you hope it will never be necessary, you can use the value of your mutual-fund holdings as collateral for a loan. If the need is short-term and you would rather not sell your funds because of tax or investment reasons, you can borrow against them rather than sell them.

Advantage #18: Mutual funds involve no personal liability beyond the investment risk in the portfolio.

Many investments, primarily partnerships and futures, require investors to sign papers wherein they agree to accept personal responsibility for certain liabilities generated by the undertaking. Thus, it is possible for investors to actually lose more money than they invest. (This arrangement is generally indicative of speculative endeavors; I encourage you to avoid such arrangements.) In contrast, this is never the case with mutual funds.

Advantage #19: Mutual-fund advisory services are available that can greatly ease the research burden.

Due to the growth in the popularity of mutual-fund investing, there has been a big jump in the number of investment newsletters that specialize in researching and writing about mutual funds. My *Sound Mind Investing* newsletter, for example, offers model portfolios geared to an investor's risk tolerance and stage of life. We provide specific fund buy/sell recommendations that are updated each month. To learn more about our service, visit our web site at www.soundmindinvesting.com. We've grown to become America's best-selling financial newsletter written from a biblical perspective because we focus on teaching our readers, in plain, everyday English, how to apply biblical principles in practical ways. (Of course, our long-term market-beating performance results don't hurt! ☺)

Advantage #20: Mutual funds are heavily regulated by the federal government.

The fund industry is regulated by the Securities and Exchange Commission and is subject to the provisions of the Investment Company Act of 1940. The act requires that all mutual funds register with the SEC and that investors be given a prospectus, which must contain full information concerning the fund's history, operating policies, cost structure, and so on. Additionally, all funds use a bank that serves as the custodian of all the pool assets. This safeguard means the securities in the fund are protected from theft, fraud, and even the bankruptcy of the fund management organization itself. Of course, money can still be lost if poor investment decisions cause the value of the pool's investments to fall in value.

Think of mutual funds as offering the convenience of something you're pretty familiar with: eating out! Someone else has done all the work of . . .

. . . developing the recipes, shopping for quality at the best prices, and cooking and assembling the dinners so that foods that go well together are served in the right proportions. For mutual funds, that's the job of the professional portfolio manager—he or she develops a strategy, shops for the right securities at the best prices, and then assembles the portfolio with an appropriate amount of diversification. And the analogy doesn't stop there. Just as there are many different dinner entrees to choose from at most nice restaurants (such as steak, seafood, chicken, pasta, and so on), there are also many kinds of mutual funds to choose from at most fund organizations. Each kind has its own "flavor."

The graphic on the next page is a partial listing of the daily mutual fund section that appears in the newspaper. Vanguard is one of the giants in the no-load fund industry, and it offers quite a "menu" for its

IN A NUTSHELL

With mutual funds . . .	With individual stocks . . .
1. The fund portfolio manager decides what stocks to buy and sell and when's the best time.	1. You decide which stocks to buy and sell and when's the best time.
2. You get the added safety that comes from diversifying among lots of different stocks.	2. You get the high-risk, high-reward potential that comes from concentrating on just a handful of stocks.
3. You can invest any amount you want (above the minimum) and receive fractional shares.	3. Stock prices affect how much you invest because you have to buy whole shares.
4. You can easily and efficiently reinvest all of your dividends.	4. It's difficult to reinvest all your dividends because the amounts are usually very small.
5. You can transfer your money between funds the same day.	5. It usually takes three business days to get your money when you sell.
6. You pay no sales charges when buying or selling no-load funds.	6. You pay brokers' commissions each time you buy or sell.

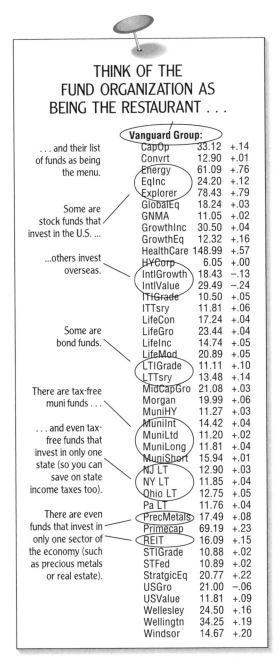

THINK OF THE
FUND ORGANIZATION AS
BEING THE RESTAURANT . . .

. . . and their list
of funds as being
the menu.

Some are
stock funds that
invest in the U.S. . . .

. . . others invest
overseas.

Some are
bond funds.

There are tax-free
muni funds . . .

. . . and even tax-
free funds that
invest in only one
state (so you can
save on state
income taxes too).

There are even
funds that invest in
only one sector of
the economy (such
as precious metals
or real estate).

Vanguard Group:

CapOp	33.12	+.14
Convrt	12.90	+.01
Energy	61.09	+.76
EqInc	24.20	+.12
Explorer	78.43	+.79
GlobalEq	18.24	+.03
GNMA	11.05	+.02
GrowthInc	30.50	+.04
GrowthEq	12.32	+.16
HealthCare	148.99	+.57
HYCorp	6.05	+.00
IntlGrowth	18.43	−.13
IntlValue	29.49	−.24
ITGrade	10.50	+.05
ITTsry	11.81	+.06
LifeCon	17.24	+.04
LifeGro	23.44	+.04
LifeInc	14.74	+.05
LifeMod	20.89	+.05
LTIGrade	11.11	+.10
LTTsry	13.48	+.14
MidCapGro	21.08	+.03
Morgan	19.99	+.06
MuniHY	11.27	+.03
MuniInt	14.42	+.04
MuniLtd	11.20	+.02
MuniLong	11.81	+.04
MuniShort	15.94	+.01
NJ LT	12.90	+.03
NY LT	11.85	+.04
Ohio LT	12.75	+.05
Pa LT	11.76	+.04
PrecMetals	17.49	+.08
Primecap	69.19	+.23
REIT	16.09	+.15
STIGrade	10.88	+.02
STFed	10.89	+.02
StratgicEq	20.77	+.22
USGro	21.00	−.06
USValue	11.81	+.09
Wellesley	24.50	+.16
Wellingtn	34.25	+.19
Windsor	14.67	+.20

investors. The point here is to show you *how many different funds you can find at a single fund organization.* Want a conservative blue-chip stock fund? Try Windsor. Perhaps something a little more aggressive? Check out Explorer or U.S. Growth. Prefer bonds instead? Vanguard has funds that specialize in corporates, governments, and tax-frees. Want short-term bonds instead of long-term? No problem—it offers funds that have different portfolio maturities for all three bond categories. The trend among fund organizations is to offer investors a choice in just about every investing specialty and risk group imaginable.

There are three primary ways you can profit from investing in mutual funds.

When you make your mutual fund investment, you will receive shares to show how much (that is, what portion) of the pool you own. The value of those shares fluctuates daily according to how well the investments in the pool are doing. (If the overall value of the stocks held in the pool goes up today, the value of the fund's shares will go up today.) The greater the volatility, the greater the risk. The price you pay for your shares is based on the worth of the securities in the pool on the day you buy in. Typically, the closing price is used for establishing their market value. For this reason, mutual funds usually are bought or sold only at the day's closing prices. This means that it doesn't matter what time of day the fund receives your order—early or late— you'll still get that day's closing price.

You can profit from your shares in three primary ways. First, the dividends paid by the stocks in the portfolio will be paid out to you periodically, usually quarterly. Second, if the portfolio manager sells a stock for more than he paid for it originally, a capital gain results. These gains will also be paid out periodically, usually annually. And third, when you're ready to sell your shares in the pool, you might receive back more than you paid for them. ◆

6

How Mutual Funds Are Sold and the Best Way to Buy Them

I.   **There are two primary ways to go about investing in mutual funds.**

    A.   "Load" fund organizations sell their shares to investors through a sales network of brokers, insurance professionals, and financial planners. A percentage of every dollar you invest (which can run as high as 8.5%) goes to the salesperson with whom you do business.

    B.   "No-load" fund organizations sell their shares to investors directly. They don't have a sales force to represent them, and so there need not be a "load" charged to the investor; 100% of every dollar invested goes to work on the investor's behalf.

II. **There are ongoing costs associated with owning mutual fund shares.**

    A.   All mutual funds charge an on-going fee for the costs associated with the services of the portfolio manager. This is the way they make their money.

    B.   All mutual funds charge an on-going fee for operating expenses such as: office, staff, equipment, bank custodial services, reporting to shareholders, and legal and auditing services.

    C.   About 70% of stock funds charge an on-going fee for marketing expenses.

    D.   Collectively, the on-going expenses cost shareholders in the average stock fund around $13 annually for every $1,000 of account value. The way this is commonly stated is that the average fund's "expense ratio" is 1.3%.

III. **You should select a fund organization based on the amount of money you have available to start, and the kinds of investments you wish to focus on.**

    A.   If you have $2,500 or less to begin, you must look for fund organizations with low account minimums. As your portfolio grows in value, you eventually may want to open accounts with more than one fund organization in order to have a greater selection of funds from which to choose.

    B.   A better approach is to use the services offered by "mutual fund supermarkets" such as Schwab and Fidelity. They offer maximum convenience, flexibility, and selection at a reasonable price.

No-Load Fund

is a mutual fund sold without a sales commission, either when you buy or sell your shares. This is usually done by the mutual fund organization selling directly to the investor rather than using a sales network.

Load Fund

is a mutual fund sold to investors through a sales network, typically by stock brokers, financial planners, and insurance agents, and for which the investor pays a markup or sales charge.

Front-Loaded Fund

is a kind of load fund where the sales commission is paid in advance at the time the shares are purchased. The shares you get when you buy front-loaded funds are typically called "Class A" shares (see page 82).

Back-Loaded Fund

is a kind of load fund where a sales commission may be owed at the time the shares are sold. The commission is deducted from your proceeds when you pull your money out. This kind of commission is sometimes called a deferred sales charge. This approach allows the firms that use them to sell shares through their commissioned brokers without charging front-loads. The firm is able to pay the brokers from these back-end loads and from the hidden 12b-1 charges (these are marketing-related charges discussed on page 83).

What does it cost to buy mutual funds?
That depends on how you buy them . . .

. . . whether *you go to them* or *they come to you*. Mutual funds earn their profits by the management fees they charge, which are based on the amount of money they are responsible for investing. The more investors' money they manage, the more they make. Naturally, they want to attract as many customers as possible.

So-called "load" funds get new customers by having a sales force of stockbrokers, financial planners, and insurance professionals sell their funds for them. These funds charge a sales fee, which is added on top of the fund's net asset value. This markup cost can run as high as 5.75% on every dollar you invest. The load applies to all purchases you make in the fund, not just the first time; some load funds even charge to reinvest your dividends for you (which I think is going a bit far). In return, the salesperson comes up with recommendations as to which funds might be best suited for your goals and completes all the paperwork to get your account opened. The load is the way the salesperson is rewarded for opening and servicing new accounts. If you would never get around to doing the research needed to select funds that are right for you, the salesperson provides an important service by doing this work for you and motivating you to action.

"No-load" funds, on the other hand, have chosen to deal directly with investors. They don't have a sales force to represent them — they believe plenty of investors are willing to do their own research and paperwork in order to save on the sales load. *They don't come to you; you go to them.* Of course, they make it as easy as possible through their advertising, websites, 800 numbers, and customer-service departments. Since they don't have salespeople to pay, they don't charge the load (thus the name "no-load"). By showing some initiative, you can save the 3.00%–5.75% load that is commonly charged. That means *all the money* you put into your fund account goes to work for *you*. I recommend you limit your investment shopping to no-load funds. You'll learn all you need to know in this book to select the funds that are right for you, and you'll save thousands of dollars in loads over the years.

But (I can hear many of you asking) what about investment performance? Is it true that load funds get better results than no-load funds?

Sometimes they do, and sometimes they don't. Let me explain it to you this way. One of the major college basketball rivalries in my part of the country is the one between the University of Louisville and the University of Kentucky. The question of who's best is settled once a year — but only briefly. Bragging rights only last until the next time they play. Since the team lineups are constantly changing, the question of superiority is fought anew each season.

If you look at the two programs over time, they're pretty evenly matched.

That's also the way it is in the great "load fund" versus "no-load fund" debate. Which kind has the better performance? The truth is they're pretty evenly matched. Neither group is inherently better than the other, just as none of the top college programs is inherently superior to the others. One year college A is best, the next year college B, and so on (although a John Wooden or a Dean Smith may come along and dominate every now and then, but that's to their credit, not the institution's).

In the same way, one year several of the no-load categories will outperform their load counterparts. The next year it could well be the other way around. Each group will have their share of winning results, and the "margin of victory" is usually quite small. They're so close that it's anyone's guess who will lead in performance in the coming year. Both load and no-load fund organizations hire top professionals in an attempt to bolster their performance results, which are, after all, what they are selling. So why should you expect either type to be inherently superior to the other? You shouldn't.

However, that doesn't mean they're equally attractive. The load that investors pay comes out upfront, which means they're "in the hole" the day their account is opened. Load funds *must* be consistently superior over time in order to be a better investment than a comparable no-load fund. This places the burden of proof on the load funds.

COSTS OF INVESTING IN MUTUAL FUNDS

Type of Fee:	Applies To:	You Pay:
Front Loads	Load funds only	When you buy
Operating Expenses	All mutual funds	A little each day
12b-1 Fees	About 70% of all funds	A little each day
Deferred Sales Charges	Load funds only	If you sell within 1 year
Redemption Fees	A few no-load funds	If you sell within 7-180 days

Don't let class confusion fool you.

To keep track of the mountain of data generated by the mutual fund industry, I subscribe to a pretty neat service offered by Morningstar, the leader among organizations that monitor the investment performance of mutual funds. For a mere $1,460 a year, I receive a computer CD each month that is packed with the equivalent of several thousand pages of data. The current one has information on more than 8,600 mutual funds (or almost 30,000 if you count different classes of shares of the same fund!).

Redemption Fees are charged by many funds. They are intended to discourage you from making frequent trades, and come into play if you sell within a specified time of buying your shares. Some funds assess the fees if you sell with 30 days. The most common time frame is 90 days.

Such fees (also sometimes called "exit" fees) can range from a low of 0.25% to as much as 2% of the money withdrawn. Like back-end loads, they are deducted from the check sent you at the time you sell your shares. Frequently with these arrangements, the fees paid by departing shareholders go into the fund assets so as to benefit the remaining shareholders. In that event, redemption fees are actually a good thing for long-term investors in the fund.

Much of this dramatic growth is attributable to a feeding frenzy on the part of investors. The public's appetite for stock investing has been huge, and fund organizations have responded in fine capitalistic fashion by meeting the demands of the marketplace. A considerable number of the new funds, however, aren't really "new" at all. They're old load funds trying to look more like no-loads by creating new "classes" of shares. If you study the offerings of load fund organizations these days, you'll often find they offer multiple ways of investing in the *same* fund.

• **Class "A" shares.** This is the traditional load fund arrangement where you pay a sales charge to the broker or financial planner who introduced you to the fund, and this charge is deducted from your investment at the time you make it. Whereas this used to run 8.50%, competitive pressures from the no-loads have taken their toll. The most common front-end load is now 5.75%, and some stock-fund loads are as low as 3.00%. In addition to this one-time sales charge, you also pay the ongoing annual operating expenses which are common to all mutual funds.

• **Class "C" shares.** At first glance, these seem the most like no-load funds. They usually have no front-end loads, and the deferred load, a relatively small 1%, usually applies only to redemptions made during the first year you own your shares. The selling broker typically gets a 1% up-front commission for selling Class "C" fund shares as well as an on-going quarterly payment which is built into the fund's expense charge and continues for as long as you own your shares.

The table at left shows the effects of various load arrangements over time on a $10,000 investment assuming an 8% average annual return. The annual expenses column is an approximate average for each group as of mid-2013.

Two kinds of no-load funds are also included for comparison purposes. One group charges 12b-1 fees (see discussion of "marketing expenses" that follows). The other group, for competitive reasons, elects not to charge 12b-1 fees. As the table makes clear, no-load fund investors enjoy the best of both worlds—no sales charges going in or coming out, and low annual expenses for as long as you stay.

Among the load funds, the advantage goes to Class "C" shares. If you hold them long enough (8+ years), Class "A" shares eventually catch up due to their lower annual expenses, but few investors hold their stock funds for a decade.

HOW VARIOUS LOAD AND EXPENSE POLICIES EAT INTO AN 8% ANNUAL RETURN

	Pure No-Load	12b-1 No-Load	Class A Load	Class C Load
Expense Ratio	1.00%	1.23%	1.26%	1.95%
Front Loads	None	None	5.75%	None
Deferred Loads	None	None	None	1.00%
Sell After Yr 1	$10,700	$10,677	$10,060 →	$10,499
Sell After Yr 2	$11,449	$11,400	$10,738 →	$11,134
Sell After Yr 3	$12,250	$12,172	$11,462 →	$11,808
Sell After Yr 4	$13,108	$12,996	$12,235 →	$12,522
Sell After Yr 5	$14,026	$13,875	$13,059 →	$13,280
Sell After Yr 6	$15,007	$14,815	$13,939 →	$14,083
Sell After Yr 7	$16,058	$15,818	$14,879 →	$14,935
Sell After Yr 8	$17,182	$16,889	$15,882 →	$15,839
Sell After Yr 9	$18,385	$18,032	$16,952 →	$16,797
Sell After Yr 10	$19,672	$19,253	→ $18,095	$17,813

What on-going costs are involved in owning mutual funds?

In addition to the sales commissions involved when investing in load funds, there are also the ongoing operating expenses that are charged by *all* mutual funds, whether load or no-load. These are the costs of owning mutual funds over the long haul.

• **Operating expenses.** First, there are the costs associated with making the investing decisions. This means paying for an experienced portfolio manager as well as a staff of financial analysts to help with all the research, and is by far the largest of the operating expenses. Second, there's a lot of administrative overhead involved in having a large office, staff, and equipment. Third, there's the cost of having a bank maintain the shareholder accounts and safeguard all the money and securities which are constantly coming and going. Fourth, there are the costs of presenting regular reports to shareholders, as well as for legal and auditing services.

• **Marketing expenses.** In addition to all the operating expenses, roughly half of all stock funds also charge some of their marketing expenses to shareholders. These expenses are referred to as "12b-1" fees because of the SEC ruling that permits them, and the money from them can be used only to advertise and sell the fund to prospective investors.

Collectively, operating and marketing expenses cost shareholders in the average stock fund around . . .

. . . $13 annually for every $1,000 of account value. The way this is commonly stated is that the average fund's "expense ratio" is 1.3%. These operating and mar-

ARE LOAD FUNDS WORTH THE EXTRA COSTS?

They're worth it for <u>some</u> people. My thoughts on this are summarized in an exchange of letters I had with a financial planner who sold load funds.

Dear Austin:

I have been in the financial services business for five years. God has blessed my business, and I am very proud of the fact that my clients place a lot of confidence in me in giving them sound, unbiased and godly financial advice. I serve most of my clients as a financial planner in the type of work I do, but I have never charged fees for this. . . .

I've seen how you recommend that people should primarily consider no-load funds. The problem I have is that no-load funds don't put bread on my family's table. I do think there are many good funds to choose from that are loaded. I tend to sell funds that are 2%–4% and not ones that are more expensive. I sell mostly larger, reputable funds with long successful track records. Yet, in all this I certainly don't feel I've done my clients a disservice, since they have not had to pay me a fee for the financial planning. I guess what I would like you to do is simply comment on how you feel about this kind of service and how I might better communicate to my clients the reasons I use load funds. —Sincerely, Alan

Dear Alan:

I understand your desire to render an honest service for a fair wage. And I know there are millions of people who are not willing to invest the time to learn the basics and become self-reliant in the area of finances and investing—they need the help of a trustworthy counselor.

A pastor once completed one of my survey forms with the comment: "I do not have the time or inclination to study financial matters, yet I know it is important." He is the kind of person who could benefit from your knowledge and objectivity. In helping him formulate a long-term plan and selecting good mutual funds (obviously, there are excellent funds to choose from in both the load and no-load camps) suited to his personal situation, you are rendering a valuable service. It is only right that you be fairly paid, and load funds make this possible.

Unfortunately, there have been so many well-publicized episodes of blatantly deceptive and self-serving brokers and planners taking advantage of trusting investors that the public is becoming cynical and wary. The primary culprit is a system that rewards stockbrokers based on their sales success (commissions earned) rather than their investment success (customers' profits). It does take a good bit of time to persuade potential clients that you are a person of integrity.

To assure that the welfare of your clients remains uppermost in your mind, I would suggest these guidelines: [1] go the extra mile to make sure the portfolio you are recommending is truly fitted to your clients' needs; [2] make sure they understand the risks and the possible worst-case scenarios if they were to withdraw their money earlier than expected; [3] put them in fund families with a wide variety of offerings to accommodate possible future changes; and [4] always remember that we live our lives moment by moment in the sight of God. "To do what is right and just is more acceptable to the Lord than sacrifice" (Proverbs 21:3). —Sincerely, Austin

If you are someone who has neither the time nor inclination to select your own mutual fund investments, then your task is to locate someone like Alan who is informed, experienced, and objective.

keting expenses are not taken out of your account all at once. Rather, in a manner that is invisible to the shareholder, they are charged daily against the fund's net asset value. The price you see in the newspaper has *already* had that day's share of the costs deducted.

Also, when you see fund rankings in financial newspapers and magazines, these expenses have already been deducted; that is, the effects of each fund's annual expenses have been taken into account. That is not usually the case, however, with respect to any sales commissions a fund might charge. Unless the article specifically states to the contrary, sales loads are typically not taken into account when fund-performance rankings are compiled. Therefore, the return you would actually receive would need to be adjusted downward by the amount of the sales load.

If you're interested in doing your own fund "shopping" and saving the costs associated with load funds, which fund organization is best?

Well, best for what purpose? How long do you expect to hold your fund investments? What kinds of funds are you interested in? Are you willing to monitor your funds' progress, or do you want to just buy a few and forget them for the next few years? There is no "best" in an absolute sense; the selection must take place within the context of your personal goals and risk tolerance. A greater number of choices, it seems, creates greater anxiety about making the right decision.

It's important to keep in mind that each fund organization has its own areas of excellence. (For example, if you're primarily going to be investing in index funds—see chapter 14—Vanguard is hard to beat.) Also, performance leadership is always changing. "Organization A" could be doing great now, but its funds could all become sell candidates a year from now. While it's important that you discipline yourself to have a long-term commitment *to the diversification strategy*, you need only make short-term commitments to individual funds and organizations.

A better alternative than going with a single fund organization is to open an investment account at a "mutual fund supermarket."

Charles Schwab pioneered its Mutual Fund Marketplace in 1992. For a small service fee, Schwab offered access to hundreds of no-load funds through one investment account. It wasn't long before Fidelity, the giant mutual fund organization, came along to one-up Schwab by offering the same service with even more funds to choose from.

Schwab struck back with its OneSource service which eliminated the service fees completely for certain fund families (the so-called "no transaction fee" funds, or NTF for short). Of course, you still had to pay a load if the fund itself charged a load, and not all no-load funds were included in the NTF offer (for those left

---

Opening A No-Load Fund Account

No-load funds attract investors through direct advertising in financial publications (such as The Wall Street Journal, Barron's, Forbes, and Money) rather than via a sales network of brokers, insurance agents, and financial planners. They typically call attention to their performance histories or variety of fund offerings in an attempt to motivate you to go to their websites or call their toll-free numbers for more information. There is no charge, either for the fund information available online or the material they send you in the mail, and they usually don't bother you with personal follow-up calls. An account application form is available online or will be included in the information package you receive by mail.

out, Schwab continued to assess a charge for processing the transaction). In 1993, Fidelity responded by introducing a similar no-transaction-fee service of its own. The battle was on! In the ensuing years, many imitators have arisen. There are now more than 20 fund supermarket services. They differ in important ways: which fund groups they offer, how many funds are available on an NTF basis, how many funds are available on a transaction basis, the amount of the transaction fee they charge, and the level of customer service.

I should point out that fund supermarkets have some drawbacks. The most significant is that the funds they offer on an NTF basis typically carry higher annual expenses than other funds. Supermarkets may not charge you for buying and selling funds in their NTF lineups, but they do charge the fund organizations. The charge can be as much as 0.40% of the asset value — this is a significant amount. The funds turn around and recapture this cost, often by passing it through to the fund shareholders as a 12b-1 marketing expense (see page 83). According to Morningstar, the fund-rating company, funds that do not participate in NTF supermarket programs charge, on average, about .25% less in annual fees than those that do. A fund supermarket can have other drawbacks, too, depending on the organization:

- It may not offer all the funds or fund families that interest you.
- You may be charged for selling a "no transaction fee" fund if you own it for less than 60-180 days, depending on the broker.
- You can expect to pay above-average management costs for their money-market and index funds.

Should you expose yourself to potentially higher costs at a supermarket when you can go directly to a no-load organization and buy its fund shares for free? Yes, for two primary reasons — greater convenience and greater selection. Because the fund supermarkets offer hundreds of different funds from which to choose, many of those funds likely will be superior performers to those of the one or two no-load organizations where you might have accounts (especially in the stock-fund categories). Also, with one toll-free call to phone lines that are answered 24 hours a day, or via the Web if you prefer, you can make changes in your portfolio. And you'll get one monthly statement that includes your transaction history, dividends, and the current market values for all your holdings.

To me, these advantages far outweigh the drawbacks. I personally have four investment accounts; three are at fund supermarkets and the fourth is at Vanguard.

The discount brokerage business, including the mutual fund supermarket niche, continues to experience consolidation. The lay of the land, as this is written in 2013, looks quite positive for consumers. Fees continue to come down, and services, particularly among the bigger brokers, continue to improve. After a period when some brokers decided they wanted to focus primarily on their wealthier clients, the pendulum has swung back in favor of the little guy.

What features should you look for when selecting a mutual fund marketplace?

My broker evaluation may well vary from others you might read. Some broker services on which others place a high value (e.g., stock research, screeners, and options trading availability) are of little importance for mutual-fund investors—especially anyone following the Fund Upgrading strategy I recommend to my *Sound Mind Investing* newsletter readers (see chapter 17). For our purposes, the critical criteria are these:

• **Selection of no-transaction-fee (NTF) funds (more is better).** These are funds you can buy and sell within your account without paying any commissions or transaction fees. You want a broker that offers an abundance of NTF funds.

• **NTF holding periods (shorter is better).** To discourage overly active trading, most brokers require you to hold NTF-fund shares for a period ranging from 60 to 180 days to qualify for the no-transaction-fee price break. In other words, if you turn around and sell your holdings too quickly you're penalized with a "short-term redemption fee." How often will that happen? It depends on your trading patterns. If you use dollar-cost averaging (investing month-by-month in funds you already hold), you are likely to incur these fees. But if you typically make a single purchase of each fund and *don't* add additional money, you rarely will pay a trading fee if you use a broker with a 90-day holding period.

• **Short-term redemption fees (lower is better).** Okay, so if you sell a no-transaction-fee fund too soon, you have to pay a fee. How much? The amount varies among brokers, from as little as $17 to $75 or more. (Note that these fees go to the broker, and are above and beyond any "early redemption" fee the fund itself might mandate.)

The dollar amount of a broker's short-term redemption fee is of particular importance to those who try to combine SMI's Upgrading strategy with dollar-cost-averaging. The reason is that fund companies apply the fee based on when you made various purchases of fund shares. For example, suppose you bought a fund in February and sold it in November. The shares purchased originally would be well beyond any 90-day (or even 180-day) holding period. But if you had invested additional money each month along the way, then selling all of your shares in November would trigger a short-term redemption fee, based on the shares purchased in the three months (or six months) prior to your "sell" date. (The ability to avoid these types of short-term redemption fees is one reason many investors who want to combine dollar-cost-averaging with Upgrading choose to invest via the SMI mutual funds. For more, go to www.smifund.com)

• **Transaction fees on *non*-NTF fund purchases (lower is better).** Any fund not labeled an NTF fund at a broker *is* nevertheless available through the particular broker, however the broker will charge a transaction fee when you buy that fund—and another when you sell. (Currently, Fidelity and Schwab are unique in charging a transaction fee only when you buy; it costs nothing to sell.)

• **Maintenance fees for smaller accounts (no fee is better).** Some brokerages discourage smaller accounts with annual or quarterly fees on accounts below a certain dollar threshold. Thankfully, these "nuisance" fees have become increasingly rare in recent years and usually can be avoided fairly easily by accepting conditions such as agreeing to receive statements and other documents electronically.

• **Customer service and website design.** There is a strong element of "you get what you pay for" when it comes to discount brokers. Generally speaking, the cheaper the broker's fees, the less service you can expect. If having ready access to a customer service rep (via phone, e-mail, or online chat) is important to you, you're likely to be disappointed with the cheaper brokers. I suspect it's worth it to most investors to pay a little more to have access to competent help when a clarification is needed or a problem arises. But like everything else, it's up to you to decide.

Here are thumbnail profiles of several leading brokers' fund supermarket offerings.

Nothing written here is intended to create the impression that you necessarily need to change brokers. If you're already dealing with a particular company and you're happy where you are, stay there. Just realize the broker that was right for you a few years ago may not be the best choice for you today.

• **Fidelity** is the biggest discount broker, with more than $3.4 trillion in assets. This isn't necessarily a plus in and of itself, but Fidelity has used its scale and resources to bring great service, tools, and depth of investment choices to its customers. Fidelity's lineup of NTF-funds is unmatched, and its shorter holding period for NTF funds in its marketplace is an industry-leading 60 days. That takes Fidelity's steep $75 short-term trading fee off the table for many investor. All of that is enough to make Fidelity my curent top recommendation for mutual-fund investors looking for a broker. And that doesn't even take into account the firm's recent expansion into the world of ETFs.

Comparing Fidelity's and Schwab's Fund-Transaction Fees

Fidelity had long been unique among discount brokers in its policy of charging a somewhat higher fee to purchase a non-NTF mutual fund, but then not charging anything to sell that fund. In other words, their stated fee was higher than the other brokers, but the other brokers charged theirs twice—once buying and once selling—whereas Fidelity charged theirs just once.

Toward the end of 2011, Schwab took a significant step in Fidelity's direction on this issue, changing their fee schedule to mimic Fidelity's policy of only charging on the buy-side of the transaction. Surprisingly though, Schwab made its purchase price $1 *higher* than Fidelity's. So on the issue of non-NTF fund pricing, the two are essentially the same now.

For Updated Information
The policies, services, and mutual-fund offetings of discount brokers are constantly changing. The recommendations made in this chapter may have changed by the time you read this. For our current broker recommendations as well as an up-to-date list of the better online resources related to mutual funds, visit the SMI website at www.soundmindinvesting.com.

• **Schwab** has raised the fees it charges mutual funds to be listed in its marketplace, and many fund families have said "no thanks." As a result, more funds are unavailable at Schwab than in the past. This trend seems unlikely to reverse. Given that fund availability is a significant component of what makes brokers attractive to fund investors, this is a strike against Schwab. With pricing that is extremely similar to Fidelity at this point but with an inferior fund lineup, there's no reason to favor Schwab.

• **Scottrade** continues to be attractive as a low-cost alternative for smaller accounts and other particularly price-sensitive readers. Scottrade's NTF and overall fund availability rivals that of the other top brokers, as does their 90-day holding period for NTF funds. Scottrade's other investment offerings are less broad than its larger competitors, and its website isn't as slick and easy to use. But the biggest continuing irritation with Scottrade is the requirement to wait up to three days between selling one fund and buying its replacement. Nevertheless, the company's fund selection and low fees (only $17 for non-NTF trades) are enough to make it a decent option for investors managing smaller amounts.

• **TDAmeritrade** was one of my recommended brokers several years ago on the basis of its low costs and great fund selection. TDA's standard fees and policies, however, have gradually become less and less appealing. The biggest strike against TDA is its NTF holding period of 180 days. Given that its other fees are relatively high, there isn't any compelling reason for a fund investor to choose TDA over Fidelity.

• **Firstrade** and **E*Trade are two more well-known options.** They're low-cost, but suffer from inferior mutual-fund lineups. There's no reason to choose either one over Scottrade (for smaller accounts) or Fidelity (for larger ones).

(The above profiles were adapted from a thorough broker review that appeared in my *Sound Mind Investing* newsletter in February 2012. Brokerage firms' policies and fees evolve over time, so you will want to verify the current status of the features inportant to you before opening an account).

There are more solid brokerage options for fund investors now than ever.

Your specific investing approach will largely dictate which broker is the best option for you. If you're choosing a broker from scratch, don't be overly concerned about making the wrong choice. You can always change later if needed. And don't feel as though you need to change brokers if you're currently satisfied. Some readers prefer continuing to pay a little more for a familiar, proven commodity rather than switching to an unknown. But it's worth reviewing your options to see if you could save money, not just in the current year but for many years to come, by moving your account to a less expensive broker that still offers the level of services you desire. ◆

7

Necessary Cautions

I. **The rapid growth of the mutual-fund industry in recent decades has created a crowded and competitive playing field.**

  A. This has led many funds to take added investment risks as they seek to gain a performance edge over their rivals.

  B. The fund industry's system for classifying risk is subjective and open to misinterpretation and abuse.

II. **The exceptional growth—and the ways in which many funds have responded to it—has raised red flags that are a cause for concern to mutual-fund investors.**

  A. Red Flag #1: You can't necessarily accept a fund's *investment objective* at face value. The investing boundaries that guide a portfolio manager have become blurred as funds have changed by-laws in order to broaden their investing horizons.

  B. Red Flag #2: You can't necessarily accept a fund's *diversification claims* at face value. Many funds, in the pursuit of higher performance numbers, sacrifice diversification by concentrating their investments in just a few sectors of the economy.

  C. Red Flag #3: You can't necessarily accept a fund's *implied performance excellence* at face value. The job of any fund's marketing department is to take that fund's performance history and make it look as good as possible. In this chapter, we look at three ways mutual funds will present their performance histories in the manner most likely to attract investors.

  D. Red Flag #4: You can't necessarily accept a fund's *performance rankings* at face value. Funds are "graded on the curve" based on the peer group they're placed in. If the risk-category definitions are inconsistent in assuring that apples are compared to apples, then the performance rankings based on them are potentially misleading.

III. **Mutual fund investors must accept the responsibility for learning how to shop intelligently. A source of information often bypassed by investors is the fund prospectus. This chaper offers pointers on how to read it for the essentials.**

Morningstar,
Lipper Analytical,
and Value Line
are large companies that are in
the business of collecting,
analyzing, and distributing
information about mutual funds.
They sell their data to financial
institutions, publishers, and
investors. When you read about
mutual fund performance in The
Wall Street Journal, Barron's,
Business Week, Money, Forbes,
or other leading financial
publications, the data shown
came from one of these three
organizations. Because of their
dominance of the industry, the
way these companies
categorize funds for risk and
performance is extraordinarily
influential in the decision-
making of millions of mutual
fund investors.

Risk Category
is a way of classifying mutual
funds that groups funds that
have similar investment
strategies and similar
possibilities of profit and loss.
The idea is that such categories
are useful in helping investors
compare "apples with apples"
when measuring mutual
fund performance.

Unfortunately, there is no
"official" list of categories used
consistently throughout the
industry. Morningstar, Lipper,
and Value Line each have their
own different (albeit similar)
ways to classify funds. Because
of the great diversity of funds,
their systems have grown to
include more than 60 different
risk categories.

In this book, I have created a
simplified system that has just
five basic categories for stock
funds and four for bond funds.
These will be explained in detail
in Section 3.

When I began my career as an investment adviser in the late 1970s . . .

. . . I chose to specialize in the study of mutual funds. Such funds offered my clients quick and easy diversification within specified boundaries, along with seasoned professional management. Plus, since there were only about 800 funds to choose from at the time (compared to thousands of common stocks), the selection process was greatly simplified.

How times have changed! The number of funds has multiplied at a phenomenal rate. Morningstar, one of the country's three leading mutual-fund reporting services, now carries data on more than 8,000 mutual funds in its database. These days the selection process is no longer a simple one. The sheer number and variety of funds has caused investors to be confused about what is available, let alone what is appropriate.

The fund industry's explosive growth has increased the complexity of monitoring mutual fund performance.

Arriving at a decision is more difficult than it used to be, not merely because you have more choices, but, regrettably, because it can no longer be safely assumed that fund managers are investing your money prudently.

Too many fund executives have made poor decisions as they attempted to gain an edge in the face of the enormous competitive pressures that now characterize the fund industry. To better understand the dynamics at work, let's use an analogy based on a business we're all familiar with—the neighborhood supermarket.

Assume that in the "old days" you had three grocery stores in your small town. There was friendly competition but enough business to go around. Then, in a period of fifteen years, the size of your town tripled. With a larger population to feed, the local grocers responded by opening additional stores. The town's growth did not go unnoticed by the grocery chains that had not previously operated in your community, and they came in with new stores as well. Now there are two dozen supermarkets—it seems like there's one on every corner.

The population tripled, but the number of grocery stores grew eightfold. The grocers know that the town can't support all of them and that a shakeout is inevitable. They also know that low prices are the key to attracting shoppers because they see their sales go up and down in direct proportion to how their prices compare to their competitors' prices. So, there is a great deal of pressure on each grocer to have his prices appear as attractive as possible. Each is determined to do what he must in order to be among the survivors, even if it means cutting a few corners here and there.

In the same way, the number of new mutual funds has far surpassed the number of new investors. Mutual fund organizations have hundreds of millions of dollars in fees riding on their ability to attract and keep customers, and the key for them isn't low prices—it's brokers' selling efforts and the emphasis on investment performance. *Fortune* once summed up the situation this way:

> In a recent Smith Barney survey of investors, when asked the single most important reason for selecting a fund, 51% looked to past performance over one to five years, not the composition of the fund portfolio or the fund's management philosophy. . . . That emphasis has sent a message to fund companies: short-term performance is paramount. . . . The trouble with this seemingly harmless focus is that fund managers can be pressured to throw caution to the wind as they try to jockey into the winner's circle for one-year performance. The swelling number of mutual fund rankings in almost every business publication has reinforced the short-term bias, moving one-year performance into an elite class. . . . Such measurements have become the standard for investors and the fund managers who serve them.

In this chapter, we're going to look at some "red flags" that should be a cause for concern to mutual fund investors. They stem, ultimately, from the way the fund industry has taken advantage of the difficulty inherent in categorizing funds by risk. Risk categories are important because they allow investors to "compare apples to apples." Let's begin by laying some important groundwork.

To analyze their performance, mutual funds are placed into groupings called risk categories.

Morningstar and the other firms place every mutual fund into one of three major camps: equity (stock) funds, fixed-income (bond) funds, and hybrid (a mix of both stock and bonds) funds. This is the easy part.

Within each of the three camps, however, there are sub-categories of risk based on a fund's "investment objective." A problem arises at this point because no official categories exist that all analysts can apply uniformly when assigning funds to a given category. The category definitions used by the Investment Company Institute—the mutual fund trade organization—and Morningstar, Lipper, and Value Line are different.

A fund is often assigned to a category that reflects the stated portfolio objectives as found in fund prospectuses, which describe a fund's theoretical goals and strategies. A fund's *actual* portfolio has tremendous room for variance while still staying within the broad, subjective guidelines given in the prospectus.

The fact that there are no official categories that everyone can agree to proves how subjective the risk-assessment process is. After reading a fund's prospectus, the Morningstar (or Lipper or Value Line) analyst assigns the fund to the risk category that accords with that rating company's set of definitions. It's often based on what the fund says it *intends* to do. Risk, like beauty, is in the eye of the beholder.

Equity Funds
are mutual funds that invest primarily in stocks.

Fixed-Income Funds
are mutual funds that invest primarily in bonds.

Hybrid Funds
are mutual funds that have characteristics of both equity and fixed-income funds.

Sector funds
specialize in just one industry (or sector) of our economy, such as banking and financial services, health care, high-tech, or precious metals. They often attract attention because they can turn in excellent performance if their sector of the economy is growing rapidly. The trade-off, however, is a much higher degree of risk due to their lack of industry diversification.

On Fund Names
Under the rules set by the Securities and Exchange Commission, a fund can name itself after a particular kind of security as long as it invests at least 80% of its portfolio in that type of security. For example, in an effort to gain a performance edge, a bond fund could invest up to 20% of its portfolio in higher-yielding, lower-quality corporate bonds and still represent itself as a super-safe "government securities" fund.

What you're looking for in a fund's stated investment objective is an indication of the road the fund is traveling in terms of risk and possible reward. If you saw your neighbor loading up the car for a trip and asked him where he was going, you wouldn't learn very much if all he said was "somewhere warm." That would eliminate a lot of places he *wouldn't* be going, but it really wouldn't pinpoint where he *was* going. That's also true of the way many mutual funds state their objectives. They tell you in very general terms what they are allowed to do, but beyond that the door is left open for a lot of "creativity" on the part of the manager. It's the irresponsible use of this creative freedom on the part of some fund managers that is a growing cause for concern, as we shall now see.

Red Flag #1: You can't necessarily accept a fund's *investment objective* at face value.

The investing boundaries that guide a portfolio manager ("it's OK for our fund to invest in this area but not in that area, to take these risks but not those") have become even more blurred as funds have changed their by-laws in order to broaden their investing horizons. Four common labels applied to stock funds by the industry are:

• **Aggressive growth:** A fund that invests in securities with *higher risk* in return for potentially *higher returns* or gains. These companies typically *do not pay dividends*, and their stock prices tend to be more volatile from day to day.

• **Growth:** A fund that invests primarily in the stocks of companies with *above-average risk* in return for potentially *above-average* returns. These companies often *pay small or no dividends*, and their stock prices tend to be more volatile from day to day.

• **Growth and income:** A fund that has a dual strategy of capital appreciation *and* current income generation through dividends or interest payments, leaning toward the growth side. Perceived to have *average risk*.

• **Equity income.** A fund that has a primary strategy of generating income by owning financially strong, dividend-paying stocks. Perceived to have *below-average risk*.

However, some funds—in seeking a performance advantage—may take risks that are not apparent to the typical investor. I have read of instances where:

• A "growth-and-income" stock fund held large positions in high-yield bonds and dropped 20% in value in six months when the junk-bond market fell.

•Two-thirds of "equity income" funds, which purportedly specialize in high-dividend-paying stocks, yielded less than 2% during the tech mania several years ago because they went for *growth* instead.

• A leading bond fund in the "high-quality corporate" category owed its superior record compared to its peers to the fact that it routinely invested about one-third of its portfolio in lesser quality bonds rated BBB or lower.

• A supposedly stable short-term government bond fund dropped 22% in one year because the manager had made a big bet on the direction of interest rates by investing heavily in "derivatives" (complicated securities — which I don't begin to understand — whose value is derived from some other underlying asset or index).

Another area where category labels can be misleading has to do with the degree to which U.S. stock funds hold shares in companies overseas. You might think that if you wanted to invest internationally you would need to choose a "global" fund (which can invest anywhere) or a "foreign" fund (which can invest anywhere except in the U.S.). Not so. There are funds in each of the four categories that have more than one-third of their entire portfolios invested outside the U.S.

Not only does this kind of behavior mean investors are taking risks of which they may be unaware, but it also makes it more difficult to evaluate the quality of the job being done by the portfolio manager. For example, if Fund A moves significantly ahead of Fund B in its performance, is it because the manager has done a better job of selecting securities, or because he ventured outside his stated objective, and made a speculative killing? In their attempts to achieve top-performing results, some funds have resorted to such high-risk strategies. Raw performance rankings, which previously implied excellence, may now merely represent temporary speculative success.

Red Flag #2: You can't necessarily accept a fund's *diversification claims* at face value.

One of the big selling points of mutual funds is that they offer lower risk due to the diversification in the portfolio. Many funds, however, in the pursuit of higher performance numbers, are turning that concept on its head by concentrating their investments in just a few sectors of the economy.

I once illustrated this in a meeting with my staff by pointing to Robertson Stephens Value + Growth, one of the leading funds in the performance rankings at that time. Whereas most funds in its peer group showed gains over the previous 12 months of 16%–28%, the Robertson Stephens fund was up a stunning 70%! It was a case where the fund's performance was *too* good. I indicated there was no way the fund could have achieved such returns without making a huge speculative bet on the high-tech sector. I hadn't looked this up; it was self-evident that the shareholders of that fund were being exposed to a high degree of risk. The Morningstar data confirmed that the fund entered that year with an 80% stake in high-tech. I wondered if the shareholders knew this. After all, the fund was categorized as a medium-risk growth fund (not a sector fund or even an aggressive growth fund). It also contains the word "value" in its name, which implies a lesser degree of risk. Now, there's nothing wrong with investing in technology. I'm merely saying that funds that have such heavy concentrations in a single area of the economy should be clearly labeled as such lest investors assume they are as diversified as their name would imply.

Another way that funds shoot for higher performance is to concentrate their holdings in a smaller number of stocks. The Fidelity Magellan fund, managed by the renowned Peter Lynch during its rise to prominence, was $10 billion in size and invested in approximately 1,000 different stocks at the time Lynch stepped down. Ten years later, its size had grown to over $100 billion, but it held only about 375 stocks under its current manager. Ten times as much money was invested in less than one-half as many stocks. That is a significant reduction in diversification with a corresponding increase in risk. This could present an especially difficult situation if the manager is forced to sell some of his holdings quickly due to shareholder redemptions.

Red Flag #3: You can't necessarily accept a fund's *implied performance excellence* at face value.

Mutual funds are promoted on the basis of how much money they've made for their shareholders. That's why their ads are usually filled with claims of "great" performance. The job of any fund's marketing department is to take that fund's performance history and make it look as good as possible. Fortunately for them, rare is the fund that hasn't hit a hot streak somewhere along the way. Using the results of the three *hypothetical* funds shown on the far right, let's look at some of the ways that mutual funds will present their performance histories in the manner most likely to attract investors.

• **Picking the best time period.** The Standard & Poor's 500 stock index serves as the benchmark to beat for most stock market professionals. If they have significantly outperformed the S&P 500 over the long haul, they will certainly trumpet that in their ads. If not, one trick is to find a shorter time period in which they had relatively good performance. Take the hypothetical Allen Fund, for example. It didn't compare too well over the past decade—the S&P grew at an average compounded rate of return of 11.0% versus just 10.1% for Allen. Shortening the time period to five years doesn't help, either, because Allen still trailed the S&P. But the final three-year period looks pretty good, thanks to a strong Year 8. In their ads, the managers of the Allen Fund play up the market conditions of recent years and proudly show off their superior performance.

• **Using average returns rather than compounded returns.** Unfortunately for the Brown Fund, it's difficult to select *any* time frame that makes it look like a particularly promising performer, so the managers adopt a different strategy in their advertising. Rather than deal in *compounded* returns as is customary, they present their gains in *average* terms. A $1,000 initial investment in Brown over the past 10 years would have grown to $2,600, a total gain of 160%. Divide that by 10 years and you get an average return of 16.0% per year. However, achieving 160% over 10 years requires a *compounded* return of just 10.0% (which was inferior to the 11.0% compounded growth turned in by the S&P). But to the casual reader of the ad, an average return of 16.0% per year sounds pretty impressive.

• **Emphasizing dollars earned rather than percentage returns.** The Cole Fund has a 10-year record that is slightly better than the S&P, but not enough to boast about. Besides, most of that was due to an exceptionally good year way back in Year 2. More recently, the fund has done relatively poorly, although it has managed to eke out some gains each year. So the managers of Cole decide to advertise their performance in dollar terms rather than in percentage terms. A shareholder who held through the entire 10-year period would have seen his initial investment triple in value, and the graph in the ad (on the left) illustrates the steady growth. To make the fund's performance appear even more powerful, the results are shown in contrast to inflation rather than the S&P 500 benchmark, which it barely surpassed. An investor coming across the Cole Fund ad would likely have reacted favorably to its performance claims. So, be alert. There's often much more than meets the eye in mutual fund performance claims.

Red Flag #4: You can't necessarily accept a fund's *performance rankings* at face value.

This problem flows logically from Red Flag #1, not being able to accept a fund's "investment objective" at face value. If you can't count on the risk categories to be consistent in comparing apples to apples, then the performance rankings based on them are potentially misleading. Assume that the ABC Fund is classified as a "large-cap *blend*" fund by Morningstar (meaning it invests in large size companies using a combina-

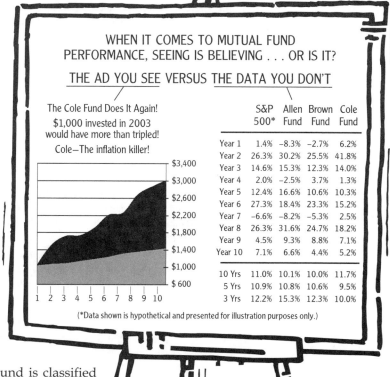

WHEN IT COMES TO MUTUAL FUND
PERFORMANCE, SEEING IS BELIEVING . . . OR IS IT?

THE AD YOU SEE VERSUS THE DATA YOU DON'T

The Cole Fund Does It Again!
$1,000 invested in 2003
would have more than tripled!
Cole—The inflation killer!

	S&P 500*	Allen Fund	Brown Fund	Cole Fund
Year 1	1.4%	−8.3%	−2.7%	6.2%
Year 2	26.3%	30.2%	25.5%	41.8%
Year 3	14.6%	15.3%	12.3%	14.0%
Year 4	2.0%	−2.5%	3.7%	1.3%
Year 5	12.4%	16.6%	10.6%	10.3%
Year 6	27.3%	18.4%	23.3%	15.2%
Year 7	−6.6%	−8.2%	−5.3%	2.5%
Year 8	26.3%	31.6%	24.7%	18.2%
Year 9	4.5%	9.3%	8.8%	7.1%
Year 10	7.1%	6.6%	4.4%	5.2%
10 Yrs	11.0%	10.1%	10.0%	11.7%
5 Yrs	10.9%	10.8%	10.6%	9.5%
3 Yrs	12.2%	15.3%	12.3%	10.0%

Graph values: $3,400, $3,000, $2,600, $2,200, $1,800, $1,400, $1,000, $600 — x-axis 1 2 3 4 5 6 7 8 9 10

(*Data shown is hypothetical and presented for illustration purposes only.)

tion of growth and value strategies) while the Lipper analyst, due to using slightly different criteria, puts it in the "large-cap *growth*" category. In that event, which is the "correct" classification to use when evaluating the excellence of the fund's performance? For example, if ABC returned 10.2% per year in 2009 (the first year of the current bull market) was that good? It depends who you ask.

Lipper would rank ABC's performance against the other funds it placed in the large-cap growth fund group. Since pure growth strategies were the big winners in 2009, let's say the average fund in that group returned 13.3% per year. Compared to that, ABC's returns were below average. Consequently, its standing in the Lipper rankings would not be very impressive. Turning to Morningstar, let's assume the average fund in its large-cap blend group returned 6.7% during the same period. ABC's average annual return of 10.2% was terrific as far as Morningstar was concerned—good enough to rank in the top 20% of its peer group—and Morningstar's rankings would reflect that. When you're being "graded on the curve," it's good to be in a class of underachievers.

This is a mighty important matter to the folks at the ABC Fund. It determines whether they can advertise their fund as an excellent performer or an also-ran. Which measurement service's rankings do you believe ABC will refer to in its full-page ads? Morningstar's, of course. In this example, the fund has done nothing wrong. It is merely taking advantage of a difference of opinion between Morningstar and Lipper. There have been instances, however, in which funds have been suspected of "gaming" the fund rankings, that is, attempting to have their fund placed in a risk category where its performance would earn it a high ranking relative to the other funds in that group. One financial magazine explained it this way:

> Fund managers can accomplish this sleight of hand in part because fund categories are so loosely defined, and because funds are commonly listed under the heading suggested by the vaguely worded investment objectives found in their prospectuses. This allows managers, in effect, to choose the heading under which their funds will be ranked, a cozy arrangement from the not-too-distant time when the whole industry was small and stodgy rather than the cutthroat world of 11,500 or more funds it has become. . . . Wall Street professionals have suspected for years that gaming was widespread. Until recently, they haven't had much evidence to back them up, but two independent studies now appear to confirm that gaming not only exists, but may be more widespread than anyone imagined. Both research efforts concluded that more than half of all mutual funds are misclassified in performance rankings. And more than one out of ten is listed inaccurately enough that investors could be misled about their true nature, according to one study.

Nevertheless, as we saw in chapter 5, mutual funds offer many advantages to the average investor. The answer is not to avoid mutual funds entirely, but rather to learn how to shop for them intelligently. This means you must accept responsibility for getting the information you need and reading it sufficiently well so that you understand the risks as well as the rewards. A good place to start, even though it has its limitations, is with the fund's prospectus.

Putting your money in a mutual fund is somewhat like taking an investment journey, and the fund prospectus . . .

. . . outlines the details of the trip—where the fund wishes to go in terms of its goal, the strategy it will use to get there, how much risk it will take on the way, and what it will charge you to ride along.

A prospectus has five sections of particular interest. Here's where you can find the essentials in ten minutes flat.

• **Investment Goals and Strategies.** This section tells you what the fund hopes to accomplish (regardless of what the name of the fund may imply). The objective is usually stated in terms of "growth" (buying securities that go up in value) and "income" (making regular dividend or interest payments to you). Here you'll also find the strategy the fund will use as it attempts to achieve its objectives. Does it have a value or growth orientation, or prefer small companies over large ones? You'll learn if the fund is *committed* to buying certain kinds of securities ("80% of the fund's assets will be invested in investment grade bonds rated AA or higher"), or merely *permitted* to buy them ("manager may engage in trading exchange-traded covered options").

• **Risks.** This is where they tell you that you can lose money owning shares in the fund. The boilerplate warnings here shouldn't come as a surprise, but read them anyway and make sure you know what the worst-case-scenario is likely to be.

• **Past Performance.** This includes the fund's annual returns to shareholders over several years, usually in comparison to a benchmark such as the S&P 500 or Russell 2000 index. Look to see if there is a great deal of year-to-year variability (big gains, small gains, and some losses all seemingly mixed together) versus consistent performance in the areas where the fund is supposed to be strong (stability, growth, or income). Does the fund have a strong record because of just one or two good years? Caution: even a good long-term record can be misleading if the manager who achieved it is no longer running the fund. Don't assume there's any correlation between the fund's past and your future.

• **Fees and Expenses.** Here's where you'll find a breakdown of the maximum sales loads (if any). Are the sales fees up front, or contingent on how long you own your shares? Do they apply to reinvested dividends as well as your initial deposit? Are there redemption fees to pay? There is also data on the annual operating expenses of the fund. These are the invisible costs that you never see on your monthly statement. As noted in chapter 6, performance numbers, such as those published in financial magazines, already take operating expenses (but not sales fees) into account.

• **Buying/Selling Shares.** This lays out how you buy/sell shares in the fund as well as services offered like reinvestment options, wire transfers, check-writing privileges, etc. The important thing here is to be clear on what you have to do to sell your shares. Can you do it over the phone or online? How long before you'll get your money? Make sure you understand this thoroughly and have any necessary forms on file with the fund.

The occasional fund scandal can be discouraging to investors. But take heart!

Later in this book, I'm going to show you how to assure that the funds you buy do *not* put you at risk of the "red flags" mentioned in this chapter *and* are suited to your personal needs.

In chapter 14 I'm going to introduce you to a special breed of mutual funds called "index" funds that, by their very nature, avoid the red flag traps we've just discussed. Then, in chapter 15, I'll show you how to assemble them into a portfolio that reflects your tolerance for risk. You need go no further than this to have a winning long-term strategy.

If you want to go beyond the basics, in chapters 17 and 18 I'll introduce you to two other strategies that I feature in my *Sound Mind Investing* newsletter. The funds recommended in those strategies have already been vetted by my staff and me, and have been selected because they are suitable for the average investor. ◆

◆
8
◆

CHAPTER PREVIEW

Income Taxes and Your
Mutual Fund Investments

I. **Mutual funds are simply conduits through which you invest. From a tax standpoint, the capital gains/losses and dividend/interest income they receive are treated as if they were yours personally.**

    A. Investment companies periodically pay their shareholders the interest and dividends the funds earn in the funds' portfolios.

    B. Investment companies periodically pay their shareholders the capital gains the funds make when the funds' investments are sold.

    C. The date on which these distributions are set aside from the fund's assets for payment to shareholders is called the "ex-dividend" date. This is the significant date as far as income taxes are concerned, not the later date on which you receive the distribution check in the mail.

II. **Tax accounting for mutual funds can be confusing, even to veteran investors.**

    A. Buying just prior to a fund distribution does not result in an actual gain; it merely results in incurring an immediate tax liability.

    B. Distributions are taxable in the year they are declared, not in the year they are received by the investor.

    C. There are two kinds of capital gains to keep in mind—those the funds earn by buying and selling within the fund portfolios, and those investors earn by selling their fund shares for more than they paid for them.

    D. The IRS recognizes three different methods for computing capital gains on fund shares. If you sell part (rather than all) of your shares in a fund, you can select the method that results in the lowest tax liability.

III. **Timing your selling so as to minimize or postpone your tax liability is a natural inclination; however, it should not supersede the normal common sense disciplines built into your long-term strategy.**

If you're tempted to skip this chapter until next year at tax time, don't do it—unless . . .

. . . your funds are held in an IRA or other retirement account, in which case fund distributions won't affect your tax situation at all.

For fund holdings in taxable accounts, however, the sooner you understand what will be needed to complete next year's 1040 form, the sooner you can begin organizing your thinking and record keeping to make things much easier on yourself. Also, you can avoid making a costly year-end investment that will unnecessarily raise your taxes (see "Common Misconceptions" #1 and #2 on pages 101-102). I promise to do my best at making this as clear as possible—but nobody can keep it from being boring! So go for a cup of coffee if need be, and get ready to make some good notes in the margins.

Mutual funds are among the most flexible of all investments from a tax standpoint. That's the good news. Calculating your taxable income, however, is made more complicated by a maze of rules and exceptions to the rules at both the federal and state levels. That's the bad news. Because tax laws vary so widely from state to state, I can't proceed very far into planning tax strategies; there are just too many possible scenarios. What I will do is give you a basic foundation so that you can read and plan intelligently in relation to your particular tax bracket and state of residence.

The first major point I want to emphasize is that mutual funds are simply conduits through which individuals invest in securities.

In the process of investing, mutual funds incur capital gains and losses and receive dividend and interest income on their investments. From a tax point of view, all of this is done on behalf of their shareholders. *It's as if you owned all the investments outright, and the gains and losses that result are all your personal gains and losses.* There are three ways mutual funds can generate profits on your behalf:

❶ They invest in stocks that pay dividends. Mutual funds collect the dividends and pay them out to you periodically.

❷ They invest in bonds or short-term debt securities that pay interest. They collect the interest and pay it out to you periodically.

❸ They sell one of their investments for more than they paid for it, thereby making a capital gain. They keep track of these gains (and offset them against any capital losses) and pay them out to you periodically, usually annually. If they end up with more capital losses than gains, they carry the losses over to the next year; you would receive no payment for the year just ending.

All of these payments to you, regardless of the source—whether dividends, interest, or capital gains—are called "distributions." The fund decides when to make these periodic distribution payments (monthly, quarterly, semi-annually, etc.).

A fund goes through a two-step process in making distributions. First, it "declares" the amount of the distribution . . .

. . . it intends to make, and sets aside the appropriate amount of cash that will be needed to write you a check. Let's say your fund declares a 25¢ per share distribution, and that there are one million shares owned by investors. This means the fund will be paying out a total of $250,000 to its shareholders at this time. Once the money is earmarked for distribution in this way, the fund no longer counts the $250,000 when it does its daily bookkeeping (see page 71). This has the effect of suddenly lowering the net asset value of the fund—one day the money was being counted as part of the fund, and the next day, the day of the declaration, it wasn't. To indicate to investors that the net asset value is lower than it otherwise would be because of the distribution, an "x" appears next to the name of the fund in the daily newspaper listings. The date this happens is called the "ex-dividend" date, *and it is the significant date as far as your taxes are concerned.*

The second step of the distribution process is when the fund actually mails your check to you. It can be anywhere from a few days to a month later. This is called the "payment date" and is important only because that's when you finally receive the cash that has been promised. The payment date has no significance when computing your taxable income.

Let's look at some of the common misconceptions that investors have about fund taxation.

Misconception #1: "It's a good idea to invest in a mutual fund just before one of its periodic distributions."

Actually, it's a bad idea because it will create an immediate tax liability for you. There is no actual profit in owning a fund on the day it goes ex-dividend because the amount the shareholders are to receive is deducted from the value of the fund that same day. If an investor buys a fund today and the fund declares a distribution tomorrow, *the investor owes tax on the amount of the distribution.* This may seem unfair, as the profits were earned by the fund long before the new investor made his purchase. Still, someone has to pay the tax on those profits, and it falls to the "shareholders of record" *at the time of the distribution* to do so.

When a fund makes a distribution, the price of its shares falls by the exact amount of the distribution. This has the effect of reducing the investor's capital gains tax liability in the future. Most funds make distributions at

HOW DISTRIBUTIONS ARE REPORTED IN THE NEWSPAPER

Monday's closing price for the XYZ Fund was $6.00 per share, up 4¢ from Friday's closing price. On Tuesday, the net asset value fell 10¢ a share due to a slight drop in the stock market that day. The fund also declared a 60¢ per share distribution on Tuesday. The listing for XYZ in the newspaper for those two days would look like this:

Monday	XYZ Fund	6.00	+ .04
Tuesday	XYZ Fund	x5.30	− .70

roughly the same time each year, and most funds announce distributions in advance. This presents an opportunity for savings. Just before purchasing shares of any mutual fund, call the fund and ask if a distribution will be made soon. If a distribution is scheduled within a few days, you may want to wait and buy your shares the day after the distribution to avoid its tax impact.

Misconception #2: "If I don't receive my distribution check until after the end of the year, I don't have to pay taxes on it this year."

From a tax standpoint, distributions fall into two classifications: (1) "capital gain" as described above, and (2) "income," a mutual fund's dividend and interest earnings, less its management fees and other operating expenses.

Your tax liability is based on the ex-dividend date, not the payment date. If the ex-dividend date is in the current year, your tax liability is also. The fund is required to prepare IRS Form 1099-DIV for everyone who was a shareholder on any day a distribution was declared. You will receive a copy (and so will the government), which lists the various distributions you will be taxed on, and where to report them on your Form 1040 return.

Misconception #3: "As long as I don't sell any of my mutual fund shares, I can't have any capital gains."

This seems logical. Assume you buy fund shares at $10 and still own them at the end of the year. Since it is too soon to know whether you will receive more or less than $10 per share when you sell them, it would seem to follow that it is also too soon to know whether you'll have a capital gain to pay taxes on. What this overlooks is that the mutual fund *itself*, within its portfolio, is continually buying and selling securities. Each time it sells one, it has another capital gain or loss. Since the tax law considers all of this as being done on your behalf, you participate in your fair share of that gain or loss *whenever a fund declares a capital gain distribution.*

When you eventually do sell your fund shares, any capital gain or loss from the original purchase must be reported on Schedule D of your Form 1040 tax return just like any other investment. One easy way to put off paying this kind of capital gains tax is simply to avoid selling mutual funds for gain just before the end of the year. If you sell in December, then taxes will have to be paid by April 15, just three and a half months later. Instead, you might wait to sell out of a profitable position until the first week of January. The tax on such gains would then not be owed until April of the following year. This postpones paying your tax liability an additional 12 months. By the same token, a good time to sell a fund if you have a loss is in December, as the loss will be deductible on the tax return filed only a few months later.

Misconception #4: "To calculate my capital gain from selling my fund shares, I subtract the amount I paid for them from the proceeds I received when selling them."

This is only true in the simplest instance—where you bought all your shares at the same time, received no distributions while you owned them, and sold them all at the same time. In that case, it's pretty straightforward as described. However, if you either receive distributions, acquire your shares over time (for example, through dollar-cost-averaging or reinvesting your dividends), or sell only part of your holdings, there is more work to be done. Let's look at the most common situations.

• **When you receive a distribution.** Keep in mind: *you aren't really gaining anything when you receive a distribution because the amount of the distribution is deducted from the value of your shares.* For example, assume you buy 100 fund shares at $8.00 each. Your total cost is $800. The value grows to $12.00 per share, and your investment becomes worth $1,200 (100 shares multiplied by $12.00 each). If a $1.00 per share dividend distribution is declared, you will receive a check for $100 (100 shares multiplied by $1.00). However, on the ex-dividend date, the value of your shares immediately drops to $11.00 each because $1.00 per share has been taken out of the fund's asset pool to be mailed to shareholders. You haven't gained; you still have $1,200 in value—$1,100 in fund shares (100 shares multiplied by $11.00) and $100 cash. The fund has merely "robbed Peter to pay Paul."

The tax consequences work like this. If you had sold your shares *before* the ex-dividend date, you would have a $400 capital gain ($1,200 proceeds minus $800 cost). If you sell your shares *after* the ex-dividend date, you would have a $300 capital gain ($1,100 proceeds minus $800 cost) *plus* $100 in dividend income; thus, you still have total taxable income of $400. The ex-dividend date didn't change the amount of your profit; it only changed the tax nature of your profit (which could be good or bad, depending on your particular tax bracket and the current tax treatment of capital gains and dividends).

• **When you reinvest your dividends.** If you routinely have your fund distributions reinvested in more shares, you must be careful to avoid double taxation. When calculating your tax liability, you must add the cost of the additional shares purchased with your dividends to the amount originally invested in the fund. This will raise your tax "basis" in the fund shares you've acquired. In this way, you'll avoid being taxed twice—initially on the dividends and again later as a capital gain when the fund shares are sold.

For example, let's take our previous example and make a change: Instead of receiving the $100 distribution in cash, you instruct your fund to reinvest it in more shares. On the ex-dividend date, the value of the fund dropped to $11.00 per share. At that price, the $100 would purchase an additional 9.09

shares, bringing your total shares to 109.09. The $100 distribution must be reported on that year's federal 1040, and taxes must be paid.

Later, you sell all of your shares for $11.00 each, which brings in proceeds of $1,200 (109.09 shares multiplied by $11.00 per share). Will you be taxed on your $400 gain? No. The total cost of the shares (for capital gains purposes) is the initial $800 *plus the $100 on which tax has already been paid,* making a total of $900. Thus, the taxable capital gain from the $1,200 proceeds received the following year is only $300 rather than $400.

• **When you dollar-cost-average.** If you routinely add to your fund holdings through frequent new purchases, you should be especially careful to keep careful records of the dates, amounts invested, and number of shares purchased. That's because you will later need detailed and accurate information concerning your many different purchases in order to compute any capital gains that might result when your shares are eventually sold. This is all the more important if you later sell part (rather than all) of your shares. See the chart at left for an explanation of the options you have under the tax laws. While you can switch between using the "first-in, first-out" method and using the "specific cost" method, if you use an "average cost" method for a particular fund, you must then use it every time you sell shares from that fund.

HOW TO COMPUTE YOUR TAXABLE GAINS AND LOSSES

	Using the First-In, First-Out Method	Using the Average Cost Method	Using the Specific Cost Method
How to Do It	Unless you say otherwise, the IRS assumes that you sell your shares in the same order as you bought them.	You calculate the average price paid for all the shares in the fund that you own. Divide the total dollars invested (including any distributions reinvested) by the number of shares you own.*	Send the fund instructions saying that you are selling the shares purchased on such-and-such a day at such-and-such a price.
Advantages and Disadvantages	If your early purchases were at higher levels, this method will give you tax losses; if your early purchases were at lower levels, this method will create taxable gains.	Could raise or lower your taxes depending on how the other alternatives work out. *A more complicated method groups shares held longer/shorter than one year.	A little more trouble, but gives you the most flexibility for managing your tax liability from year to year.

As you can see, dealing with mutual fund distributions in a taxable account can get fairly involved, particularly when you have distributions reinvested automatically. Because of this, I typically advise investors with taxable accounts to *not* reinvest their fund distributions. While this does require the owner to occasionally reinvest any cash received from distributions, it can greatly simplify tax reporting when a fund is sold.

Under the general heading of "other assorted things you should know" are the following items.

• The IRS is available year-round to answer your tax questions. Call their help line at 1-800-829-1040. It also offers free materials on various topics — call 1-800-829-3676 to request IRS forms and publications be sent to you in the mail, or download them at www.irs.gov. You can begin with publication 910, which is an explanation of all the *other* publications that are available.

• The best tax advantage available for mutual fund investing is to carry out as much of your long-term program as possible within an IRA or other tax-deferred type of account.

• The lower tax rate available on dividends does not apply to bond funds. Their monthly "dividend" payments are actually distributions of interest income.

• Whenever you "switch" between funds at the same mutual fund organization, it's the same as selling your shares in the fund you are leaving. Calling it a switch doesn't change the fact that you are selling one fund and buying another. In a taxable account, every switch has tax consequences unless you are moving out of a money market fund.

• Using the special checks your bond fund might supply also has tax consequences. That's because the fund sells some of your shares in order to honor your check. As a result, you'll have a taxable gain or loss on the shares sold. This is not the case with money market funds because they always maintain a level $1.00 per share value.

• Investors in tax-free funds don't completely avoid dealing with tax considerations. For example, capital-gains distributions from the funds and capital gains you might make on the sale of your shares are taxable just as with any other security. "Tax-free" income is generally free from federal tax, but not all the dividends you receive will necessarily be exempt from state tax; check with your fund if in need of clarification. Also, special rules apply under a variety of situations (for example, investors who receive tax-exempt income from shares in a municipal bond fund that was held for six months or less and sold for a loss). Request IRS Publication 564 for more information on the taxation of mutual funds.

• If you invest in international stock and bond funds, mutual funds are to notify you if you are entitled to claim a tax deduction for taxes that the fund paid to a foreign country. For more information, request IRS Publication 514.

• The tax documentation you will receive from your mutual fund each year includes: confirmation statements telling you the date, price, and number of shares transacted when buying and selling fund shares; form 1099-B reports the proceeds from selling shares during the year, as well as cost basis information for any shares purchased in 2012 or later (used to help you compute your capital gains or losses); and form 1099-DIV reports the details of dividend and capital gain distributions for which you owe taxes.

I felt it was important to equip you with some basic tax-planning knowledge. My recommendation, however, is that you not buy or sell primarily for tax reasons.

Although I acknowledge that it is legitimate to minimize one's tax liability by using any of the applicable strategies mentioned here, a preoccupation with taxes can be counterproductive. Sometimes a few days in the market can make a big difference as to the price you pay or receive for your shares. Don't let tax considerations sidetrack you from following the disciplines you will be building into your long-term strategy. ◆

CHAPTER PREVIEW

All About Exchange-Traded Funds (ETFs)

I. ETFs are basically mutual funds that trade like individual stocks.

    A. The simplest way to understand ETFs is to first think of an index fund. Most ETFs track a particular market index, such as the S&P 500. (We'll look at index funds in greater detail in Chapter 14.)

    B. Although nearly 1,500 exchange-traded products are on the market, roughly 200 of them dominate the market.

II. ETFs offer several advantages to investors.

    A. ETFs trade like individual stocks, allowing you to buy and sell them throughout the day.

    B. There's tremendous variety within the ETF universe. If there's a market that tracks something, chances are good an ETF exists to follow it.

    C. ETFs are more tax efficient than traditional funds due to their structure. This is of particular importance to investors with taxable accounts.

    D. Unlike traditional mutual funds, ETFs have no minimum investment requirement.

    E. Compared to actively managed traditional mutual funds, ETFs have much lower average expense ratios. This advantage is diminished when compared to traditional index funds.

III. ETFs have disadvantages as well, and trade-offs must be considered.

    A. The fact that ETFs can be bought and sold throughout the day can foster a trading mentality.

    B. Trading ETFs is more complicated than buying and selling traditional funds.

    C. ETFs are vulnerable to pricing glitches. This concern can be greatly diminished by sticking with the larger, more-liquid ETFs and staying away from the smaller and more thinly traded ones.

    D. ETFs can be expensive to trade for smaller amounts, because of commissions and the potentially costly "spread."

Let's begin by taking a brief look at the ETF industry and its history.

In chapters 5 through 8, I've explained the nature and advantages of mutual funds. Make that *traditional* mutual funds. In recent years a new kind of mutual fund has come into its own. It's the "exchange-traded" fund, commonly referred to as an ETF.

It's been 20 years since the first ETF opened to investors. Few imagined at the time that ETFs would significantly alter the way individuals invest. Despite the rapid growth of the ETF industry since then, these products remain something of a mystery to many investors. As recently as 2011, more than six in 10 investors surveyed said they didn't invest in ETFs because they "don't know what they are." And of those respondents who owned stocks or mutual funds, only 17 percent said they were "comfortable" investing in ETFs.

Generally speaking, *retail* investors have been slow to embrace ETFs. Nevertheless, the industry has grown explosively in recent years due to *institutional* investors. Nearly $200 billion flowed into ETFs in 2012, a new record. With roughly $1.4 trillion in assets, ETFs now account for 13 percent of the overall ETF/mutual fund pie (excluding money-market fund assets).

Although nearly 1,500 exchange-traded products are on the market, that large number obscures the fact that the ETF industry is composed of about 200 big funds with the rest being relatively small. The general rule is that an ETF needs at least $100 million in assets to be profitable, yet more than half of ETFs have assets less than that. Another 29 percent have assets between $100 million and $1 billion. Then come the big players: the 13 percent of ETFs (191 total funds) that have assets greater than $1 billion. When broken down by trading volume, the statistics are even more stark: more than 87 percent of the daily ETF trading volume occurs in only 69 funds.

These stats explain why a consolidation phase is occurring in the industry—closings and mergers are outnumbering new ETFs coming to market. That's a healthy development for this maturing industry. These numbers also illustrate that while the ETF marketplace may appear huge due to the large number of products available, the number of "key" products is much more manageable.

The simplest way to understand ETFs...

...is to first think of an "index" fund. (In chapter 14 we'll take a more in-depth look at index funds as I teach you an investing strategy that is easy to understand and implement—it relies on index-fund ETFs exclusively.)

Like traditional index-based mutual funds, most ETFs are designed to track a particular market index or sector of the economy. (Recently, a small

This Chapter Was Written in the Fall of 2013.

The ETF segment of the mutual-fund industry continues to evolve rapidly. The information provided in this chapter was accurate in late-2013, but will change as the industry continues to grow. For current articles and links to updated information, visit my web site at www.soundmindinvesting.com.

number of "actively managed" ETFs have appeared on the scene, but that's a more complicated subject for another day.) The particular index that an ETF tracks may be something broad and well-known, such as the S&P 500. Or it may be something extremely narrow that you've never heard of, like the price of goat cheese in Albania (okay, I'm exaggerating—but not by much).

Like traditional mutual funds, exchange-traded funds offer a convenient way to invest in a pre-assembled basket of stocks. But this is where the similarities end and the differences begin. Whether these differences make ETFs more (or less) attractive than traditional funds depends on the circumstances of each investor. Here are the pros as a typical investor would likely evaluate them.

ETFs offer many advantages relative to regular mutual funds.

• **Advantage #1: ETFs trade like individual stocks.** ETFs and traditional index funds are similar in how they are constructed, but different in how they trade. Traditional mutual funds are *priced once per day*—after the market closes, when the prices of all the fund's holdings are known. All orders placed for a traditional index fund throughout the day receive the same end-of-day price, which is called the NAV (net asset value). ETFs, in contrast, are *priced and traded continually throughout the day*, in the same way individual stocks are. Buying a particular ETF in the morning will likely garner a different price than buying the same ETF in the afternoon (or, for that matter, even buying it a few minutes later). This greater flexibility is a key selling point of ETFs. They offer other "stock-like" attributes too—you can buy them on margin, "short" them, and use more sophisticated order types to buy and sell them (such as limit and stop orders).

While these advantages are certainly appealing to active traders and professionals, they are of less value to most "average" investors. Being able to buy at different prices throughout the day is usually of little importance to those following a long-term investing plan. In fact, trading like an individual stock introduces a level of complexity that some investors would just as soon do without.

• **Advantage #2: There's an ETF for virtually anything you want to index.** The stock market is like baseball—there's a statistical measurement for everything that happens. As a result, there are many different stock indexes, each measuring a slightly different slice of the market. As ETFs have become increasingly popular, the companies that create them have responded by designing ETFs to track almost any index available (and creating new indexes that track things they want to create an ETF for!). Therefore, it's easier to invest in certain market niches using ETFs than via traditional index funds, simply because in some cases there aren't any index funds following the less-prominent market segments.

But, again, for the average investor, the relevant question is how finely do you need to slice the market? With only 69 ETFs accounting for nearly 90 percent of the dollar volume of ETF trading, it's clear that most investors are sticking with the mainstream options. That said, specialized ETFs are like specialized hand tools—you may not use them often, but they sure are nice to have when the need arises. Still, for most investors the tremendous variety of ETFs available is simply overkill.

• **Advantage #3: ETFs are more tax efficient than traditional funds.** This isn't a huge distinction relative to traditional *index* funds, which are tax efficient by their very nature because they rarely sell stocks from their portfolio. But relative to *actively managed* funds, the tax efficiency of ETFs can yield quite a cost savings. Most traditional funds are required to distribute capital gains to shareholders as the fund sells holdings at a profit each year, whereas ETFs, due to structural differences, don't.

For example, while many traditional funds distributed capital gains to shareholders in 2012, 275 of the 280 iShares-brand ETFs had none (the five that did were all bond funds, and all five distributed less than 0.5% of NAV). In short, ETF owners generally pay taxes only when they sell the ETF, whereas traditional mutual-fund owners sometimes have to pay tax on distributions from funds they still own. Again, this is largely an "indexing vs. active-management" issue, but it's clearly one in which ETFs come down on the more advantageous side.

• **Advantage #4: ETFs require no minimum investment.** This is nice for investors who want diversification across various funds but don't have a large amount of money to invest. This may primarily affect new investors, but it's still an area where ETFs have a clear advantage over traditional funds.

• **Advantage #5: ETFs have lower expense ratios.** The average ETF's expense ratio is roughly 0.6% while the average actively managed fund's is 1.4%, leading many to believe that ETFs offer a tremendous cost savings. And they do, if one is willing to make the change from actively managed traditional funds to indexed ETFs. In reality, most ETFs carry only slightly lower expense levels than their traditional index fund counterparts, so lower expenses are often overrated as a comparative benefit.

For example, the expense level on Vanguard's S&P 500 ETF is 0.05%, as compared to 0.17% for the "Investor" share class of its Vanguard 500 index fund. However, a shareholder investing at least $10,000 can buy the "Admiral" share class of the traditional fund, which carries an identical 0.05% expense ratio. So the worst case is an investor pays an additional $12 per $10,000 invested, and many will avoid that by using the lower-cost Admiral shares. The low fees are great, but aren't typically dramatically better than the leading index funds.

While there is indeed much to like about ETFs, they aren't without disadvantages. Consider...

• **Disadvantage #1: ETF's trade like individual stocks.** That's right, the top advantage of ETFs can be their primary disadvantage as well. While the flexibility of being able to buy and sell any time during the trading day *sounds* like a plus, there's also a downside. I share the concern of Vanguard founder John Bogle that the trade-anytime emphasis placed on ETFs can foster a trading mentality that works against the "slow and steady" long-term approach I think is best for most investors.

• **Disadvantage #2: Trading ETFs is more complicated.** Beyond that philosophical point though, since ETFs are traded continuously on the open market, buying and selling them is more complicated than buying and selling traditional funds (see sidebar at right). This diminishes one of the chief virtues of mutual-fund investing: simplicity. Buyers of traditional mutual funds know that everyone buying on a particular day gets the same price, calculated based on the value of the underlying holdings at the end of the day. Not so with ETFs, where you pay a fluctuating "market price" rather than one based solely on the value of the portfolio.

• **Disadvantage #3: ETFs are vulnerable to pricing glitches.** Another concern is that ETFs seem particularly vulnerable to intraday price anomalies, such as occurred in the May 2009 "flash crash." Granted, the flash crash was an unusual occurrence, but there have been subsequent disturbing episodes, such as the glitch in October 2010 that dropped an ETF based on the S&P 500 Stock Index (ticker: SPY) by almost 10% in the blink of an eye. Part of the problem is that ETF owners often use trading instructions such as "stop-loss" orders (which I suggest never be used in conjunction with ETF shares) in an attempt to protect holdings from declining too much during a selloff. However, in these periods of intraday volatility, these stop orders can result in market orders that execute in the midst of a sudden downturn. This can lead to unpredictable prices for ETFs, which temporarily can vary widely from a reasonable valuation of the ETF's underlying holdings. When these pricing anomalies occur, the computerized trading that has come to dominate the market can produce unsettling results.

• **Disadvantage #4: ETFs can be expensive to trade for smaller amounts.** Commission costs for ETFs used to be a significant problem and in some case still can be when investing small investment amounts (such as in a dollar-cost-averaging strategy). For most investors, however, this problem has greatly diminished in recent years. Not only have most brokers dropped their regular ETF commissions below $10 per trade, some—including Fidelity, Schwab, and TD Ameritrade—now offer an assortment of no-commission ETFs. Originally each company offered their own ETFs for free, e.g., Vanguard custom-

How to Buy or Sell an ETF

1. Go to your broker's Web site. Open the Stock and ETF trading page, rather than the usual mutual-funds trading page.

2. Get a price quote. Each broker's process is different, but there's likely a "Quote" or "Symbol" box available somewhere on the screen. Enter the ticker symbol. For example, entering the symbol for the Vanguard S&P 500 Index ETF (VOO) might produce a quote showing the current "Ask" price is $60.46 per share. That's the lowest amount any seller is currently willing to accept.

3. Determine how many shares to buy. Let's say you have $5,000 to invest in this ETF. Divide $5,000 by the Ask price of $60.46. Doing so results in an answer of 82.7 shares. If your account is at Fidelity, you need to account for a $7.95 commission (check at your broker to see how much is charged for stock/ETF commissions), so you should round down to 82 shares. Enter that in the "number of shares" field.

4. Choose the type of order. Choices are normally "Market" (the trade will be filled right away at the next available price), "Limit" (the trade will be made at a specified price or better within a specified time frame), or some variation of "Stop" (the trade will be made when the security's price surpasses a certain point). For most purposes, a market order is fine. For more on limit orders, see the discussion on page 112.

ers could trade Vanguard ETFs for free, and so forth. But the menus of commission-free ETFs have expanded dramatically, with TD Ameritrade and Schwab each offering more than 100 different ETFs from *different* fund companies. Fidelity recently enlarged its commission-free program to 65 iShares ETFs (offered via Fidelity's ETF partner, iShares).

While free ETF trades sound like a great deal, it's important to recognize the potential pitfalls of such a policy.

I've already noted more than half of all ETFs lack sufficient assets to be profitable. One great way to gather the additional assets they need to put them in the black is to pay to be listed on a "free ETF" platform at a brokerage heavyweight such as Schwab. When investors see that they can trade a certain ETF for free and that it covers the segment of the market they were looking to invest in, they often ignore the fact that the fund's operating expenses are higher. An even more subtle cost is the burden posed by "the spread" — it's often so wide that the commission savings on the "free" ETF are completely eliminated.

The spread is the difference between the best available "Bid" and "Ask" prices for a security at any given point in time. The bid is the highest price a buyer is willing to pay, and the ask is the lowest price a seller is willing to accept. On stocks and ETFs that trade many shares every day, the spread is typically quite low, often just a single penny. But on lower-volume securities (and at times of market disruption), the spread can be much wider. Investors benefit from narrow spreads, but incur more cost from wider spreads.

When you place a market order for a stock or ETF, you typically will pay at least part of the spread, and possibly the whole amount. Think of this as a "convenience fee" for getting your entire order filled immediately. Alternatively, you can enter a "limit" order where you specify the price you are willing to pay. As a buyer, you can set your limit price at the current ask price and avoid paying any of the spread — *if* your order gets filled. The danger is that by limiting the price you are willing to pay, the price of the security you are trying to buy may move higher, causing your order to go unfilled. So using a limit order can often save you a bit of money, but it comes with the risk of having to spend even more to chase the price higher. That's why I have generally suggested using market orders and keeping things simple. But it's true that using limit orders when trading ETFs is the safest way to protect yourself from bad pricing, which is of particular concern with less liquid ETFs.

All of this is relatively moot if you use the biggest, most liquid ETFs.

On an ETF with substantially lower trading volume, the spread typically is going to be wider, and thus the hidden costs higher. In my *Sound Mind Investing* newsletter, I recommend only the most liquid ETFs. However, many of my readers are tempted to substitute different "no fee" ETFs in place of the officially recommended ones in an effort to avoid commissions. That's when the spread can become a cost issue, and not in the beneficial way the readers are expecting!

Here's an example of how that can backfire. One of our strategies uses the SPDR S&P 500 (SPY). On one occasion, the quote for SPY showed a bid price of $151.59 and an ask price of $151.60. The spread is only a penny, so even the worst case of using a market order and potentially paying the full spread would result in the trade "costing" an extra penny per share. A person wanting to invest $25,000 would divide that amount by the $151.60 ask price to determine that they could afford 164 shares. At a penny per share, the maximum cost of the spread on this trade is only $1.64. As noted earlier, a limit order priced at $151.59 could be used to potentially eliminate that cost, but for the extra $1.64, most investors would likely prefer to simply place a market order and be done with it.

Here's where Schwab's "free ETFs" enter the picture. Schwab doesn't make SPY available for free, but it does offer its own Large-Cap ETF (SCHX) for free. Based on the similarity of their returns in recent years, they seem to be roughly comparable in terms of holdings. And SCHX's expense ratio is even a touch lower, at 0.05% per year, than SPY's 0.09%.

It seems that this is a good substitution, but we still need to consider the hidden cost of the spread. The quote showed SCHX trading with a two-cent spread between the $36.27 bid and $36.29 ask prices. Dividing the $25,000 investment amount by $36.29 shows that approximately 688 shares can be purchased (a higher number than SPY due to the lower price per share). With the two-cent spread per share, the spread on this trade would cost as much as $13.76.

All together, a Schwab investor using market orders and paying the full spread to buy SPY would pay an $8.95 commission plus another $1.64 spread cost, for a total of $10.59. To buy the "free" SCHX, they pay no commission but a potential spread cost of $13.76. So much for the free-commission ETF always being the better deal. It depends on the size of the investment being made and the prices of the two ETFs being compared. As the amount being invested decreases, the balance gradually tips in favor of the free ETFs (assuming they have equally good liquidity).

ETFs are playing an increasing role in the strategies I recommend in my newsletter.

With both commissions and expense ratios falling drastically, the ETF landscape has changed dramatically in recent years. Along with ETFs becoming cheaper and easier to buy, the fact that more of them now have longer-term performance histories to compare against conventional mutual funds has caused me to give them a more prominent role in our investing strategies.

• **Just-the-Basics** (which we'll discuss in chapter 14). I use ETFs exclusively. This allows newer investors to set up their investing plans without getting caught on the required investing minimums of conventional mutual funds. Also, Vanguard makes trading their own ETFs free for those with accounts at Vanguard, thus eliminating the recurring cost hurdle for those regularly adding to their accounts. And the expenses of the ETFs are so low that they offer the best deal—the same low expense ratios as Vanguard's Admiral shares (available to those with larger mutual-fund accounts).

• **Fund Upgrading** (which we'll discuss in chapter 17). I have long made use of ETFs as recommended funds within the Upgrading strategy. The frequency of their use has increased slightly in recent years, mostly because of the growing number of ETFs that meet the diversification criteria for my Upgrading recommendations. In 2012, I officially switched the *bond* portion of our Upgrading recommendations from Vanguard's traditional bond mutual funds to the ETF share classes of those same funds. Most of the same advantages described above apply here as well: elimination of required fund minimums, cheap/free commissions at Vanguard and other brokers, and the lowest expense ratios available among any Vanguard share class.

• **Dynamic Asset Allocation** (which we'll discuss in chapter 18). This advanced strategy is based entirely upon the use of ETFs. DAA is a more active strategy, and occasionally requires us to sell a holding after owning it for a short time. Selling quickly would cause problems if we were to try such a thing with traditional mutual funds, but it's having this flexibility that makes DAA so effective in weak markets. The maturing of the ETF industry is a key part of what makes this strategy possible.

You don't need to use ETFs to be a successful investor. But...

...they are quickly becoming a mainstream investing tool, so having at least a basic familiarity and comfort level with them is a good idea. ETFs are still new enough that the conventional wisdom regarding their use is still evolving as they are tested under a greater variety of real-life conditions. For example, due to a regular stream of pricing irregularities, some people are questioning the stability of the ETF structure for investing in illiquid market segments (such as municipal and high-yield bonds).

I'm comfortable enough with ETFs to recommend some of the bigger and most heavily traded ones to my newsletter readers. I continue to be cautious regarding ETFs that are thinly traded, as this appears to be where many of the unusual trading situations have occurred. But if you stick with the larger, high volume issues, ETFs can offer flexibility and rock-bottom expenses. That combination can be very helpful when implementing certain investing strategies, making ETFs a useful tool for your investing toolbox. ◆

Your Most Important Investing Decision

The plans of the diligent lead to profit
as surely as haste leads to poverty.

Proverbs 21:5

"I'm relaxing in the jacuzzi watching t.v. when one of those financial interview shows comes on. They're talking about how easy it is to boost your returns in sub-prime mortgages. By that time I've already sold my company and am pretty well set financially, ya know, but of course, who can't always use a little more? So..."

CHAPTER PREVIEW

What Investing Is — and Why It's Actually Quite Simple

I. **Investing occurs when you put your money to work in a commercial undertaking subject to modest levels of risk. You expect a reasonable return over time.**

   A. It is not the same as speculation, which also puts your money to work in a commercial undertaking but involves a very high level of risk. Speculation offers the possibility of a very large return in a relatively brief period of time.

   B. It is not the same as gambling, which subjects your money to a very high level of risk in an attempt to profit from the outcome of a contest or game of chance. With gambling, there's a possibility of an unusually large return in an exceptionally brief period of time.

II. **Investing is simple because you have only two basic choices.**

   A. With some investments, you become a lender.

      1. These are generally the lower-risk kind. The primary risk to watch out for is that you might get locked in to a poor rate of return for many years, so the financial strength of the borrower is of great importance.

      2. The most common borrowers include (1) banks and savings and loans, (2) local, state, and federal governments, (3) large corporations, and (4) insurance companies.

   B. With other investments, you become an owner.

      1. These are generally the higher-risk kind. The primary risk here is that the value of what you own could fall, so the economic outlook and its effect on your holdings is of great importance.

      2. The most common investments where you become an owner include common stocks, real estate, precious metals, and collectibles.

   C. How you divide your money between these two basic choices has a greater impact on your eventual investment results than any other single factor.

III. **The one fundamental rule of investing you should never, ever, *ever* forget is:**

   A. The greater the return being offered, the greater the risk you're taking.

   B. This is always the case—whether those making the offer tell you or not, whether it's obvious or not, and whether you know it or not.

**I've been an investment adviser for more than 30 years.
During that time, I've had the courage of my convictions
(some might say audacity) to go to people and say . . .**

. . . "You can trust me with your hard-earned money. I'll protect it while I make it grow." There have been good years, accompanied by rankings in the top 5% of money managers nationwide. It seemed as if everyone was my friend, and I loved coming to work in the morning. I thought, *What a great business to be in!*

Th ere have also been years when I was too conservative. My clients' profits were not as high as they might have been. I made money, but not as much as some of my competitors made that year. Asking, "What have you done for me lately?" many of my clients left in search of greener pastures. After several months of this, I dreaded coming to work in the morning. I thought, *What a terrible business to be in!*

Most people seem to have the impression there's something special about being an investment adviser. I've been at social gatherings where people who throughout the evening had hardly noticed me suddenly came alive when they learned that I manage investments for a living. Judging by their new interest in me, I have been instantly transformed from my usual self into someone of great charisma and charm. What accounts for this?

**I've come to believe it's because people secretly think
of investing as being like magic.**

It's the kind of "wow" reaction a magician receives when, after placing a little kitten into a cage and covering it, he removes the cover to reveal a growling, full-grown tiger. "Amazing—did you see *that*? How'd he do that?!" Where did the kitten go? Where did the tiger come from? What happens under that cover, anyway? It's amazing and mysterious!

Isn't this similar to the kind of reactions we have when we read of the futures trader who made millions in a single week? Or the real-estate tycoon who always seems to know where to buy next? Or the college student who started out buying stocks in meager amounts and a few years later is worth more than $20 million? It all seems so impossible. How do they ever do it?

Our imaginations and curiosities are kindled. Unlike the kitten, which doesn't actually turn into a tiger, the modest sums of these gifted individuals actually do turn into fortunes. But—and here's where the misconception comes in—it's a mistake to call what they do "investing." It's "speculating."

• *Investing* occurs when you put your money to work in a commercial undertaking, subject to modest levels of risk, and expect a reasonable return over a long period of time. What's reasonable? About 3%–5% more than the rate of inflation.

• *Speculating* also involves putting your money to work in a commercial undertaking, but it involves a level of risk so great that it's theoretically possible to lose most or all of your capital (the actual amount you invested). In return for this high risk, the speculator has the possibility of making an unusually large return (perhaps doubling or even tripling his/her money) in a relatively brief period of time—usually a couple years at most. This is also frequently accompanied by borrowing additional sums for the undertaking and accepting personal responsibility for repaying those sums regardless of the outcome of the venture. Financial options, commodity futures trading, and leveraged real estate projects are common forms of speculation.

• *Gambling* subjects your money to an *exceedingly* high level of risk in an attempt to profit from the outcome of a contest or game of chance. There is the possibility of an unusually large return in an exceptionally brief period of time—perhaps measured in minutes or hours. A sure sign that an activity falls under the "gambling" heading is when *the activity exists solely for the sake of creating wagering opportunities.* For example, apart from wagering, there would be no reason for casinos, horse racing, or lotteries to exist.

Gambling should be avoided by all. Speculating should be avoided by all except those with a professional interest and degree of expertise. But investing is an activity that all of us, as stewards of God's resources, are unavoidably called to. Once you understand that investing involves taking only prudent risks and seeking reasonable returns, it takes a lot of the magic and mystery out of it.

Do not wear yourself out to get rich; have the wisdom to show restraint. Cast but a glance at riches, and they are gone, for they will surely sprout wings and fly off to the sky like an eagle.
Proverbs 23:4–5

People who want to get rich fall into temptation and a trap and into many foolish and harmful desires that plunge men into ruin and destruction. For the love of money is a root of all kinds of evil. Some people, eager for money, have wandered from the faith and pierced themselves with many griefs.
1 Timothy 6:9–10

Like it or not, as a steward of God-given time, talents, and resources, you're an investor.

Investing is simply giving up something now in order to have more of something later. When you put your money into a savings account, you are making an investment decision (less spendable money now in order to have more spendable money later). When you volunteer your professional services or personal talents now in order to serve in a ministry, you're making an investment decision (less free time or current income now in order to have a greater sense of fulfillment and eternal gains later). When you take a day off without pay in order to spend time with your family, you're making an investment decision (less income now in order to have stronger family ties and happy memories later).

Your investing goals seem reasonable: Make as much as you can but don't lose any of your capital. You're eager for good advice but wonder whom you can trust. You would like to feel confident but usually feel a little confused. You are caught in the constant tension between risk and reward. If you feel this way, I have good news!

Investing is actually quite simple . . .

. . . because you only have two basic choices: investments where you become *a lender to someone* and investments where you become *an owner of something*.

Investments where you *lend* your money are generally the lower-risk kind. Assuming you do a good job of checking out the financial strength of the borrower, the primary risk is that you might get locked in to a poor rate of return for many years. We'll cover investing-by-lending in detail in chapter 11.

Investments where you *own* something are generally the higher-risk kind. The primary risk here is that the value of what you own could fall, so the economic outlook and its effect on your holdings is of great importance. We'll be looking at investing-by-owning as it pertains to the stock market in chapter 12.

**What I'm about to tell you is very important,
so please pay close attention: The way in which . . .**

. . . you divide your investment capital between these two basic choices of "loaning" or "owning" *has a greater impact on your eventual investment returns than any other single factor*.

INVESTING BY LENDING

| **Banks and Credit Unions** (which you lend to when you open savings accounts and buy their certificates of deposit) | **Large Corporations** (which you lend to when you give your money in return for corporate IOUs— commercial paper and bonds) | **The Federal Government** (which you lend to when you give your money in return for Treasury IOUs—bills, notes, and bonds) | **Local and State Governments** (which you lend to when you give your money in return for their IOUs—that is, bonds—which pay tax-free interest) | **Insurance Companies** (which you lend to when you give your money in return for insurance company IOUs—cash value life insurance and fixed annuities) |

Think of your investments as being like a garden. Some people like to grow flowers and others prefer to grow vegetables. Some enjoy doing both. The one decision that has the greatest influence over what your garden looks like and the kind of harvest you'll ultimately have is this: How much of your garden should you devote to flowers and how much to vegetables? Once you decide that, you know a lot about what to expect in terms of the risks involved and the potential results even if you haven't yet decided *which kinds* of flowers or vegetables you're going to plant. Once you decided how you were going to allocate the space in your garden, the kind of harvest you were going to have was, to a great extent, already predetermined.

Now, let me shift your thinking to the investment arena. Studies have shown that 80% or more of your investment return is determined by how much of your portfolio is invested in stocks (flowers) versus bonds (vegetables), and only about 20% is determined by how good a job you did at making the individual selections. This surprises most people, because the investment industry gives far more attention to telling you about hot stocks and mutual fund performance rankings than to explaining the critical importance of asset allocation (that is, how much room you make in your investment garden for stocks versus how much you

INVESTING BY OWNING

Stocks	**Real Estate**	**Oil & Gas Syndications**	**Precious Metals**	**Farmland**
(where you become part owner of a business—"preferred" stock shares give you first claim on dividends)	(where you become an owner of land and/or buildings purchased primarily for their income-generating potential)	(where you pool your money with other investors and head for the great outdoors in search of undiscovered sources of energy)	(where you become an owner of actual gold, silver, or platinum—some investors prefer to hold gold/silver in the form of coins)	(where you become an owner of land used for growing crops—typically held for future price appreciation rather than income)

THE RISKS AND RETURNS OF OWNING VS. LOANING OVER VARIOUS 5-YEAR HOLDING PERIODS

5 Year Period	"Own" (Stocks)	"Loan" (Bonds)	50% Each
1955–1959	15.0%	−0.3%	7.8%
1956–1960	8.9%	1.4%	5.7%
1957–1961	12.8%	3.8%	8.8%
1958–1962	13.3%	3.6%	9.0%
1959–1963	9.9%	4.5%	7.5%
1960–1964	10.7%	5.7%	8.5%
1961–1965	13.2%	3.8%	8.8%
1962–1966	5.7%	2.9%	4.6%
1963–1967	12.4%	0.3%	6.6%
1964–1968	10.2%	0.4%	5.5%
1965–1969	5.0%	−2.2%	1.6%
1966–1970	3.3%	1.2%	2.5%
1967–1971	8.4%	3.3%	6.1%
1968–1972	7.5%	5.8%	6.8%
1969–1973	2.0%	5.6%	3.9%
1970–1974	−2.4%	6.7%	2.4%
1971–1975	3.2%	6.0%	5.0%
1972–1976	4.9%	7.4%	6.5%
1973–1977	−0.2%	6.3%	3.4%
1974–1978	4.3%	6.0%	5.5%
1975–1979	14.8%	5.8%	10.4%
1976–1980	13.9%	2.4%	8.4%
1977–1981	8.1%	−1.3%	3.7%
1978–1982	14.0%	5.6%	10.2%
1979–1983	17.3%	6.9%	12.5%
1980–1984	14.8%	11.2%	13.4%
1981–1985	14.7%	17.9%	16.4%
1982–1986	19.9%	22.5%	21.4%
1983–1987	16.5%	14.1%	15.4%
1984–1988	15.4%	15.0%	15.2%
1985–1989	20.4%	14.9%	17.7%
1986–1990	13.1%	10.4%	11.9%
1987–1991	**15.4%**	**10.4%**	**13.0%**
1988–1992	15.9%	12.5%	14.3%
1989–1993	14.5%	13.0%	13.8%
1990–1994	8.7%	8.4%	8.6%
1991–1995	16.6%	12.2%	14.4%
1992–1996	15.2%	8.5%	12.0%
1993–1997	20.2%	9.2%	14.8%
1994–1998	24.1%	8.7%	16.4%
1995–1999	28.6%	8.4%	18.5%
1996–2000	18.4%	5.8%	12.5%
1997–2001	10.7%	7.7%	9.8%
1998–2002	−0.6%	8.3%	4.7%
1999–2003	−0.5%	7.2%	4.2%
2000–2004	−2.3%	10.7%	4.8%
2001–2005	0.5%	9.3%	5.5%
2002–2006	6.2%	7.8%	7.6%
2003–2007	12.8%	5.1%	9.1%
2004–2008	-2.2%	5.8%	2.5%
2005–2009	0.4%	4.7%	3.4%
2006–2010	2.3%	5.9%	5.0%
2007–2011	-0.3%	8.8%	5.1%
2008–2012	1.7%	10.5%	6.9%

allocate to bonds). We'll look at this in great detail in chapter 14 where I'll teach you a very simple strategy which puts your focus on "how much you put where" rather than "which ones."

For now, I just want you to recognize that the economic forces that influence the two basic choices are different. It's possible for you to invest-by-lending your money to a financially strong company such as General Electric in return for one of its bonds and, even in the midst of a deep recession, earn a nice return. On the other hand, it's also probable that if you chose to invest-by-owning stock of the same corporation and thereby become one of its part owners, the same recession would have caused serious harm—hopefully temporary—to the company's earnings and dividend payments. As a part owner of the business, you would have likely watched your investment in the company lose value even while its creditors (like the investors who bought GE's bonds) were happily collecting their interest payments.

Of course, that's just looking at the risk part of the equation. The other side of that coin is that the owners of a company can enjoy great prosperity during those times in the business cycle when the economy is healthy and growing. The creditors, meanwhile, continue receiving only the interest payments to which they are due.

The reference table of annualized returns (at left) illustrates this risk/reward relationship. Consider the five-year period from 1987 to 1991. The table indicates that investors who allocated 100% of their capital to being owners (by investing in the shares of stocks in those blue-chip companies that are part of the Standard & Poor's 500 Stock Index) would have received a total return of 15.4% *per year* during that time. This is despite the fact that the crash of 1987 occurred early in the period. By comparing the "own" column with the "loan" column, you can also readily see that, with a few exceptions (notably during the bear markets of 1973-74, 2001-02, and 2008-2009), stockholders who hold for at least a five-year period typically do far better than bondholders during the same period.

Investors who decided to allocate 100% of their money to becoming lenders would have earned 10.4% per year during the 1987–1991 period. (This assumes their returns were similar to the bonds included in the Salomon Brothers Long-Term High-Grade Corporate Bond Index, which is an average of more than 1,000 publicly issued corporate debt securities.) They would have made less money and taken less risk. The final column on the right shows the experience of investors who don't want to cast their lot entirely with either camp, but choose to split their capital equally between the two basic choices—50% in stocks and 50% in bonds. (The reason the 50/50 column is not simply the average of the other two columns is due to the effects of reallocating the portfolio back to one-half of each kind of investment at the beginning of each new year. This annual process is often referred to as "rebalancing.") You'll note that this middle-of-the-road course has consistently been profitable.

All investing eventually finds its way into the American economy. It provides the essential money needed for businesses to be formed and grow — for engineering, manufacturing, construction, and a million and one other services to be offered and jobs to be created. You can either be a part owner in all this, tying yourself to the fortunes of American business and sharing in the certain risks and possible rewards that being an owner involves. Or, you can play the role of lender, giving your money to others in order to let *them* take the risks and knowing you are settling for a lesser, but more secure, return on your money.

How to divide your funds between these two kinds of endeavors is your first and most important investing decision. Everything else is fine-tuning.

Of course, no discussion of investing is complete without including the potential risks involved . . .

. . . in making an investment. There is one fundamental rule that you should never, ever, *ever*, forget — the greater the potential reward being offered, the greater the risk involved in making that investment. Let me say that again. The greater the potential reward being offered, the greater the risk involved in making that investment. Or, in everyday plain English, *There's no free lunch*. Countless people have learned this simple lesson only after losing thousands (and often hundreds of thousands) of dollars in an investment that was "just as safe" as a money-market account but offered a higher return. The truth is that the link between risk and reward is as certain as the link between sowing and reaping. It's inescapable. Anyone who tells you differently is either self-deceived or is trying to deceive you.

THE POTENTIAL FOR HIGHER RETURNS ALWAYS CARRIES A PRICE TAG

You reap what you sow.

There's no free lunch!

The greater the reward, the greater the risk.

Think about it for a second. The world's safest and most liquid investment is a 90-day U.S. Treasury bill. Investors in T-bills are lending money to the U.S. government (which represents the world's largest economy and has never defaulted on its debts). They'll get it back in just three months, not a very long period of time. It's the closest thing to a "sure thing" that the world of finance has to offer. Let's say the U.S. government will pay you a 3% annualized return. Anyone else competing with the U.S. government for your investment dollar will have to offer you more than 3%; otherwise, you have no incentive to do business with them. Why not? Because by definition they are not as creditworthy and represent a greater risk. Anyone else who wants your money *will have to* offer you a better return just to get your attention.

Every investment involves your parting with your money and handing it over to others who are going to use it for their own purposes. In return, it will cost them something. Naturally, they want their costs to be kept as low as possible. That is, they don't want to give you a dollar more than is absolutely necessary. But, as we've just seen, it *is* absolutely necessary to offer you more than you can get by investing in risk-free U.S. T-bills. In fact, it's necessary to offer you more than you can get from *any* lower-risk alternative. Otherwise, you'll always select the lower-risk alternative.

If they promise you 8%, it's only because *they have to*. They're not just being nice. There's something about the investment—credit risk, market risk, interest-rate risk, lack of liquidity, something—that makes their investment less attractive than other investments you could make which would pay you, say, 6% with less uncertainty.

This relationship between risk and reward is one of the fundamental truths you must accept in order to succeed in investing.

As we go along, I'll be giving you basic rules concerning this and other investing truisms. My goal will not be just to help you understand them—I want you to "own" them. I want you to develop convictions concerning them. It will be the strength of these convictions that, in future years, will continue to provide you with a reliable compass for navigating the often turbulent waters of economic life. ◆

11

CHAPTER PREVIEW

The Basics of Bonds

I. **Bonds are merely long-term IOUs.**

   A. They are a promise to repay the amount borrowed at a specific time in the future. Bonds pay a fixed rate of interest that doesn't vary over the life of the bond. They carry higher risks than money-market funds due to their longer average maturities.

   B. There are two major risks associated with investing in bonds, both of which can be neutralized.

      1. The first risk is that you might lend to a business or other entity that is not creditworthy. This risk is neutralized by lending only to the federal government and financially strong corporations. Investing in a bond mutual fund adds safety through diversification.

      2. The second risk is that you could get locked into a below-market rate of return. This risk can be neutralized by lending only for the short term. The advantage of longer maturities is that you receive a higher yield than when lending for shorter terms. The disadvantages of longer maturities are that the value of your bonds can go down, due to either their quality rating being lowered or rising interest rates.

II. **By using the two main influences on risk, we can create a "risk profile" for categorizing bond funds that greatly simplifies the process of selecting the bond funds that are best for you.**

   A. This results in four distinct categories (or "peer groups"), each having its own risk characteristics in terms of quality and average maturities.

   B. The risk profile enables us to build a "risk ladder." In this chapter, I provide 10-year performance histories for each of the four risk categories. I also point out risk characteristics you should understand.

III. **Tax-free bonds are issued by state and local governments. The interest received from tax-free bonds is exempt from federal income tax, and also exempt from state income tax in the state in which the bond was issued.**

IV. **Although bond *funds* have advantages, investing in them has two drawbacks that don't apply to investing in *individual bonds*: bond funds never reach maturity, and, under certain conditions, they may have tax disadvantages.**

Bonds
are IOUs in the form of investment certificates.

Issuer
is the business or government that is borrowing the money.

Maturity Date
is the time at which the borrower is due to pay the bond in full.

Coupon Rate
is the percent of interest stated on the bond that the borrower agrees to pay to investors. It stays fixed throughout the life of the bond.

Par
is the face value on the bond, usually $1,000. This is what investors are to receive when the bond matures.

Deep Discount Bonds
are those that can be purchased far below their par value. This means investors receive, in addition to the regular interest payments, the added benefit of getting back much more at maturity than they paid for the bond originally. This extra enticement is needed either because the coupon rate being paid is below the current levels available to investors or because the issuer's credit rating has slipped and full payment at maturity is in doubt.

Average Maturity
is the average number of years it will take for all the bonds in a bond fund portfolio to mature. As a general rule, the longer the average maturity, the greater the risk in the portfolio.

Greater self-confidence — the kind needed to take charge of your financial future — comes with *knowledge* and *experience*.

In this book, I'm working on adding to the first, *but you're the only one who can add to the second.*

Let me encourage you to keep at it. It's worth the effort because nobody will take as much of a genuine interest in your finances as you will. And, of course, you know yourself better than anyone else does. You know how much money you have to work with and whether you're really willing to risk losing any of it. You know how much you'd reasonably like to make, how much time you have before you need it, and how much patience you bring to the task. Most people know, perhaps even subconsciously, what's best for them.

I've seen this demonstrated time and again in the counseling sessions I have with my readers. After listening to them explain the various alternatives they have, I usually ask, "What would you *like* to do?" The responses are almost always reasonable and carefully thought out. They knew the answers; they just wanted me to confirm them. In the same way that most of us know which foods we *should* be eating and how much exercise we *should* be getting, we also generally know how much risk we should be taking.

You'll find that all of this isn't as complicated as it might sound, especially when you follow the proven investing strategy I'm going to lay out for you in the next section. I call the strategy Just-the-Basics because I devised it for people who are relatively new to investing and find themselves a bit overwhelmed by the idea of diversifying across the full risk spectrum. To make matters easier for them, I created a simplified diversification strategy that uses just four exchange-traded mutual funds (ETFs). It's the epitome of simplicity and low maintenance. I'll explain it in detail in chapter 14, but first I need to lay a little more foundation so you'll be able to clearly understand what I'll be telling you. That requires two brief primers, one on bonds and bond funds (that's this chapter) and one on stocks and stock funds (coming in the next chapter). So, let's get started!

America's largest banks and corporations (not to mention our local, state, and federal governments) need your help . . .

. . . they'd like to borrow money from you. For a few months or, if you're willing, for several decades. To make sure you get the message, their ads are everywhere. The government promotes safety of principal and has created certain kinds of bonds with special tax advantages. Banks want your deposits and want you to know your money is safe with them because it's "insured." Bond funds tantalize you with suggestions of still higher yields, although in their small print they remind you that "the value of your shares will fluctuate." And of course, insurance companies promote the tax-deferred advantages of their annuities. You're in the driver's seat. To all these institutions, you're a Very Important Person.

Does the thought of "renting" out your money seem strange? Chances are, you do it all the time. You probably think of it as buying a certificate of deposit (or Treasury bill, bond, or fixed annuity), but actually, you're making a loan. The "rent" you're being paid is called interest. In the financial markets, investors with extra money (lenders) rent it out to others who are in need of money (borrowers). The borrowers give their IOUs to the lenders.

Bonds are basically IOUs.

They are a promise to repay the amount borrowed at a specified time in the future. The date on which the bonds will be paid off is called the maturity date and may be set at a few years out or as many as (believe it or not) one hundred years away. At that time, the holder of the bond gets back its full face value (called par value). In order to make bonds affordable to a larger investing public, they are usually issued in $1,000 denominations.

Bonds promise to pay a fixed rate of interest (called the coupon rate) until they mature (are paid off). *This rate doesn't vary over the life of the bond.* Remember that. Once the rate is set, it's permanent. That's why bonds are referred to as "fixed-income" investments. As we'll soon see, it's the unchanging nature of the interest rate that causes bonds to go up and down in value.

Why buy bonds?

If you want to protect your principal and set up a steady stream of income, then bonds, rather than stocks, are the answer. Current income is traditionally the most important reason people invest in bonds, which usually generate greater current returns than CDs, money-market funds, or stocks.

They also can offer greater security than most common stocks since an issuer of a bond will do everything possible to meet its bond obligations. (Even Donald Trump accepted a humbling at the hands of his banks to gain the money necessary to meet his bonds' interest payments.)

The interest owed on a corporate bond must be paid to bondholders before any dividends can be paid to the stockholders of the company. And it's payable before federal, state, and city taxes. Being first in line helps make the investment safer.

Bond funds carry higher risks than money-market funds (see pages 52-56). The primary difference has to do with . . .

. . . the *average maturity* of the portfolio. Bond funds diversify among a great many individual bond issues, each of which has its own maturity date. By adding up the length of time until each issue matures and then dividing by the total number of bonds owned, you learn the average amount of time needed for the entire portfolio to be paid off.

While time is passing, many things can happen to interest rates or to the bond issuer (whoever borrowed the money from investors in the first place) to affect the value of the bonds. The more distant the maturity date, the more time for things to potentially go wrong. That's why bond funds with longer maturities carry more risk than ones with shorter maturities.

WHAT BOND RATINGS MEAN

Standard & Poor's and Moody's are the two leading credit-rating agencies. They use slightly different rating terminology. Below, S&P is shown on the left (AAA) and Moody's on the right (Aaa). The lower the rating, the higher the risk <u>and</u> the higher the interest rate the borrower will have to pay to attract investors.

AAA / Aaa
Highest rating; extremely strong capacity to pay interest and repay principal; smallest degree of investment risk.

AA / Aa
High quality; very strong capacity to pay interest and repay principal; safety margins are strong, differing from highest rating only in small degree.

A / A
Upper-medium grade; strong capacity to pay interest and repay principal but somewhat more susceptible to adverse economic circumstances.

BBB / Baa
Medium grade; adequate capacity to pay interest and repay principal; however, no room for error. Any further deterioration and these will no longer be considered investment-grade bonds.

BB / Ba
Only moderately secure, issuer faces major ongoing uncertainties and exposure to adverse business, financial, or economic conditions.

B / B
More vulnerable to adverse conditions than BB-rated bonds. Lacks the safety of a desirable investment for average investor.

CCC / Caa
Currently vulnerable with significant risk. Favorable conditions must develop to meet financial commitments. May be in danger of default.

CC / Ca
Currently highly vulnerable, major risk of default.

D / C
Has failed to pay one or more of its financial obligations. Poor prospects for improvement.

Any drop in the value of the bonds is offset against the fund's interest income. If these losses are greater than the interest received by the fund, the price of the bond fund drops that day. *That's why it's possible for investors in a bond fund to get back less than they put in!*

Let's learn how bond values fluctuate by working through an example. Assume XYZ Inc. wants to borrow $200 million for advanced research . . .

. . . and doesn't want to have to pay the loan back for 30 years. Banks generally don't like to lend their money out for such long periods of time, so the company decides to issue some bonds.

Let's say that XYZ agrees to pay a coupon rate of 7% annual interest and repay the loan in 2043. Bond traders would call these bonds the "XYZ sevens of 2043." No matter what happens to interest rates over the next 30 years, XYZ is obligated to pay investors 7% per year on these bonds. No more. No less. If you purchase one of these new XYZ bonds, you will receive $70 per year from XYZ on your $1,000 investment (7% times $1,000). Since bond interest is usually paid twice a year, you would receive two checks for $35 spread six months apart.

The simplest transaction would work this way. Assume that when XYZ first sells its bonds (through selected stock brokerage firms), you buy one of these brand-new bonds at par value. In effect, you lend XYZ $1,000. You collect $70 interest every year for 30 years. It doesn't matter how high or how low interest rates might move during this period, you're still going to get $70 a year because that was the deal that you and XYZ agreed to. Finally, in 2043, XYZ pays back your $1,000. You made no gain on the value of the bond itself; your profit came solely from the steady stream of fixed-income you received over the 30 years.

There are two major risks to watch out for in the world of bonds. The first is that you might not get all your money back.

The pros call it the "credit risk" because you're depending on the creditworthiness of the borrower. You're taking the risk that the issuer of the bond might go into default. This means the borrower is not able to keep up its interest payments or even pay off the bonds when they mature. This is the worst-case scenario that faces all bond investors.

To help evaluate this risk, ratings are available that help determine how safe the bonds are as an investment. Standard & Poor's and Moody's are the two companies best known for this. There are nine possible ratings a bond can receive (see sidebar notes, page 128). Most bond investors limit their selections to bonds given one of the top four ratings. As you might expect, the lower the quality, the higher rate of interest investors demand in order to reward them for accepting the increased risk of default.

By definition, all other borrowers are less creditworthy than the U.S. government. Therefore, borrowers who are in competition with the federal government for your money *must* pay you more in order to give you an incentive to lend to them instead of Uncle Sam. That's why U.S. Treasury bills establish the floor for interest rates. Other rates are higher than the T-bill rate depending on how creditworthy the borrower is.

If XYZ gets into trouble due to poor management and earnings, its ability to pay off its bond debts . . .

. . . may come into question. Assume its quality rating is lowered from AAA to A, and that shortly thereafter you need to sell your XYZ bond to meet an unexpected expense. A buyer of your bond will now want a greater potential profit to reward him for the possibly greater risk of default. As a practical matter, it may seem to be a very minor increase in risk, but the buyer will want compensation nevertheless.

But remember, the interest that XYZ pays on these bonds is fixed at $70 per year and can't be changed. The only way anyone buying your bond can improve his profit potential is *if you will lower the price of your bond.* Then, in addition to the interest received from XYZ, the buyer will also reap a profit when he ultimately collects $1,000 (if all goes well) for a bond he bought from you for only, say, $900.

Thus, as the quality rating of a bond falls, sellers must lower their asking prices in order to make the bond attractive to potential buyers. Always remember that a bond can become completely worthless if the issuer gets into financial difficulty and defaults.

How can you minimize the credit risk? One way to *eliminate* it altogether is to stick solely with U.S. Treasuries. The drawback, however, is that because U.S. government bonds are widely regarded as the world's safest fixed-income investments, the interest rates they pay investors are lower than those of corporate bonds. The most common way to *minimize* the credit risk is to add safety through diversification. Spread your holdings out among many different bond issues. That's where bond funds (which we'll discuss shortly) can play a helpful role.

How "Yield" Is Different from "Gain" and "Total Return"

Bear with me for a little history lesson. In the late 1980s, as interest rates fell for both bank CDs and money-market funds, savers went in search of higher returns. They saw that some highly publicized bond funds were "yielding" 12% and more, so off they went. When the junk-bond market crashed, investors found they could be receiving a great yield yet still lose money! The average high-yield bond fund fell about 10% in value in 1990. A few dropped more than 20%. Focusing on yield alone can be dangerous because the highest-yielding funds are the ones with the lower quality ratings or the longest average maturities.

When evaluating whether an investment has been successful, there are two questions to be addressed. First, how much income from your investment did you receive? And second, did you get back more than you put in, less than you put in, or the same as you put in?

The income you received while your money was tied up is called the yield and is always expressed in annualized terms. If you invest $1,000 in an XYZ bond and it pays $90 every year in interest, it is yielding you 9.0% ($90/$1,000). Now, when you eventually sell your investment, if you receive back more than you paid for it, you have a capital gain. Let's say your $1,000 investment is sold after three years for $1,300, giving you a $300 gain.

Both the yield and the gain represent partial returns; only when you combine them do you get the total picture, hence the name total return (usually expressed in annual compounded terms). In our example, you invested $1,000 and received back a total of $1,570 over three years ($270 in dividends plus the $300 gain).

To learn what your total return was in annual terms, you ask, "What rate of growth is needed to turn $1,000 into $1,570 in three years?" By using a financial calculator that can perform time-value-of-money computations, you learn that it takes about a 16.3% per year rate of growth to do that. In other words, if you could invest $1,000 at 16.3% for three years, you'd have approximately $1,570 at the end of that time. In the example, you know that part of the growth came from that 9% annual yield. But how did you get from 9% to that 16.3% total return? By selling for a gain and picking up that extra $300. The 9% yield that you received as you went along, plus the $300 gain at the end, made it possible for you to achieve a very nice 16.3% annualized total return.

But what if the bond had gone down $300 instead of up $300. That makes the result look quite different. You invested $1,000, and after three years have just $970 ($270 in dividends minus a $300 loss) to show for your efforts. Your total return is now negative; while you were collecting your 9% yield with the thought that you were making money, you were actually losing, on average, about 1% per year!

The second major risk facing bondholders, and the one that is the greater of the two, is that you could get locked into a below-market rate of return.

The pros call this the "interest-rate risk." It's the same dilemma you face when trying to decide how long you should tie up your money in a bank CD, but it has even greater significance when investing in bonds. If you invest in a three-year CD when it turns out that a six-month one would have been better, you're only missing out on better rates for 30 months. But if you buy a 30-year bond, you're stuck with inferior returns for *decades*. That gives you an idea of how painful it can be when holding long-term bonds during a period of rising interest rates.

A fear of inflation leads to rising long-term interest rates. Just for the moment, assume that you're back in 1980 and inflation is running at 12% per year. Now ask yourself this question: Would you be willing to pay full price for a 30-year, $1,000 bond with an 7% coupon rate? Not likely. The bond would only be paying you $70 in interest per year at a time when you need $120 just to keep up with inflation. You'd be agreeing to a deal that would guarantee you a loss of purchasing power of $50 each year. Eventually, you'd get your $1,000 back, but it wouldn't buy nearly as much in the future as it does now.

But what if the seller would lower the price of the bond so you could buy that bond at a big discount? If you only had to pay $585 for a $1,000 bond, it might make economic sense. The $70 interest per year—remember, the coupon rate stays fixed throughout the life of the bond—would represent a 12% return ($70 received in interest divided by the $585 invested). Now, at least you're even with inflation. Plus, when the bond matures 30 years down the road, you get a full $1,000 back for your $585. That's 70% more than you paid for it.

So you can see that high inflation (or even the fear of high inflation) causes bond buyers to demand a higher return on their money in order to protect their purchasing power. And in order to create that higher return, bond sellers must lower their asking prices. That's why the bond market often goes down when any news comes out that could reasonably be interpreted as leading to higher consumer prices.

Here's how this affects your XYZ bond. Although you originally intended . . .

. . . to hold onto your XYZ bond for the full 30 years, real life is rarely quite that simple. Very few investors hold onto their bonds for so long a period of time. Let's say that you decide to sell your XYZ bond and use the money for a really worthwhile purpose—like buying tickets to the Final Four basketball championship. You want your money back *now*, not in 2043.

Where do you sell it? In the bond market where older bonds (as opposed to new ones just being issued) are traded. Your stockbroker can handle it for you. Assuming that XYZ is still in tip-top financial condition with a AAA credit rating, you might expect to get all of your $1,000 back. Well, maybe you will, and maybe you won't. The big question is: *what is the rate of interest being paid by companies that are now issuing new bonds?*

If the rate of interest being paid on new bonds is higher than what your bond pays, you've got a problem. Assume that interest rates have gone up since you bought your

XYZ bond, and that new bonds of comparable quality are now paying 8%. Why would any investor want to buy your old XYZ bond that will pay him just $70 per year in interest when he can buy a new one that will pay $80? Obviously, if both bonds cost him the same price, he wouldn't. So, to sell your bond you will have to reduce your asking price below $1,000 to be competitive and attract buyers.

On the other hand, if interest rates have *fallen*, to let's say 6%, then the shoe is on the other foot. Your old bond that pays $70 per year looks pretty attractive compared to new ones that pay only $60. This means you can sell it for a "premium," meaning more than the $1,000 par value you paid.

Here's the lesson: anytime you sell a bond before its maturity date, it will either be worth less than you paid for it (because interest rates have gone up since you bought it) or worth more than you paid for it (because interest rates have gone down since you bought it).

UNDERSTANDING BOND LISTINGS

These listings are for bonds issued in the past that are now being bought and sold in what's called the "secondary" market (the primary market is when new bonds are sold to investors when they are first issued). The secondary market is the place to sell a bond you acquired when it first came out, but then you changed your mind and decided you don't want to hold onto it for 20 years after all. Your broker can sell it for you—just like a stock.

Company	Coupon	Maturity	Last Price	Yield to Maturity	Est $ Volume
Viacom	5.850%	Sept 2043	97.405	6.038%	411,700
Apple	2.400%	May 2023	89.104	3.750%	382,927
Wells Fargo	4.125%	Aug 2023	98.000	4.374%	373,757
Bank of America	4.100%	July 2023	96.808	4.502%	287,705
Toyota	2.800%	Jan 2018	104.498	0.897%	145,740
BurlingtonNorth	5.150%	Sept 2043	97.888	5.291%	135,945
Oracle	2.375%	Jan 2019	99.962	2.382%	135,722
BostonScientific	4.125%	Oct 2023	97.695	4.409%	135,610
Kroger	3.850%	Aug 2023	97.430	4.168%	121,659
GE Capital	3.100%	Jan 2023	92.089	4.125%	108,603

Name is the company that borrowed the money initially and is (1) responsible for paying the interest regularly and (2) paying the amount owed on the bond when it matures.

Coupon Rate is the interest the borrower pays to the bondholder. It stays constant throughout the life of the bond. Since bonds usually come in $1,000 denominations, this Toyota bond pays $28.00 per year interest (2.800% x $1,000).

Maturity Date is when the bond matures and the investor receives the face value of the bond. This Kroger issue would be known as the "three eighty fives of twenty-three" and would mature in 2023.

Last Price is the price at which the bond changed hands on its final trade of the day. Also called the closing price. This Boston Scientific bond closed at $976.95 per $1,000 of face value.

Yield to Maturity is the number you're interested in as a buyer. It tells what your return would be if you bought at yesterday's last price and held the bond until it matures. It includes the interest you receive as well as any gain or loss between your purchase price and face value.

You can see that the longer-term bonds maturing in 2043 yield more than the shorter-term bonds maturing in 2023. That's to compensate the buyer for the higher risk.

Volume is the dollar value (expressed in thousands) of all the bonds of this issue traded yesterday. $287,705,000 of this Bank of America bond traded. The bigger the better, because it means a more efficient market.

That's why it's possible to lose money even with investments such as U.S. Treasury bonds. For example, 30-year Treasuries suffered losses of 15% in value in only six months during the first half of 2009 when the interest rate pendulum began to swing in the direction of higher rates. They're safe from default, but nobody can protect you against rising interest rates.

Of course, if you hold onto your XYZ bond until it matures in 2043, it will be worth $1,000. At that time, XYZ will repay the par value to whoever owns its bonds. The closer you get to a bond's maturity date, the more the bond's price reflects its full face value. That's why interest rates eventually lose their power to affect the market value of a bond.

The longer you have to wait until maturity, the longer you are vulnerable. How can you shorten the wait (and therefore reduce the risk)? Buy old bonds that were issued many years back and are now only a few years from their maturity. The shorter the maturity, the less volatile a bond's price will be.

Short-term bonds, then, represent a middle ground between the money market and the long-term bond market. They have much less interest-rate risk than long-term bonds and still pay higher yields than money-market funds.

How do you distinguish among the large number of bond mutual funds and select the ones most appropriate for you?

There are many varieties of bond funds. They differ in whether they're committed to investing in high-quality bonds or will specialize in higher-risk, higher-yielding ones of lower quality. They differ in the maturities of their portfolios—some seek to keep their average weighted maturities at four years or less, others want to keep theirs at no less than 20 years. Some generate taxable dividends, others tax-free dividends. Some limit themselves to the U.S. market, whereas others are permitted to invest overseas. Now imagine that you started mixing and matching all these possibilities to see how many different combinations are possible. The answer? A lot! More than you want to read about—one writer on the bond market published a book spanning 1,426 pages!

To bring some kind of order out of this chaos, I've grouped bond funds in a way that should be most helpful for beginners. These aren't the "official" groupings used for comparing risk and performance among mutual funds. In fact, there's no such thing. The Investment Company Institute, which is the trade association for the mutual-fund in-

BOND PRICES FALL WHEN INTEREST RATES RISE

This graph shows the various effects on short-term, medium-term, and long-term bond portfolios when interest rates go up. The point is not only that interest rates and bond prices move *opposite* to each other, but also that the longer term the bond, the greater the price movement.

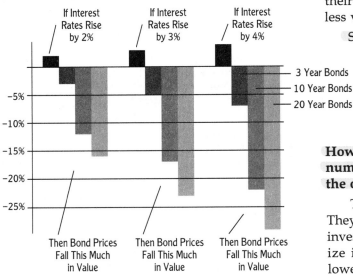

dustry, has its way of grouping fixed-income funds. Morningstar and Lipper, the two major mutual fund reporting services, have their own ways — and each is different from the other. Their classification systems are rather complicated; I wouldn't even consider trying to explain them to you or using them in this book. Instead, I have created my own way of classifying bond funds that I believe you will find relatively easy to understand and use. Here's how it works.

First, I divide all U.S. bond funds into two groups. One group is composed of those funds that invest in a diversified portfolio of bonds that are taxable and have no unusual features. These are the funds I regard as primary when assembling a bond portfolio. The other group includes what I call "special purpose" bond funds because they invest in bonds with distinctive features. This group includes mortgage-backed bonds (pages 55-56), zero-coupon bonds (see sidebar at right), tax-exempt bonds (pages 137-138), convertible bonds, and international bonds.

I'll illustrate bond-fund risk by using a graphic device that I call a "risk profile."

As we've discussed, there are two major threats facing lenders (i.e., bond investors). The first is the risk that the bonds will go into default. The extensive diversification you achieve in a bond mutual fund virtually eliminates this risk as a meaningful threat.

Bonds are issued by borrowers from all across the "credit-worthiness" spectrum. The U.S. government is regarded as the borrower highest on the quality scale. Even there, many experts make a distinction between direct obligations of the U.S. Treasury versus those of government agencies, the latter being considered as ever so slightly lower in quality.

Then come corporate bonds issued by financially strong companies that receive "investment grade" ratings (AAA, AA, A, and BBB — see page

WHEN IT COMES TO BONDS THAT CARRY A HIGH INTEREST-RATE RISK, ZERO-COUPON BONDS ARE THE ULTIMATE!

Would you be interested in buying bonds that pay "zero" interest? That's right, no interest at all. Doesn't sound very appealing, does it? But what if I was willing to sell you a three-year $1,000 zero-coupon bond for $760? Invest $760 for three years and get $1,000 back. If you said yes, good move! Although you would be receiving no interest for three years, when you finally got your $1,000 it would represent an effective yield of +9.58% per year before taxes.

Zeros are a special breed of bond that pay no current interest. They retain the interest you earn and automatically reinvest it. When the bond matures, you receive all the interest and principal at one time.

Zeros were created in the early 1980s by the brokerage community for large pension investors who needed to know exactly how much they would be getting back at specific times. Zeros make this possible by hedging what is called the "reinvestment risk." With normal bonds, when you receive your semi-annual interest payments, you are faced with the task of reinvesting. If interest rates have fallen, you won't get as attractive a rate on your reinvested amounts as you did on the original bond. That's the reinvestment risk. Zeros eliminate this concern because the issuer, in effect, makes you this offer: "I promise to let you reinvest at the initial rate throughout the life of the bond. But to keep things simple, rather than mail you a check and have you mail it back, I'll just keep the interest money here and reinvest it for you."

Zeros are especially suited for those investors who plan on holding their bonds to maturity. Because you know up front the rate at which your money will be reinvested over the life of the bond, you can calculate a predictable rate of return for the entire period. This makes planning easier.

Zeros have two unpleasant drawbacks. First, the IRS taxes you on the interest you earn from your zeros each year even though you won't receive it until the bonds mature. That makes them better choices for tax-sheltered accounts such as IRAs and 401(k)s. Second, zeros are very sensitive to changes in interest rates. In fact, they are the ultimate in high "interest-rate risk" bonds. Their market prices rise and fall much more dramatically than regular bonds as rates fluctuate. If all goes well with the issuer, the bonds will be worth their full face value when they mature, but if you need to sell them prior to maturity in a climate of rising interest rates, you might be shocked at how much they have dropped in value.

I'm not that excited about zeros. But if you truly desire to buy some, here are my suggestions: (1) wait until you have reason to believe that interest rates are at or near a peak; (2) buy only the U.S. Treasury kind; (3) buy only as many as you are fairly certain you can afford to hold until they mature; and (4) buy them only in your IRA or other tax-deferred accounts in order to escape the income taxes.

128 for definitions of bond ratings). The subtle credit distinctions among investment-grade bonds may be of interest if you're buying only a few issues, but they are less important when buying into a mutual-fund portfolio. Defaults are rare events at this level of quality, and even if one should come along, the investor is well protected by the diversification.

BUILDING A RISK PROFILE FOR BOND FUNDS: STEP #1

Separate funds according to the credit-worthiness of their portfolios

Mixed Quality ❹

High Quality ❸   High Quality ❷

High Quality ❶

For purposes of assessing the credit risk, I don't make a distinction between funds investing only in U.S. government-backed bonds versus those that also invest in high-quality corporate bonds. Taken individually, of course, the government bonds are of higher quality. But, as a practical matter, in a diversified portfolio that includes a sampling of BBB-rated bonds, the differences in risk are insignificant. Even the so-called "general corporate" bond funds will invest to some extent in Treasury securities (to balance out some of their risk as well as put idle cash to good use in case they can't find enough of the lesser-grade bonds they like). Since they obviously can own large amounts of government bonds, we shouldn't think of them as buying only bonds issued by businesses. Therefore, I'm treating funds that invest in any of the above kinds of bonds the same. Their overall credit quality will range from AAA to BBB, and they will be placed in one of the three lower diamonds in our risk profile (see step one in sidebar at left).

BUILDING A RISK PROFILE FOR BOND FUNDS: STEP #2

Separate funds according to the average maturities of their portfolios

Various Maturities ❹

Long Term ❸   Medium Term ❷

Short Term ❶

That leaves the bonds of weaker companies, the so-called "junk" bonds, that must pay higher yields to attract investors.

BUILDING A RISK PROFILE FOR BOND FUNDS: STEP #3

Combine criteria to create four distinct risk categories based on overall credit quality and average portfolio maturities

Mixed Quality Various Maturities ❹

High Quality Long Term ❸   High Quality Medium Term ❷

High Quality Short Term ❶

Junk bonds are corporate bonds that have been given low ratings by independent grading firms such as Moody's and Standard & Poor's. The ratings are intended to evaluate a company's financial strength and, accordingly, its ability to pay both the principal and interest on its debts as they come due. Generally, bonds rated in the top four categories are considered "investment grade" quality. Only several hundred of the strongest companies qualify for these high ratings.

That leaves several thousand companies stuck with the "junk" label, although naturally differences in financial strength exist even here. There are distinctions between those companies that just barely failed to qualify for an investment grade rating and those that have problems so severe that they have already filed for bankruptcy protection. If you want the higher yields that these companies offer (to entice investors to buy their bonds), the trick is to sort through these lower-rated offerings and pick the strongest of the weak. That's the task of the fund manager.

Junk-bond investors are realistic enough to expect some of their holdings to eventually default. Studies have shown that it's normal for 1.5% to 2.5% of junk bonds to default in any given year. That's why the diversification provided by the fund is so essential—it spreads out this risk over a sufficiently large number of bonds to reasonably assure that its default experience will be in this range. The higher yields paid by junk bonds compensate investors for this expected small loss of capital.

Here's how it might work. Say the average yield in the fund portfolio is 12% on junk bond holdings of $1 million. That means the fund would receive $120,000 in interest payments throughout the year. Assume that the fund experiences a 2.5% default rate ($25,000 of their bond holdings). Even in a default, bonds don't typically become worthless; bondholders usually recoup 40%–50% of the principal value of the bonds. If the fund recouped 40% of its investment in the bad bonds, it would get $10,000 of its capital back. That means the fund lost $15,000 on the defaulting bonds, which would be offset against the interest income. After all is said and done, the fund would still come out $105,000 ahead for the year.

A healthy economy is very important to buyers of junk bonds because it helps maintain a positive cash flow that enables even weaker companies to keep up with their interest payments. While a recession spells trouble for everybody, it can be especially devastating for companies with high debt loads. It's the same problem faced by families with high credit-card and other consumer debt.

With this in mind, it's easy to see why junk bond funds often respond to economic events more like stock funds do. For instance, *high-quality bond funds* returned about 14% in 2009. But stock and *junk-bond funds*, even though the economy was just beginning to emerge from The Great Recession, returned a surprisingly strong 28% and 46%, respectively. Why? Because, like the stock market, junk bonds are valued based on anticipated strength in corporate earnings six to nine months away. Investors began expecting the recovery to kick in and greatly improve the cash flow of the companies that had issued the bonds. This appeared to lower the risk, and the high yields looked great in comparison to other savings-type investments, which had fallen to extremely low levels.

Due to their high risk, funds that invest in junk bonds will be placed in Category 4, the uppermost of the four diamonds in the risk profile on page 134. Step one (upper left) summarizes the placement of funds based on the risk of default.

The second major threat facing bond owners is that of rising interest rates — as rates go up, bond prices go down.

A bond fund's average portfolio maturity tells us more about the risk of that fund than just about any other factor. As you move toward longer maturities, the risk of being hurt by rising interest rates increases. The sooner the bonds in your portfolio mature, the sooner your fund manager can go out and buy bonds paying the new higher rates. It follows, therefore, that the shorter the average portfolio maturity of a bond fund, the less its price volatility.

We reflect this in the second step of building our risk profile. Because the short-term portfolios pose the least risk, we assign them to the lowest diamond; the medium-term funds go into Category 2; and the long-term portfolios, which have the highest risk among high quality bond funds, are placed in Category 3.

Now to put all this together. As you can see in step three, the two fundamental risk considerations combine to create four distinctive risk categories. The diamond that is positioned lowest in the profile (Category 1) is also the category with the lowest risk because it combines the safety of high-quality bonds with shorter maturities. The category that is positioned highest in the profile (Category 4) is the category with the highest risk because it features bonds of mixed quality that also have medium-to-long-term maturities. The two diamonds in the center are for bond funds with risk in between the two extremes. Once you know which of these four risk categories a bond fund falls in, you know a lot about that fund's likely volatility as well as its potential for gain or loss.

Let's apply the lessons you've learned about bonds as we study the "risk ladder" for bond funds below.

It's called a risk ladder because it's safest at the bottom, and each step up to the next rung increases your risk. The statistics were compiled from the Morningstar database.

• Notice there's normally a stair-step pattern to returns as you move up the risk ladder. In a typical year, the Category 1 funds have the lowest returns, the Category 2 funds slightly better retuns, and the Category 3 funds the best returns. This is a reflection of the increasing level of risk, as evidenced by the same stair-step pattern in the "standard deviation" (a measure of volatility) column. There are occasional exceptions (see 2006 and 2009) when rising interest rates, which lead to lower bond prices, are too much for the longer maturities to overcome.

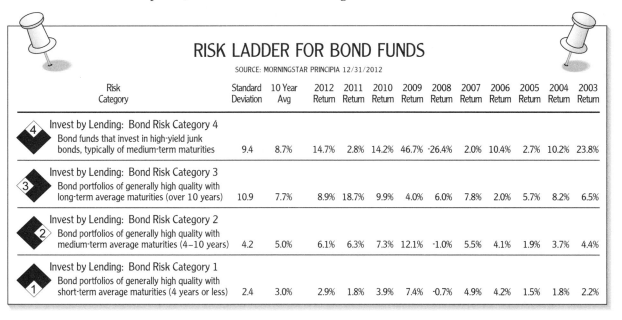

RISK LADDER FOR BOND FUNDS
SOURCE: MORNINGSTAR PRINCIPIA 12/31/2012

Risk Category	Standard Deviation	10 Year Avg	2012 Return	2011 Return	2010 Return	2009 Return	2008 Return	2007 Return	2006 Return	2005 Return	2004 Return	2003 Return
4 Invest by Lending: Bond Risk Category 4 — Bond funds that invest in high-yield junk bonds, typically of medium-term maturities	9.4	8.7%	14.7%	2.8%	14.2%	46.7%	-26.4%	2.0%	10.4%	2.7%	10.2%	23.8%
3 Invest by Lending: Bond Risk Category 3 — Bond portfolios of generally high quality with long-term average maturities (over 10 years)	10.9	7.7%	8.9%	18.7%	9.9%	4.0%	6.0%	7.8%	2.0%	5.7%	8.2%	6.5%
2 Invest by Lending: Bond Risk Category 2 — Bond portfolios of generally high quality with medium-term average maturities (4–10 years)	4.2	5.0%	6.1%	6.3%	7.3%	12.1%	-1.0%	5.5%	4.1%	1.9%	3.7%	4.4%
1 Invest by Lending: Bond Risk Category 1 — Bond portfolios of generally high quality with short-term average maturities (4 years or less)	2.4	3.0%	2.9%	1.8%	3.9%	7.4%	-0.7%	4.9%	4.2%	1.5%	1.8%	2.2%

• Notice that the high-yield Category 4 funds march to a different drummer. As mentioned above, there is a relatively consistent pattern that shows up when comparing the year-by-year results of the funds in Categories 1 through 3; however, the performance of the Category 4 funds seems almost random. That's because, as I pointed out earlier in this chapter, junk bonds often behave more like stocks because of their sensitivity to the strength in the economy. You'll also see that, due to the weak returns during the 2008 stock market downturn, the group failed to achieve its customary position as the best-performing of the four groups, but bounced back strongly when the 2009 bull market in stocks began.

Tax-free bonds: they're not for everybody . . .

. . . but if I'm going to talk about them in this book, it's now or never—after all, this is the bond chapter.

Here's the deal. You work hard, live frugally, save your money, and invest it carefully. Then, when the fruit of your labor and sacrifice—your interest check—arrives, state and federal tax agents show up and demand their cut. Their combined share (for most families) starts at about one-fourth and can easily climb to one-third of your investment earnings. Obviously, any investment that can avoid such a heavy penalty is worth knowing about.

Tax-free bonds (also called "municipal" bonds) are debt securities issued by state and local governments. By law, the interest earned on such bonds is exempt from federal taxes. If the issuer is a city in your state, or the state itself, the interest is also exempt from the state income tax. Because of the value of these tax benefits, issuers of tax-free bonds can borrow money at interest rates lower than those paid by other borrowers. That means they won't pay as much in interest, but what tax-free funds do pay, you can keep entirely!

Would you benefit from investing in tax-free bonds? That depends on your "marginal" tax bracket. At present, the federal tax law provides for several tax brackets—10%, 15%, 25%, 28%, 33%, 35%, and 39.6%—to be applied against your taxable income. Different rates apply for singles and married persons. (See the table at right for the tax brackets as they were for 2013.) The brackets are adjusted annually for inflation. How high up the tax ladder does your income take you? As your income increases, each $1 of additional income is subject to the higher rates *according to the bracket within which it falls*. The highest rate you pay is called your marginal rate.

UNDERSTANDING TAX BRACKETS

Taxable income is what is left after reportable income is offset by your exemptions, deductions, and other permitted subtractions.

2013 Brackets (For Filing 4/15/14)	For Single Taxpayers	Married, Filing Jointly
10%	Up to $8,925	Up to $17,850
15%	$8,925–$36,250	$17,850–$72,500
25%	$36,250–$87,850	$72,500–$146,400
28%	$87,850–$183,250	$146,400–$223,050
33%	$183,250–$398,350	$223,050–$398,350
35%	$398,350–$400,000	$398,350–$450,000
39.6%	Above $400,000	Above $450,000

There's an easy calculation you can make to see if you're better off receiving a higher rate of interest that is taxable or a lower return that is tax-free (see page 48). Due to a provision in the tax code that affects the deductibility of itemized deductions, tax-frees are even more attractive than the formula would imply if your adjusted gross income rises above the $250,000 (for individuals) to $300,000 (for joint filers) levels.

If you believe you would benefit from investing in tax-frees, I strongly encourage you to diversify widely to minimize the risk of defaults. This can be accomplished easily by investing in *three* no-load muni funds rather than putting all your money into just one. I suggest staying with top-quality bonds rated A or better (see sidebar, page 128). When considering a fund, look at a breakdown of the quality ratings of their holdings. This is often called a credit analysis, and it will tell you how much (by percentage) the fund has in AAA-rated bonds, AA-rated bonds, and so on. (You can get this analysis from the fund, or online at morningstar.com—just type in a fund's five-letter ticker symbol and look in the "portfolio" section.)

There is even more incentive to switch to tax-frees if you live in a high-tax state. So-called "single state" tax-exempt funds invest solely in tax-free securities issued from within that one state. This means the interest income is *double tax-free:* from state income taxes as well as federal ones. For example, New Yorkers investing in a New York-only tax-free fund that yields 3.2% would be getting the equivalent of a before-tax return above 6% (1 minus a total federal-state tax burden of 47% = .53, then 3.2 divided by .53 = 6.04%). Since this is significantly higher than comparable taxable bonds, such a bond fund makes sense from a tax point of view for some investors.

Be aware, however, that a huge amount of diversification protection is lost with this approach. It seems to me this is a significant drawback—you'll have all your muni investments riding on the financial condition of your state. With concerns mounting about the financial health of several major cities and states, I question the wisdom of placing much of one's savings at higher risk merely to save a percent or so on taxes.

To combat the inflation problem for fixed-income investors, the U.S. government introduced Treasury Inflation Protected Securities (TIPS) in the late 1990s.

Like traditional government bonds, TIPS are assigned a fixed interest rate at the time they are originally issued. This is the rate that is used to determine their semi-annual interest payment. All TIPS pay interest twice a year—six months from issue and on the anniversary date of issue. This interest is treated as interest income and is subject to federal income tax, but it is exempt from state and local taxes.

The key differentiating feature of TIPS is that the face value of the bond itself increases based on changes in inflation. Suppose you own a $1,000 TIPS with an interest rate of 3%. The first interest payment would be $15 ($1,000 x 3% = $30 annually, which is $15 semi-annually). If inflation were 5% during the first year, the face value would be adjusted upward by 5% to $1,050. The face value is the amount you'd get back when the bond matures.

But the increase in face value is only half the story. Each increase in the face amount also results in an increase in the amount of your semi-annual interest payment—the fixed rate of 3% is now multiplied by the new, higher face value. Thus, the next payment would be $15.75 ($1,050 x 3% = $31.50 annually, which is $15.75 semi-annually). In this way, both your principal and interest payments are protected from inflation. This makes TIPS especially attractive for investors such as retirees who want to draw income from their investment while preserving the purchasing power of their principal.

There is a drawback, however, and it is a significant one: the increase in the face amount (the $50 in our example) has to be reported annually on your taxes as interest income even though you do not receive it until the bond matures. For this reason, many investors choose to hold TIPS in a tax-advantaged retirement account. That's a potentially costly solution, because it nullifies the benefit of the state and local tax exemption.

A convenient way to invest in TIPS is through a mutual fund. This enables many different issues of varying rates and maturities to be held. It also means you don't have to worry about investing bits and pieces of interest income as it comes in. One good option worth investigating is Vanguard's Inflation-Protected Securities Fund (VIPSX).

In concluding this chapter on bond-market basics, let's look at how investing in a bond fund differs from investing in a portfolio of individual bonds that you put together yourself.

Investing in a pre-assembled portfolio via a bond fund offers convenience and professional management, but there are some drawbacks.

1. Bond funds never reach maturity. The job of the bond-fund manager is to maintain the fund's average maturity at the level stated in its prospectus. For example, the Vanguard Long-Term Investment-Grade Bond Fund is committed to keeping the average weighted maturity of its portfolio between 15 and 25 years. As time goes by and maturities shorten, the manager will need to replace some of the shorter-term bonds with longer-term ones to stay within the stated range. Although time is passing, the fund never gets close to the day when the entire portfolio matures and every shareholder will cash out whole.

This is different from what takes place if you buy an individual bond. Assume you invest in one which has a 15-year maturity. Each year, it moves closer to the date when it will be paid off. That means the tendency of your bond to experience wide price swings in its market value is reduced year by year. Eventually, there will come a time when you will receive all your money back. This is not an assurance that investors in bond funds have (zero coupon bond funds are an exception to this).

2. Bond funds may rob Peter to pay Paul. Typically, bond fund investors are seeking regular income. This leads most bond funds to distribute income to their shareholders on a monthly basis. Because their portfolios are constantly undergoing change, bond funds don't receive the same amount of interest income on their holdings every month. That means the amount of income they distribute varies slightly from month to month. Or at least it should. But shareholders prefer that the amount of the monthly check they receive be predictable and consistent. Some bond funds have responded to this by paying out a set amount. The problem arises when the set amount turns out to be more than the fund actually earned. Assume the portfolio manager finds it reasonable to believe that the fund's earnings will be approximately $1.20 a share over the coming year. Accordingly, he sets a monthly payout of 10¢ per share.

Now, suppose his estimate is off. Perhaps interest rates have fallen and the new money coming into the fund can't be invested at the formerly high rate. If so, the fund manager has two options. One, he can invest the new money at the lower rates. Then, the fund's income per share will come in below expectations. The monthly payout will have to be reduced (because the earnings won't be there to support it) and shareholders will be disappointed.

Alternately, he can invest the new money in "premium" bonds. These are bonds which were issued a year or two earlier when interest rates were still high, and because they carry such attractive coupon rates, they sell in the marketplace at a premium over par value (say $1,150 for a $1,000 bond). The trade-off is obvious—in order to have more income now (i.e., maintain the high payout rate), the manager will have to settle for less later (because he is guaranteed to lose $150 in value per bond between now and the maturity date). If he chooses this course, the losses in the premium bonds will gradually eat away at the price per share of the fund and shareholders will be disappointed.

Individual bonds, on the other hand, don't require any special action to assure that the interest income received is predictable and consistent. They're that way by design. Most bonds make regular interest payments at six-month intervals, and the amount of the payment is always the same. A 30-year $1,000 bond with a 4% coupon rate will make payments of $20 every six months for the next 30 years.

Buying premium bonds is not a "bad" strategy per se. After all, you have a higher level of income to offset the losses in market value. The significance has more to do with the taxes paid by investors. Buying premium bonds has the effect of adding to current income and taking away from capital gains. As long as income is taxed at higher rates than capital gains, this works to the detriment of the shareholder. This problem is neutralized if the shares are held in a tax-sheltered account such as an IRA, 401(k), or 403(b) plan.

What kinds of bonds should you buy, since you don't know (and neither does anyone else!) where interest rates are headed?

I suggest that you make your mistakes on the side of caution. To minimize risk, don't go further out than about 10 years—the reward just isn't worth the risk. According to the respected Ibbotson Associates research firm, since the late 1920s, intermediate-term Treasuries (average maturities near five years) have averaged 5.4% per year (with only nine losing years) versus 5.7% for the higher-risk long-term bonds (average maturities near 20 years) which had 22 losing years. Additionally, the returns of the intermediate-term bonds were only 63% as volatile as those of the long-term group. Thus, the gains on five-year Treasuries have been equal to 95% that of 20-year bonds but with 37% less risk.

In our Just-the-Basics strategy, we'll use a middle-of-the-road approach by investing in a bond fund that typically has an average maturity of about eight years. On the bond risk ladder (see page 136), it falls into Category 2. For the 15 years ending October 2013, it generated an average annual return of 5.1%, which slightly exceeded the 5.0% turned in by the average Category 2 bond fund. More significantly, it did so with less volatility (a standard deviation of 3.5 compared to 4.2 for the average fund). An equal or better return at less risk—such a deal!

We'll talk more about this fund in chapter 14. For now, it's time to turn our attention to the stock market. ◆

CHAPTER PREVIEW

Stock Market Basics

I. **Stock shares represent part ownership in a business.**

  A. As an owner, you have the right to participate in the future growth of the company. You will receive dividends if the company decides to distribute money to shareholders rather than retain it for future growth needs.

  B. The stock market is where the buying and selling of part ownerships in businesses takes place. Stock market prices rise and fall for the same reasons other prices do: from supply and demand forces that reflect economic conditions.

II. **There are two major risks to your capital when you invest in stock shares and become a part owner in a company.**

  A. The first is that the company might fail and your investment be totally lost. This risk can be controlled through prudent selection and diversification.

  B. The second is that the entire market for stocks can be adversely affected by economic conditions that may have nothing to do with your company. This risk can't be avoided, but can be minimized by holding your shares through a complete economic cycle.

III. **When assessing risk, knowing the average size of the companies in which a fund invests as well as the investing "style" used by the fund manager provides helpful guidance.**

  A. *Large* companies generally are safer to invest in than *small* companies, although they typically don't have the capital-gain potential of smaller firms.

  B. The two major styles of investing are *value* and *growth*. The value approach is the more conservative because of its emphasis on looking for bargains and getting your money's worth.

  C. The funds with the lowest risk/reward characteristics will be those that follow a large company/value strategy. The highest risk/reward potential is found among funds that employ a small company/growth strategy.

IV. **Major market uptrends are called "bull markets" and downtrends are called "bear markets." In an attempt to avoid losses during bear markets, many investors practice market timing, a strategy not recommended for the average investor.**

Common Stock
is the term used to describe the units of ownership in a corporation.

Initial Public Offering (IPO)
is when a corporation offers to sell its stock to investors for the first time. The proceeds, minus what the company owes for the broker's services, go to the company.

Secondary Offering
is when a corporation offers to sell previously issued stock which is held by founders and other insiders. The proceeds, minus what is owed for the broker's services, go to the individuals who are selling, not to the company.

Limited Liability
is one of the attractions of stock ownership. It means that shareholders have no financial obligation to assist the company should it be unable to pay its liabilities.

Preferred Stock
is a special class of stock that pays dividends at a promised rate. Holders of preferred stock must receive their dividends before any may be paid to common shareholders. They also take preference over common shareholders in receiving back the par value of the stock in the event the company is liquidated. Preferred stock typically does not carry voting rights.

Par Value
is the face value printed on a security. In the event of a corporate liquidation, preferred shareholders receive preference over common shareholders to the extent of receiving back the par value of their preferred shares.

What we call "stocks" are actually pieces of paper that represent ownership in a company.

When corporations desire to raise money from investors for long-term working capital, they have two choices. One, they can borrow it by selling bonds. This approach means that the company will have to make regular interest payments to the bondholders, as well as pay all the money back some day. The investors play the role of lenders.

Or two, the company can sell part ownerships in the company by offering *stock*. In that case, the investors play the role of owners. They are usually entitled to voting rights (which allow them to participate in electing the board of directors who oversee the running of the company, to vote on whether to merge with or sell to another company and under what terms, etc.), and they share in any dividends the board of directors may decide to pay out. However, they will not receive any interest payments on their investments (because they are owners, not lenders) and cannot necessarily count on ever getting their investment money back. Their fortunes are tied in with the future success or failure of the company.

When you decide to invest in shares of stock, you've actually made a decision to "go into business." Just as with any business owner . . .

. . . you're last in line when it comes to dividing up the money that's (hopefully) pouring in from happy customers. Your company has to pay the suppliers that provide a variety of needed goods and supporting services. It has to buy equipment and then keep it well maintained. It has employees' salaries, related payroll taxes, health insurance, and retirement benefits to support. It needs to carry property, liability, and workman's compensation insurance. It regularly needs financial and legal services and must continually deal with government reporting requirements and other red tape.

Depending on the business, it might also need to invest large sums in product research and development, or massive sums for sales and marketing. And if it has borrowed any money for expansion or seasonal cash flow needs, it must pay the interest in full. Finally, if your company manages to pay all these bills and still has any money left over at year's end, governments at the local, state, and federal level all show up demanding a share of the profits.

All of this happens before you, the owner, receive a penny. Nobody said it would be easy. Whatever money is remaining at the very end, if any, is called the net profit. What you are hoping for is that there will be some net profits every year, and the net profits this year will be greater than the net profits last year. If these two things happen consistently—and despite the odds, they occasionally do—then you have a good chance of prospering along with the company.

Investors buy stock with the hope of either (1) sharing in the company's profits while they own the stock, or by . . .

. . . (2) eventually selling their shares for more than they paid. For example, you might receive cash payments from the company as it distributes some of its accumulated profits to the owners—that's called dividend income. Or the board of directors might decide it's better to pay little or no dividends for the time being, preferring instead to keep the money to use for the additional expansion of the company. As the company's sales and profits grow over time, the price of its shares will likely gain in value as well—that's called capital growth. Dividend income and capital growth are the two primary rewards investors hope to receive in return for the risks they assume when they become shareholders in companies.

Newcomers to stock investing are often confused as to what it is that makes the price of shares go up or down each day.

Perhaps you've seen scenes of the stock trading activity at the New York Stock Exchange (NYSE) on the news and wondered what's going on down there. Well, "what's going on" is that thousands of investors worldwide have sent buy and sell orders through their brokers for stocks listed on the NYSE, and they all collide in a kind of controlled chaos.

Come along, and I'll take you through a typical trade. Let's start by assuming that you own 100 shares of stock in McDonald's (symbol: MCD). As a shareholder, you are one of the owners of MCD. Perhaps not a major owner, but an owner nevertheless. As a part owner, you share in MCD's profits, if any. When MCD pays its shareholders a dividend, all the owners receive some money in proportion to how much of MCD they own.

As it so happens, there are new people every day who decide they, too, want to own stock in MCD. Perhaps they are portfolio managers who have extra money from investors to put to work and believe that MCD is the best value in the restaurant industry. Or, perhaps they are people who like the fact that MCD pays an annual dividend of $3.00 per share. If they buy shares for $100 each, that $3.00 represents a yield of 3.0% on their money. For whatever reason, they want to buy shares in MCD.

It is also apparent each day that some of the current part-owners of MCD decide they don't want to be part owners anymore. Let's say you're one of them. Perhaps you've decided that ever-increasing competition in the restaurant industry is going to cut into MCD's market share. Or maybe you still like MCD's competitive position in the industry but fear the economy is heading into a recession that will hurt MCD's profits and possibly cause the company to reduce its $3.00 dividend. Or maybe it has nothing to do with MCD or the economy; you just need the money for a down payment on a house, or for college tuition, or something else.

Leverage

means owning a larger amount of securities than you can pay for in cash. This is accomplished by borrowing a portion of the purchase price. Leverage can greatly magnify gains and losses, and is considered a high-risk strategy.

Short-Selling

is the practice of borrowing (from a broker) shares in a company and selling them at the current price. This is done in the hope the price will fall, allowing you to repay the borrowed shares with shares repurchased at a lower price.

Stock Exchange

is an organized marketplace where the shares of companies that meet certain criteria—with respect to company size and shares outstanding—are traded among its members. Such shares are said to be "listed" on the exchange.

Over-the-Counter

is a market where securities are traded through a dealer network rather than on an organized exchange.

Secondary Market

involves the trading of securities—on stock exchanges and over-the-counter—that takes place after the securities are originally issued. The proceeds from such transactions go to the investors who are selling, not to the companies that originally issued the securities. For example, when Ford stock is traded daily on the New York Stock Exchange, the money paid by buyers goes to the investors who are selling, not to Ford. Ford Motor Company received its money when the shares were initially sold in the "primary" market.

**Dow Jones
Industrial Average**

(DJIA) is the oldest and most
widely quoted of all market
indicators. It is an average of the
stock prices of 30 of the nation's
strongest blue-chip companies.
Unfortunately, the DJIA was
originally conceived as a "price-
weighted" index. This means
higher priced stocks have more
influence than lower priced ones.
For this reason—and the fact that
only 30 stocks are included—
some analysts consider the Dow
one of the least representative
measures of daily market action.
This is ironic in light of the
stature it enjoys.

**Standard & Poor's
500 Index**

(S&P 500) is a market-weighted
index published by Standard &
Poor's, another giant financial
news and information company.
It represents about 80% of the
market value of all NYSE-traded
stocks. Composed of 500 large
companies from all the major
sectors of the economy, it is
more representative than the
DJIA as to what the overall
market did on a certain day. As
such, it has long been used by
investing professionals as the
benchmark against which they
measure their own investment
performance results. Further
testimony to its perceived
accuracy, the U.S. Commerce
Department has selected this
index to represent the stock
market in its Index of Leading
Economic Indicators.

Russell 2000 Index

measures the performance of
2,000 smaller-size companies.
This index, not widely followed
by the general public, is the
benchmark against which the
performance of small-company
oriented mutual funds is
compared. It is to small-stock
money managers what the S&P
500 is to large-stock managers.

The point is you want to sell your shares in McDonald's. Where do you find all those new buyers I said were out there? For the most part . . .

. . . on the trading floor (or computer network) of the NYSE where part ownerships in companies are bought and sold all day. That's where your broker comes in. All the major brokerage firms are members of the NYSE, and they have connections there that enable them to carry out your trading instructions.

So, you enter an order online (or call your broker, if you're old-school) with instructions to sell your 100 shares immediately at the best price available. In the old days, that order would be sent to a floor worker, and when the market opened at 9:30 Eastern Time, he would go to the place on the floor where MCD stock is traded. When the worker would arrive, he or she would encounter workers from other firms also carrying customer instructions to sell or buy MCD shares. While this still happens, the reality is that most trading these days occurs automatically on computerized networks. Either way, for the sake of our example, on this particular morning let's assume there are many more shares of MCD ready to be sold than there are to be purchased. In other words, the current supply of MCD stock for sale is greater than the demand for MCD stock at the current price. Although MCD last traded the day before at $100, it seems the most any buyer will offer this morning is $99. Since that's the best price available, your order to sell is matched with the best available offer to buy and the transaction takes place. Immediately, the last traded MCD price shown in computerized quotes around the world changes to $99.00, recording the fact that 100 shares of McDonald's just changed hands at $99 a share.

Who decided the price of MCD should drop that morning? The free market did—that is, the collective decisions of buyers and sellers (like you) from all over the world acting in their own self-interest made it happen. At the old price of $100, there were more shares of MCD to be sold than there were buyers for them; to attract more buyers, a lower price was necessary.

Throughout the day, shares of MCD will change hands many thousands of times. The price of the very last transaction of the day will appear in the next morning's paper as the "closing price." If that closing price is less than the previous day's closing price, then MCD will be said to have gone down that day.

What does it mean when we say that "the market was up" today?

McDonald's is just one of more than 6,000 stocks for which daily price quotes are available. In order for the stock market to "go up," do all of them have to go up, or just a majority, or just a few of the important ones?

In a sense, there's no such thing as "the stock market." The term is so broad that it's misleading. It sounds so singular, as if all stocks were moving as one. In fact, they rarely do. Some stocks go soaring to the heights while others are disappearing into bankruptcy. Some represent companies that are larger and more powerful than many countries, whereas others are little more than wishful thinking disguised as businesses.

Asking what the stock market did yesterday is akin to asking what the weather was like yesterday. In some places it was unseasonably warm and others below zero; some places it was wet and others dry. To make sense of the question—and get a meaningful answer—you have to be much more precise: "What was the weather like *in Atlanta* yesterday?"

To help investors speak about the stock market with greater precision, market "averages" (or "indexes") were devised.

Stock indexes attempt to measure changes in value, over time, of a specific group of stocks. Some are very broad-based (Wilshire 5000), which means they communicate information in only the most general of terms. Others are more narrow in their focus (Dow Jones Utilities), which makes them more useful for understanding how stocks with specific characteristics are performing.

Indexes serve as benchmarks against which you can evaluate the investment performance of the stocks or mutual funds you own, but it's important to use one that is similar in content to your portfolio to be sure you're comparing "apples to apples." There are dozens of stock market indexes, but there are only five you need to become familiar with initially (see sidebars).

Owning a business carries two major risks. In our imaginary sale of McDonald's stock, we saw both come into play.

First, there's the risk that *the company you own* will fall on hard times. This is called the "business risk." In the example, this was manifested by concerns of sellers that the constant movement of new restaurant chains into the marketplace could cut into MCD's sales and profits. Or the concerns might center around poor management, technological obsolescence, a shift in cultural behavior patterns, changing government policies, or any number of things. Considering all the things that can go wrong, it's a wonder that there are a large number of successful businesses. Separating the future winners from losers requires knowledge, experience, wisdom, and a fair amount of good fortune. It is very difficult to do well on a consistent basis. If it were not, we'd all be making easy money in the stock market.

The second major risk of owning stocks is called the "market risk." This refers to those times when the stock market *as a whole* is being adversely affected by economic events. This takes place

Wilshire 5000 Composite Index

is the broadest of all the market indexes. If you had to pick one index that most closely represents the behavior of the entire U.S. market, this would be the one. It represents the value, in billions of dollars, of all the New York Stock Exchange (NYSE), American Stock Exchange (AMEX), and over-the-counter (Nasdaq) stocks for which quotes are available. The Wilshire 5000 represents approximately 99% of the total investable U.S. market. Like most stock indexes, it is "market-value weighted" (see table below).

Nasdaq Composite Index

is named for the National Association of Securities Dealers Automated Quotation system. It reflects the price behavior of the nearly 3,000 domestic and international-based companies traded on the NASDAQ system. It is regarded as an indicator of the performance of stocks of technology companies and growth companies. It is "market-value weighted."

MARKET-WEIGHTED INDEXES

A stock's total market value—also referred to as its market capitalization—is what it would cost you to buy all the shares outstanding at the current price. In an unweighted index, each stock has an equal weight. However, in a market-value weighted index, which most of the leading indexes are, each stock influences the index <u>in proportion to its total market value</u>. In this hypothetical example, Microsoft accounts for almost 60% of the movement in the index.

Company	Unweighted Index	Share Price	Total Shares Outstanding	Total Market Value	Market Value Weighted Index
McDonald's	33.3%	$98	1,000 million	$98.00 billion	21.8%
Microsoft	33.3%	$32	8,370 million	$267.84 billion	59.7%
American Express	33.3%	$75	1,106 million	$82.95 billion	15.8%
	100.0%			$448.79 billion	100.0%

during the periodic recessions that the American economy goes through. In our example, it could be that MCD as a company is doing great, but lots of people still want to sell their MCD shares because they (1) fear a recession is coming and don't want to own any stocks, (2) have already been hurt by a recession and need to sell some of their stock to raise cash for living expenses, (3) have seen a recession drive down home prices and interest rates and are going to sell their stock in MCD to come up with the down payment money for a new house, and so on and so on.

As you can see, people often sell stock shares for reasons that have nothing directly to do with the prospects of the company. Many times, the sale of stock reflects the unfolding realities in the American and world economies and the level of interest rates. At other times selling takes place for purely emotional reasons. It has been said that "fear" and "greed" are the two primary forces that continually drive market activity. It's important to understand that ultimately your shares are worth what the market says they're worth, regardless of how seemingly well or poorly the company itself may be doing.

There's a tendency to view the stock market as moving in lockstep, but behind the scenes . . .

. . . there are performance differences among various groups (as reflected in the results of leading stock indexes — see bottom of page). The rally in the stock market in 2010 was led by strength in the shares of smaller companies. What determines a "small" company versus a "large" one? Is size measured by the number of employees? The most sales? Or profits? Or perhaps the amount of assets? All of these are meaningful indications, but the measure most commonly used by investing professionals is "market capitalization" (or "market cap" for short). This merely refers to the current market value of all a company's outstanding stock. In other words, how valuable is the company? If you could buy *every one of its shares* at today's closing price, how much would it cost you? By this criteria, America's largest company in 2013 was Apple, which had a market capitalization of more than $400 billion.

Larger companies, such as those included in the Dow Jones Industrial Average and the S&P 500 index, usually are stronger in terms of market penetration and financial muscle. Their

DIFFERENT INDEXES FOLLOW DIFFERENT GROUPS OF STOCKS

Index	Characteristics	2012	2011	2010	2009	2008	2007	2006	2005
Wilshire 5000	Very broad-based; includes almost entire stock market	16.1%	0.6%	17.9%	29.4%	-37.3%	5.7%	15.9%	6.3%
Russell 3000	Very broad-based; includes almost entire stock market	16.4%	1.0%	16.9%	28.3%	-37.3%	5.1%	15.7%	6.1%
Russell 1000	Reflects the price movements of 1,000 large companies	16.4%	1.5%	16.1%	28.4%	-37.6%	5.8%	15.5%	6.3%
Standard & Poor's 500	Reflects the price movements of 500 large companies	16.0%	2.1%	15.1%	26.5%	-37.0%	5.5%	15.8%	4.9%
Dow Jones Industrials	Reflects the price movements of only 30 large companies	7.3%	5.5%	11.0%	18.8%	-33.8%	6.4%	19.1%	1.7%
Nasdaq Composite	Medium to small companies, but tech heavy	15.9%	-1.8%	16.9%	43.9%	-40.5%	9.8%	9.5%	1.4%

This table illustrates how indexes can be useful in understanding where the strength is in the market. Consider 2010 when the smaller companies in the Russell 2000 turned in far better performance numbers than the larger companies in the S&P 500. In 2011, the opposite happened. Some years there is not a material difference between the various indexes—in 2012, for example, the performance of large- and small-company stocks was similar. The Dow Jones Industrials, which includes only 30 large companies, and the Nasdaq Composite, which is heavily weighted with high-tech stocks, usually march to their own drummers.

earnings may be temporarily affected by competitive pressures, technological developments, or a recession, but they are expected to survive and prosper. They have limited potential to grow quickly in size, however; their glory "growth" days are largely behind them.

Smaller companies (sometimes called "small caps") carry higher risk because they are more easily devastated by economic setbacks. On the other hand, they have the potential to grow to 10, 20, or 50 times their present size. The time to "get in on the ground floor" is when they're still small. Of course, the worst-case loss scenarios from investing in smaller companies is greater, especially for one-year holding periods.

One group is not "better" than another. They offer different strengths which are suitable for different investing needs. Large companies typically offer higher dividends and greater price stability; smaller companies offer higher long-term growth potential. Economic factors influence whether large companies or smaller companies are popular with investors at a given time.

• **Interest rates.** In order to grow, small companies need (1) money and (2) a healthy economy. Larger companies are financially stronger. Smaller companies are more easily devastated by high interest rates or a recession; they need a healthy economy and affordable interest rates to prosper.

• **The strength of the U.S. dollar.** In 2006-2007, a weak dollar helped large multinational companies that have business abroad (often 20%–40% of total sales). A rebounding dollar cuts the other way. Lower profits for large companies make small companies look relatively more attractive. One example: during the March-September 2008 period, the dollar rallied strongly, gaining more than 12%. At the same time, the large-company S&P 500 stock index lost ground but the small-company Russell 2000 index gained about 9%.

Let's begin building a risk profile for stock funds.

As we did with bonds (page 134), we'll divide a large diamond into four smaller compartments. The idea is to place all stock funds into one of the four compartments using criteria that have the greatest bearing on risk (see diagram on page 149). In this way, we can get a quick insight into the general riskiness of a fund just by seeing in which of the four compartments it is placed. In step one, we'll take the size of the companies in the portfolio into consideration.

It's now common in the industry to use as many as *five* size categories — micro-cap (companies whose stock is worth under $250 million in market value), small-cap ($250 million to $1 billion), mid-cap ($1 to $5 billion), large-cap ($5 to $ 50 billion), and giant (over $50 billion). But Morningstar, the industry leader in measuring and reporting on mutual fund performance, doesn't go that far. They have *three* categories: small (which combines micro and small), mid, and large (which combines large and giant). To decide which funds go into which category, Morningstar first looks at all the stocks in a fund's portfolio and calculates the average (or "median") size of those companies. Then, to determine their cutoff points, their analysts employ a somewhat sophisticated methodology that adjusts to an ever-changing market. Typically, their upper limit for defining small companies hovers around $1.5 billion.

HISTORICAL RETURNS FROM MUTUAL FUNDS INVESTING IN LARGE vs SMALL COMPANIES

Source: Morningstar

Year	Large	Small
1993	10.8%	17.0%
1994	−1.3%	−1.0%
1995	31.7%	27.2%
1996	20.4%	21.2%
1997	27.0%	24.0%
1998	21.2%	−1.8%
1999	19.1%	27.8%
2000	−2.9%	5.4%
2001	−13.1%	4.4%
2002	−23.0%	−20.1%
2003	28.2%	45.4%
2004	11.0%	16.7%
2005	6.6%	6.7%
2006	13.3%	13.9%
2007	7.5%	1.9%
2008	-38.0%	-37.1%
2009	30.6%	35.2%
2010	15.0%	26.8%
2011	-0.7%	-3.7%
2012	15.0%	15.1%
5Yr Avg	1.2%	3.6%
10Yr Avg	7.0%	9.6%
20Yr Avg	7.3%	9.5%

Rather than confront you with as many as five stock risk categories based on size, let me explain the process I use for my newsletter readers. For them, I assign stock funds to either a "small" or "large" category. To do this, I combine the micro-, small-, and mid-size companies into the same "small" category. I do this because an examination of the history of the three groups shows they behave relatively similarly in terms of volatility and returns (in comparison to the large- and giant-sized companies, which are placed into the same "large" category). I'm cheating a bit here, because the differences in performance among funds in the same groups is occasionally significant. But what we lose in precision, we gain in simplicity. This is a tradeoff I have found most SMI readers are quite happy to make.

For the most part, investing strategies (or "styles") used by portfolio managers of stock funds can be grouped into two major camps—value investing and growth investing.

The "value" camp emphasizes how much you're getting for your investment dollar. This kind of manager primarily considers the present state of a company's assets, earnings, and dividends in arriving at an assessment of its stock's intrinsic value. Value managers prefer to bargain-hunt, and they often end up buying unglamorous, unappreciated companies (because that's where the bargains are). Value managers are serious about getting their money's worth. If a bear market comes along, they shouldn't get hurt as badly because many of the stocks they buy have already been beaten down in price (which is when *they* bought them) and hopefully won't fall much further. The table at left shows how well value stocks weathered the 2000-2002 bear market. The drawback is that the reason a stock is bargain priced in the first place is that it either has operating problems or is simply out of favor with investors. It often takes *years* for such stock purchases to bear fruit. This approach is the more conservative, but requires great p-a-t-i-e-n-c-e.

The other style of stock investing is the *growth* camp. The managers using this strategy would say, "Look at all the great things the company has going for it! It has a tremendous future ahead." A great deal of their success hinges on the ability to accurately predict corporate earnings a few years into the future. When measured in terms of the company's current earnings and dividends, the stock may appear expensive at present, but if the company can achieve its potential, today's share price will look like a bargain a few years from now. When they're right in their projections and they've got a good economy to work with, growth managers can hit home runs. These are the funds that can gain 50% to 100% and more in a single good year. But this approach carries more risk because growth stocks typically *are already priced* on the assumption that all the future good news will come to pass. If there are disappointments along the way, the share prices of growth stocks have a lot of room to fall.

HISTORICAL RETURNS
FROM MUTUAL FUNDS
INVESTING IN
VALUE vs GROWTH
STRATEGIES
Source: Morningstar

Year	Value	Growth
1993	15.4%	12.8%
1994	-1.1%	-1.6%
1995	28.3%	35.0%
1996	21.0%	18.7%
1997	27.3%	20.1%
1998	11.6%	18.7%
1999	14.9%	57.2%
2000	12.7%	-7.9%
2001	3.8%	-17.3%
2002	-15.8%	-27.1%
2003	33.0%	35.6%
2004	16.2%	11.3%
2005	6.7%	7.9%
2006	17.7%	9.1%
2007	-0.2%	12.9%
2008	-35.9%	-40.5%
2009	30.6%	37.2%
2010	18.0%	21.1%
2011	-2.0%	-2.4%
2012	15.5%	14.6%
5Yr Avg	2.3%	2.0%
10Yr Avg	8.0%	8.3%
20Yr Avg	7.5%	8.9%

How are you to know which style of investing a particular fund is following?

I begin with the Morningstar analysis that applies various valuation formulas (such as a stock's price-to-earnings ratio, price-to-book value ratio, and dividend yield, to name a few) to each fund's current stock portfolio. Morningstar then assigns every fund to one of three different style categories: value, growth, and "blend"(which is a combination of value and growth). To adapt this concept to our easy-to-understand risk profile approach, we do not follow Morningstar's use of a "blend" category. Instead, we assign such funds to the value category. This is done because my studies show that so-called "blend" funds, as a group, have historically moved more in harmony—in terms of risk and reward— with value funds than they have with growth funds. Again, this makes the guidelines somewhat less precise but gains in simplicity and ease of use. In general, value-oriented funds are those which own stocks with aver- age or below-average prices in relation to earnings expecta- tions, book value, cash flow, and dividends. Funds that own stocks with above-average prices in relation to these items are regarded as more growth-oriented.

BUILDING A RISK PROFILE FOR STOCK FUNDS: STEP #1

Separate funds according to the average size of the companies in which they invest

Historically, both value and growth ap- proaches have made money, but no investment style results in top performance year after year. As we go through the recurring growth-recession cycle, economic events favor different styles at different times (see performance data, far left). So, the point is not neces- sarily to try to pick one style over the other—both will have their "day in the sun" at various times. In fact, structuring your portfolio so as to include stock funds using each style is a sensible diversification move.

BUILDING A RISK PROFILE FOR STOCK FUNDS: STEP #2

Separate funds according to whether they use a value- or growth-oriented philosophy of investing

When we put it all together as shown on the right, we have four distinct types of fund portfolios from which we can choose . . .

BUILDING A RISK PROFILE FOR STOCK FUNDS: STEP #3

Combine criteria to create four distinct risk categories based on the size of companies in the portfolio and the investing style

. . . with some degree of confidence that we under- stand the investment strategy and risk of loss associated with each. The risk is lowest at the bottom of the profile (funds that invest in large companies and use a value strategy) and greatest at the top (funds that invest in small companies and use a growth strategy). Bear in mind that funds are as- signed to one of the four groups based on the most current information available. Mutual fund portfolios change on a daily basis, so it's possible for a fund to move to a different risk category periodically as its portfolio holdings change.

    The risk ladder at the bottom of this page shows the risks and rewards in recent years from investing in mutual funds assigned to each category. The numbers reflect *the average of all the funds in each group*; individual funds will vary. That's the trick, of course—picking the funds in advance that will be above average in their respective risk categories. It's a very tough thing to "beat the market" on a consistent basis as we'll discuss in the next chapter.

If you're beginning to think that the risks of owning stocks are considerable, that's good. You must . . .

    . . . have a realistic view of this! The decade of the 1990s provided such a positive economic environment for stocks that many people lost sight of the fact that stocks can lose value as well as gain it. That truth was painfully rediscovered during the bear markets of 2000-2002 and 2007-2009, the worst since the Great Depression. Let's take a look at the historical record to put things into perspective. "Major Price Trends" (page 152) shows stock price movements over the past 40+ years. I've simplified the picture by drawing in only the major price moves of 20% or more. The accompanying tables explain the letter codes on the graph, showing the amount of each move and how long it lasted. For example, the bull market indicated by the letters *A-B* gained 80% (as measured by the S&P 500 stock index) over a 44-month period.

    Notice two key elements in the graph. First, the overall trend is up. Even the long sideways movement of the 1960s and 1970s had an upward bias. This upward trend reflects the underlying strength of American free-enterprise capitalism. As long as the economy is healthy and the population expanding, businesses have a favorable environment in which they can prosper and grow. That means more profits. And more profits means more dividends being paid to the owners.

SMI'S RISK LADDER FOR STOCK FUNDS

SOURCE: MORNINGSTAR PRINCIPIA 12/31/2012

Risk Category	Standard Deviation	10 Year Avg	2012 Return	2011 Return	2010 Return	2009 Return	2008 Return	2007 Return	2006 Return	2005 Return	2004 Return	2003 Return
4 Invest By Owning: Stock Risk Category 4 Stock funds that invest in smaller companies and employ a growth-oriented strategy	19.2	9.3%	13.7%	-3.1%	25.8%	37.6%	-40.8%	11.2%	10.4%	8.4%	13.9%	42.3%
3 Invest By Owning: Stock Risk Category 3 Stock funds that invest in smaller companies and employ a value-oriented strategy	19.1	9.5%	15.1%	-4.7%	23.8%	38.6%	-36.3%	-0.4%	15.8%	7.5%	18.6%	41.1%
2 Invest By Owning: Stock Risk Category 2 Stock funds that invest in large companies and employ a growth-oriented strategy	16.4	7.2%	14.9%	-2.1%	15.7%	34.7%	-39.2%	12.6%	9.2%	7.3%	9.4%	30.1%
1 Invest By Owning: Stock Risk Category 1 Stock funds that invest in large companies and employ a value-oriented strategy	15.5	6.8%	13.8%	-0.4%	13.9%	27.3%	-36.1%	3.3%	16.2%	6.0%	12.3%	29.0%

Stock prices, ultimately, must reflect the earnings and dividends of the underlying companies.

Second, bear markets, on average, don't last as long as bull markets. They tend to be more abrupt and relatively brief. With instantaneous communication of financial news, everyone trying to act on the same news at the same time creates a traffic jam. Because markets aren't always capable of absorbing a high volume of sell orders quickly, large price markdowns are often needed in order to entice a sufficient number of potential buyers off the sidelines. After the sellers have been satisfied, the way is clear for a new bull market to begin.

To deal with these occasional bear markets, many investors are attracted to a strategy known as "market timing" where they attempt to move out of stocks . . .

. . . near market highs and buy back in near market lows. Market timing is a strategy where, in its purest form, the idea is to be invested in stock, bond, or gold mutual funds *only* during favorable market periods when prices are rising, and then moving all your capital to a haven of safety such as a money-market fund (a non-stock mutual fund that provides a temporary holding place for cash—see chapter 3) when prices are falling.

Because "buying low and selling high" is every investor's dream, market timing can sound an alluring call. But is it just another investing fantasy? Superstar investors such as Warren Buffett don't even attempt it. The *Harvard Business Review* called it "folly," and *Money* magazine frequently ridicules it. Why are these knowledgeable observers lined up against it? They say it's too difficult to be done *on a consistently* profitable basis, and that newsletter writers have grossly exaggerated its value in order to sell more newsletters. While it sounds good in theory, they submit it doesn't deliver as advertised.

Enter Mark Hulbert, publisher of *The Hulbert Financial Digest*. For nearly 30 years, Hulbert's work has served as a kind of *Consumer Reports* of the investment newsletter field. Over time, his research, performance statistics, and writing has gained a wide following. What has Mark Hulbert's years of tracking newsletter recommendations taught him about market timing? In his words:

> It is an undeniable fact that some newsletters have beaten a buy-and-hold approach with their timing. . . . The proportion of timing newsletters which have beaten the market is significant and can't be explained away as just luck. . . . One goal is to beat the market—to do better than simply buying and holding. But the other goal, which is far less widely recognized, is to reduce risk. Whatever else one might say about the market timing newsletters, this is a goal on which they can, and have, delivered. . . . More than half of the market timing newsletters beat the market on a risk-adjusted basis in each of the three time periods measured. This is a very impressive achievement.

Hulbert's findings are in line with my own experience—that market timing can indeed reduce risk while improving returns; however, it's not as easy as some would have you believe and it's often mentally and emotionally exhausting. I gained this insight the old-fashioned way—I earned it.

In 1978, a close friend and I decided to launch an investment advisory service based solely on market timing. We were one of the early entries in what eventually became a crowded field. During periods of market weakness, we performed exceedingly well for our clients due to our ability to sell out and move quickly into money market funds. When the eventual rallies occurred, we were nimble enough to get back in and enjoy most (but not all) of the ride up. Our strategy generated returns which saw our average managed account more than triple in value during our first five years of operations.

Our "glory days" faded during the bull market of the mid-1980s. Market timing doesn't work well in bull markets because the occasional moves out of the market eventually prove unnecessary, and you often find yourself buying back in at higher prices. Investors become impatient with these miscues; during bull markets they forget the need to be ready with a defensive game plan. The summer of 1987 still stands out in my memory as one of the worst periods of my professional life. I'll share the grim details with you in chapter 28.

For now, just accept my word for it that successful market timing demands enormous self-control, more than most people are conditioned to give. I'm not a proponent of average investors attempting a market timing strategy on their own. It's just too challenging emotionally. First, there's our natural greed. Peering blind-eyed into an impenetrable future, we talk ourselves into expecting the best. So if our trade turns into a loss and our timing system says to sell, we tend to hope, *Surely the market won't go straight down from*

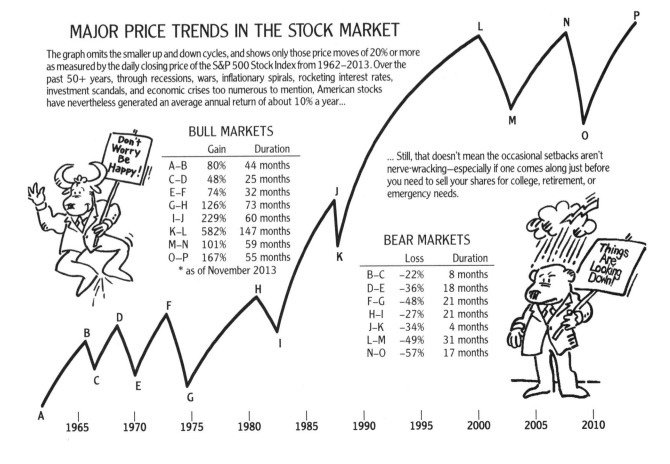

MAJOR PRICE TRENDS IN THE STOCK MARKET

The graph omits the smaller up and down cycles, and shows only those price moves of 20% or more as measured by the daily closing price of the S&P 500 Stock Index from 1962–2013. Over the past 50+ years, through recessions, wars, inflationary spirals, rocketing interest rates, investment scandals, and economic crises too numerous to mention, American stocks have nevertheless generated an average annual return of about 10% a year...

... Still, that doesn't mean the occasional setbacks aren't nerve-wracking—especially if one comes along just before you need to sell your shares for college, retirement, or emergency needs.

BULL MARKETS

	Gain	Duration
A–B	80%	44 months
C–D	48%	25 months
E–F	74%	32 months
G–H	126%	73 months
I–J	229%	60 months
K–L	582%	147 months
M–N	101%	59 months
O–P	167%	55 months

* as of November 2013

BEAR MARKETS

	Loss	Duration
B–C	–22%	8 months
D–E	–36%	18 months
F–G	–48%	21 months
H–I	–27%	21 months
J–K	–34%	4 months
L–M	–49%	31 months
N–O	–57%	17 months

Don't Worry Be Happy!

Things Are Looking Down!

1965   1970   1975   1980   1985   1990   1995   2000   2005   2010

here. There's bound to be at least a little bounce and I can get out without a loss. How many times have you decided to sell an investment "just as soon as the price gets back up to what I paid for it?"

Second, there's simple fear. Your system says "buy," but you're convinced by what you've been reading and hearing to expect further weakness instead. This causes you to lack confidence in your system's signal. You decide that if the market can prove itself by rising to Point X, *then* you'll buy. When Point X is reached, you feel better about the market's prospects, but don't want to pay the higher price. Your plan becomes, "I'll buy on a pullback to Point Y." Assume you are given this second chance and Point Y is reached. Perversely, the very weakness that you were hoping for now causes you to doubt the authenticity of the rally. You again hesitate. While you're racked with indecision, the market roars off without looking back. When last seen, you were still trying to muster the courage to re-invest.

Despite bountiful experience to the contrary, millions of investors expect to be able to select the cream of the investment crop, ride their holdings to the crest of a glorious bull market, and then wisely take their profits. They'll move to the sidelines and let other (presumably less savvy) investors suffer the frustrations of the inevitable correction that follows. Unfortunately, they're living, like children, in a fantasy world.

Many would object at this point and say, "I know that's unrealistic. I don't try to do that." But what then is the motivation, conscious or subconscious, behind the most common questions investors ask, such as: *When* will the rise in interest rates stop? Where is the market headed *next*? Should I buy tech stocks *now*? These are the questions the financial media constantly raise, appealing to our natural desire to make profitable decisions. Yet, they are largely irrelevant to the investor with his eyes fixed on the distant horizon. The long-term investor is asking a different set of questions: Is it even appropriate for me to take on the risks of investing in securities that fluctuate in value? If so, how should I divide my capital between the different kinds of investments (stocks, bonds, real estate, etc.)? What are the growth prospects for the next five years, both in America and various overseas economies? Am I getting good value for my money?

We need to say, along with the apostle Paul, *"When I was a child, I talked like a child, I thought like a child, I reasoned like a child. When I became a man, I put childish ways behind me"* (1 Corinthians 13:11). To be profitable, we need to put away childish things—such as demanding immediate gratification—and invest by using our reason rather than our emotions.

Every successful investing strategy requires self-discipline.

Self-discipline is the ability to do the right thing at the right time every time. By the "right" thing, I don't mean always making the most profitable decision. That's

---

Price/Earnings Ratio

The price-to-earning ratio (P/E) is a popular value benchmark used by investors to assess whether a stock is reasonably priced. It's calculated by dividing the price of a stock by its reported earnings for the past four quarters. If your favorite stock, Can't Miss, Inc., is selling for $32 a share and has reported earnings for the past 12 months of $2 per share, it is said to have a P/E of 16 ($32/$2). Historically, a P/E ratio between 10 and 20 has been considered "normal." The P/Es of growth stocks tend to be considerably above-average while those of value stocks are below-average.

When evaluating a stock, it's helpful to determine the current P/E in relation to its historical range. For example, if a stock's P/E over the past 15 years has ranged between 15 and 30 and it's currently at 28, you know the stock is relatively expensive at present.

A problem with using earnings as a guide to stock valuation is that they are very susceptible to manipulation by the company. Accounting principles and IRS rules offer a variety of ways to deal with depreciation, research and development expenses, marketing expenses, inventory costs, and so on. Another problem with using earnings is that optimistic investors often tend to justify higher stock prices by using projected future earnings rather than current earnings when computing the P/E.

impossible. Rather, I mean the right thing is to ignore the distractions of news events and well-intentioned advice and stay with your plan. This is more difficult than it sounds because the markets don't always offer positive reinforcement. In the short run, you can lose money following your plan or you can make money deviating from it. When that happens, "good" behavior is penalized and "bad" behavior is rewarded. It weakens your commitment to following your strategy. If this continues, it isn't long before you're back where you started—making every decision on a what-seems-best-at-the-moment basis. Unless you have a rare and natural gift for investing, that's the last place you want to be.

In the next section, I'm going to offer you a strategy designed to minimize the wear and tear on your emotions by making it easier for you to exercise self-discipline and do "the right thing." It's been my experience that:

• **Doing the right thing is easier when the strategy is simple.** Our Just-the-Basics portfolios use relatively few ingredients, and I use plain-English explanations to tell you what to do and why we're doing it. The simplicity lets you see how everything fits together, so you can feel more comfortable making decisions.

• **Doing the right thing is easier when the rules are clear-cut.** Just-the-Basics offers specific guidelines that determine your mix of stocks and bonds and fund selections. You can have more confidence when you know you're making buy/sell decisions that fit into a coherent plan.

• **Doing the right thing is easier when it's not time consuming.** You don't need to read *The Wall Street Journal*, monitor the mutual-fund rankings, keep daily charts, calculate moving averages, or anything else. Just-the-Basics requires only an hour or two once a year, usually in January, to perform a little routine maintenance.

• **Doing the right thing is easier when you know you're in for the long haul.** You needn't be overly concerned about the quarterly performance in your Just-the-Basics portfolio. There will be occasional setbacks. But we're realistic and understand that's going to happen from time to time. Investing often involves taking two steps forward and one step back. But that needn't alarm us because we've got time on our side.

This book, as well as my monthly newsletter, gets its name from 2 Timothy 1:7. In the New King James Version, it reads: *"For God has not given us a spirit of fear; but of power and of love and of a sound mind."* It's interesting that the New International Version translates "sound mind" as "self-discipline." We can look forward to maturing in our faith beyond childish things because *"His divine power has given us everything we need for life and godliness through our knowledge of him who called us by his own glory and goodness. . . . For this very reason, make every effort to add to your faith . . . self-control"* (2 Peter 1:3, 5-6). ◆

13

Selecting the Portfolio Mix Best Suited to Your Risk-Taking Temperament and Current Season of Life

I. **All of us have "money personalities" that reflect our attitudes toward earning, spending, saving, and investing money.**

   A. Psychologist Kathleen Gurney has conducted nationwide surveys and found that people have a "financial self" and use money as a means to gain security, freedom, love, respect, power, and happiness.

   B. Gurney notes nine distinct money personality types; I have combined several in developing the four investing temperaments in this chapter.

II. **Meet the Preserver, Researcher, Explorer, and Daredevil.**

   A. Each of these investing personalities reflects a different emotional reaction to risk taking.

   B. A series of "attitudinal snapshots" should enable you to select the one that is closest to the way you feel about financial security and the tradeoffs between risk and reward.

III. **For financial planning purposes, life can be divided into four phases.**

   A. Laying the foundation: Typically runs up into your 40s.

   B. Accumulating assets: Your 40s and 50s.

   C. Preserving assets: Your 60s and into your 70s.

   D. Distributing assets: Age 75 and beyond.

IV. **These two factors—your temperament and your current "season of life"—come together to determine how much risk is appropriate for your situation.**

   A. The "controlling your risk" matrix presented in this chapter shows how I suggest dividing your investments between stocks (investing-by-owning) and bonds (investing-by-lending).

   B. This matrix provides a rational basis for dealing with the constant tension between the need for capital growth and the fear of capital loss that confronts every investor.

"Not only do we have a physical self, an emotional self, and a social self, but we have a financial, or money, self.

"This money self is an integral part of our behavioral repertoire and influences the way we interact with our money. In other words, your money personality is a major factor in how you utilize your money. Most of us fail to realize the extent to which our money personality impacts our financial habits and affects the degree of satisfaction we get from what money we have. There is an inseparable link between our unconscious feelings about money and the way in which we earn it, spend it, save it, and invest it."

This observation is made by Kathleen Gurney in her book *Your Money Personality*. She adds that psychologists believe that money is a kind of "emotional currency" that symbolizes many of our unconscious needs and desires, among them:

- **Security** (If I have enough money, I'll always be safe. No person and no catastrophe can harm me.)

- **Freedom** (If I have enough money, I can freely choose my jobs or choose not to work; my options are open.)

- **Love** (If I have enough money, more people will care about me. Money makes relationships a lot easier.)

- **Respect** (If I have enough money, everyone will recognize that I have merit, that I accomplished what I set out to do.)

- **Power** (If I have enough money, nobody will ever push me around. I will be strong and have total control over my life.)

- **Happiness** (If I have enough money, I will truly be happy. I can finally relax and enjoy life.)

Dr. Gurney suggests that as many as nine different investment personality types exist (which she discusses in detail). To simplify matters, I have combined them in order to consider just four. There's nothing "official" about these. I devised them simply to help make this process easier and perhaps a little more fun. We all probably have some elements of each of the four types within us, so don't think I'm saying that any one type will fit you perfectly. But you may find that you identify with one temperament more than the other three. If so, you can learn something about yourself from this exercise.

I call the most aggressive investors "Daredevils." They enjoy the investment "fast lane" . . .

. . . and are often found playing the markets on a short-term basis. They have plenty of self-confidence. The markets for new issues, stock and index options, and commodity futures would be areas of interest to Daredevils due to the opportunities they offer to make a lot of money quickly.

They often resist advice to diversify into more prudent, less colorful investments. Yet, even Daredevils need a solid, conservative base to counter their occasional impulsiveness and higher-risk tendencies. If they're not careful, they'll reach their retirement years with little to show for a lifetime of wheeling and dealing.

Daredevils could really benefit from the Just-the-Basics approach where we emphasize putting first things first. The use of highly diversified mutual fund portfolios, while not as high-stakes as some of their other investments, would bring a much-needed balance to their overall investment picture. It would go a long way toward countering their natural inclinations to "go for it."

"Explorers" are fascinated by the money-making potential of investing . . .

. . . but if they lack confidence in choosing the best path, they often take refuge in the safety of following the crowd. They are attracted to the latest trendy investments that are dominating the news. The "thrill of the hunt" is the fun part for them.

Explorers can be impetuous and often hop aboard a new investment without fully understanding just how serious the risks might be. As a result, their holdings are frequently a random assortment of moderate- to high-risk "good deals" collected over the years. Such a portfolio likely lacks balance and has no long-term focus. Explorers would benefit from a systematic, controlled-risk way of moving toward their long-term goals.

"Researchers" also tend toward caution, but their self-confidence enables them to overcome their concerns . . .

. . . if they feel they have done sufficient investigation. Simply reading in this book that a certain mutual fund is recommended may not be good enough for Researchers; they may want to know more about that mutual fund and why I recommend it. They are willing to immerse themselves in facts and figures in order to get a thorough understanding of the strengths and drawbacks of the investments they are considering.

They can easily postpone making commitments because they want more information. Up to a point, this caution serves them well. If overdone, their ability to make decisions is paralyzed because they will never know for sure that they have all the relevant information. Researchers appreciate the self-discipline imposed by following an objective set of guidelines. In addition, they have the long-term mind-set and patience necessary to stay with their game plan for many years in spite of occasional setbacks.

The Psychology of Investing

Most people are willing to invest time and expense in gaining a good understanding of market fundamentals (knowledge) and work at assembling that knowledge into a proven strategy (technique). Unfortunately, these are not the only attributes needed for success—if they were, we'd all be millionaires!

The quality that separates the top professionals from the rest of us is one that takes years to develop: emotional self-control. Our emotions interact with news and market events in ways that incline us to act at exactly the wrong time. We all want to "buy low and sell high," but experience shows that most investors do the opposite. That is likely because, emotionally, it's quite difficult to "buy low." The reason that prices are low is that the news is bad and people are pessimistic. They become fearful about the future. Investors feel pressured, and under pressure, emotions tend to dictate our actions.

As our fears increase, so do our anxieties, and we can become paralyzed. We know what we should do, but we "tighten up." Athletes call it "choking." A short putt to a golfer or free throw to a basketball player is no big deal in a friendly pick-up game. But with huge television audiences looking on and millions of dollars at stake, it's a far different story. Why? Emotions.

If you'd like to know more about the psychological side of investing, you might enjoy a book by market veteran Justin Mamis called The Nature of Risk. It offers interesting insights into why we behave as we do in making investing decisions. This is not casual reading, so be prepared for your thinking to be stimulated and challenged.

"Preservers" tend to worry about their investments . . .

. . . because the risk of losing their capital is very real to them. As a result, they are usually quite cautious, favoring CDs, government bonds, and only the highest-quality blue-chip stocks. This approach helps them to preserve their wealth but may not provide enough growth to achieve reasonable performance goals.

Sometimes their desire to be cautious makes it difficult for them to make any investment decisions at all. If they can find advisers in whom they have confidence, they are frequently willing to rely on them heavily to assist with investment decisions. Realizing that they are safety conscious and must accept lower returns as part of the trade-off for safety, they usually have realistic expectations with regard to how much they can reasonably hope to make.

If you're a Preserver, the basic philosophy underlying all of your investing decisions is to preserve capital. You would agree with Warren Buffett, a legendary investor of our time, when he said there were only two really important rules of investing. Rule #1 is "Don't lose any money," and Rule #2 is *"Never* forget Rule #1."

You're now ready to select the investment temperament that best describes your attitudes toward . . .

. . . monetary risk-taking and its possible rewards. On pages 160-161, you'll find each of the four investment temperaments listed along with their corresponding attitudes on risk and profit expressed in a variety of ways. Read each of them carefully and thoughtfully. You may want to pencil in checkmarks next to the statements that you identify with. Which of the four temperaments has the most check marks? (If you're married, you should ask your spouse to study them as well.)

It's been my experience that most people have little trouble seeing themselves in one of the four. The identification is usually almost instantaneous. However, if you narrow it down to two and have trouble deciding between them, my suggestion is to select the one on the right, the more conservative one (risk decreases as you move from left to right). Err on the side of safety and prudence rather than risk-taking.

Once you identify your money personality, I encourage you to stay within the boundaries it implies if at all possible. James Dale Davidson and Sir William Rees-Mogg, in their best-selling investment book, *Blood in the Streets,* stated well what usually happens to those who play a high-stakes game for which they are temperamentally unsuited:

Nothing is more surely condemned to failure than a high-risk strategy pursued by a low-risk man; he will always flinch at the point before the strategy has succeeded, and will throw away his potential gains in an attempt to leap back to the security he actually prefers. . . . To be a successful investor you have to be right, but in your own way. It is not only a matter of knowing yourself. It is even more important to be yourself.

There's always a tension between our *need for capital growth* **and our** *fear of capital loss.*

Obviously, it would be great if we could make all that we need on our investments without taking any risk. A relatively small number of multimillionaires might be able to live comfortably off the interest paid by their T-bills, but the rest of us aren't so fortunate. Without taking away from the importance of "being yourself" as stated above, we must sometimes learn how to live with a little more risk than we would like.

Many readers of my newsletter became so committed to their comfort levels that they were not making sufficient progress in building their capital. To remedy this, I developed guidelines for helping them decide how to balance their holdings between stocks and bonds. They're based on the "seasons of life" through which we all travel. The four temperaments still play an important role, but a new dimension has been added—the need for capital growth at various phases of life:

Phase 1: Laying the foundation. This is the starting point for most of us. We spend the greater part of our 20s and 30s acquiring transportation and a residence, paying off student and other loans, and building a contingency reserve. There may not be much in the way of monthly surplus left to invest for retirement (which is still 25 or more years away). The money we do put aside can be invested aggressively because we have a very long time frame in which to work. This is the phase where we can afford to take our greatest risks.

Phase 2: Accumulating assets. Most of us experience our peak earning years during our 40s and 50s. At the same time, our expenses should be falling as the house gets paid for and the kids are raised. Retirement is now more than a distant concept; we see it as an economic reality that we will actually experience. Fine-tuning our financial plans and following a workable strategy takes on a new importance.

Phase 3: Preserving assets. Unbelievably, retirement is just around the corner

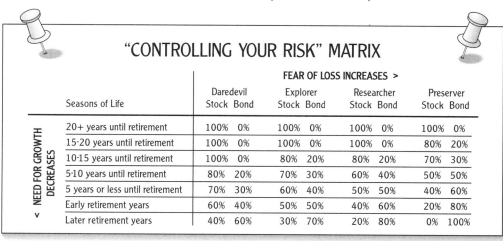

"CONTROLLING YOUR RISK" MATRIX

		Daredevil Stock	Daredevil Bond	Explorer Stock	Explorer Bond	Researcher Stock	Researcher Bond	Preserver Stock	Preserver Bond
	Seasons of Life				FEAR OF LOSS INCREASES >				
	20+ years until retirement	100%	0%	100%	0%	100%	0%	100%	0%
	15-20 years until retirement	100%	0%	100%	0%	100%	0%	80%	20%
NEED FOR GROWTH DECREASES	10-15 years until retirement	100%	0%	80%	20%	80%	20%	70%	30%
	5-10 years until retirement	80%	20%	70%	30%	60%	40%	50%	50%
	5 years or less until retirement	70%	30%	60%	40%	50%	50%	40%	60%
	Early retirement years	60%	40%	50%	50%	40%	60%	20%	80%
	Later retirement years	40%	60%	30%	70%	20%	80%	0%	100%

The Daredevil

The Explorer

The Daredevil	The Explorer
❏ If I believe an investment has a chance of really paying off big, I'm willing to take the chance that I could lose a large part (maybe even all) of my money.	❏ I'm willing to take a greater-than-average amount of risk in return for the possibility of having my portfolio grow substantially.
❏ I can accept losses in the value of my investments, even if they continue for several consecutive years. The end result is all that really matters!	❏ I can accept an occasional year where I lose money on my investments, but I wouldn't like it if I had two of them back-to-back.
❏ I almost always prefer to make my investing decisions on my own.	❏ I occasionally make my investing decisions all on my own, but usually I prefer to let my broker bring me what he thinks are his best ideas.
❏ The amount of current income I receive from an investment is not a factor in my decision making.	❏ It would be desirable to receive some current income from my investments, but I don't insist upon it in every case.
❏ Inflation is the number one threat. I think it's essential that you beat inflation, and that means you don't have the luxury of playing it safe all the time.	❏ Inflation is a genuine concern, so I'm willing to invest where there's a good chance of getting a "real" return even though there's a little more risk.
❏ I've had some super results on a few high-risk situations. Of course, I've had my share of big losers, too. To really make money, you've got to risk money.	❏ I think exploring new financial territory is exciting. When I hear about the latest "hot" investment area, I like to take a look.
❏ For me to risk 10% of my net worth in an investment that seemed to have a 90% chance of success, the potential profit would have to be at least equal to the amount I put at risk.	❏ For me to risk 10% of my net worth in an investment that seemed to have a 90% chance of success, the potential profit would have to be at least twice as much as the amount I put at risk.
❏ I suppose I'm optimistic (and a tad impulsive at times), but I don't usually worry about my investment decisions once they're made.	❏ I don't have time to bury myself in the details like some people. I keep my ear to the ground and think I have pretty good intuitive insights.
❏ It's important to me, perhaps even a source of pride, that my portfolio does better than the stock market over the course of an economic cycle.	❏ I do tend to compare the results in my portfolio with what the overall stock market did. It's a good feeling to know that you "beat" the market.
❏ If a stock doubled in price a year after I bought it, I'd buy some more shares in that company.	❏ If a stock doubled in price a year after I bought it, I'd hold on and hope for still more gains.

The Researcher

The Preserver

The Researcher	The Preserver
❏ I'm fairly conservative, but am willing to take a greater-than-average amount of risk with part of my portfolio in order to boost its growth potential.	❏ I'm very conservative, and am much more concerned about protecting what I already have than in taking risks to make it grow.
❏ I can handle the month-to-month ups and downs of investing, but I wouldn't want to end up losing any money for the entire year.	❏ It's important to my peace of mind to have stable, consistent year-to-year results.
❏ I prefer to make my own investing decisions, but am always open to ideas from the "experts" which I search out in magazines, books, and television/radio.	❏ Making investing decisions all on my own makes me a little nervous. I tend to rely a lot on others to help me.
❏ It's fairly important that I receive current income from my investments, but I'm willing to accept some uncertainty as to the amount.	❏ The amount of current income I receive from an investment is important to me; if possible, I'd like to know the amount in advance.
❏ Inflation is a genuine concern, but gains lower than the rate of inflation are acceptable if it means I can keep my risk down.	❏ Preserving my capital and knowing how much current income I'll receive are much more important to me than beating inflation.
❏ I want to make my decisions based on a solid understanding of all the facts. I don't believe in investing in something just because everyone else is doing it.	❏ News about such things as the bank failures, our trade deficits, or the losses in "junk bonds" are a little scary and confusing.
❏ For me to risk 10% of my net worth in an investment that seemed to have a 90% chance of success, the potential profit would have to be at least four times as much as the amount I put at risk.	❏ No amount of potential profit is worth risking the loss of 10% of my net worth.
❏ Once I make a decision, I have a lot of confidence in it, which enables me to stay with it even if others around me are changing their minds.	❏ Making investment decisions is hard for me; I'm never quite sure I have all the facts. I wish I could be sure what the best investments are for me.
❏ I keep an eye on what the overall stock market is doing during the year. Naturally, I'd like to do even better, but it's not a major factor in my thinking.	❏ It's irrelevant to me whether my portfolio does better than the stock market over the course of an economic cycle.
❏ If a stock doubled in price a year after I bought it, I'd sell half my shares and lock in part of my profits.	❏ If a stock doubled in price a year after I bought it, I'd sell all my shares.

(or already here)! Our need for preserving capital and generating current income has risen, and if we've done our job well, our need for additional growth in our capital base has abated. Our time horizon, which used to allow us the luxury of decades to bounce back from bear market losses, has shrunk dramatically. The situation calls for more fixed-income investments and fewer stocks.

THE PERSONALITY TRAITS UNDERLYING THE FOUR TEMPERAMENTS

The temperaments were developed by factoring in one's willingness to lose money in the quest to make more money. You might say it's a question of whether optimism or caution is the governing emotion.

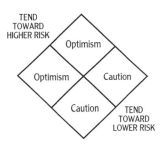

Then, we divide the diamond to show the levels of self-confidence in making one's own financial decisions versus the tendency to rely on others.

Phase 4: Distributing assets. We're in the home stretch of life, and can envision it won't be too long before we'll experience the joy of what Scripture means when it teaches that "to be away from the body" is to be "at home with the Lord." As much as prudently possible, we'll want to give away our surplus capital to our children and the Lord's work. At this point, unnecessary risk-taking should be avoided.

Locate your investing personality in the "controlling your risk" matrix on page 159. Then, select the financial season of life that best describes your situation. If your recommended stock/bond mix requires a greater commitment to stocks than you've been comfortable with in the past, you've got a judgment call to make. You can use a dollar-cost-averaging approach (see chapter 15) for making the transition from where you are now to where you want to go.

The matrix reflects my personal sense of risk. Some investment advisers might encourage you to take more risk than I suggest, others might recommend less. All of us are being arbitrary to a degree. The point is that as the time to begin drawing on the investments draws ever nearer, you should move increasingly to a more conservative approach. If you have 10 or more years, you can afford to take more risk if you want to—but do you want to? It's up to you.

Another very important reminder: After you select guidelines that you feel comfortable with, *stick with them!* There will be temptations from your broker, well-meaning friends, the media, and your own desires for higher returns that will encourage you to "make an exception" or abandon your guidelines altogether. You do so at your own peril.

Being realistic in your expectations is an important part . . .

. . . of your investment planning process. Making assumptions (often known as "wild guesses") about the future is an unavoidable part of planning and budgeting. One fundamental question that needs answering is: "How much of a return can I reasonably expect from my investment portfolio?"

It's important that your answer be grounded in reality and not wishful thinking. To this end, on page 173 I provide annual performance data for the Just-the-Basics portfolios. Bear in mind that the past 20 years saw both periods of stock market prosperity (2003-2007, 2009-2013) as well as the worst bear markets since the Great Depression (2000-2002, 2008). These cycles are common in stock market investing, yet the performance numbers for

A Strange Sounding Bit of Wisdom: Make Sure Your Decision-Making Is Inside-Out

One of the more counterintuitive propositions that I regularly put forth in these pages is the idea that one's investing decisions usually can be made with little regard for what's currently going on in the investment markets. Let me once again make my case, and then we'll apply it to the question of deciding whether now is a good time to sell some or all of your stock holdings.

Typically, where do ideas for your investment decisions originate? For many investors, the starting point of the process is found in the impersonal "outside" world of current events, magazine articles, and brokers' recommendations. Their decisions are primarily guided by outside considerations. As they respond to all the data thrown at them—sometimes buying, sometimes selling—their personal "inside" financial worlds take shape. Their thinking is "outside-in." They need a continual stream of news and information to provide stimulation and provoke them to action. Decision-making would be impossible without it.

For other investors, the starting point of their decision-making is "inside" information. The focus is on their own financial needs and a personalized long-term strategy designed to meet those needs. Their buy/sell decisions are made based on what's required to make sure their financial holdings are in accord with the game plan. The "outside" world of investment professionals comes into the picture only because assistance is needed in executing decisions already made. This is "inside-out" thinking, where decisions are primarily shaped by inside considerations. Thus, current market fads, pressures and so-called expert opinions are largely irrelevant to inside-out investors. As you have probably guessed by now, I'm encouraging you to be an inside-out thinker.

In other words, make your investing decisions as you do other consumer purchasing decisions. For example, if your family has grown to the point you need a spacious minivan to haul everyone around, you wouldn't buy a new Mini Cooper instead merely because an article in Money magazine said they're exceptionally "hot" at the moment. Or, if you need a medicine that lowers your blood pressure, you wouldn't let a glowing recommendation from your druggist convince you to bring home the leading antihistimine for allergies instead. It would be foolish to let irrelevant external influences (outside-in thinking) steer you into making such inappropriate purchases. Instead, you make your decisions based on your needs at the time, irrespective of what the marketplace would like to sell you.

This is obvious, you say. Yet, many people have a difficult time applying this consumer mindset to their investing decisions. One of the most frequently-asked questions I receive is a variant of "The market seems overvalued, and I've read where many experts are sounding an alarm. Is this a good time to sell my stocks?" These folks may decide whether to reduce their stock holdings depending on how volatile the market has been, what the business magazines say, what the Federal Reserve may do to interest rates, or—heaven help them—what my opinion might be.

Outside-in thinking will never tell you whether it's a "good time" to sell stocks because no one knows what the market will do in coming months (as evidenced by the continual reporting of conflicting opinions from Wall Street's bulls and bears).

Here's a checklist an inside-out investor might run through in deciding the "Is it a good time to sell?" question.

☐ Is my financial foundation still rock solid? That is, am I still debt-free (chapter 1) and is my contingency fund still sufficient (chapter 3)? If not, I should sell enough stock to repair the cracks in my foundation.

☐ Are my earlier assumptions about my lifetime earnings, retirement and lifestyle goals, health needs, life expectancy and emotional tolerance of risk still acceptable (chapters 13,19)? If not, perhaps I should reconsider the way I have divided my portfolio between stocks and bonds.

☐ Are my protective boundaries still in place (chapter 27)? If not, what adjustments should I make at this time?

☐ Can I commit the monies I have at risk in my stock holdings for at least another five years? If not, how long can I commit? Are the risks of loss for such a time frame acceptable (see table on page 274)?

☐ Am I meeting my giving goals? Am I now in a position so I can give even more? Perhaps I should give some of my stocks that have gone up in value to my church or favorite mission organization (chapter 25).

☐ Has my portfolio grown enough so that I can now achieve my long-term goals with less risk? If so, perhaps I should convert a portion of my stock holdings into fixed-income securities (chapter 22).

Notice that the focus is on the personal needs and circumstances of the individual, not on the headlines of the day which almost never tell you anything that will enhance the quality of your decision-making. While current events may provoke you to run through your personal list of review questions, they should not dictate the answers.

From the Sound Mind Investing newsletter.
To learn more about the monthly SMI newsletter, visit our website at www.soundmindinvesting.com.

the entire 20 years were roughly in line with the stock market's *average* historical return of about 9% per year—the 100% stock portfolio averaged 8.6% from 1993-2012. Dramatic ups and downs in the market, such as the mania that led to the dot.com bubble and was followed by the severe 2000-2002 bear market, tend to cancel each other out . . . but not completely. The stock market, due to the strength and resilience of our free enterprise economy, has a long-term upward bias.

To provide a guide as to what you might expect in the future, I would suggest that you have performance expectations that are in line with the 20-year averages shown, but recognize that those gains come in fits and starts, not smoothly year after year. We know that if a penny is tossed 1,000 times, it's likely to land heads up about half the time. However, you can't count on these probabilities asserting themselves if you toss a penny *only twice*. It could easily come up tails twice in a row. In the same way, the longer you stay with your investing program, the more likely you are to get these kinds of returns.

THE RESULT IS FOUR RISK PROFILES WITH DISTINCT STYLES OF INVESTMENT DECISION-MAKING

TEND TOWARD HIGHER RISK

Daredevil
Optimistic and exhibits self-confidence in decision-making

Explorer
Optimistic, still tends to rely on "experts" for investing advice

Researcher
Cautious, but exhibits self-confidence in decision-making

Preserver
Cautious, tends to rely on "experts" for investing advice

OPTIMISM

SELF-CONFIDENCE

CAUTION

RELY ON "EXPERTS"

TEND TOWARD LOWER RISK

What the next decade will produce in the way of dramatic change in the financial markets . . .

. . . is anyone's guess. The 1970s gave us listed stock options and the birth of money-market funds. The 1980s produced a veritable explosion of offerings in the fixed income investments and mutual fund industries. The 1990s ushered in the era of the Internet and on-line transactions with banks and brokers, and ended with a buying mania (and subsequent crash) centered around the "new economy" dot.com stocks. And the first decade of the 21st century saw a dramatic market selloff following 9/11, followed by an exceptionally strong bull market that was ended by a crisis in subprime mortgages and massive government intervention to stablize the financial markets. After a period of severe market weakness in 2008, the market roared to life and, as of this writing in late-2013, hasn't looked back.

But in terms of the potential risks and rewards for the average investor, the importance of the advantages offered by the Just-the-Basics strategy—sufficient diversification for safety and a risk level designed to fit your individual situation—hasn't changed. Assemble a portfolio tailored to your financial personality and long-term goals, and peace-of-mind investing can become a reality for you. ◆

Choosing an Investment Strategy

Jesus went on to tell them a parable, because...the people thought
that the kingdom of God was going to appear at once. He said:
"A man of noble birth went to a distant country to have himself
appointed king and then to return. So he called ten of his servants...
'Put this money to work,' he said, 'until I come back.' "

Luke 19:11-13

"I'm sorry, but Mr. Hutton left very strict orders
he couldn't take any drop-in appointments with clients today."

14

CHAPTER PREVIEW

A Winning Long-Term Strategy
Designed to Keep Pace with the Market

I. **Historical data shows that, over time, it's common for a majority of professional money managers to fall short in "beating the market."**

   A. A "loser's game" is that kind of competition in which the winner is determined primarily by mistakes made by the loser *rather* than the skill of the winner. Investing can be approached as a loser's game.

   B. The path to success when playing a loser's game is to play a passive, patient game where the emphasis is on minimizing one's mistakes.

II. **The mutual-fund world offers a product perfectly suited to playing a loser's game. It's called an "index" fund.**

   A. An index fund doesn't try to beat the market. Its goal is to *equal* the market by replicating the performance of a major market index, such as the S&P 500.

   B. The growth in index funds has been explosive. Pension funds, insurance companies, and other large institutional investors, recognizing how difficult it is to regularly outperform the market, have placed huge sums in index funds.

III. **Our Just-the-Basics strategy uses no-load stock and bond index ETFs in various combinations to create six portfolios with varying degrees of risk.**

   A. Your most important investing decision is how you divide your money among stocks, bonds, and cash reserves. This "allocation" decision has far more influence on your final investment results than any other single factor.

   B. An advantage of Just-the-Basics is that its primary focus is on this all-important asset-allocation decision rather than on which mutual funds to purchase. The Just-the-Basics strategy also helps guard against sub-par investment returns. Other advantages include lower expenses, fewer taxable distributions, and easy accessibility.

IV. **Just-the-Basics also includes a provision for investing outside the U.S. In this chapter, we discuss the pros and cons of adding an international fund to your portfolio.**

Traditional money management is founded on the questionable assumption that . . .

. . . professional managers can consistently beat the market through research, intelligent risk-taking, and exploiting the mistakes of others. But what if this assumption is false?

We'll begin our study with an analogy from the world of tennis. In my younger days, I spent many an afternoon risking bodily injury and public humiliation on the tennis courts. As a beginner, I concentrated my efforts on trying to learn how to hit the ball correctly. My pregame strategy had little to do with specific plans for hitting the ball to my opponent's forehand or backhand or placing it shallow or deep. My primary concern was pretty simple: Try to keep the ball in bounds! I lost many more points due to the mistakes *I* made than as a result of the actions of my opponents.

In his book on tennis strategy, *Extraordinary Tennis for the Ordinary Player*, Dr. Simon Ramo describes the kind of amateur tennis I play as a "loser's game." By that he means it is the kind of competition *in which the winner is determined by the behavior of the loser*. The amateur doesn't win by defeating his opponent; he wins by letting his opponent defeat himself.

Ramo contrasted this with the "winner's game" played at the professional tennis level. In professional matches, we are accustomed to seeing consistently precise serves, stunning recoveries, and long, dramatic rallies. Eventually, one player takes a calculated risk and attempts to put his opponent away with an exceptionally powerful or well-placed shot. At the expert level, it is the successful winning of points that drives the action and determines the outcome. In a winner's game, the outcome is determined by the *correct actions of the winner*. In a loser's game, the outcome is determined by *mistakes made by the loser*.

OK, so what does this have to do with selecting a mutual-fund portfolio? In his highly acclaimed book, *Winning the Loser's Game* (McGraw-Hill, 2013), money-manager Charles D. Ellis applied Ramo's work to the investing arena. When Ellis studied the investment markets, he saw that it was not uncommon for a majority of the managers of stock and bond mutual funds to underperform their respective markets:

> *Over one year, 60 percent of funds underperform; over 10 years, 70 percent underperform, and over 20 years, about 80 percent underperform their chosen benchmarks.... Unhappily, the basic assumption that most institutional investors can outperform the market is false.*

In their efforts to "score" for their shareholders, they were hitting the ball into the net or out of bounds far too often.

Believing that investing had become a loser's game, Ellis drew this conclusion: Just as the path to victory in amateur tennis is to play a passive, patient game while letting your opponent take the risks, so the logical strategy for the amateur investor should be the same game plan of avoiding mistakes.

There are advantages to playing a loser's game.

Most investors, consciously or subconsciously, are caught up in playing a winner's game. They're trying to "beat the market." They buy financial magazines and investment newsletters that offer a dizzying array of stock recommendations and mutual-fund rankings, and they feel they must respond to fast-breaking news events and trade with a short-term perspective. Theirs is an active strategy where they work harder and take extra risks in what is usually a futile attempt to "win." One investor/writer expressed his frustration over the investing rat race this way:

> I could keep my money in stocks, either in many companies or in just a few good ones; I could invest abroad or bring my money home; I could buy and hold or entrust portfolio choices to hot mutual funds; I could shift to bonds; I could prepay my mortgage; or, last — and in the view of Wall Street wisdom, unutterably stupid — I could simply sit on my cash. Like other investors, I balance my fears against my greed, my distrust in easy money against my belief in the eternal upward movement of the market. Like others, I tramp from sage to wizard to priest, gathering portents and signs, each more bewildering than the last, always believing that ahead lies a successful end. In other words, I am a fool. (Ted C. Fishman, "The Bull Market in Fear," Harper's magazine, October 1995.)

In a loser's game, the strategy is more passive (and relaxing!). The path to victory lies in minimizing one's mistakes and being patient. This describes our Just-the-Basics portfolios where we refuse to play the performance game. Instead, we simply invest in selected "index" funds, which, by definition, are going to give us returns similar to the market as a whole.

An index fund is a special kind of mutual fund that has only one objective: to mirror the performance of a market index . . .

. . . such as the Standard & Poor's 500 stock index. The portfolio manager invests in the same securities that are used in calculating the index. The fund will make or lose money to the same extent that the index after which it's patterned shows gains or losses. For example, if the S&P 500 gains (or loses) 15% in a given year, then any S&P 500 index fund should also gain (or lose) about 15% that year. From an investing point of view, what could be simpler?

The growth in the number and size of index funds has been explosive over the past 25 years, thanks to the interest shown by pension funds, insurance companies, and other big institutional investors. More than $1.6 *trillion* has been invested in stock index funds, and much of that is invested in S&P 500-type index funds because it is still the benchmark against which most investors compare themselves. All of this "smart" money going into index funds shows how difficult it can be to outperform the market. If it were a simple matter to invest in the right stocks (or bonds) at the right time, everyone would be wealthy.

An investment in an index fund is another way of saying, "It is so hard to consistently do better than the market averages! I'll give up the potential to make *more* than the overall market in return for knowing that I won't make *less.*" Once you create your Just-the-Basics portfolios, there's nothing further to do throughout the year (other than a few hours of annual paperwork) except sit back, relax, and hopefully enjoy the ride. By using index funds, we keep pace with the markets virtually without effort. And, by getting the same returns as the overall market, we'll outperform the majority of professional investors. Ironically, we win by *not trying* to win.

Now, let's take a look at how I suggest you use index funds in a Just-the-Basics strategy.

Many fund organizations offer index funds, but the ones from the no-load Vanguard Group are especially well suited to this approach.

Vanguard has also created ETFs (see chapter 9) of many of their index funds, which is great for beginners investing smaller amounts. For purposes of explanation, I'll use the traditional Vanguard index funds — their long performance histories are helpful in illustrating what the results have been from this strategy. Later in the chapter, we'll switch to the ETF versions of these funds when it comes to actually implementing Just-the-Basics.

HISTORY OF THE FOUR
JUST-THE-BASICS FUNDS

| | ------- Vanguard Funds ------- | | | |
	500 Index	Extend Market	Total Intl	Total Bond
2003	28.5%	43.4%	40.3%	4.0%
2004	10.7%	18.7%	20.8%	4.2%
2005	4.8%	10.3%	15.6%	2.4%
2006	15.6%	14.3%	26.6%	4.3%
2007	5.4%	4.3%	15.5%	6.9%
2008	-37.0%	-38.7%	-44.1%	5.1%
2009	26.5%	374%	36.7%	5.9%
2010	14.9%	274%	11.1%	6.4%
2011	2.0%	-3.7%	-14.6%	7.6%
2012	15.8%	18.3%	18.1%	4.0%
10 Yrs	7.0%	10.6%	9.4%	5.1%

The 10 year annualized return is for the period ending December 31, 2012.

Let's start with the Vanguard 500 fund. This fund attempts to duplicate the performance of Standard & Poor's 500 stock index. It invests in all 500 companies in the same proportion as the weight they carry in the index. Vanguard 500 has been around since 1976 and has done an excellent job of fulfilling its mandate. For the 10 years ending 12/31/2012, the fund gained 7.0% per year versus 7.1% per year for the S&P 500 index itself. The small difference is attributable to the costs of operating the fund.

Another Vanguard stock fund will play an important role too: Vanguard Extended Market Index Fund. This fund attempts to provide investment results that correspond to the price and yield performance of 4,500+ smaller-to-medium-sized U.S. companies. Naturally, it can't invest in all 4,500, but by using some fancy computer-driven statistical techniques, it buys about 1,200 stocks plus a representative sample of the remainder so that, when taken together, the portfolio acts pretty much the same as if all 4,500 were present and accounted for.

Now, here's the neat thing about these two funds: *none of their holdings overlap!* This means that if you invest in both of them, you are essentially investing in 5,000+ different stocks ranging from the very small to the very large. *The end result is that you've pretty much invested in the entire American stock market.*

To gain a global flavor, we'll use a third Vanguard stock fund — the Total International Stock Index fund. This fund is authorized to invest in stocks anywhere in the world outside the U.S. Finally, we need to add the Vanguard Total Bond Market Index Fund to our arsenal. This fund employs an indexing investment approach designed to track the performance of the Barclays U.S. Aggregate Float Adjusted Bond Index. This index measures a wide spectrum of public, investment-grade, taxable, fixed-income securities in the United States — including government, corporate, and international dollar-denominated bonds. The fund has an average bond quality rating of AA and weighted maturity of seven to eight years.

We'll put together these funds in different combinations . . .

. . . so as to produce six portfolios of varying degrees of risk. The portfolio at the low end of the risk scale is invested 100% in the bond fund. This one is designed to incur minimum risk in an attempt to preserve capital while generating current income. As we've discussed, investing by lending is the lowest-risk kind of investing.

By increasing the stock allocation in incremental steps of 20%, we begin moving up the risk scale until we reach the high end — a portfolio invested 100% in the stock funds. I suggest that the stock portion of the portfolio be invested two-fifths in the S&P 500, two-fifths in the Extended Market, and one-fifth in International. The table on the next page shows the six Just-the-Basics portfolios and their performance characteristics over the past 10 years.

When you combine the four Vanguard funds in these various ways, you get the potential rewards of stock ownership along with a reduction in risk due to the less volatile bond portion. Sometimes the funds will move together, but it will often be the case that the bond fund will move opposite the stock funds, and the international stock fund will behave differently from the two U.S. stock funds. When that happens, the price changes somewhat cancel each other out. The effect of this is to increase the price stability of the overall portfolio. Thus, although you are less likely to score a huge gain in any one year when holding a combination of the four funds, you are also less likely to incur a huge loss. This improved price stability (which equates to lower risk) is one of the primary advantages for the average investor of diversifying through mutual funds.

As we saw in chapter 13, the portfolio that is best for your situation depends on two factors — your emotional tolerance for risk and the season of life you are now in. Using what you learned in that chapter, you can select which of the six portfolios is best for you.

The use of index funds as your core holdings merits your serious consideration. Here are several advantages they offer:

• **A correct emphasis.** Your most far-reaching investing decision involves how you allocate your money among stocks, bonds, and cash reserves. In *Bogle on Mutual Funds*, Vanguard founder John Bogle quotes a well-known study in claiming that the allocation decision "has accounted for an astonishing 94% of the differences in total returns achieved by institutionally managed pension funds....The 94% figure suggests that long-term fund investors might profit by concentrating more on the allocation of their investments between stock and bond funds and less on the question of *which particular* stock or bond funds to hold" (emphasis added). Other research has indicated that the 94% number is too high—perhaps 60%-70% is closer to the truth. Whatever the actual number may be, virtually everyone agrees that the allocation decision is the most influential one. An indexing strategy forces the investor to focus on the most relevant issue.

• **To guard against sub-par investment returns.** Index funds help assure that your results are in line with those of the general market. They can be counted on to closely track the market at which they're targeted. If, for example, the stocks in the S&P 500 index continue to return their historical rate of return of about 10% annually over the next decade, it's reasonable to expect that an S&P 500 index fund will also gain roughly 10% per year during the period.

• **Lower expenses.** One reason it's difficult for mutual funds to consistently outperform the averages is that they have to overcome the costs of running the fund. The operating expenses (for management fees and other expenses) for the average stock fund amount to about 1.2% a year. Plus, money spent on commissions when the fund does its buying and selling adds another 0.5% to 1.0% per year (depending on how active the portfolio manager is in buying and selling). Thus, the shareholders' profits in the typical fund are reduced by 1.7%-2.2% per year due to operating and transaction costs. Index funds, on the other hand, have very low expenses. Management fees are nominal because the fund can essentially be run by a computer, and transaction costs are quite low because index funds require relatively little buying and selling within the portfolio. The expenses of Vanguard's index ETFs run 0.1% per year, about one-twelfth of what a typical stock fund might incur.

OVERVIEW OF THE SIX JUST-THE-BASIC PORTFOLIOS • 2003-2012

Portion Allocated to Stocks:	Portion Allocated to Bonds:	Breakdown				Your Need for Growth of Capital:	Your Need for Current Income or Protecting Capital:	10-Year Annualized Return:	Best 12 Month Return:	Worst 12 Month Return:	Volatility Compared to the Market
		S&P 500	Extend Market	Total Intl	Total Bond						
100%	None	40%	40%	20%	None	Maximum	None	9.0%	62.0%	−45.4%	14% More
80%	20%	32%	32%	16%	20%	High	Little	8.7%	49.9%	−36.3%	10% Less
60%	40%	24%	24%	12%	40%	Moderate	Modest	8.1%	38.6%	−27.1%	33% Less
40%	60%	16%	16%	8%	60%	Modest	Moderate	7.3%	28.1%	−17.6%	54% Less
20%	80%	8%	8%	4%	80%	Little	High	6.3%	18.2%	−8.2%	71% Less
None	100%	None	None	None	100%	None	Maximum	5.1%	13.8%	−1.0%	76% Less

Risk is usually defined in terms of the potential an investment has for wild swings up and down in its market value. The term "volatility" refers to the extent of these price swings. An investment with high volatility (meaning very wide, often abrupt, swings in its market value) is defined as high risk. An investment with low volatility (meaning narrow, usually gradual, swings in its market value) is thought of as having low risk. From following the financial news, you may already have a rough idea how volatile the overall market is on a day-to-day basis. The table shows how volatile each portfolio is in relation to the market (as measured by the S&P 500 index).

• **Fewer taxable distributions**. Like individual investors, mutual funds aren't taxed on their "paper profits." A taxable event takes place only when securities are sold and the paper gains are realized. The fact that index funds require fewer transactions means there are fewer occasions when stocks are sold and the paper profits converted to taxable profits. This reduces the amount of capital gains taxes, a significant advantage if you're investing taxable dollars, i.e., outside a tax-deferred retirement account.

• **Easy accessibility**. Index funds, especially those based on the S&P 500, are frequently offered in 401(k)s and variable annuities. That makes it easier to include your retirement assets in your overall allocation strategy.

If indexing is so great, why doesn't everybody do it?

Index funds have long been used by large pension funds in a major way, yet they account for a relatively small percentage of the assets of stock mutual funds. Although growing in popularity among individual investors, index funds have had to battle for acceptance despite their many advantages. Here are some guesses as to why that has been the case.

Index funds conflict with our desire for security. The most significant drawback is that index funds offer no protection during periods of market weakness. They are fully invested in a portfolio of stocks that reflects the index they are designed to mimic, and they *stay* fully invested at all times. When the 2008 bear market took the S&P 500 stocks down 37%, the Vanguard S&P 500 index fund fell 37% right along with them. This is a scary thought. As long as we're actively buying and selling, we hope to somehow have the insight, impulse, or just plain luck to stand aside in time to avoid the carnage.

HISTORY OF THE SIX JUST-THE-BASICS PORTFOLIOS

	All Stocks	80% 20%	60% 40%	40% 60%	20% 80%	All Bonds
1993	18.7%	16.9%	15.1%	13.3%	11.5%	9.7%
1994	−0.1%	−0.6%	−1.1%	−1.6%	−2.2%	−2.7%
1995	31.5%	28.8%	26.2%	23.5%	20.8%	18.2%
1996	19.1%	16.0%	12.9%	9.8%	6.7%	3.6%
1997	24.8%	21.7%	18.6%	15.6%	12.5%	9.4%
1998	18.2%	16.3%	14.3%	12.4%	10.5%	8.6%
1999	28.2%	22.4%	16.6%	10.8%	5.0%	−0.8%
2000	−11.5%	−7.0%	−2.4%	2.2%	6.8%	11.4%
2001	−12.3%	−8.1%	−4.0%	0.2%	4.3%	8.4%
2002	−19.6%	−14.1%	−8.5%	−2.9%	2.7%	8.2%
2003	35.7%	29.3%	23.0%	16.6%	10.3%	4.0%
2004	15.6%	13.3%	11.0%	8.8%	6.5%	4.2%
2005	9.0%	7.7%	6.4%	5.0%	3.7%	2.4%
2006	17.2%	14.6%	12.0%	9.4%	6.8%	4.3%
2007	7.1%	7.1%	7.0%	7.0%	7.0%	6.9%
2008	−39.3%	−30.4%	−21.6%	−12.7%	−3.8%	5.1%
2009	33.9%	28.3%	22.7%	17.1%	11.5%	5.9%
2010	20.0%	17.3%	14.6%	11.9%	9.1%	6.4%
2011	−3.4%	−1.1%	1.3%	3.7%	5.4%	7.6%
2012	17.6%	14.9%	12.1%	9.4%	6.8%	4.0%
10 Yrs	9.0%	8.7%	8.1%	7.3%	6.3%	5.1%
20 Yrs	8.6%	8.5%	8.2%	7.7%	7.0%	6.2%

The 20/10 year annualized returns are for the periods ending December 31, 2012.

Because they're on automatic pilot, index funds are said to be "passively managed" funds. The managers of "actively managed" stock funds, on the other hand, can take defensive measures such as increasing their holdings of cash or high-dividend-paying stocks. Such efforts may or may not help cushion the fall, but at least the managers are trying.

Our Just-the-Basics strategy deals with these drawbacks by combining several index funds into one portfolio. By adding a bond fund, we hope to provide a cushion to bear-market weakness. By adding Vanguard's Extended Market Index fund and the Total International Index fund, we increase our diversification by adding small-company and foreign stocks to the mix. These additional funds will not enhance performance every year, but they do add stability to the portfolio over the long haul.

Index funds conflict with the financial interests of the investing industry. Indexing threatens the profits of most investment advisers, stockbrokers, and financial magazines and newsletters. These companies, for the most part, prosper from the public's natural desire for above-average returns. That's why there's always a sense of urgency surrounding their advertising—the emphasis is on what's new and changes you should make *now*. If their customers began relying on indexing, buying and selling activity would greatly diminish and their profits would as well.

Index funds conflict with common sense. The success of index funds is not something you'd expect. How can doing nothing be better than doing something? How can expert advice be worse than no advice at all? And more mysteriously, how can you win by refusing to even play? Yet, the facts speak for themselves. Beating the market for a single year or two is not too hard. Beating it consistently over many years, as Charles Ellis points out, "is so very difficult to do—but it's so easy, while trying to do better, to do worse."

Index funds conflict with human nature. Who wants to settle for "average" when being "above average" doesn't really seem that hard? Most people are optimistic and see themselves as having a good chance of being in that select group who can consistently outperform the market—either through their own skills or by selecting and relying on the right advisers. Contrary to their ambitions and best efforts, however, most investors are not beating the market. The market is beating them.

According to the latest "Quantitative Analysis of Investor Behavior" study by Dalbar Inc., fund investors have significantly underperformed the S&P 500 over the past 3, 5, 10 and 20 years. While average stock-fund investors did almost match the S&P 500's 16% total return in 2012, they lagged the index by nearly 4 percentage points per year from 1993 to 2012. — Forbes

	S&P500 Index Fund	Avg Foreign Fund	Foreign Differs By
2003	28.5%	37.9%	+9.4%
2004	10.7%	19.3%	+8.6%
2005	4.8%	16.6%	+11.8%
2006	15.6%	25.0%	+9.4%
2007	5.4%	12.2%	+6.8%
2008	-37.0%	-44.6%	−7.6%
2009	26.5%	38.6%	+12.1%
2010	14.9%	13.9%	−1.0%
2011	2.0%	-13.6%	−15.6%
2012	15.8%	18.8%	+3.0%
10 Yrs	7.0%	9.2%	+2.2%

Note: The average foreign fund performance is based on the results from 172 stock funds that invest outside the U.S. and are not restricted to any particular region of the world. Source: Morningstar.

Many beginning investors hesitate to invest in companies located outside the U.S. Let's briefly discuss the pros and cons of that.

For years, it's been the conventional wisdom that a well-diversified portfolio should include foreign companies, and results from the past decade continue to make the case. The average foreign stock fund has outperformed Vanguard's S&P 500 index fund seven times in the past 10 years (see nearby table). While some advisers are contending that international diversification isn't necessary, most argue that diversifying abroad remains an important factor in reducing risk. Here are some of the key points made by those *in favor of investing outside the U.S.:*

❶ *"Invest abroad because the diversification will help balance out the ups and downs in your portfolio. Because stock prices in other countries are affected by local factors, they will rally and fall at different times than U.S. stocks. When the U.S. market is weak, growth in other regions will help stabilize your portfolio."* Response: As never before, governments are working together in implementing their economic and trade policies. Furthermore, many of the barriers that previously served to restrict the flow of money across national boundaries have been removed. As a result, the world markets are so interconnected now that weakness in the U.S. is contagious. One academic study of the 20 worst declines in the S&P 500 since 1970 showed that stocks worldwide (as measured by the widely-used EAFE index from Morgan Stanley) gained on only four occasions. Six times the EAFE index went down *even more* than the S&P 500. We saw this "foreign did even worse" scenario repeated in 2008.

❷ *"Invest abroad because it gives you more exciting growth opportunities. From 2003-2012, the average foreign fund (investing worldwide outside the U.S. but not limited to any one region) returned 9.2% compared to 7.8% for the broad U.S. market. As strong as the U.S. is, it still represents just a fraction of the world economy. The action over the next decade is going to be in the emerging markets in Asia."* The response to this is: "Are you kidding? Are you saying there's not enough opportunity right here in the U.S. when our economy, despite the challenges to our financial system in 2008, leads the world in technological change, health research, and creative entrepreneurship? The average person couldn't begin to investigate all the exciting investing opportunities. Gimme a break!"

Those *against investing outside the U.S.* fight back with these arguments.

❸ *"Keep your money home because you should stay with what you know. Information is plentiful, analysis is easier, and you don't have to worry about currency exchange rates."* Response: Sure, it's hard to make good decisions without good information, but the converse isn't true—merely possessing good information doesn't automatically translate into higher profits. After all, the average U.S. stock fund, run by the most data-rich, informed money managers in history, still can't consistently outperform the "dumb" index funds.

❹ *"Keep your money home because America has the world's strongest economy."* This is the continuation of the response to point number two. The rebuttal is a simple but powerful one: Remember Japan at the end of the 1980s? With the second largest economy in the world, Japan seemed ready to overtake the U. S. for the number one position. At that time, few Japanese investors bought shares in U.S. blue chip companies. Why bother? There seemed to be unlimited opportunity in the Japanese market. But the Japanese Nikkei index started falling, on its way from 39,000 yen to 14,000. The average return in Japanese stock funds over the following decade (from 1989-1998) was a loss of 3.4% per year. As we now know, diversification would have been a smart move, no matter how great things looked at home.

❺ *"Keep your money home because the U.S. offers a better trading environment. Our accounting practices are standardized and regulated, so you'll get fuller disclosure and more accurate information. Your commissions will be lower. Because our markets are more liquid, you'll get better executions. To keep the playing field level, our brokers aren't allowed to trade for their own accounts. We offer legal protections to investors, and we've got political stability. You can't take these things for granted when you venture outside our borders."* The fund industry got a black eye during the scandals of 2003-2004, but on balance the above claim is true, which makes it even more sensible to use mutual funds and their experienced managers and analysts to navigate those potentially treacherous foreign waters.

How would the performance in a Just-the-Basics strategy be affected if you left out the foreign stock component?

	100% Stocks Portfolio with Foreign	100% Stocks Portfolio without Foreign
2003	36.8%	36.0%
2004	16.2%	14.9%
2005	9.4%	7.8%
2006	17.5%	14.9%
2007	7.4%	4.8%
2008	−39.6%	−38.0%
2009	33.5%	32.5%
2010	19.3%	22.0%
2011	−4.4%	−1.4%
2012	17.4%	17.3%
10 Yrs	9.0%	6.8%

The 10-year returns are for the period ending December 31, 2012.

The table on the left shows the results from two Just-the-Basics portfolios that are invested 100% in stocks. The first one includes the standard 20% allocation to Vanguard Total International Index fund; the second one omits the foreign stock fund and divides the portfolio 50% in the 500 Index fund and 50% in the Extended Market Index fund. As you would expect, given the news on the previous page that foreign funds have been outperforming their U.S. counterparts, the first portfolio has won the performance race in recent years.

I favor some international diversification, primarily because I agree with point one and the cautionary tale included in point four (pages 174-175). As for point one, our foreign holdings may not fully protect us against a slide in the U.S. markets, but then neither would adding to our U.S. holdings!

Of course, it's your call if you prefer to omit an international emphasis. However, by doing so you'll be surrendering some diversification as well as the potential to benefit from the more rapidly growing economies and companies in our increasingly globalized financial world.

Now that I've explained Just-the-Basics strategy in concept, let's look at the specific exchange-traded funds (ETFs) you'll use when implementing it.

A significant challenge new investors commonly face when their account balances are small is meeting the initial investment minimums for any fund they want to buy. A new Vanguard investor would face at least three separate $3,000 minimum amounts to fully fund the Just-the-Basics strategy using traditional mutual funds (four, if they allocate part of their portfolio to bonds). What if the investor doesn't have $9,000 (or $12,000) to start with? This isn't uncommon, as many investors start with a single IRA contribution, or similar small amount.

In 2001, Vanguard began introducing ETF versions of their various index funds. (I wrote about exchange-traded funds in chapter 9 if you want a quick refresher.) By 2011, all four of the Just-the-Basics index funds were available in an ETF version. With the introduction of these ETFs, minimums are no longer an issue. You can begin by simply purchasing the ETF versions of the Vanguard index funds that comprise Just-the-Basics in whatever amounts you can afford. And because Vanguard customers can invest in Vanguard-brand ETFs without being charged a commission, investing small amounts on a monthly basis is very cost effective.

If you want to implement Just-the-Basics but your account isn't at Vanguard, you have a decision to make.

Let's say you have an account at Fidelity or Schwab. They have "house brand" equivalents of each Just-the-Basics ETF which you'll be able to trade for free.

But instead you may want to consider buying the Vanguard ETFs through your broker and pay a small commission on each trade ($7.95 at Fidelity, $8.95 at Schwab). The reason to consider this is that there's no guarantee that Fidelity and Schwab's funds will perform as well as Vanguard's.

Although Schwab's ETFs haven't been around long enough to compare, Fidelity's free ETFs have—and they haven't performed as well as Vanguard's. (Fidelity is using the popular iShares ETFs as their free equivalent brand.) Here are a couple of examples. The S&P 500 iShare used by Fidelity trailed Vanguard's 500 Index ETF by a 4.70% to 4.64% annual margin over a recent 10-year period. That's not too bad—a total difference of less than $100 on a $10,000 investment over 10 years. But their Extended Market equivalent, the iShare Russell 2000, trailed by an 8.00% to 6.17% annual margin. That's a $3,391 difference over 10 years on an investment of $10,000. It clearly would have been worth paying a $7.95 commission up front for the better fund in that case!

TICKER SYMBOLS FOR THE ETFS USED IN JUST-THE-BASICS			
ETF	Vanguard	Fidelity	Schwab
Total International	VXUS	ACWX	SCHF
Extended Market	VXF	IWM	SCHA
S&P 500	VOO	IVV	SCHX
Total Bond	BND	AGG	SCHZ

Part of the decision whether to choose the no-commission house brand at your broker or the Vanguard ETFs may involve where you are in your investing life cycle. If you're regularly adding to your investments, you might lean toward the no-transaction-fee house brands. That's because your regular investments in the Vanguard ETFs will incur repeated commissions at other brokers. On the other hand, paying the Vanguard commissions is less of a big deal if you'll be setting up your Just-the-Basics funds once and then leaving them alone for a year until your rebalancing occurs.

When you've spent a decade (or more!) investing in traditional mutual funds, it can seem a bit scary jumping out into the world of ETFs with their stock-like trading characteristics. But ETFs continue to gain ground on traditional funds, in part because of policy changes such as we've seen at Vanguard, Fidelity, and Schwab—allowing free ETF trading of their house brands. With the lowest expenses and free trades, it's hard not to like the flexibility offered by these ETFs. The tickers for the Just-the-Basics ETFs at these three brokers are shown above.

I encourage you to give the Just-the-Basics strategy a serious look, and consider using it as the foundation of your long-term strategy.

Of course, indexing need not be an "all or nothing" proposition. Many of my newsletter readers use the Just-the-Basics funds as basic all-season holdings to anchor their portfolios. For example, you could divide your portfolio between a Just-the-Basics mix of funds—perhaps one-half of the total value—and then be a little more flexible with the rest. You could either be more adventurous (by investing the remaining one-half in the Fund Upgrading or Dynamic Asset Allocation strategies I'll explain later in this section) or more conservative (by adding Treasuries, CDs, or other money-market holdings). ◆

CHAPTER PREVIEW

Getting Started on the Road to Financial Security

I.   **There are six key principles I believe should be incorporated into every investment strategy, all of which are reflected in the Just-the-Basics strategy.**

    A.   Your investing plan must reflect your current financial limitations.

    B.   Your investing plan should incorporate a high degree of diversification.

    C.   Your investing plan must have easy-to-understand clear-cut rules.

    D.   Your investing plan must keep you within your emotional "comfort zone."

    E.   Your investing plan must be realistic about the level of return you can reasonably expect.

    F.   Your investing plan must allow you to begin investing in small amounts so that you can get started right away and take full advantage of the tremendous power of compound interest.

II. **The Just-the-Basics strategy can be implemented at most brokers, but I recommend opening an investing account with the no-load Vanguard Group.**

III. **After your Just-the-Basics portfolio is in place, it requires you to take further action only once a year. This annual "rebalancing" process restores your portfolio allocations to their target percentages.**

IV. **Dollar-cost-averaging is a widely practiced "formula" strategy for investing that automates decision making.**

    A.   Dollar-cost-averaging requires investing a set amount of money in the same investment at regular time intervals.

    B.   This approach forces you to do what every investor seeks to do: buy more shares when prices are low and fewer shares when prices are high.

V.   **A strict buy/sell discipline, as provided by formula strategies, is essential for successful investing.**

    A.   Formula strategies need not be "perfect" to be highly profitable.

    B.   A disciplined strategy is essential to protect you from unexpected swings in the market and from your own emotions.

"The spontaneous tendency of our culture is to inexorably add detail to our lives: one more option, one more problem, one more commitment, one more expectation, one more purchase . . .

. . . one more debt, one more change, one more job, one more decision. We must now deal with more 'things per person' than at any other time in history. Yet one can comfortably handle only so many details in his or her life. Exceeding this threshold will result in disorganization or frustration. It is important to note here that the problem is not in the 'details.' The problem is in the 'exceeding.' This is called overloading."

In Dr. Richard Swenson's interesting book *Margin*, he says that margin is the space that once existed between us and our limits. It's the gap between rest and exhaustion, between peace and anxiety. He thinks most of us don't have enough margin, and he has written his book to provide a prescription for the dangers of overloaded lives. I've found it fascinating so far, and I intend to finish it as soon as I can find the time!

Dr. Swenson lists 23 specific types of overload. I was struck by how many of the items also could appear on a list of frustrations that often overwhelm average people as they attempt to manage their *financial* lives. A few of them include: choice overload (too many possible investments clamoring for attention), education overload (too much to learn), expectation overload (we're told we can have "wealth without risk"), hurry overload (investing ads are presented as if it's essential to "act now"), information overload (research, articles, and opinions coming at us faster than we can possibly absorb them), and media overload (thousands of experts writing thousands of books and appearing on thousands of radio and TV programs).

It was to help eliminate this sense of overload and the paralysis it can cause that I suggested a set of financial priorities.

For perspective on where we now stand on our journey toward sound mind investing, let's review what we've covered thus far.

• In Section One, we considered the two "financial-fitness tests" you should pass before using your monthly surplus to invest in the stock and bond markets: getting debt-free (chapter 1) and saving for future needs (chapter 3). Along the way we discussed why having a spending plan is essential; the costs and dangers of credit cards and how to handle them wisely; the best kinds of investments for your *emergency* fund, as well as the investment options for your *accumulation* fund; where paying off a house mortgage fits into your long-range plans (chapter 2); and finally we considered the rising cost of college and how to plan for it (chapter 4).

• In Section Two, we moved out into the world of Wall Street, where I introduced you to mutual funds and the advantages they offer the average investor (chapter 5); how funds are sold and the best way to buy them (chapter 6); necessary cautions that should be understood about their risks (chapter 7); the tax consequences of owning mutual funds (chapter 8); and I provided a primer on exchange-traded mutual funds (ETFs) that can be bought and sold like stocks (chapter 9).

• In Section Three, we took a look at what investing is and why it's actually quite simple (chapter 10); examined some of the basic things you should know about the nature of bonds (chapter 11) and stocks (chapter 12); and concluded with guidelines for controlling your risk by personalizing the all-important decision as to how much of your investment portfolio should be invested in stocks versus bonds (chapter 13).

• In this Section, I began by introducing you to a "no muss, no fuss" approach to putting together a long-term stock and bond portfolio that I've dubbed Just-the-Basics because of its simplicity and low maintenance requirements (chapter 14). I explained how it works and why it gives better results than the majority of professional money managers typically achieve over time.

Now it's time to equip you with the remaining specifics you need to launch your own Just-the-Basics strategy. I am going to start by showing how Just-the-Basics reflects the six principles I believe every investment strategy should follow. Whether you're single or married, young or nearing retirement, investing for college or buying your first house, this strategy is flexible enough to work well for you! Here are the six principles.

Principle #1: Your investing plan must reflect your current financial limitations.

Your plan should effectively prevent you from taking risks you can't afford. The words "higher risk" mean that there's a greater likelihood that you can actually lose part or all of your money. Every day, people who mistakenly thought "it will never happen to me" find just how wrong they were. Investing in the stock market is not a game where gains and losses are just the means of keeping score. Money is not an abstract commodity. For most of us, it represents years of work, hopes, and dreams. Its unexpected loss can be devastating.

That's why the sound-mind approach sets getting debt-free and building your emergency reserve as your two top priorities. Only then are you financially strong enough to bear the risk of loss that is an ever-present reality in the stock market. I encourage you: do not invest any discretionary funds in the stock and bond markets until your debt and savings goals are fully met. (Investing in a 401(k) plan at work where your employer matches your contributions is an exception to this general rule.) When you're ready to invest, refer to the "controlling your risk" matrix (chapter 13) for guidelines that reflect the growth needs appropriate for your current season of life.

Principle #2: Your investing plan should incorporate a high degree of diversification.

Success in investing comes not in hoping for the best, but in knowing how you will handle the worst. Always remember: nobody *really* knows what's going to happen next. Some things can be predicted; most things can't. The tide tables, for example, can be prepared far ahead of time because they are governed by physical laws. The investment world is a colossal engine fueled by human emotions. Millions of people make billions of decisions all reflecting their feelings of fear or security, hardship or prosperity. To attempt to make reliable forecasts in the face of this staggering complexity is foolhardy.

Therefore, since none of us knows what is going to happen next year, next month, or even next week, a good plan must allow for the fact that the investment markets will experience some unexpected rough sledding every now and then. That's where diversification comes in. The idea is to pick investments that "march to different drummers." This means your strategy involves owning a mix of investments that are affected by different economic events. For example, you might invest in both a bond fund and a gold fund. When inflation really heats up, bonds go down (due to rising interest rates) while at the same time gold often goes up (because investors want a secure "store of value"). To the extent that the price changes in the two funds offset each other, you have added stability to your overall portfolio. Surprisingly, it is possible to assemble some lower-risk investment combinations that give pretty much the same returns over time as higher-risk ones. When that is done, such a mix of investments is said to be more "efficient" because it accomplishes the same investment result while tak-

ATTITUDE CHECK

As concerns mounted throughout 2008 about the collapse of the housing bubble and the losses being incurred in sub-prime mortgages, investors grew increasingly wary. The Dow Industrials stood at 11,715 in late August, having slowly fallen from above 14,000 during the previous 12 months. Then, as the potentially calamitous nature of the financial crisis became more apparent, the stampede out of stocks began in earnest. By late November, the Dow had sunk to 7,552. It had lost 36% of its value in only a three-month period. Were you among the millions of investors who watched the value of their hard-earned investment portfolio lose so much of its value so quickly? Which of these statements would best reflect your reaction to what was happening in the financial markets? Your choice reflects your investment temperament.

❑ "You never know when something like this could happen. That's why I don't put much of my money in the stock market. I'm very conservative and am more interested in holding on to what I have than in taking risks that might make my money grow" (Preserver).

❑ "I realize that things like this are going to happen from time to time. That's why I'm careful to investigate before I invest. I'm fairly conservative but am willing to accept some risk of loss in return for greater growth potential. My long-term plan is still sound. I'm going to stay calm and ride this out" (Researcher).

❑ "My broker said he was recommending that his clients buy call options on some beaten down stocks. I've never invested in options before, but this sounded like a good time. I'm willing to risk losing a fair amount of my capital in return for the possibility of having it grow substantially" (Explorer).

❑ "What a great opportunity! Stocks are really taking a beating. By jumping in quickly, a person has a chance to double his money pretty fast. I'm willing to risk losing all of the money I put at risk if I'm convinced that the investment has a chance of paying off really big" (Daredevil).

ing less risk. Just-the-Basics offers you portfolios that combine stocks and bonds in various ways in order to reduce volatility and risk while still achieving attractive long-term returns.

Principle #3: Your investing plan must have easy-to-understand, clear-cut rules.

There must be no room for differing interpretations. You must be able to make your investing decisions quickly and with confidence. This means reducing your decision making to numerical guidelines as much as possible. A strategy that calls for a "significant investment" in small-company stocks is not as helpful as one that calls for "30% of your portfolio" to be invested in small-company stocks.

Insofar as possible, your strategy should not only tell you *what* to invest in but also offer precise guidance in telling you *how much* to invest and *when* to buy and *when* to sell. With Just-the-Basics you'll always know exactly where you stand and what you need to do to stay on course.

Principle #4: Your investing plan must keep you within your emotional "comfort zone."

Your investing plan should prevent you from taking risks that rob you of your peace. Consider the four responses given in the Attitude Check (far left). These are likely reactions from our four investment temperaments. The amount of risk you take should be consistent with your temperament. You shouldn't adopt a strategy that takes you past your good-night's sleep level! If you do, you will tend to bail out at the worst possible time. A Just-the-Basics portfolio, used in conjunction with the risk matrix shown on page 159, will reflect your investing personality and current season of life.

Principle #5: Your investing plan must be realistic about the level of return you can reasonably expect.

I receive letters asking me to recommend safe investments that will guarantee returns of 12%, 14%, and more. If by "safe" it is meant that there's absolutely no chance of the value of the investment falling, then I must answer that I don't know of any investments like that. The ones that I do know about that are "safe" in that sense pay much less than 12%.

The reason any investment offers a potentially higher rate of return is that *it has to* in order to reward investors for accepting a higher level of risk. My goal is to help you get started in the right direction, incurring the least risk possible that will still get you to your destination safely. The tables on page 173 provided the historical performance results of each of the Just-the-Basics portfolios to let you know ahead of time what are reasonable expectations with respect to rates of return.

Principle #6: Your investing plan must allow you to begin investing in small amounts so that you can get started right away and take full advantage of the tremendous power of compound interest.

Remember the story of Jack and Jill in chapter 3? Who would you have expected to have the larger retirement fund at age 65 — Jack, who put $13,200 in as a young paperboy, or Jill, who put in $120,000 over the 40 years of her working life? Weren't you surprised to learn that Jack was the winner? His fund had grown to more than $894,000, an amount almost 68 times more than he put in as a child! Jack's earlier start, even with much smaller amounts and for far fewer years, was too much for Jill to overcome, thanks to the tremendous power of compounding.

That's why it's important to start investing early and to add to your program regularly. The Vanguard organization offers an automatic investing plan for amounts as low as $50 per month. Even such small amounts can grow to substantial sums over many years. Every dollar makes a difference!

Here's how you can get started with your Just-the-Basics strategy.

For this strategy, I suggest you open a brokerage account at Vanguard. As I explained in the last chapter, you can begin purchasing the ETF versions of the Vanguard index funds that comprise Just-the-Basics in whatever amounts you can afford. And Vanguard customers can invest in Vanguard-brand ETFs without being charged a commission. This makes it very cost effective for those investing small amounts on a monthly basis.

Vanguard is one of the largest and most respected no-load mutual fund organizations in the investment industry. The company has a reputation for giving excellent service while keeping administrative costs low. Also, if you want to branch out beyond the ETFs you'll use in Just-the-Basics, Vanguard offers an exceptional variety of ETFs and traditional mutual funds from which you can choose. As with all no-load funds, there are no commissions charged, either when you invest or when you take your money out. You can move your money from one of its funds into another via telephone or the Internet at no cost. Vanguard brokerage accounts can be opened with as little as $3,000.

To open an account, go to www.vanguard.com (or call 1-800-662-7447). If you like, you can open an account online (it takes about 15 minutes), or you can fill out forms and mail them in. (It's possible to move your current IRA or SEP-IRA account to Vanguard. If interested, download the necessary forms from their web site, or request them by phone.) Just follow the step-by-step instructions. You'll need to have some basic information handy, such as beneficiary details and your Social Security number. Some of the questions request that you make choices (which can be changed at any time) among different convenience options. You can call Vanguard toll-free, if you need to, for help in completing the form.

Just-the-Basics at Schwab or Fidelity

While Vanguard is my preferred broker for this strategy, it's also possible to implement at other brokers.

See the discussion on page 177 regarding the use of house-brand ETFs at Schwab and Fidelity.

Also, see pages 112-113 for a review of the importance of using highly liquid ETFs.

The automatic investment plan is especially helpful for automating your program. By providing the information about your local bank, you can have your bank send the amount you choose directly to your Vanguard account every month. Vanguard will take care of the arrangements. I also suggest that you sign where indicated and apply for check-writing privileges. Vanguard will send you checks, which will come in handy in case you need to quickly transfer your money from Vanguard to your home bank.

Initially, I suggest you deposit all of your money into the Vanguard Prime Money-Market Fund.

It pays competitive short-term interest rates with virtually no risk. Once your account is established, your initial deposit will be sitting in your new money-market account. Then, you can go online or make a phone call with instructions to move the money out of the money-market fund and into our recommended funds in accordance with the portfolio mix you have selected.

There are many different ways to achieve the various portfolio mixes. The ones shown on the chalkboard (below) are offered as guidelines. For example, if you open your account with $5,000 and choose the 80% stocks, 20% bonds mix, you would invest $800 in VXUS (16% of $5,000), $1,600 in both VXF and VOO (32% of $5,000), and the remaining $1,000 (20% of $5,000) in BND.

For tax-deferred accounts, I recommend you instruct Vanguard to have all income and capital-gains distributions reinvested. However, for taxable accounts, I suggest *not* doing this. Instead, ask that they be deposited into your Prime money-market account where you can reallocate them among the various ETFs at a convenient time. This will simplify your tax accounting.

Keep in mind that the advantages of index-fund investing—keeping costs low, for example—manifest themselves over time. So, don't focus too much on short-term performance. Carefully review the information on Vanguard's web site to be sure you clearly understand the pros and cons of investing in index funds.

HOW I SUGGEST DIVIDING YOUR MONEY UNDER THE JUST-THE-BASICS STRATEGY

(SEE RISK MATRIX ON PAGE 159)

Percentage of stocks:		100%	80%	60%	40%	20%	0%
Percentage of bonds:		0%	20%	40%	60%	80%	100%
Total International	VXUS	20%	16%	12%	8%	4%	0%
Extended Mkt Index	VXF	40%	32%	24%	16%	8%	0%
S&P 500 Index	VOO	40%	32%	24%	16%	8%	0%
Total Bond Market	BND	0%	20%	40%	60%	80%	100%

One of the periodic housekeeping chores investors must deal with from time to time is "rebalancing" their portfolios.

It's like four people playing a game of Monopoly. Everybody starts out with 25% of the money, but after a few rounds of play, some are richer and some poorer. To get back where you started, you'd have to "rebalance" by taking money from some players and giving it to others. Here's how that applies here.

Assume you invest along the lines recommended for those desiring a portfolio mix of 80% stocks and 20% bonds, and divide your money among the four Vanguard ETFs as shown in the table on the previous page. In the months that follow, as some ETFs do better than others, the percentages you started with begin to change. If Extended Market does better than Total International, for example, it may soon represent 40% of your total holdings while Total International falls to only 12%. How long do you let this continue before you step in and sell some Extended Market in order to return its value to just 32% of your portfolio? I suggest rebalancing during the first week of each new year. Emotionally, January is a good time for new beginnings and fresh starts. Also, if you have taxable gains, waiting until January postpones paying the tax for a year.

AN EXAMPLE OF THE ANNUAL REBALANCING PROCESS

Ticker/Name	Desired Mix	Initial Purchases	End Of Period	Desired Balances	Changes Needed
VXUS/Total International	16%	$800	$700	$960	+260
VXF/Extended Market	32%	1,600	2,400	1,920	–480
VOO/S&P 500	32%	1,600	2,100	1,920	–180
BND/Total Bond Mrkt	20%	1,000	800	1,200	+400
Total Holdings	100%	$5,000	$6,000	$6,000	

The table shows a theoretical example of how the rebalancing computation is made. The initial purchases were made based on a portfolio mix of 80% stocks, 20% bonds as shown in column one. At the end of the year, the account balances have changed due to market fluctuations (and possibly because you added some new money during the year). Going into the new year, you want to get your portfolio back to the desired 80/20 levels. To do this, you simply multiply the percentage in column one for each ETF times the new total value of your holdings (circled). In the example, the new target level for Total International is $960 (16% x $6,000). To restore the fund to its proper level, you must buy $260 in new shares ($960 desired level minus $700 actual). This purchase (as well as the one for the bond ETF) is paid for by selling off shares in the Extended Market and S&P 500 ETFs.

You will notice that rebalancing takes money away from your star performers and gives it to the poorer performing groups.

A common question is: "Why are we buying more shares in last year's losers at the expense of last year's winners? Since they've done so poorly, wouldn't it be better to put less emphasis on them for the coming year?" If "better" means "more profitable," then the answer is that some years it would be better; but in most years it would not. Market performance leaders change as the economy goes through the various stages of its cycle.

For example, in 2007, the best performance among the four Vanguard Just-the-Basics funds was Total International, which gained 15.5% (see page 170). If you had not rebalanced and reduced that portion of your portfolio back up to its recommended percent allocation, you would have been overinvested in that fund in 2008 when it turned in the worst performance of the four (-44.1%). Similarly, from 2003-2007, the worst performer was Total Bond Market, which provided only modest returns while the others were generally turning in much healthier gains. If you had not rebalanced at the end of 2007, you would have missed out on having a full bond allocation in 2008's top performer among Just-the-Basics funds when the Total Bond Market fund gained 5.1% while the others were brought down by the financial crisis.

This kind of thing can happen at any time. If it didn't, wouldn't the markets be a great place to make easy money?

One knowledgeable writer called dollar-cost-averaging a long-term investment technique that "beats the market...by ignoring the market."

A consistent theme of the Sound Mind Investing philosophy is the importance of taking charge of your own financial future by becoming an "initiator" rather than a "responder." Initiators don't let others shape their course; *they* set the pace. Action is taken as a result of specific guidelines from a specific strategy coming into play. They "plan their work and work their plan."

In devising your plan, consider making use of a systematic "formula" strategy. Such an approach can be quite useful in helping you stay focused on your long-term goals because it requires you to make your buying and selling decisions based solely on mechanical guidelines. There is no judgment involved; it's all automatic. Such guidelines are helpful because they protect you against your own emotions and the tendency to go along with the crowd. Such strategies fit well into the disciplined framework for decision making desired by initiators.

We'll talk about two such strategies later in this section when I explain Fund Upgrading (chapter 17) and Dynamic Asset Allocation (chapter 18).

Probably the best-known formula strategy is dollar-cost-averaging (DCA). It's not complicated. It's not time-consuming. In fact, nothing could be simpler. Here's all you do: (1) invest the *same amount* of money (2) at *regular time intervals*. For example, you might choose to invest $300 once a month. The amount and frequency are up to you. The important thing is to pick an amount you can stick with faithfully over many years.

The beauty of DCA is that it frees you from . . .

. . . the worry of whether you're buying stocks at the "wrong" time. Your constant dollar investment forces you to buy more shares when the price is low and to buy fewer shares when the price is high. In effect, you are buying more shares at bargain prices and fewer shares at what might be considered high prices. Of course, only when you look back years from now will you know when prices really were bargains and when prices were too high.

It is critically important to ignore all market fluctuations when employing a dollar-cost-averaging strategy. Most investors who obtain poor returns in the market are victims of their own emotions. Only after stock prices have been rising sharply do "responders" work up enough courage to buy stock-fund shares. And about the only time they ever sell shares is when they become especially fearful after prices have plunged. The consequence is that they buy high and sell low, the very opposite of their ambition. It is important, then, not to let your emotions control you. You must exercise the discipline of maintaining your systematic investment program.

Dollar-cost-averaging doesn't protect you against losses.

It does result in your average cost per share being lower than the average price of the shares over time. But in a bear market, you still can have temporary losses.

Furthermore, DCA is a two-edged sword. It can lower your potential profits as well as losses. If your fund's share prices had risen all year long, you would obviously show greater gains if you had made a single large investment early on. In fact, academic studies have appeared purporting to show that DCA is a bad idea. Why? Because the market has a long-term upward bias. Over time, the market has always moved higher. The implication is that, on average, you're going to be paying more for your shares if you stretch your buying out than if you go ahead and invest as much as you can as soon as possible.

That's all well and good when you're looking back over a 40-year period with 20/20 vision. It ignores the fact that there are bear-market periods along the way when it's quite easy for investors to be frightened out of the markets altogether. If you invest your $50,000 inheritance just before a bear market wipes out $10,000 of it, who's to say you're going to have the stomach for staying around and waiting for the next bull market to recoup your losses and then some? The academics may have it right in theory, but in the real world, DCA makes it easier for investors to overcome their fears and make the difficult decision to put their limited (and therefore, precious) savings at risk.

In summary, DCA is the systematic investing of a fixed amount of money on a regular basis, usually monthly. I especially like it when used in conjunction with no-load funds and 401(k) plans (or IRAs) for these reasons:

• It eliminates the need to ask the question, "Is this a good time to buy

DCA Math

The benefits of DCA can be illustrated with a simple example. Let's assume you can afford to invest $100 every month in your stock fund program. At the time of your first new investment, the fund shares sell for $10.

(I'm going to exaggerate the amount of market volatility in order to show the mathematical effects.)

The next month, the market soars and you pay $14 for your shares. Finally, the third month the market falls back, and your fund retreats to $12, midway between your two buying levels.

Ordinarily, that would put you at break-even. But look at what has happened. The first month you were able to buy ten shares at $10 per share. The second month you acquired only 7.1429 shares at $14 per share. Now, at $12 each, your 17.1429 shares are worth $205.71 rather than the $200 you invested. Instead of being at break-even, you have a small profit.

stocks?" As far as DCA investors are concerned, every month is a good month.

• It imposes a discipline, forcing you to make regular "installment" payments on your future financial security.

• It will cause you to buy relatively more fund shares when prices are low and fewer shares when prices are high.

• Using no-load funds eliminates commission costs and provides sufficient diversification to reflect the stock market at large.

Let's walk through an example of some of the decisions involved in executing a DCA strategy.

Before getting started, let me note that if you're starting a Just-the-Basics investing strategy with a sufficient amount of capital, you may want to follow a slightly different approach than I have outlined thus far. Rather than investing via ETFs, it will be more efficient for you to use Vanguard's traditional mutual-fund counterparts (see sidebar). Traditional mutual funds allow for the purchase of fractional fund shares and therefore put all of your money to work in stocks immediately. (ETFs are not sold in fractional shares.)

My general approach in this book, however, is to write for beginning investors who—because they are just starting—may not have much to invest. The example below is based on the assumption that an investor is beginning with a relatively small amount. That being the case, we're using ETFs because they have no investment minimums.

Because ETFs don't allow for purchase of fractional shares, the rare distributions from ETF investments cannot always be immediately reinvested. This is simply because the cost of new shares and the amount you have to invest may not match. Don't worry about that. These distributions can be placed in the Vanguard Prime Money-Market Fund so as to be available for investing in ETFs the following month. Now, on with the show!

In this hypothetical example, I'll assume...

...that you've gone through the exercises in chapter 13 and determined that a "100% stocks" portfolio is appropriate for you given your current season of life and risk-taking temperament. You have $5,000 available to launch your program. Creating your personal versions of the worksheets shown on pages 192-193 can help you deal with adjustments for dividends and annual rebalancing. The worksheets are intended to be read from far left to far right as if they were all on the same page; it might be helpful to use a ruler to guide your eyes as you follow along with the example I've created.

In what I hope will eventually prove reassuring, I've decided to let you begin your program at a particularly bad time—just as the market was about to plummet due to the banking crisis brought on by the bursting of the hous-

---

Ticker Symbols for Vanguard's Traditional Just-the-Basics Mutual Funds

For those starting their Just-the-Basics strategy with at least $10,000 to invest in each fund, I recommend using the traditional stock fund counterparts to the ETFs. Their ticker symbols are:

Total International	VTIAX
Extended Market	VEXAX
S&P 500	VFIAX
Total Bond	VBTLX

Remember the cautions concerning many of today's mutual funds which I alerted you to back in chapter 7?
At the end of that chapter, I promised to "introduce you to a special breed of mutual funds . . . that, by their very nature, avoid the red flag traps we've just discussed." Let's briefly look at how index funds and the Just-the-Basics strategy protect you from the abuses explained in chapter 12.

· Red Flag #1: You can't necessarily accept a fund's "investment objective" at face value. You don't have to worry about an index fund broadening its investing horizons (and taking on more risk in the process), because that would be self-defeating. An index fund doesn't have any investment objective other than to replicate the performance of the index it's based on.

· Red Flag #2: You can't necessarily accept a fund's diversification claims at face value. For an index fund to concentrate its holdings in a relatively few stocks would also be self-defeating. Unless, of course, the fund is based on an index, such as the Dow Industrials, which itself encompasses a small number of stocks. In that case, the fund would be doing exactly what it is supposed to do.

ing bubble and subsequent sub-prime debacle. Before all that happened, the market hit its highs in October 2007, and you have the misfortune of launching your new portfolio at the beginning of September that year.

❶ Since we're using ETFs, we don't need to concern ourselves with fund minimums. You can buy them in any amount you wish. After your initial deposit, your Prime MMF account shows a $5,000 balance (column 7).

We'll divide our initial $5,000 according to the guidelines suggested for a "100% stocks" profile—40% large-company stocks, 40% small-company stocks, and 20% international stocks. We make these investments by transferring the appropriate amounts out of Prime and into the three ETFs (column 11 for each ETF).

Because you can only buy ETFs in whole shares, you're not able to invest the entire $5,000. In fact, your stock investments total $4,814 (the sum of column 13 for each ETF). That means you have $186 remaining in your Prime account (column 8).

At the end of each month, you can see the number of shares owned for each ETF (column 14), the value of those shares (column 15), and the value of your total portfolio (column 5). You can also gauge the progress of your account since you began your plan (column 6) in comparison to the change in the S&P 500 (column 2).

❷ You plan on adding $400 a month during the first year (with the hope of increasing your monthly deposit by $50 every 12 months). For purposes of this illustration, I'll assume you make your regular investments on the first trading day of the month. At the beginning of October, you make your $400 deposit. This is added to the small balance remaining from September, raising your available funds to $586 (column 7). You should attempt to invest this in the 40-40-20 ratio you've adopted, but this is not always possible because you can only buy ETFs in whole shares. The ratio implies an investment in the ETF for the S&P 500 of $235 ($586 times 40% as shown in column 11). However, with that ETF priced at $140+ (column 9), you can only afford to buy a single share (column 12). Similarly, you are unable to invest the full allocation in the other ETFs as well. Not to worry— the unused amounts can stay in Prime until you repeat the process next month. When all the buying is done, there remains $120 in the Prime account.

❸ You notice on your December statement that your ETFs paid dividend distributions that were deposited in Prime. These occasional deposits are the reason that your month-ending Prime balance is more than you would expect based solely on the buying activity shown in the worksheet.

❹ It's the beginning of a new year and usually the time for your annual rebalancing to get your ETF values back in line with your original 40/40/20 allocation. However, since you just began your strategy a few months ago, you're still pretty close to the original percentage allocations, so we'll forego that process this first year.

❺ At the end of September 2008, you've completed your first year of making regular monthly investments, and what do you have to show for your efforts?

A big loss! So far, you've pumped in $9,800 (column 4) but your portfolio finishes the month at a mere $6,545 (column 5). You've lost about one-third of your money. Sure, the S&P 500 has had a rough 12 months—it's down 21% (column 2), but that's little consolation. Despite your concern and doubts, you soldier on. You know it's important to stay with your program regardless of what the market's doing, so you begin the next month by raising your investment $50 as planned. You send in $450 (column 3). With the price down, you're getting a lot more for your money!

❻ It's the beginning of a new year and time for your annual rebalancing. Rather than making purchases based on your usual 40-40-20 ratio, you make the changes needed to *restore the overall portfolio* to the 40-40-20 mix.

With a portfolio value at the end of December of $6,238 (column 5) and a January deposit of $450, your portfolio starts the new year at $6,688. Allocating 40% of that amount to the S&P 500 ETF means you should have $2,675 invested there. Its starting value in January is $2,659 (column 10), so you only add $16 to that ETF. However, a single share is $83 (column 9). That means you can't add any to that particular ETF in January.

The Extended Market ETF also has a target 40% allocation of $2,675. With a starting value in January of $1,958 (column 10), it requires an investment of $717 (column 11) to bring that ETF up to the target level. With that budget, you're able to buy 22 shares for $695; the rest remains in the Prime account.

The Total International ETF has done well. In fact, its value of $1,489 is $151 above the 20% target allocation ($6,688 total value x 20% = $1,489). This means you need to sell a few shares. At $10.79 per share, you sell 14 shares. The proceeds from the sale go into the Prime account.

Every January you go through a similar calculation to restore your total portfolio to the 40-40-20 allocation you want.

❼ At the end of September 2009, you've been making monthly investmens for two years. At $13,040, your account is still underwater, but you've made progress. You're down 14%, which is better than the S&P 500's decline of 28% during this period and a great improvement from being 33% down a year earlier. Your consistent purchases at low prices during a weak market are paying off!

❽ By the end of December 2010, your investments totaling $22,850 are worth $25,367. During the same period, the S&P 500 fell from 1,489 to 1,258, a drop of 15%. Yet, you have made money. How is this possible? It happened because, while other investors were wringing their hands over the uncertainty surrounding the economy and the financial crisis, you were busily buying up shares at low prices month after month. When the inevitable rebound finally arrived, you were in a position to profit. And it only took a few minutes each month. Despite beginning your DCA at a very inopportune time, you persevered through a brutal bear market and now you have a profit. Congratulations!

There are hundreds of variations on how DCA investments can be made.

· Red Flag #3: You can't necessarily accept a fund's implied performance excellence at face value. There's no incentive for an S&P 500 index fund to claim a gain of 15% in a year when the S&P 500 gained only 10%. It would serve to reveal that the fund manager had done a poor job of tracking the index and make the manager look inept rather than insightful.

· Red Flag #4: You can't necessarily accept a fund's rankings at face value. Performance rankings are a function of which peer group a fund is in and how well it performs in that group. There's no disagreement among industry observers as to which peer groups the various index funds should be placed in. Relative rankings of index funds may not always be in the top quartile, but they will at least be honest.

The four red flags are all symptoms of the same problem: Mutual funds function in a highly competitive marketplace, and their managers are under tremendous pressures to outperform the competition. Take away the need to outperform, and you take away the stimulus for the abuses. Index funds are appreciated for the fact that, while they don't strive to outperform the markets, neither do they have the misfortune of significantly underperforming it.

Month Year	(1) S&P 500 Index End of Month	(2) Change From Start	(3) Total Monthly Deposit	(4) Total Amount Invested	DCA IN ACTION (5) Portfolio Value End Of Month	(6) Change From Start	(7) Prime MMF Begin Balance	(8) Prime MMF Ending Balance		S&P 500 ETF (TICKER: VOO) (9) Share Price Begin Month	(10) Value Account Before Deposit	(11) Amount Avail Begin Month	(12) New Shares Bought	(13) New Shares Cost	(14) Shares Owned End Of Month	(15) Value Account End Of Month
Sept 2007	1526.75	4%	$5,000	$5,000	$5,190	4%	$5,000	$186	❶	$135.75	$0	$2,000	14	$1,901	14	$1,969
Oct 2007	1549.38	5%	$400	$5,400	$5,744	6%	$586	$120	❷	$140.61	$1,969	$235	1	$141	15	$2,142
Nov 2007	1481.14	0%	$400	$5,800	$5,846	1%	$520	$176		$142.83	$2,142	$208	1	$143	16	$2,190
Dec 2007	1468.36	-0%	$400	$6,200	$6,171	-0%	$576	$182	❸	$136.85	$2,190	$230	1	$137	17	$2,298
Jan 2008	1378.55	-6%	$400	$6,600	$6,132	-7%	$582	$138	❹	$135.15	$2,298	$233	1	$135	18	$2,286
Feb 2008	1330.63	-10%	$400	$7,000	$6,409	-8%	$538	$123		$127.02	$2,286	$215	1	$127	19	$2,335
Mar 2008	1322.70	-10%	$400	$7,400	$6,755	-9%	$523	$129		$122.89	$2,335	$209	1	$123	20	$2,435
Apr 2008	1385.59	-6%	$400	$7,800	$7,530	-3%	$529	$126		$121.75	$2,435	$212	1	$122	21	$2,681
May 2008	1400.38	-5%	$400	$8,200	$8,155	-1%	$526	$102		$127.67	$2,681	$211	1	$128	22	$2,845
June 2008	1280.00	-13%	$400	$8,600	$6,216	-28%	$502	$183		$129.31	$2,845	$201	1	$129	23	$2,710
July 2008	1267.38	-14%	$400	$9,000	$6,520	-28%	$583	$164		$117.83	$2,710	$233	1	$118	24	$2,804
Aug 2008	1282.83	-13%	$400	$9,400	$6,912	-26%	$564	$151		$116.85	$2,804	$226	1	$117	25	$2,964
Sept 2008	1166.36	-21%	$400	$9,800	$6,545	-33%	$551	$153	❺	$118.54	$2,964	$220	1	$119	26	$2,792
Oct 2008	968.75	-34%	$450	$10,250	$5,632	-45%	$603	$56		$107.37	$2,792	$241	2	$215	28	$2,502
Nov 2008	896.24	-39%	$450	$10,700	$5,585	-48%	$506	$56		$89.34	$2,502	$202	2	$179	30	$2,488
Dec 2008	903.25	-39%	$450	$11,150	$6,238	-44%	$506	$132		$82.93	$2,488	$203	2	$166	32	$2,659
Jan 2009	825.88	-44%	$450	$11,600	$6,088	-48%	$582	$38	❻	$83.09	$2,659	$16	0	$0	32	$2,435
Feb 2009	735.09	-50%	$450	$12,050	$5,882	-51%	$488	$66		$76.10	$2,435	$195	2	$152	34	$2,312
Mar 2009	797.87	-46%	$450	$12,500	$6,875	-45%	$516	$48		$67.99	$2,312	$207	3	$204	37	$2,717
Apr 2009	872.81	-41%	$450	$12,950	$8,265	-36%	$498	$59		$73.44	$2,717	$199	2	$147	39	$3,138
May 2009	919.14	-38%	$450	$13,400	$9,330	-30%	$509	$56		$80.46	$3,138	$204	2	$161	41	$3,484
June 2009	919.32	-38%	$450	$13,850	$9,761	-30%	$506	$85		$84.98	$3,484	$202	2	$170	43	$3,643
July 2009	987.48	-33%	$450	$14,300	$11,105	-22%	$535	$63		$84.72	$3,643	$214	2	$169	45	$4,101
Aug 2009	1020.62	-31%	$450	$14,750	$11,959	-19%	$513	$51		$91.14	$4,101	$205	2	$182	47	$4,438
Sept 2009	1057.08	-28%	$450	$15,200	$13,040	-14%	$501	$45	❼	$94.42	$4,438	$200	2	$189	49	$4,775
Oct 2009	1036.19	-30%	$500	$15,700	$13,056	-17%	$545	$43		$97.45	$4,775	$218	2	$195	51	$4,877
Nov 2009	1095.63	-26%	$500	$16,200	$14,189	-12%	$543	$59		$95.63	$4,877	$217	2	$191	53	$5,372
Dec 2009	1115.10	-24%	$500	$16,700	$15,278	-9%	$559	$231		$101.35	$5,372	$223	2	$203	55	$5,647
Jan 2010	1073.87	-27%	$500	$17,200	$15,184	-12%	$731	$87		$102.67	$5,647	$664	6	$616	61	$6,037
Feb 2010	1104.49	-25%	$500	$17,700	$16,192	-9%	$587	$71		$98.97	$6,037	$235	2	$198	63	$6,428
Mar 2010	1169.43	-21%	$500	$18,200	$17,814	-2%	$571	$69		$102.03	$6,428	$228	2	$204	65	$7,002
Apr 2010	1186.69	-19%	$500	$18,700	$18,746	0%	$569	$63		$107.73	$7,002	$228	2	$215	67	$7,332
May 2010	1089.41	-26%	$500	$19,200	$17,652	-8%	$563	$47		$109.43	$7,332	$225	2	$219	69	$6,947
June 2010	1030.71	-30%	$500	$19,700	$17,194	-13%	$547	$96		$100.68	$6,947	$219	2	$201	71	$6,739
July 2010	1101.60	-25%	$500	$20,200	$19,050	-6%	$596	$81		$94.91	$6,739	$239	2	$190	73	$7,413
Aug 2010	1049.33	-29%	$500	$20,700	$18,609	-10%	$581	$39		$101.55	$7,413	$232	2	$203	75	$7,271
Sept 2010	1141.20	-23%	$500	$21,200	$21,055	-1%	$539	$77		$96.95	$7,271	$216	2	$194	77	$8,090
Oct 2010	1183.26	-20%	$550	$21,750	$22,455	3%	$627	$60		$105.06	$8,090	$251	2	$210	79	$8,614
Nov 2010	1180.55	-20%	$550	$22,300	$23,106	4%	$610	$85		$109.04	$8,614	$244	2	$218	81	$8,832
Dec 2010	1257.64	-15%	$550	$22,850	$25,367	11%	$635	$314	❽	$109.04	$8,832	$254	2	$218	83	$9,613

Month Year	EXTENDED MARKET ETF (TICKER: VXF)							TOTAL INTERNATIONAL STOCK ETF (TICKER: VXUS)						
	(9) Share Price Begin Month	(10) Value Account Before Deposit	(11) Amount Avail Begin Month	(12) New Shares Bought	(13) New Shares Cost	(14) Shares Owned End Of Month	(15) Value Account End Of Month	(9) Share Price Begin Month	(10) Value Account Before Deposit	(11) Amount Avail Begin Month	(12) New Shares Bought	(13) New Shares Cost	(14) Shares Owned End Of Month	(15) Value Account End Of Month
Sept 2007	$107.34	$0	$2,000	18	$1,932	18	$2,001	$19.62	$0	$1,000	50	$981	50	$1,034
Oct 2007	$111.18	$2,001	$235	2	$222	20	$2,277	$20.67	$1,034	$117	5	$103	55	$1,204
Nov 2007	$113.85	$2,277	$208	1	$114	21	$2,248	$21.89	$1,204	$104	4	$88	59	$1,233
Dec 2007	$107.05	$2,248	$230	2	$214	23	$2,418	$20.89	$1,233	$115	5	$104	64	$1,273
Jan 2008	$105.15	$2,418	$233	2	$210	25	$2,453	$19.89	$1,273	$116	5	$99	69	$1,255
Feb 2008	$98.12	$2,453	$215	2	$196	27	$2,600	$18.19	$1,255	$108	5	$91	74	$1,351
Mar 2008	$96.30	$2,600	$209	2	$193	29	$2,759	$18.25	$1,351	$105	5	$91	79	$1,431
Apr 2008	$95.14	$2,759	$212	2	$190	31	$3,112	$18.12	$1,431	$106	5	$91	84	$1,611
May 2008	$100.38	$3,112	$211	2	$201	33	$3,475	$19.18	$1,611	$105	5	$96	89	$1,733
June 2008	$105.31	$3,475	$201	1	$105	34	$1,658	$19.47	$1,733	$100	5	$97	94	$1,666
July 2008	$48.75	$1,658	$233	4	$195	38	$1,844	$17.72	$1,666	$117	6	$106	100	$1,707
Aug 2008	$48.53	$1,844	$226	4	$194	42	$2,080	$17.07	$1,707	$113	6	$102	106	$1,717
Sept 2008	$49.53	$2,080	$220	4	$198	46	$2,023	$16.20	$1,717	$110	6	$97	112	$1,577
Oct 2008	$43.97	$2,023	$241	5	$220	51	$1,758	$14.08	$1,577	$121	8	$113	120	$1,316
Nov 2008	$34.47	$1,758	$202	5	$172	56	$1,714	$10.97	$1,316	$101	9	$99	129	$1,326
Dec 2008	$30.61	$1,714	$203	6	$184	62	$1,958	$10.28	$1,326	$101	9	$93	138	$1,489
Jan 2009	$31.59	$1,958	$717	22	$695	84	$2,437	$10.79	$1,489	($151)	-14	($151)	124	$1,178
Feb 2009	$29.01	$2,437	$195	6	$174	90	$2,353	$9.50	$1,178	$98	10	$95	134	$1,151
Mar 2009	$26.14	$2,353	$207	7	$183	97	$2,739	$8.59	$1,151	$103	12	$103	146	$1,371
Apr 2009	$28.24	$2,739	$199	7	$198	104	$3,415	$9.39	$1,371	$100	10	$94	156	$1,652
May 2009	$32.84	$3,415	$204	6	$197	110	$3,792	$10.59	$1,652	$102	9	$95	165	$1,998
June 2009	$34.47	$3,792	$202	5	$172	115	$3,965	$12.11	$1,998	$101	8	$97	173	$2,067
July 2009	$34.48	$3,965	$214	6	$207	121	$4,562	$11.95	$2,067	$107	8	$96	181	$2,378
Aug 2009	$37.70	$4,562	$205	5	$189	126	$4,915	$13.14	$2,378	$103	7	$92	188	$2,555
Sept 2009	$39.01	$4,915	$200	5	$195	131	$5,431	$13.59	$2,555	$100	7	$95	195	$2,789
Oct 2009	$41.46	$5,431	$218	5	$207	136	$5,308	$14.30	$2,789	$109	7	$100	202	$2,828
Nov 2009	$39.03	$5,308	$217	5	$195	141	$5,722	$14.00	$2,828	$109	7	$98	209	$3,037
Dec 2009	$40.58	$5,722	$223	5	$203	146	$6,287	$14.53	$3,037	$112	7	$102	216	$3,113
Jan 2010	$43.06	$6,287	$24	0	$0	146	$6,078	$14.41	$3,113	$43	2	$29	218	$2,982
Feb 2010	$41.63	$6,078	$235	5	$208	151	$6,594	$13.68	$2,982	$117	8	$109	226	$3,098
Mar 2010	$43.67	$6,594	$228	5	$218	156	$7,320	$13.71	$3,098	$114	8	$110	234	$3,423
Apr 2010	$46.92	$7,320	$228	4	$188	160	$7,885	$14.63	$3,423	$114	7	$102	241	$3,466
May 2010	$49.28	$7,885	$225	4	$197	164	$7,477	$14.38	$3,466	$113	7	$101	248	$3,182
June 2010	$45.59	$7,477	$219	4	$182	168	$7,113	$12.83	$3,182	$109	8	$103	256	$3,246
July 2010	$42.34	$7,113	$239	5	$212	173	$7,849	$12.68	$3,246	$119	9	$114	265	$3,707
Aug 2010	$45.37	$7,849	$232	5	$227	178	$7,602	$13.99	$3,707	$116	8	$112	273	$3,696
Sept 2010	$42.71	$7,602	$216	5	$214	183	$8,702	$13.54	$3,696	$108	7	$95	280	$4,186
Oct 2010	$47.55	$8,702	$251	5	$238	188	$9,323	$14.95	$4,186	$125	8	$120	288	$4,458
Nov 2010	$49.59	$9,323	$244	4	$198	192	$9,828	$15.48	$4,458	$122	7	$108	295	$4,360
Dec 2010	$51.19	$9,828	$254	4	$205	196	$10,664	$14.78	$4,360	$127	8	$118	303	$4,775

There's no single "right" way to do this, so don't second guess yourself or let small things distract you from the big picture. *The important thing is that you get started and stay with it.* Being consistent in putting money into the market and keeping your transaction costs under control are more important factors than maintaining your allocations precisely. Mechanical strategies such as DCA are designed to make investing easier for you by removing your emotions from the equation. So don't stress out over the details. Relax, and enjoy the ride!

Reviewing the market lessons of years gone by only renews my commitment to the discipline . . .

. . . imposed by having a specific, well-researched strategy in place — a strategy that has *objective* decision-making criteria. Such discipline is essential to your investment survival for four reasons:

• **Every investment strategy involves some capital risk.** There's no way around it: to live is to take risks. In the same way, financial life has risks. Investing your capital involves accepting some risk of losing part or all; not investing invites the risk of losing buying power to inflation.

• **No one really knows what's going to happen next.** No one. Some things can be predicted. We know precisely when the sun is going to come up each morning, for instance. The investment world, on the other hand, is about people and their attitudes about money. It's primarily a world governed by human emotions and behavior and, as such, cannot be predicted with certainty by anyone or any method.

• **The market won't present a clear warning when it's time to act.** The reality is that you cannot know in advance how long a good thing is going to last. It might last a long time. On the other hand, it might end tomorrow. Systematic investing will help balance the up and down swings in your portfolio.

• **Our emotions naturally cause us to postpone committing ourselves.** First, there's our natural optimism. Second, there's simple greed. And third, there is an enormously powerful influence felt by every investor: the "fear of regret." It's this fear of doing the wrong thing that can paralyze us and prevent us from taking prompt action.

The key to successful investing is having the self-discipline to stick to your strategy.

It's not that any strategy is perfect: there's no such thing. But a strategy doesn't have to be perfect to be profitable over time. The value of discipline and how it can protect us, from the markets and from ourselves, cannot be overstated. Keep that in mind as you risk your capital in what can be a high-risk endeavor. ◆

CHAPTER PREVIEW

Making the Transition:
How to Get from Where You Are
to Where You Want to Go

I. **The "right" portfolio moves can't be evaluated simply in terms of maximizing profits. Rather, such changes take into account your spiritual, intellectual, and emotional priorities.**

   A. No investment portfolio can be consistently positioned to maximize profits from coming events.

   B. The right portfolio move is one consistent with a specific, long-term, biblically sound strategy that you've adopted.

   C. The right portfolio move is one you understand.

   D. The right portfolio move is one that is prudent under the circumstances. It passes the "common sense" test.

   E. The right portfolio move is one that is consistent with your "investing self"—it fits comfortably.

   F. The right portfolio move is one for which you've taken plenty of time to pray and to seek trusted, experienced Christian counsel.

II. **A remodeling worksheet can provide an overview of how you go about making the transition.**

   A. The worksheet will list current equity and fixed-income holdings and allow you to conveniently calculate the percentage allocations between the two.

   B. The worksheet will show you which changes in holdings are necessary to alter your portfolio from its present structure to one that matches your investment temperament and long-term goals.

"Future shock is the disorientation that affects an individual when he is overwhelmed by change and even the prospect of change. It is the consequence of having to make too many decisions . . .

. . . about too many new and unfamiliar problems in too short a time. . . . We are in collision with tomorrow. Future shock has arrived." — Alvin Toffler

Do you ever feel like that? As if the decisions you are required to make, especially about your finances, are coming at you at an ever faster and more confusing rate? A great many people today are finding it increasingly difficult to know the "right" step to take. They wonder:

"Is this a good time to buy stocks?"

"Which mutual funds would be best?"

"Should I sell some of my employer's stock in order to diversify?"

"My CDs mature soon. Should I renew them for 90 days or a year?"

"How much of my retirement plan should I put in stocks versus bonds?"

"If I sell this losing investment and buy something else, will I be better off?"

Since we cannot know the future with certainty, it's obvious that no investment portfolio that any of us comes up with will ever be *perfectly* positioned to profit from upcoming events. As the future unfolds, it will always be possible to point to ways by which we could have made more money than we did—and some of them will appear incredibly obvious in retrospect! *This means it's pointless to think of the "right" investment portfolio simply in terms of maximizing profits. If that is your approach, you will always be frustrated and second-guessing your decisions.*

The "right" portfolio is one that realistically faces where you are right now, looks years ahead to where you want to go, *and has a high probability of getting you there on time.* As you consider "remodeling" your current holdings, let's look at some of the characteristics of the "right" steps to take.

• The right portfolio move is one that is consistent with a specific, long-term, biblically sound strategy you've adopted.

A trait I find among many of those I counsel is that their current investment portfolio tends to be a random collection of "good deals" and assorted savings accounts. Each investment appears to have been made on its own merits without much thought of how it fit into the whole.

I find savings accounts (because the bank was offering a "good deal" on CDs), company stock (because buying it at a discount is a "good deal"), a savings bond for the kids' education (because they read an article that said they were a "good deal" for college), a universal-life policy (because their insurance agent said it was a "good deal" for someone their age), a real-estate partnership (which their broker said was a "good deal" for people in their

The plans of the diligent lead to profit as surely as haste leads to poverty.

Proverbs 21:5

tax bracket), and 100 shares of XYZ stock (because their best friend let them in on this *really* "good deal").

As we've discussed, I want you to become an *initiator* (one who develops an individual investing strategy tailored to your personal temperament and goals) rather than a *responder* (one who reacts to sales calls, making decisions on a case-by-case basis). Then you can select the appropriate investments accordingly. The right investment step is the one that *you* seek out purposefully, knowing where it fits into the overall scheme of things.

• The right portfolio move is one you understand.

This typically involves at least two things. First, it's relatively simple. It's not likely that your situation requires exotic or complicated strategies. In fact, the single investment decision of greatest importance is pretty easy to understand. Do you know what it is? We covered it in chapter 13. It's deciding what percentage of your investments to put in stocks (where your return is uncertain) as opposed to bonds and other fixed-income investments (where your return is relatively certain). *This one decision has more influence on your investment results than any other.*

And second, you've educated yourself on the basics. When you're able to give a simple explanation of your strategy to a friend and answer a few questions, you've probably got at least a beginner's grasp. The right investment step is the one in which you understand what you're doing, *why* you're doing it, and how you expect it to improve matters. That's the least you should expect of yourself before making decisions that can dramatically affect your life and the lives of those you love.

The heart of the discerning acquires knowledge; the ears of the wise seek it out.
Proverbs 18:15

• The right portfolio move is one that is prudent under the circumstances. Does it pass the "common sense" test?

How much of your investing capital can you afford to lose and still have a realistic chance of meeting your financial goals? The investments that offer higher potential returns also carry correspondingly greater risks of loss. The right portfolio for you is not always the one with the most profit potential.

For example, it's usually best to not have a majority of your investments in a single asset or security. For that reason, people who have large holdings of stock in the company they work for often sell some of it in order to diversify. If the stock doubles after they sell it, does that mean they did the "wrong" thing? No, they did the right thing. After all, the stock could have fallen dramatically as well as risen. What would a large loss have done to their retirement planning? The right investment step is the one that protects you in the event of life's occasional worst-case scenarios. Generally, this moves you in the direction of increased diversification.

A simple man believes anything, but a prudent man gives thought to his steps.
Proverbs 14:15

• **The right portfolio move is one that is consistent with your "investing self"—will it fit comfortably?**

I developed the structure of the four Sound Mind Investing temperaments to illustrate that, as part of our separate God-given identities, we each have different capacities to accept risk and uncertainty. Some people seem to be energized by the thrill of adventure, whereas others prefer more secure, predictable surroundings. If you make investments that violate your natural temperament, you are much more likely to react emotionally when the occasional setbacks occur and objective decision making is needed.

When someone presents me with two investing alternatives and invites my opinion, I often ask, "Which one would you prefer to do, and why?" This is my way of learning more about that person's investing temperament. Unless I find a grievous flaw in their financial logic, I encourage taking the course of action the person intuitively leans toward. An investor is more likely to stick with a strategy over the long term and exercise the self-discipline to be successful if he or she is *comfortable* with a portfolio. The right investment step is the one that enhances your ability to make calm and well-reasoned decisions.

Do not be anxious about anything, but in everything, by prayer and petition, with thanksgiving, present your requests to God. And the peace of God, which transcends all understanding, will guard your hearts and your minds in Christ Jesus.
Philippians 4: 6–7

• **The right portfolio move is one for which you've taken plenty of time to pray and to seek trusted, experienced Christian counsel.**

Because your decisions have long-term implications, take all the time you need to become informed. Don't be in a hurry; there's no deadline. A good friend once commented to me: "The Christian life isn't a destination; it's a way of travel." Likewise, you're not under pressure to predict the best possible portfolio for the next six months or make this year's big killing. You're remodeling in order to settle in for a comfortable investing lifestyle that will serve you well for decades.

Besides, prayer takes time. You need time to pray, ask for the counsel of others, and reflect. You should consider the alternatives, examine your motives, and continue praying until you have peace in the matter. If you're married, you should pray with your spouse and talk it out until you reach mutual agreement. You're in this together and, rain or shine, you both must be willing to accept responsibility for the decision. The right investment step is the one that results from careful and prayerful consideration. This will add to your steadfastness during the occasional rough sledding along the way.

The way of a fool seems right to him, but a wise man listens to advice.
Proverbs 12:15

With these points in mind, it's time to walk through a "remodeling" project that revamps an investment portfolio. I have designed it . . .

. . . to teach by example. Carefully follow the steps taken by Tom and Marilyn Randolph as they adjust their portfolio to achieve the mix that they have decided is best for them given their tolerance for risk and current stage of life—40% invest-by-owning (usually stocks) and 60% invest-by-lending (bonds and savings). In developing this example, I assumed that Tom's 401(k) plan offers the typical choices: company stock, blue-chip stock fund or S&P 500 index fund, long-term bond fund, and money-market fund.

As you begin, keep in mind these two guiding principles:

• You don't need to *perfectly* achieve the recommended percentages for the various risk categories. It's good enough to come close; when in doubt, go with less risk.

• You don't have to change things all at once. Take it in steps over many months (or even a few years) as your comfort level grows.

Step 1: List the current values of your assets.

Basically, this means writing down the investments over which you exercise control. Divide them into two groups: investments where you are an owner and investments where you are a lender (see the notepad at right). There are two exceptions. Do not count the savings set aside for your contingency fund—they are not part of your long-term risk-taking strategy. Also, do not include money set aside for the children's education. These assets should go through their own remodeling process once you understand how to do it.

If you're married, put down both spouses' investments. Married couples are in this together— I discourage attempts to keep "his" money separate from "her" money. Also, as you can see from Tom and Marilyn's list, you don't need to distinguish between retirement or current savings, or when you bought them or what you paid. Nor do you care whether the investment is held in a normal brokerage account, an IRA, a 401(k), a variable annuity, or any other legal structure in which investments are placed. The goal is to list on paper your various investments and the amount you would expect to receive if you sold or exchanged them.

INVESTMENT HOLDINGS OF TOM AND MARILYN RANDOLPH

INVESTMENTS WHERE WE ARE OWNERS

$6,000	Marilyn's pension plan invested in a growth fund
8,300	Tom's 401(k) at work invested in the "S&P 500" portfolio
15,800	Tom's 401(k) at work invested in G.E. stock
4,300	Goodyear shares inherited from Marilyn's mother
3,300	Utility shares inherited from Marilyn's mother
$37,700	Equity portion is 62% of total holdings

INVESTMENTS WHERE WE ARE LENDERS

$1,900	Tom's 401(k) at work invested in long-term govt bonds
6,200	Marilyn's pension plan invested in long-term corp bonds
3,000	IBM bond inherited from Marilyn's mother
4,600	Tom's 401(k) at work that's invested in the money market
2,400	Credit union passbook joint savings account
2,600	Tom's IRA invested in a bank money market account
2,600	Marilyn's IRA invested in a bank money market account
$23,300	Fixed income portion is 38% of total holdings
$61,000	Total Investment Holdings

When you're finished, add up the totals and calculate the percentage each group represents in your total holdings. This is your first insight into how much risk you're taking in your portfolio. If you're like most people, your investments carry a higher overall risk level than you expected.

Step 2: Determine what dollar changes are needed.

Now that the Randolphs know their current mix (62% equity and 38% fixed income), they can compute the dollar amount of the change needed to achieve the mix they seek (40% equity and 60% fixed income). Obviously, they will need to decrease the equity portion and increase the fixed-income portion.

Here's how they calculate the dollar amount. They take the total value of their holdings of $61,000 and multiply it times 40% to arrive at the equity portion goal—$24,400. They then subtract this from their current equity portion of $37,700 to learn how much of a decrease is needed.

This tells them that they need to sell $13,300 worth of securities from the equity side and reinvest it over on the fixed income side. This will decrease their equity portion to $24,400 (current $37,700 less sales of $13,300) while increasing the fixed-income portion to $36,600 (current $23,300 plus new investments of $13,300). Once this is done, their desired mix will have been accomplished.

Step 3: Decide which holdings to sell in order to meet your dollar goal.

They say that "timing is everything." When it comes to investing, the timing of buy orders gets all the attention. Many forces work to incline us toward making an investment (e.g., friends, relatives, brokers, and financial planners), but few return with the message "It's time to sell that stock I told you about!"

The Randolphs now know they need to liquidate $13,300 worth of their equity holdings—but which ones? Here are a few guidelines that may be of help in deciding.

• Keep in mind any limitations imposed by your pension holdings. For example, if Tom sells some of his 401(k) equity holdings, he can reinvest the money only in *other* 401(k) offerings. This limits the number of possible ways he can accomplish his goal.

• Move toward increased diversification. This means that Tom's large holding in his employer's stock (G.E.) could prudently be reduced.

• Sell the losers. The alternative is to sell the winners—the strong companies that have fulfilled your hopes and expectations. Why would you want to unload the winners and hang on to the disappointments? Go ahead and acknowledge that they didn't work out. If the stock is not being held in a tax-deferred account, you can take advantage of the loss for tax purposes.

• Sell a stock when the reason you bought it is no longer valid. For whatever reason (the expected new product didn't pan out, the merger was called off, they didn't land the big government contract, etc.), the original case for investing in the stock no longer holds true.

• Sell stocks whose earnings have fallen. Any company looks bad if it reports lower earnings, so its management will go to great lengths (and accounting mischief) to avoid doing so. Only when they exhaust all their options for disguising their deteriorating profits will management generally report earnings that are down (for the most recent 12-month period compared with the previous 12 months). It may be a good time to exit.

• Don't worry. Many people fear "being wrong" and selling something that later goes higher. They're right to expect it, but wrong to think there's anything they can do about it. You can't know the future, so be realistic and accept your limited vision—don't let it paralyze you.

The Randolphs decide to sell their Goodyear and utility stocks plus however many of Tom's G.E. shares are necessary to reach a total of $13,300. These moves are steps toward achieving greater diversification.

Step 4: Decide in which risk categories to make your new purchases.

Now that they've raised the $13,300 to add to their fixed-income portion, how do they decide *exactly* where to put it? Again, there are no absolute rules that govern this. There isn't just one "right" way to do your portfolio fine-tuning.

Let's assume that Tom and Marilyn decide to deal with the risk of rising interest rates by having roughly equal portions of their fixed income holdings in long-term bonds (over 10 years), medium-term bonds (over four years but less than 10 years), and money-market funds and savings accounts. That means allocating $12,200 (one-third of their fixed income portfolio of $36,600) to each of the three categories. The targets were attained as follows:

LEVELS OF INVESTMENT RISK

Investing by Lending (your fixed-income holdings)	Investing by Owning (your equity holdings)
Zero-coupon bonds	Oil and gas partnerships
High-yield "junk" bond funds	Gold/silver coins/bars
Long-term high quality bond funds	Real-estate partnerships
Long-term tax-free bond funds	Individual shares in small companies
High-yield "junk" tax-free bond funds	Sector funds
Fixed annuities	Small-company/growth funds
Medium-term high quality bond funds	International stock funds
Medium-term tax-free bond funds	Rental property
Govt-backed mortgage bond funds	Small-company index funds
Short-term high quality bond funds	Small-company/value funds
Short-term tax-free bond funds	Individual shares in large companies
Money-market mutual funds	Large-company/growth funds
Bank CDs/money market accounts	S&P 500 index fund
U.S. Treasury bills	Large-company/value funds
Volatility and risk is lowest at the bottom.	Volatility and risk is lowest at the bottom.

❶ They raised $7,600 by selling the Goodyear and utility stock, then invested in a new medium-term no-load bond fund at Vanguard.

(Note that once the Randolphs knew the *kind* of investments they wanted to make, they selected a no-load mutual fund organization *that offered funds with demonstrated performance excellence in their area of interest* — bonds.)

❷ The $3,000 IBM bond was sold and the proceeds added to the new Vanguard bond-fund account also. This increased the Randolphs' diversification.

❸ They withdrew $1,600 from their credit-union savings and also added to the new Vanguard bond-fund account, making the total $12,200.

❹ In Tom's 401(k) plan, he sold $5,700 worth of G.E. shares, transferring $4,100 of it into the long-term bond fund and $1,600 into the money-market fund. Note that none of this money left the 401(k), but was moved around *within* it.

The "remodeling" worksheets the Randolphs used are shown on pages 204-205. Each of the above numbered steps is shown in the "changes needed" columns. The final result is summarized on the notepad on page 203. Notice that they didn't feel they needed to follow my allocation suggestions "to the letter of the law." They had the flexibility of adjusting their bond holdings to fit their personal situation and preference.

To help you begin your own remodeling project, you'll find blank forms on pages 206-207.

It's at this stage that investors often "freeze up."
Many people seem to find investing to be a nerve-racking . . .

. . . if not downright scary experience. Making investment decisions, and then watching the results unfold, can be stressful. Do you become anxious when circumstances compel you to make important investing decisions? Most of us do to one degree or another. If my mail is any indication, a great degree of financial fretting is common. Three recurring comments lead the list of ways my readers express their concerns.

• "There's so much at stake. I'm afraid I'll make the wrong decision."

• "I don't have much experience. I'm afraid I'll make the wrong decision."

• "My savings aren't making enough now, but if I make a change I'm afraid I'll make the wrong decision."

What is the "wrong" decision, anyway? If you feel a wrong decision is like saying 2+2=5, then you're off track; such thinking implies investing decisions can be made with mathematical certainty. They can't. This doesn't mean the economy and investment markets are completely random, only that you're dealing with *probabilities*, not certainties and predictable events. Scientists can predict with great accuracy when the next eclipse of the sun will occur years into the future, yet they can't tell you if the sun will be "eclipsed" by clouds and ruin next week's picnic.

All of this is actually good news. It means anybody can play. It's like learning to drive a car. After a couple of lessons, you know enough to travel around town if you follow a few basic safety guidelines. After all, you're not trying to qualify for the Indy 500 — you just want to reach your destination. In the same way, once you understand the concepts in this book, you're fairly well equipped for making whatever decisions you face.

Pretend you're in a contest in which...

...you are to travel from coast to coast before the current interstate system was built. You can choose any route (but they're almost all two-lane roads), travel any speed, and take as much time as you want. There are no bonus points for getting there first — *the only goal is to arrive safely.* Everyone who does that "wins."

As you drive along, you constantly must make decisions. Should you take the route to the left or to the right? Is there construction or traffic up ahead? Will there be a motel with a vacancy? There are no scientific answers to these questions. Every decision requires some powers of observation, the ability to learn from your experiences, and a little common sense. You rarely come to a point where the decision is obvious. It would always be helpful to have "just a little more" information — but the challenge of the trip is the necessity of making choices *without having all the information. No one ever has all the relevant information.*

INVESTMENT HOLDINGS OF TOM AND MARILYN RANDOLPH AFTER REBALANCING

INVESTMENTS WHERE WE ARE OWNERS

$6,000	Marilyn's pension plan invested in a growth fund
8,300	Tom's 401(k) at work invested in the "S&P 500" portfolio
10,100	Tom's 401(k) at work invested in G.E. stock
$24,400	Equity portion is 40% of total holdings

INVESTMENTS WHERE WE ARE LENDERS

$6,000	Tom's 401(k) at work invested in long-term govt bonds
6,200	Marilyn's pension plan invested in long-term corp bonds
12,200	Vanguard intermediate-term bond index fund
6,200	Tom's 401(k) at work that's invested in the money market
800	Credit union passbook joint savings account
2,600	Tom's IRA invested in a bank money market account
2,600	Marilyn's IRA invested in a bank money market account
$36,600	Fixed income portion is 60% of total holdings
$61,000	Total Investment Holdings

Investing is a lot like our hypothetical road-trip contest. You can't know for certain what lies ahead; anyone who would have you believe otherwise is lying to you. It's *because* we can't know the future that we diversify and stay flexible. This brings us to one of the few rules that investing has: protect your capital! That's the only prerequisite for "arriving safely." When in doubt, take the safe route.

			INVEST-BY-OWNING		
			(Risk Generally Decreases as You Move Down the Page)		
What Goes Here	Your Current Holdings	Current Value		Changes Needed	After Rebalancing
Include in this section any investments that are not specifically named in the SMI strategy					
	Total				
Special purpose equity investments					
	Total				
International equity investments					
	Total				
Investments that fall into Stock Risk Category 4: Small companies + "growth" characteristics	Marilyn's pension plan	6,000			6,000
	Total	$6,000	9.8%		$6,000 9.8%
Investments that fall into Stock Risk Category 3: Small companies + "value" characteristics					
	Total				
Investments that fall into Stock Risk Category 2: Large companies + "growth" characteristics	Tom's 401(k) S&P 500 portfolio	8,300			8,300
	Tom's 401(k) G.E. stock	15,800		❹ −5,700	10,100
	Goodyear shares	4,300		❶ −4,300	
	Total	$28,400	46.6%		$18,400 30.2%
Investments that fall into Stock Risk Category 1: Large companies + "value" characteristics	Utility shares	3,300		❶ −3,300	
	Total	$3,300	5.4%		
	INVESTING BY OWNING	$37,700	61.8%	−$13,300	$24,400 40.0%

INVEST-BY-LENDING
(Risk Generally Decreases as You Move Down the Page)

What Goes Here	Your Current Holdings	Current Value	Changes Needed	After Rebalancing
Include in this section any investments that are not specifically named in the SMI strategy				
	Total			
Special purpose bond investments				
	Total			
Investments that fall into Bond Risk Category 4: Lower quality high-yield (junk) bonds				
	Total			
Investments that fall into Bond Risk Category 3: Long-term bonds of generally high quality	Tom's 401(k) long-term govts	1,900	❹ +4,100	6,000
	Marilyn's pension plan	6,200		6,200
	Total	$8,100 13.3%		$12,200 20.0%
Investments that fall into Bond Risk Category 2: Medium-term bonds of generally high quality	Vanguard Intermed-term Index		❶ +7,600	
	Vanguard Intermed-term Index		❷ +3,000	
	Vanguard Intermed-term Index		❸ +1,600	12,200
	Total			$12,200 20.0%
Investments that fall into Bond Risk Category 1: Short-term bonds of generally high quality	IBM bond (matures 6/2020)	3,000	❷ −3,000	
	Total	$3,000 4.9%		
Cash-equivalent investments like savings accounts, CDs, T-bills, and money market funds	Tom's 401(k) money market	4,600	❹ +1,600	6,200
	Credit union joint savings	2,400	❸ −1,600	800
	Tom's IRA bank money market	2,600		2,600
	Marilyn's IRA bank money market	2,600		2,600
	Total	$12,200 20.0%		$12,200 20.0%
	INVESTING BY LENDING	$23,300 38.2%	+$13,300	$36,600 60.0%

INVEST-BY-OWNING
(Risk Generally Decreases as You Move Down the Page)

What Goes Here	Your Current Holdings	Current Value	Changes Needed	After Rebalancing
Include in this section any investments that are not specifically named in the SMI strategy				
	Total			
Special purpose equity investments				
	Total			
International equity investments				
	Total			
Investments that fall into Stock Risk Category 4: Small companies + "growth" characteristics				
	Total			
Investments that fall into Stock Risk Category 3: Small companies + "value" characteristics				
	Total			
Investments that fall into Stock Risk Category 2: Large companies + "growth" characteristics				
	Total			
Investments that fall into Stock Risk Category 1: Large companies + "value" characteristics				
	Total			

INVEST-BY-LENDING				
(Risk Generally Decreases as You Move Down the Page)				
What Goes Here	Your Current Holdings	Current Value	Changes Needed	After Rebalancing
Include in this section any investments that are not specifically named in the SMI strategy				
	Total			
Special purpose bond investments				
	Total			
Investments that fall into Bond Risk Category 4: Lower quality high-yield (junk) bonds				
	Total			
Investments that fall into Bond Risk Category 3: Long-term bonds of generally high quality				
	Total			
Investments that fall into Bond Risk Category 2: Medium-term bonds of generally high quality				
	Total			
Investments that fall into Bond Risk Category 1: Short-term bonds of generally high quality				
	Total			
Cash-equivalent investments like savings accounts, CDs, T-bills, and money market funds				
	Total			

You control the level of risk you take by deciding how you divide your money between the two choices—to invest by lending (lower risk) and to invest by owning (higher risk). Don't make decisions in isolation (e.g., "Should I renew this CD?" or, "Should I change the mix in my 401(k) plan?") without taking into account how the decision affects your overall mix.

Scripture teaches that *"to the LORD your God belong the heavens, even the highest heavens, the earth and everything in it"* (Deuteronomy 10:14). God has ownership rights; we have management responsibilities. That's why, whether you have many or few investments, doing your best to manage them in a God-pleasing manner is a task that must be taken seriously. It's a lifelong calling. ◆

CHAPTER PREVIEW

Performance Momentum and SMI's Fund Upgrading Strategy

I. **A Just-the-Basics strategy (chapter 14) is a "passive" strategy that seeks to match the performance of the overall stock market through the use of index funds. A "Fund Upgrading" strategy, in contrast, invests the stock portion of one's portfolio in "actively managed" mutual funds in an effort to *beat* the market's return.**

    A. Economic conditions and expectations are constantly shifting. Predicting future market movements is nearly impossible to do with any consistency.

    B. Rather than try to predict what the market will do next, a better approach is to seek to follow already-established short-term market trends. In investing, this type of approach is referred to as a "momentum strategy."

II. **Fund Upgrading is based on two key findings:**

    A. Performance results that are more than one year old are no longer very meaningful or predictive of future performance.

    B. Short-term recent performance from the past year is predictive of short-term future performance. This short-term performance, then, becomes our guide to selecting which mutual funds to own.

III. **Fund Upgrading is a "mechanical" (i.e., unemotional) process for selecting funds to purchase, as well as for determining when a fund should be sold.**

    A. More than 1,000 stock funds are given a performance-momentum score based on their most recent 3-, 6-, and 12-month history.

    B. All funds are then categorized according to the risk-category system described in chapter 12.

    C. Top-performing funds in each risk category are purchased, and held until a fund's momentum score falls out of the top 25% of its risk category. At that point, the fund is sold and a new top-peforming fund is purchased.

IV. **This simple process requires monthly attention and a subscription to the *Sound Mind Investing* newsletter. It has paid off exceedingly well for readers in the past, making it my newsletter's most popular strategy.**

In chapter 14, I discussed a Just-the-Basics strategy that utilizes index funds in an effort to match the stock market's overall results. If that's all you're looking for, you can skip this chapter. But for those investors willing to take a more active role...

...the possibility exists of not only matching, but *exceeding,* the market's rate of return. The primary strategy I've used in my *Sound Mind Investing* (SMI) newsletter to accomplish this is called "Fund Upgrading." It requires a few minutes of time each month and a subscription to SMI. But, as I will show in this chapter, it has repaid the time and expense of SMI readers many times over.

Investors have always wanted to believe the myth of the market wizard...

...who can peer into the future and reliably predict what will happen next. At the start of the 1980s, the reigning media investment superstar was Joe Granville. When he predicted market weakness and told his followers to sell everything, the stampede to the exit door caused the Dow Jones Industrial Average to fall more than 3% on the heaviest volume of trading in the history of the New York Stock Exchange up to that time.

But Granville failed to foresee the great 1980s bull market. On the contrary, as it began his skepticism was so great that he advised his followers to "go short" (selling shares with the expectation of buying them back later at lower prices). This was a costly and lengthy disaster for Granville's followers. Later, after missing the major market advance of the early 1980s, he turned bullish—right at the top of the market before the crash of 1987. His reputation never recovered.

Robert Prechter replaced Granville as the leading forecasting guru. He captured center stage with forecasts based on a rather mysterious theory of market movements and mass psychology called the Elliott Wave. He was the first to call for a Dow move to the then-incredible heights of 2700+, a forecast that was widely derided as absurdly optimistic. As that goal was approached, he raised his sights to the 3600+ area. There is some controversy as to whether he changed his mind in time to get his followers out before the 1987 crash. He expected the 1990s to be disastrous for the stock market and advised, "The 1990s will be the decade of cash. Stay in U.S. treasury bills." Not surprisingly, when the 90s turned out to be a great decade for owning stocks, he lost the influence he once commanded.

We could also add:

• Elaine Garzarelli (who gained prominence when she advised getting out of the market shortly before the '87 crash and then faded from public view when she couldn't sustain a guru-level of omniscience);

• Mary Meeker (queen of the Internet analysts who could cause dot.com stocks to skyrocket with a mere favorable mention, but then let her followers lose 80%-90% of their capital by silently standing by as the mania collapsed); and,

• the Gardner brothers of Motley Fool fame (who eventually threw in the towel on their "Foolish Four" strategy when it misfired for several years).

One respected Wall Streeter says: "Investors are always looking for a messiah. The system will always produce a new superstar, and inevitably, the star will fall flat on his or her face."

It's impossible to predict future market movements with consistent accuracy. That's why "market gurus" come and go, and it's also one of the reasons that a majority of actively managed stock mutual funds (those funds with a manager who tries to select the stocks that will perform best) nevertheless underperform the general market averages (as we discussed in chapter 14).

Another reason the average actively managed fund trails the overall market, often touted by indexing advocates, is cost. To understand why this is true, recognize that the returns of *all investors* combine to make up "the market." Consequently, the return of *all mutual funds* taken together will, by default, be very close to this overall market average. Thus, after subtracting operating expenses of 1%-2% per year plus commission costs, it's easy to see why most funds trail the market. Rarely are managers able to add enough value through their management to overcome these costs. This is why if you are planning to buy and hold one particular fund for several years, you are very unlikely to keep up with the market indexes.

Does this mean that there is no reason to invest in actively managed mutual funds? At first glance, that may seem to be the case. There are, in fact, two ways to keep ahead of the average mutual fund. One is to concede that the cost hurdle is too difficult, and simply invest primarily in index funds as called for in the Just-the-Basics strategy. Then you'll know that the results in your portfolio will be similar to (if not slightly better than) the market as a whole. More often than not, this means you'll do better than the "average" fund.

If you're not willing to settle for the market's average return...

...your other option is to *continually* stand ready to adjust your holdings so as to own only those funds that are demonstrating relatively superior results *at that time*. This fine-tuning process, whereby you initially invest in the top performers of recent months and then sell them when they surrender their place of leadership, is what I call "fund upgrading."

Upgrading is necessary because, as economic conditions and expectations change, market leadership rotates among large-, medium-, and small-sized companies. Furthermore, as this rotation takes place, it naturally favors some strategies over others. At times, a cautious value strategy is best; other times aggressive-growth investors are rewarded. But although market conditions are constantly changing, fund managers rarely change with them. What I mean is that most managers who are trained to invest in large "growth" companies (for example), can't change their philosophical stripes overnight and turn into small-cap "value" managers just because that sector of the market is strong at this stage of the cycle. For the most part, they just keep doing what they believe in—investing in the shares of large-growth companies.

That's why performance leadership among mutual funds is constantly rotating, and why numerous academic studies have shown that very few funds can consistently perform in the top ranks year after year. By implication, then, these studies indicate that there is very little predictive value in using a fund's long-term past performance as a forecaster of its future performance.

The best approach, therefore, is *not* trying to select one super-great fund in order to hold it for many years. Investing in a particular fund and staying with it for the long haul is unlikely to result in outstanding performance over the entire period. Strategies that lead you on a search for all-weather performers that you can supposedly buy and forget about—such as *Forbes* Honor Roll, *Consumer Reports* recommended funds, or Morningstar's well-known "star system"—do not result in superior performance.

The origins of "upgrading" go back at least 40 years...

...to a man named Burton Berry, founder of a helpful mutual-fund ranking newsletter called *NoLoad FundX*. Berry performed an interesting study of mutual-fund performance. He identified the 25 funds that had the best track records over a recent five-year period and posed this question: how many of these funds will be in the top-performing group again next year? *The surprising answer was only two of the 25.* He tried it again for a different five-year period, and the answer was *none*. Altogether, he checked out 17 different five-year periods and found that, on average, only two of the top 25 performers of the past five years made the list again the following year.

These facts offer persuasive evidence that selecting mutual funds on the basis of their recent five-year track records is not likely to identify the best funds for the coming year. However, several studies have shown there to be value in concentrating on a fund's *more-recent* track record as a predictor of future success. Therefore, it seems prudent to initially invest in a top-performing fund that has been doing an excellent job of late. But, when the fund falters (as it inevitably will), stand ready to exchange it for one of the new leaders. How do you do this? In his newsletter, Berry proposed a way to measure fund performance that would pinpoint how to make the necessary changes.

He devised a strategy which he called "upgrading." His basic assumptions, which my years of experience bear out, were that (1) performance results that are more than one year old are no longer very meaningful, and (2) more recent months should be weighted more heavily than distant months. These assumptions led Berry to develop a methodology for evaluating mutual-fund performance based on each fund's most recent 1-month, 3-month, 6-month, and 12-month performance. His approach also involved a "star system" where he awarded extra rating points for funds that place in the top of their peer group for each of the time frames being measured.

Building on Berry's two assumptions, I developed a similar, simpler formulaic approach for my newsletter readers (which I call "performance momentum") that I use to evaluate and rank the performance of mutual funds. These momentum-based rankings are available to my subscribers and form the basis for my fund selection within a Fund Upgrading strategy.

The performance-momentum rankings are the key to Fund Upgrading's success. And the key to these rankings...

...is that they focus *exclusively* on how a fund has performed lately. When assessing an investment's track record, the first question to be settled is "which period of time are we evaluating?" Last month? Last year? The last full market cycle? *The answer to this question has more influence on the outcome of a fund's ranking than any other single factor.* Most financial magazines use quite lengthy time frames when measuring performance and compiling their ratings. *Forbes, Business Week,* and *Consumer Reports* all use periods of at least five years. This is much longer than is either necessary or beneficial. In my Fund Upgrading strategy, I look only at the past 12 months, giving greater weight to the more recent months.

Look at it this way. As the baseball season hits the mid-way mark, who do you think is more likely to win the league pennant this year—the team that has done the best over the past 5 years, the team that won last year, or the team that has been the most dominant this year and is currently leading the league? In sports, the teams that have been strongest of late are the more likely winners in the coming months. The same is true in the world of mutual funds, and the momentum calculation is one good way to identify the contenders for the performance title.

The momentum score itself is easy to calculate—simply add up a fund's most recent 3-month, 6-month, and 12-month performance. As you do, notice that the most recent three months' performance is reflected in all three statistics. It represents 100% of the first number, 50% of the second number, and 25% of the final number. In this way, a fund's more recent performance is given greater weight. Stated another way, momentum counts each fund's most recent three-month performance 3 *times more* than it does the 12th month back. This formula takes into account both assumptions mentioned earlier: that results older than 12 months aren't very relevant, and that more recent months should be weighted more heavily than distant months.

My approach to this calculation is slightly different from Mr. Berry's.

The major differences are, first, I omit the 1-month performance results and the star system for awarding extra rating points. This change reduces the higher turnover that results from weighting the most recent month's performance so heavily in the calculation. And second, I assign funds to risk categories using the risk ladder discussed in chapter 12, which is based on the nature of a fund's portfolio holdings. I made this change to get a clearer picture of how each fund compares against its peers within the same risk category.

I make no claim that my approach is superior to Burton Berry's, and remain indebted to him for introducing me to the "upgrading" concept.

Applying the momentum rankings *within* each stock-risk category, and thereby rating a fund only against other funds of the same type, is an important part of the process. Doing so assures that we stay reasonably diversified, and not end up owning a portfolio of funds all invested in similar types of stocks. As important as it is to make good fund selections, two decisions are even more important: the asset allocation decision—what percentage of your investments should be in stocks and what percentage in bonds—and the decision of how much to invest in each stock and bond risk category. Chapter 13 explained how to make these critical decisions for yourself in light of your personal risk tolerance and season of life.

Here's an overview of the process...

...my newsletter staff uses to identify the funds we recommend in the SMI newsletter's model portfolios:

(1) Using data from Morningstar's extensive database of mutual-fund performance, we place all the funds that we follow (well over 1,000) in each fund's proper risk category. Then we rank them according to their most recent performance momentum.

(2) Initially, we begin with the top 5-10 in each risk category and start a process of elimination. We rule out funds with characteristics that make them unsuitable for our purposes, such as those that charge loads, are closed to new investors, are not available through the brokerage firms where we recommend our readers have their accounts, and those with a higher risk than seems appropriate for that particular category. Our winnowing criteria are appropriate for making recommendations to thousands of SMI newsletter readers who don't wish to trade a lot; it doesn't mean the funds eliminated in this way won't prove to be good performers in the coming months. We settle on four finalists that make our recommended list.

(3) As long as our current recommendations continue to be ranked in the top one-fourth of their peer group, we hold them. Funds that fall out of the top quartile usually are sold. This unemotional selling discipline is

HOW THE PERFORMANCE OF JUST-THE-BASICS AND FUND UPGRADING COMPARE TO THAT OF THE MARKET

	Overall U.S. Market	Just-the-Basics	Fund Upgrading
1998	23.4%	18.2%	9.3%
1999	23.6%	28.2%	30.7%
2000	−10.9%	−11.5%	−2.7%
2001	−11.0%	−12.3%	4.8%
2002	−20.9%	−19.6%	−14.1%
2003	31.6%	35.7%	46.7%
2004	12.5%	15.6%	17.3%
2005	6.4%	9.0%	12.0%
2006	15.8%	17.2%	17.4%
2007	5.6%	7.1%	14.3%
2008	−37.2%	−39.3%	−38.8%
2009	28.3%	33.9%	33.6%
2010	17.2%	20.0%	17.8%
2011	1.0%	−3.4%	−5.3%
2012	16.1%	17.6%	14.1%
Total	**104.0%**	**124.4%**	**236.4%**

a vital part of the Upgrading process. It keeps us from continuing to hold funds long after they've lost their upward momentum.

(4) When we need a replacement, we begin the process again.

As you can see, following the Fund Upgrading strategy requires an on-going monthly time commitment. Unlike Just-the-Basics, which allows you to set your portfolio mix at the beginning of the year and forget it until the following year, Upgrading requires you to monitor your holdings each month and replace funds as they drop off the recommended list. It also requires you to have a subscription to *Sound Mind Investing* to receive the monthly ongoing updates (visit www.soundmindinvesting.com for details on how to become a subscriber).

Thankfully, the actual Upgrading process is quite simple. When each month's issue of the SMI newsletter is released, readers check to see if any of the specific recommended funds they own have been replaced. If so, they simply log in to their brokerage account, sell the old recommendation and buy the new replacement. That's all there is to it.

The extra effort involved in Upgrading has paid off in a big way.

SMI's Fund Upgrading strategy doesn't beat the market every year, but it has managed to put together an impressive track record over time. As the table on the far left shows, over the past 15 years (1998-2012), Upgrading's total gain was 236.4%, more than twice that of the U.S. stock market's total gain of 104.0% (as measured by the Wilshire 5000). Said differently, if an investor had started that period with $100,000, they would have ended it with roughly $336,000 if they had invested it using Fund Upgrading, compared to $204,000 if it had earned the U.S. market's rate of return. This is depicted in the graph below.

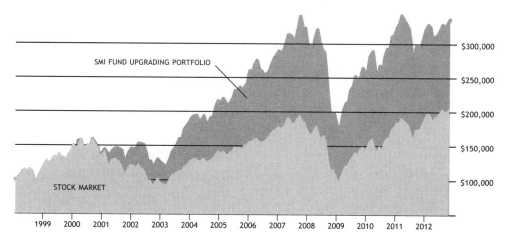

For those who want a one-time "set it and forget it" approach...

...to investing, the Just-the-Basics strategy discussed in chapter 14 is tough to beat. Likewise, for those with extremely limited investment choices (such as within a college 529 plan or some small 401(k) plans), that indexing-based strategy makes a lot of sense.

However, as the data on pages 214-215 make clear, significant improvements over the market's rate of return are attainable for those willing to invest just a little time each month. The combination of relative simplicity and excellent returns has made Upgrading my newsletter's most popular investment strategy.

As the bear market of 2008 made clear, however, even a great strategy such as Upgrading can't always protect against severe downturns. To do that, a different type of approach is required, one that is more defensive in nature. We offer such a strategy in the SMI newsletter, and call it "Dynamic Asset Allocation." That strategy is the subject of our next chapter.

18

Dynamic Asset Allocation:
A Lower-Risk Investing Strategy

I. **Economic uncertainty is always present, but today's level of economic uncertainty is unlike anything most of us have experienced.**

   A. Federal Reserve actions have pushed bond yields to unnaturally low levels, setting up the likely prospect of poor bond returns, or possibly even losses, over the second half of the decade.

   B. The uncertain prospects for bonds, which are traditionally considered the "safe" part of a portfolio, has created an appetite among investors for alternative approaches to the standard stock/bond portfolio construct.

   C. Rather than holding an unchanging combination of stocks and bonds regardless of the current economic climate, one approach that has shown great promise is to only own those asset classes currently showing strength.

II. **Dynamic Asset Allocation (DAA) is a strategy designed to rotate among six distinct asset classes—U.S. stocks, foreign stocks, real estate, gold, bonds, and cash.**

   A. The goal is to own those classes currently showing the greatest strength—and just as importantly, to avoid those asset classes showing weakness.

   B. Each asset class is represented by a specific ETF (see chapter 9) that does a good job capturing the returns of that class.

   C. DAA evaluates the recent momentum of each asset class monthly, always owning the top three performing asset classes. A DAA portfolio, then, will always consist of three ETFs, re-evaluated monthly.

III. **Testing of this approach over 30+ years showed DAA would have provided returns superior to those of the stock market overall, while being markedly less volatile. DAA would have lost money over a calendar year only once since 1982.**

IV. **DAA is appropriate as a stand-alone strategy, or in combination with another core SMI strategy, such as Just-the-Basics or Fund Upgrading.**

   A. DAA is exceedingly *simple* to implement. But that doesn't mean it will be emotionally *easy* to follow.

   B. That said, the risk/return profile of DAA is such that it should prove to be a much easier strategy than most for investors to stick with over time.

The traditional method of fine-tuning risk has been to adjust how much of a portfolio is invested in stocks and how much in bonds (as I explained in chapter 13). This has worked beautifully...

...over the past three decades as declining interest rates have added an extra kick to bond returns. However, in response to 2008's financial crisis and recession, the Federal Reserve embarked on an unprecedented campaign to drive interest rates down to levels never previously witnessed.

By the middle of 2012, the 10-year Treasury bond, which acts as a benchmark of sorts for a wide variety of other financial instruments, was yielding only 1.4%—a huge drop from the 6.6% average yield of the past 50 years. Remember the most important principle you need to know about investing in bonds: their yields and prices *always* move in opposite directions (chapter 11). That means the historically depressed bond yields we've seen from 2008-2013 can mean only one thing for future bond prices: as those yields eventually rise back toward "normal," the prices of those bonds are going to fall.

But it wasn't only bonds that had seen a huge run up in prices since the dark days of the financial crisis. Stocks more than doubled from the 2009 bear market lows, and gold had made a major move up over the prior decade. The million-dollar question investors were asking themselves was this: Where does one invest in a world where everything looks expensive?

My SMI newsletter team and I spent a lot of time pondering this...

...problem during 2011-2012 in connection with the needs of our over-50 readers. One of the foundational investing rules is that the older you get, the more your investments should shift away from stocks and toward bonds. This advice has worked beautifully in recent decades as bond yields have fallen from the mid-teens to the low single-digits, causing the prices of previously issued bonds to rise and producing year after year of strong, stable returns.

However, as bond yields continued ever lower during this period, we wrestled with a growing unease regarding our traditional stock/bond portfolio framework. Specifically, we grew increasingly concerned that bonds will no longer provide the downside protection—the safe-haven aspect—that investors count on them to provide. With bond prices at all-time highs as a result of the Federal Reserve pushing yields to unnatural lows, it's safe to say the U.S. bond market had never been as overvalued as it was at that point.

Meanwhile, government borrowing has exploded. Our concern was that, like a rubber band wound tighter and tighter, a limit will eventually be reached. At some point, lenders will look at the massive debt loads that even "credit-worthy" borrowers such as the U.S. government are carrying and demand higher returns (that is, higher interest rates) for the added risk. Bond yields will eventually rise, and bond prices will eventually fall. The only question is when.

Unfortunately, there's no such thing as a permanent safe haven in investing.

This may come as a surprise to those who have watched money flood into U.S. Treasury bonds at every sign of trouble over the past decade. But we're reaching the point when government finances become the *source* of the trouble. That point has arrived in Europe already, and eventually it's coming to America.

(Reader alert: To lay the groundwork for the rationale behind the strategy I'll be explaining in this chapter, I must venture briefly into the realm of politics and economics. I apologize ahead of time.)

The dominant financial issue of our time is how to deal with the massive amount of debt that governments around the world have amassed. This problem has been building for decades, but the tipping point was reached in the aftermath of 2008's financial crisis. The pressure is on to reduce these debt loads as a percentage of national income.

This process of reducing debt in relation to income is called "deleveraging." It can be attempted in various ways. One way is to cut spending, which is often referred to as "austerity." This has been the approach taken in Europe the past few years. What we've learned from watching their efforts is that austerity in the face of an already weak economy is painful. This path has caused dramatic recessions in much of Europe, creating a vicious cycle of lower income, leading to lower tax revenues, leading to even greater government debt. This process is deflationary by nature, meaning prices and wages fall as unemployment rises and demand for goods declines.

Not only does austerity cause great economic pain, it also gets democratically elected politicians voted out of office! This lesson hasn't been lost on politicians in other countries, as we've witnessed in recent U.S. elections and during negotiations regarding the federal budget, taxes, and spending. Significant spending cuts, in today's environment, have been viewed as politically ill-advised by many in Washington. The "powers that be" aren't going to surrender without fighting for more deficit spending.

An alternative approach to stimulating an economy has been to increase the amount of money in circulation through what central banks have been doing with their "quantitative easing" programs. From 2008-2013, these massive efforts barely succeeded at keeping the global economy slightly above stall speed. The risk is that eventually inflation will be ignited by these stimulative measures that, in creating more money, essentially devalue the money already in circulation.

This hadn't happened by 2013 because the deflationary impact of recessions and deleveraging have overwhelmed these otherwise inflationary policies. But this could change, perhaps without much warning, particularly if real economic growth picks up once again. Ironically, governments currently welcome modest inflation, as it helps them repay their debts in cheaper dollars. But this is a dangerous game, as inflation is not easily tamed once unleashed.

Trying to predict the economic future is a losing game. But, given the aforementioned valuation extremes in the bond market, the stakes have rarely been higher. If bonds are no longer an adequate safe haven, where else can one turn?

The answer is that we turn, intially, to Harry Browne's theory.

In the late 1970s, an investment adviser named Harry Browne began promoting an investing strategy he called the "Permanent Portfolio" (PP). His main observation was that economic conditions change over time, cycling unpredictably through extremes of prosperity, inflation, recession, and deflation.

Each of these phases produces specific investment winners and losers. What you want to own during a recession may well be the opposite of what will perform well during an economic recovery, and so on. Browne's solution was to divide a portfolio into four equal investments, each highly uncorrelated with the others (meaning they each "march to different drummers").

The portfolio was to be divided into four equal pieces—stocks, bonds, gold, and interest-earning short-term investments such as U.S. Treasury bills (referred to as "cash" for short). These were selected because each would excel under a different economic extreme. Thus, the portfolio would always have at least one of the four pieces completely in tune with the current environment. Other than rebalancing periodically, this four-equal-pieces approach was unchanging, thus the Permanent Portfolio name.

This exceedingly simple strategy has performed quite admirably over the past three decades. From 1982-2011, such a portfolio gained roughly 8.2% per year. The S&P 500 gained 11.0% per year, but did so with significantly greater volatility and risk. Remember, only 25% of the PP was in stocks. The real virtue of this approach was how little volatility it generated: only two years of negative returns, and the worst (2008) was just -7.2%. This type of smooth ride has appealed to investors who lost more than 30% in stocks during 2008 alone, not to mention three consecutive years of losses between 2000-2002.

My team and I liked the main idea of the PP strategy, but there seemed to be two significant downsides.

First, while our goal was to create a strategy that would satisfy safety-conscious investors, the PP was more conservative than most investors need. Allocating one-fourth of one's portfolio to cash may have made sense in the late 1970s when that would earn 15% in a money-market fund. Today, cash earns virtually nothing, so permanently fixing a quarter of the portfolio there is a non-starter. If this type of approach was going to work for our readers, we clearly were going to need to broaden the basket of asset classes beyond the four proposed by Harry Browne.

The second problem has less to do with the portfolio and more to do with human nature. The PP has looked great over the past decade or so, due to stocks being weak while bonds and gold have been soaring. It will always look its best following sharp bear markets in stocks, of which we've had two in the past dozen or so years. But there have been long stretches when the PP lagged the stock market badly.

I've watched investor behavior closely over the past few decades, and know how few have the willpower to stick with an approach like this when stocks are crushing the returns of their PP. Stocks gained more than 20% for five straight years from 1995-1999, while the PP earned more than 11% only once! Investors, even conservative ones, simply don't stick with systems at times like those—the emotional component is simply too powerful. And yet, the years that followed were *exactly* the time to embrace the Permanent Portfolio! If a PP investor, tired of missing the gains of great years such as 1995-1999, were to give up and move into stocks at the end of that period, he or she would have done so just in time to experience the sharp losses of 2000-2002.

It seemed that a timing mechanism of some sort would be needed.

While a pure application of the PP wasn't going to work for us, it did spark our thinking about working with asset classes that weren't correlated to each other. The breakthrough came when we started testing what happens when we own *only the asset classes showing upward momentum at that particular time.* Sound familiar? It should—we were simply applying an Upgrading-like momentum rating (see chapter 17) to the Permanent Portfolio idea.

After much testing and many iterations, we emerged with a simple but powerful strategy. Our roster of asset classes eventually expanded to six: the PP's original four, plus foreign stocks and real estate. Using these six asset classes, we applied a momentum screen at the beginning of each month, identifying the three asset classes we wanted to be in and—perhaps more importantly—the three we wanted to avoid. Each month we ran the numbers again and adjusted our holdings as needed. The results, shown on the next page, were very encouraging.

We called the strategy "Dynamic Asset Allocation," DAA for short.

It's "dynamic" in the sense that it's active, requiring continuous monitoring (as opposed to the passive PP which required no ongoing attention). And "asset allocation" is Wall Street jargon referring to how you divide your portfolio into various kinds of asset classes.

It's natural to scan the year-by-year results (see table at left) and focus on the final results at the bottom of the columns. Yes, DAA's 13.6% annualized return for the 30+ years is significantly better than the Wilshire 5000's 10.9%. That's great, but it's hardly the main story.

Remember, the beginning point of this journey was to find a replacement for bonds as a safe haven for risk-averse investors. If boosting a portfolio's bond allocation wasn't going to provide the safety from future market storms that we've counted on in the past, we needed something else that would. That's the real value of this new strategy.

Compare each year's returns for DAA vs. the market. A few things should stand out. First, DAA has only had one losing year, a loss of -6.6% in 1990. Now look specifically at 2000-2002 and 2008. While stocks were plummeting and investors were full of panic and fear, DAA investors would have been breathing easy.

(It's important to understand I'm not saying there won't be any losing years going forward with DAA. This is merely the picture of what has happened in the past using the mechanical rules we've established for the DAA strategy.)

The key to DAA's success is *winning by not losing*. By dramatically reducing losses, the strategy is able to come out ahead in the long run, even though it doesn't earn as much when stocks are soaring. Most importantly, this is a strategy that risk-averse investors can stick with. That's crucial, as even the most profitable systems are worthless if investors can't handle the volatility they experience along the way and sell everything out of fear. From 2000-2012, a period with two huge bear markets, DAA outperformed the stock market while being *42% less volatile!* That's a stunning combination. Slow and steady really does win the race!

The good news is this is an extremely *simple* strategy to implement. That doesn't mean it will be *easy*, but we'll get to that in a moment.

Here's how to implement the DAA strategy.

For each of the six asset classes, a single ETF is used (as shown in the table on the next page). Each month, we post on the *Sound Mind Investing* website which three ETFs are to be owned for the coming month. This means an SMI subscription is required to follow this strategy using the timing mechanisms that produced the history shown in the table. Of course, investors with a bent for research can attempt to develop their own timing indicators.

It's not the precise timing of making these changes that is the key to the strategy. Rather, *the key is being out of the weakest asset classes during their periods of decline or underperformance.*

Once an SMI subscriber learns which three ETFs to own for the month, the next step is to divide his or her portfolio (or the portion of the portfolio being

	Overall U.S. Market	DAA Strategy
1982	18.7%	23.3%
1983	23.5%	13.0%
1984	3.0%	7.9%
1985	32.6%	30.7%
1986	16.1%	28.7%
1987	2.3%	15.4%
1988	17.9%	7.8%
1989	29.2%	13.9%
1990	−6.2%	−6.6%
1991	34.2%	23.2%
1992	9.0%	10.9%
1993	11.3%	17.1%
1994	−0.1%	1.2%
1995	36.4%	20.8%
1996	21.2%	17.8%
1997	31.3%	20.3%
1998	23.4%	11.5%
1999	23.6%	12.5%
2000	−10.9%	7.1%
2001	−11.0%	4.0%
2002	−20.9%	10.4%
2003	31.6%	22.4%
2004	12.5%	19.3%
2005	6.4%	8.6%
2006	15.8%	25.7%
2007	5.6%	10.1%
2008	−37.2%	1.3%
2009	28.3%	17.6%
2010	17.2%	20.3%
2011	1.0%	1.4%
2012	16.1%	12.3%
30+ Yrs	**10.9%**	**13.6%**

THEORETICAL PERFORMANCE OF DAA COMPARED TO THAT OF THE MARKET

These are backtested results using mechanical formulas. From 1982-2005, the results are those from investing in the asset-class benchmarks; from 2006-2012, the results are those from investing in the actual ETFs (most of which didn't exist prior to that time).

allocating to DAA) into three equal amounts. Each of the three ETFs selected will get one-third of the money to be invested. Much as with Fund Upgrading, once the first three holdings are purchased, the SMI website is then checked each month to see if any of the ETFs are being replaced.

Many months, there won't be any trades to make, as the three currently recommended ETFs continue to be held. When a change is made, it usually will be one ETF at a time, as opposed to replacing all three at once. But whenever a change is called for, those following DAA will simply sell their total holdings of that ETF and use the proceeds to buy the new one.

Asset Class	Name of ETF	Ticker
U.S. Stocks	SPDR S&P 500 ETF	SPY
Foreign Stocks	iShares MSCI EAFE	EFA
Gold	SPDR Gold Trust	GLD
Real Estate	Vanguard REIT ETF	VNQ
Bonds	Vanguard L-T Bond	BLV
Cash	iShares Barclays TB	SHY

It's worth noting that implementing this strategy prior to the invention of ETFs several years ago would have been difficult. That's because DAA investors occasionally may be required to sell an ETF purchased only a month earlier. Traditional mutual funds, because of commonly required holding periods, don't allow such nimble moves; ETFs, in contrast, allow quick selling with no questions asked (see chapter 9 for more on ETFs). While a small commission may be required, many brokers now allow some ETFs to be traded commission-free. Those that aren't comission-free typically cost less than $10 per trade, again making this approach more feasible than it would have been in the past.

(A brief note about ETF substitutes: In some cases, substituting one ETF for another may be fine. For example, the iShares S&P 500 ETF, ticker IVV, may be free to trade at your broker, whereas our recommendation, SPY, is not. This substitution is fine because their long-term performance records are extremely similar. But be careful—not all similar sounding fund names have truly similar performance. Always check longer-term performance at a site such as Morningstar.com before substituting one ETF for another. While the most important thing is being in the right asset class, with ETF commissions being so low these days, you don't want to be penny-wise and pound-foolish by using an inferior ETF.)

Warning: DAA is *simple*, but following it won't always be *easy*.

Dynamic Asset Allocation is not a difficult strategy to understand or implement. The instructions are clear and SMI subscribers always know exactly what the strategy is calling for them to do.

However, *actually following through and doing it is another matter entirely!* The battle will be one of the mind and emotions. Right from the start, some readers will have a difficult time putting one-third of their portfolio into a single security, particularly one like GLD (gold)! At some point, you'll likely be told to sell an ETF at a loss that you just bought the month before. Are you mentally prepared to do so immediately without questioning the system or the signal?

I know this is difficult because, before founding SMI, I worked for more than a decade as a professional money manager (see chapters 27-28). During that time, I relied primarily on a market-timing strategy. As a result, I'm very aware of the emotional difficulty many investors have following even the most successful systems. Like any system, DAA is going to be wrong from time to time, and will require prompt action to quickly sell an ETF recently purchased. It won't always be easy to stick with the system, particularly if you're the one entering every order and seeing each whipsaw along the way.

Another difficulty arises from the fact there will be times when DAA lags the market for extended periods of time. Consider 1988-1991 or 1995-1999 (see backtesting results on page 222). This will inevitably cause some to drop the strategy, likely right before it would help them the most.

Whether to use DAA is not an all-or-nothing decision.

As with Just-the-Basics and Fund Upgrading, the DAA strategy can safely be used in as much of your portfolio as you feel comfortable with. It wouldn't concern me to have someone follow DAA as a primary (or even sole) strategy, given its superior performance *and* risk profile. The real question isn't whether DAA is safe, it's can you faithfully implement the system's signals?

Be aware, however, this strategy doesn't fit within your usual stock/bond allocation framework. Because it will steer you in and out of both stocks and bonds when appropriate, the best way to handle it is as a separate portfolio altogether. In other words, I suggest you determine what portion of your total portfolio, if any, to devote to DAA. Set that amount aside, take what's left and apply your normal asset allocation guidelines (as discussed in chapter 13) to that remaining part. For example, someone with a $180,000 portfolio might decide to put $80,000 in DAA and $100,000 in Upgrading (chapter 17). The investor would take the $80,000 and begin following DAA with that portion, then take the remaining $100,000 and divide it using his or her normal stock/bond allocation and the standard Upgrading process.

Conclusion

No one knows what the coming years will hold for the economy, or by extension, for the investment markets. Will we see growth or recession? Inflation or deflation? In the past, planning for these outcomes and the impact each would have on specific types of assets was problematic. Dynamic Asset Allocation frees us from that difficulty, equipping us with a tool to position our portfolios in the right place at the right time. With a risk profile that the most cautious investor can be comfortable with and a track record any investor can get excited about, it's a welcome breakthrough for such a time as this. ◆

Looking Toward Retirement

Go to the ant, observe her ways and be wise, which
having no chief, officer or ruler, prepares her food in
the summer and gathers her provision in the harvest.

Proverbs 6:6-8

"The Social Security system calls it quits.
Details at 11:00. And now, sit back and enjoy tonight's movie . . ."

CHAPTER PREVIEW

The High Cost of Living in Prime Time

I. **As the baby-boomer generation moves into retirement, the 65-and-over age group will grow from 12% of the total population to 20%. The need for adequate retirement planning will grow too.**

   A. Today's retirees are the wealthiest in U.S. history. With life expectancies of about 15 years following retirement, the vast majority of them live out their lives quite comfortably.

   B. As life expectancies continue to increase, the baby-boomer generation can reasonably expect to live 20 to 25 years past retirement.

   C. Longer life expectancies and the increasing cost of health care indicate that today's workers must plan carefully to be sure of financial security during retirement.

II. **Projecting your financial needs for a secure and comfortable retirement involves making many financial assumptions concerning inflation, future rates of return, and your life expectancy. Worksheets included in this chapter will help you through the process.**

III. **The truth about Social Security is that it is a wealth-transfer program, much like welfare. It takes money from one group of citizens (active workers) and gives it to another group of citizens (retirees).**

   A. It is not an "insurance" program because the amount you put in has no correlation to the amount you receive back. It does not "entitle" you to benefits because Congress can legally reduce them any time it chooses. Workers do not make "contributions" that "earn" them protection. Workers pay taxes that earn them nothing.

   B. When the baby-boomer generation enters retirement, there will be an inadequate number of active workers to tax. To balance the books, changes will be needed. You can expect a continuing national dialogue in coming years on various reform proposals. It's in your financial interest to become educated on the issues and participate in the debate.

When I was a small child, perhaps five or so, it used to fascinate me to think that someday I'd be "old" like my parents.

My mother was 21 when I was born, and I used to say to her (proud of my newly acquired ability to add numbers), "Mom! When I'm 21, you'll be 42!" And she'd answer back, "And when you're 42, I'll be 63!" Knowing it was my turn to go next, I would usually begin giggling at what to me was a really silly idea; namely, that I would *ever* be 63 or that she would *ever* be 84!

I could imagine being old enough to go to high school someday, and maybe college after that. I could almost imagine being old enough to get married, although I wasn't at all sure why I would ever want to. But picturing myself as being over 60, like my grandparents, was simply incomprehensible, beyond the limits of my youthful imagination.

I recalled my little childhood game recently as I read some fascinating statistics on what has been called "the graying of America." Did you know that today's generation of retirees (I'll call them "prime-timers") are the wealthiest in U.S. history? They participated in the postwar economic boom, watched their homes greatly escalate in value during the inflationary 1970s, and paid far less into pension plans and Social Security than they are now taking out in indexed benefits. At the same time, their cash flow needs are past their peak—the children are grown and out on their own, most mortgages are paid off, and work-related expenses are no longer a drag on the family budget.

The majority of Americans 65 and older are living relatively comfortably. According to the most current data available. . .

. . . from the U.S. Census Bureau, they had a median net worth of around $170,000 per household, well above the median for the general population of $69,000. Their median annual income was $33,100 (including Social Security and other government transfer payments), and more than 80% own their own homes.

The number of those joining the ranks of the retired is increasing at twice the rate of the overall population. By 2030, the post-WWII "baby boomers" will raise the prime-timer population to 72 million. This translates to about one out of every five Americans, up from only one in every seven now. What will retirement be like for us newcomers? (Although I was born a year too early to officially be a boomer, I'm taking a little editorial license and including myself.) Will we have it as good? The trends are not encouraging.

Somewhat paradoxically, the problem has to do with the fact that life expectancy continues to make remarkable gains. This increasing longevity is due mainly to the continuing improvements in health care; also contributing to longer lives is the American public's discovery of the benefits of nutrition, physical fitness, and healthier lifestyles. About three-fourths of prime-timers consider their health to be good-to-excellent. A significant decline in activities and interests doesn't generally occur until age 85 and later.

It now seems that moving into the 85-plus group has the "elderly" connotation formerly associated with the 65-plus group. One expert refers to them as "old-olds" to distinguish them from the "young-olds" who are *only* 65 to 84. The old-olds population is growing fast, projected to exceed 8.9 million by 2030. The U.S. Census Bureau projects that one in nine baby boomers will live into their late 90s. The number of centenarians (100 or older) is expected to grow six-fold from the current level of about 75,000 to nearly 450,000 by 2050!

In short, we'll all be living longer. And let's face it: living costs money. Of course, the longer the life, the greater the likelihood that support services will be needed; families now stand a greater chance than ever before of having a disabled elderly relative to support. More than 80% of us will enjoy reasonably good health, but even so, it's estimated that health care for prime-timers costs three-to-four times what it costs the rest of the population. Then there are the other niceties of everyday life, such as food, shelter, clothing, and recreation.

A fundamental fact of retirement life is that you don't want your money to run out before you do! For a reasonable guess as to how long you'll live in retirement, let's consider the case of 65-year-old males as shown in the table at right. On average, a man who lives to age 65 goes on to live another 17 years. Roughly half of this age 65 group will live more than 17 years and half will live less. To be on the safe side, financially speaking, you have to assume you'll be in the surviving group. If you make it to age 85, your expected life span is increased another six years. That means, in the absence of health reasons to the contrary, your goal should probably be to have enough money to support yourself (and your spouse, if married) into your 90s.

LIFE EXPECTANCIES		
Age	Men	Women
30	47 more years	52 more years
35	42 more years	47 more years
40	38 more years	42 more years
45	33 more years	37 more years
50	29 more years	33 more years
55	25 more years	28 more years
60	21 more years	24 more years
65	17 more years	20 more years
70	14 more years	16 more years
75	11 more years	13 more years
80	8 more years	10 more years
85	6 more years	7 more years
90	4 more years	5 more years
95	3 more years	4 more years

So that brings us to the big question: how much is all this going to cost, anyway?

If you're feeling a sense of urgency about learning the answer, good! I've got your attention. Now you're ready to make the effort needed to come up with a reasonable approximation of how much you should be budgeting for your own prime-time experiences. My goal is to help you understand what it will take to get you "in shape" financially in preparation for your retirement years. The process will involve making a series of assumptions. As we go along, I will explain the reasoning for the ones I make, but feel free to change them to fit your own sense of what is appropriate.

Getting in shape is not a particularly enjoyable process. It requires us to consistently sacrifice *certain* enjoyments now in return for *uncertain* benefits in the future. Watching my diet and scheduling regular workouts is, for me, extremely easy to postpone. Retirement planning, and the goal of getting in shape financially, is similar. It's no fun, it requires short-term sacrifice with little immediate positive reinforcement, and the benefits can seem a long way off. That may explain why too many of us arrive in our 60s ill-prepared—in both body and bank account—to get the most from our retirement years. You need not let this happen to you and your family.

We'll now turn to a step-by-step process that will help you see where you are now in relation to your long-term retirement needs.

The series of worksheets on the following pages is designed to serve only as a very general tool to help you think through your personal retirement planning responsibilities. It is based on a variety of assumptions concerning inflation and the rates of return you will earn on your investments. The closer you are to retirement, the more accurate it is likely to be. It's a good idea to run the numbers anew every year or two to keep them reasonably on target.

Unless noted, I've made no special attempt to take one's normal annual income-tax obligations into consideration. All the financial goals and standard of living assumptions are based on "before tax" dollars. My hypothetical couple, the Millers, have a current income of $50,000 before income taxes. The dollars they have remaining after they pay their income taxes are sufficient to support a certain standard of living. I assume the same will be true during their retirement. That is, they will have to pay their income taxes out of their projected retirement income just as they do their other living expenses. I took this approach because it was impossible to accommodate all of the various state and federal income tax rates currently in effect, let alone guess what they might be years into the future.

Let me warn you ahead of time that you might be tempted to feel discouraged when you complete step 11. That's the point at which you discover how much money you'll need in order to live comfortably for the rest of your life once you retire (based on assumptions you will have made regarding lifestyle costs, inflation, and your life expectancy). It will be a huge number. But don't stop there. By the time you factor in Social Security and your other pension and retirement assets, you'll likely find that the amount you need to save between now and retirement (step 45) is manageable.

But given Social Security's widely-publicized short-comings, is it realistic . . .

. . . to count on receiving your Social Security retirement benefits? That depends on how close *you personally* are to the day you switch teams—leaving the ranks of the people paying in and joining those in that happy state of grace where you receive monthly income for life far in excess of your earlier contributions. If you are planning to retire in the next 10 years, you're in pretty good shape. There may be minor adjustments to your benefits along the way, but congressional hypocrisy and cowardice is probably good for another decade of failure to face up to Social Security's monumental problems.

The rest of us are probably going to be pretty unhappy about whatever "fix" Congress finally comes up with (see page 241), and the younger we are now, the more unhappy we're likely to be. In the past, each generation of workers was asked to support the benefits for the previous generation. But it is falling to the baby-boomer generation and their children to pay for the retirement of not only the earlier generations but also to provide trillions in additional taxes for their own retirement as well.

According to government figures, the Social Security "trust fund" had a surplus on hand of $2.6 trillion at the end of 2012. This is supposed to be reassuringly good news, but it's not. The surplus is a drop in the bucket compared to the level of benefits already promised. Here's the coming scenario according to the *2013 Annual Report of the Board of Trustees of the Federal Old-Age and Survivors Insurance Fund and Federal Disability Insurance Trust Funds.*

• **The present situation.** Since 2010, taxes paid into the system by current workers have not been enough to pay promised benefits. Social Security has been using some of the interest income it receives from its Treasury IOUs to make up the difference. Think of it as a family spending all its regular income, and needing to use part of its interest income to support its standard of living.

• **From 2021 until 2033.** In 2021, the interest income will no longer be sufficient to make up the difference between tax revenue coming in and benefits being paid out. To continue paying benefits, Social Security will need to draw on its trust-fund assets. This has two important implications: (1) the Treasury Department will need to begin paying off its IOUs to the Social Security Administration, and (2) as the IOUs are paid off and the money distributed to retirees, there will be fewer IOUs left in the Social Security fund to earn interest for the coming years. In effect, our "family" is now beginning to spend the investment capital that has been providing the essential interest income. A downward spiral has begun.

• **2033 and later.** The surplus is gone; the trust fund is empty. All the IOUs have all been paid (don't ask me where the Treasury got the money) and the money spent. There is no interest income. And the tax money coming in covers only about three-fourths of the need. Our spendthrift family is broke.

RATES OF INFLATION / TABLE ONE

YEARS UNTIL RETIREMENT	3.0%	3.5%	4.0%	4.5%	5.0%	5.5%	6.0%
5	1.159	1.188	1.217	1.246	1.276	1.307	1.338
6	1.194	1.229	1.265	1.302	1.340	1.379	1.419
7	1.230	1.272	1.316	1.361	1.407	1.455	1.504
8	1.267	1.317	1.369	1.422	1.477	1.535	1.594
9	1.305	1.363	1.423	1.486	1.551	1.619	1.689
10	1.344	1.411	1.480	1.553	1.629	1.708	1.791
11	1.384	1.460	1.539	1.623	1.710	1.802	1.898
12	1.426	1.511	1.601	1.696	1.796	1.901	2.012
13	1.469	1.564	1.665	1.772	1.886	2.006	2.133
14	1.513	1.619	1.732	1.852	1.980	2.116	2.261
15	1.558	1.675	1.801	1.935	2.079	2.232	2.397
16	1.605	1.734	1.873	2.022	2.183	2.355	2.540
17	1.653	1.795	1.948	2.113	2.292	2.485	2.693
18	1.702	1.857	2.026	2.208	2.407	2.621	2.854
19	1.754	1.923	2.107	2.308	2.527	2.766	3.026
20	1.806	1.990	2.191	2.412	2.653	2.918	3.207
21	1.860	2.059	2.279	2.520	2.786	3.078	3.400
22	1.916	2.132	2.370	2.634	2.925	3.248	3.604
23	1.974	2.206	2.465	2.752	3.072	3.426	3.820
24	2.033	2.283	2.563	2.876	3.225	3.615	4.049
25	2.094	2.363	2.666	3.005	3.386	3.813	4.292
26	2.157	2.446	2.772	3.141	3.556	4.023	4.549
27	2.221	2.532	2.883	3.282	3.733	4.244	4.822
28	2.288	2.620	2.999	3.430	3.920	4.478	5.112
29	2.357	2.712	3.119	3.584	4.116	4.724	5.418
30	2.427	2.807	(3.243)	3.745	4.322	4.984	5.743
31	2.500	2.905	3.373	3.914	4.538	5.258	6.088
32	2.575	3.007	3.508	4.090	4.765	5.547	6.453
33	2.652	3.112	3.648	4.274	5.003	5.852	6.841
34	2.732	3.221	3.794	4.466	5.253	6.174	7.251
35	2.814	3.334	3.946	4.667	5.516	6.514	7.686
36	2.898	3.450	4.104	4.877	5.792	6.872	8.147
37	2.985	3.571	4.268	5.097	6.081	7.250	8.636
38	3.075	3.696	4.439	5.326	6.385	7.649	9.154
39	3.167	3.825	4.616	5.566	6.705	8.069	9.704
40	3.262	3.959	4.801	5.816	7.040	8.513	10.286

RETIREMENT PLANNING WORKSHEET: SECTION 1 **How much annual income will you need during prime time?**			
Overview	Step by Step	Millers	Yourself

To project the amount of annual income you are likely to need each year during retirement, we start by considering how your income needs will change as you enter retirement. The good news is that you can expect to maintain approximately the same standard of living you have now in spite of the fact you will have a lower income after you retire. There are several reasons for this:
    1. You won't have work-related expenses such as commuting, eating away from home, and wardrobe maintenance.
    2. You won't have the children to feed, clothe, transport, and educate.
    3. You won't have to pay Social Security and other payroll taxes (although, depending on your income situation, your SS benefits may be taxed).
    4. You won't be contributing to your personal and employer's retirement plans.
    5. And, assuming you arrive at retirement debt-free, you won't have home mortgage payments, car payments, or credit card payments to make.
    Of course, as I've already pointed out, you'll be facing increased health care costs, and since you'll have more free time, you're also likely to spend more on recreation. But all in all, most experts say that if your retirement income is around 80% of what you're earning now, you'll be in good shape; however, they warn that you're likely to face financial difficulties if it drops below 50% of what you're now making.
    Let's see how this works. I'm going to pick a family out of the mid-range of the census data and assume we are preparing a projection for them. Let's call them the Millers. The husband and wife are both 35 years old and have current income (before taxes) of $60,000 per year. What will their annual income needs be when they retire? To be on the conservative side, I'm going to use 90% as their "lifestyle maintenance" assumption; that is, the Millers' retirement income needs will be equal to 90% of their current level of income. By multiplying the lifestyle maintenance assumption times their current income (90% x $60,000), we learn that the Millers will need to generate $54,000 per year in income (before taxes) during their prime-time years.
    Of course, that's in today's dollars. How can we adjust this number so that it will have the same buying power during retirement that is does today? Continue on to the next page.
	1. Enter <u>your current before-tax annual income</u>, or if you wish to plan for a higher standard of living than you now enjoy, enter an amount that you believe would provide that standard of living.
	
	2. Enter <u>your lifestyle maintenance assumption.</u>
	
	3. Multiply Item 1 by Item 2. This provides an estimate of how much <u>annual income (before taxes) you will need during retirement</u> to maintain your standard of living.
		$60,000
		
		×90%
		
		= $54,000	

RETIREMENT PLANNING WORKSHEET: SECTION 2
What about the effects of inflation?

Overview	Step by Step	Millers	Yourself
The Millers' $54,000 will not always buy for them what it can buy today. We must take the $54,000 per year we projected as the amount of annual income the Millers will need during retirement and translate that to a higher number to allow for the fact that the value of the dollar shrinks a little every year. To do that, we refer to the inflation chart on page 231. For the Millers, I'm assuming that long-term inflation will average 4% per year. That's close to what it was for the final two decades of the 20th century. You're free to change the inflation assumption if you wish. Because your family's spending pattern is unique, your personal inflation experience will be different from any theoretical number computed for the "typical" American family. Choosing a higher rate, for example, is for the extra cautious person who wants to be doubly careful to arrive at retirement with a sufficient nest egg built up. Choosing a lower rate is for those who think I'm being too pessimistic—after all, inflation averaged just 2.5% annually for the 10 years ending in 2012. Since the Millers have 30 years to go before they retire at age 65, we look down the left-hand column until we come to the number "30." Then, we go over three columns to find the number listed under the 4% heading. The number we find is 3.243. Now, here comes the scary part. We multiply $54,000 times 3.243 to learn what the Millers' income will need to be when they retire in 30 years in order to maintain the standard of living they enjoy today. The answer is $175,122 per year! Sort of overwhelming, isn't it? It's difficult to imagine that the day will come when a family would need that much money every year just to maintain a modest lifestyle.	3. From page 232. 4. Enter the rate of inflation assumption which you are making for planning purposes. 5. Enter the number of years remaining until you retire. 6. Enter the inflation adjustment factor from the table on page 231. This factor reflects your assumption concerning the rate of future inflation and the years remaining until you retire. 7. Multiply Item 3 by Item 6. This is an estimate of the amount of income you will need during your first year of retirement to sustain your desired standard of living.	$54,000 4% inflation 30 years x 3.243 = $175,122	

RETIREMENT PLANNING WORKSHEET: SECTION 3
Will you have enough to sustain you through a normal life expectancy?

Overview	Step by Step	Millers	Yourself

An essential part of your planning is to come up with a reasonable estimate of how long you (and, if married, your spouse) will live. The table of life expectancies on page 229 is a good starting point. You can make adjustments based on your current state of health and family history.

We use this information to project how much income you'll need <u>during the whole</u> of your retirement years. This is a function of your standard of living, life expectancy, and the rate of inflation after you retire.

The table below has been designed to do the math for you. In the Millers' situation, I'm being cautious and assuming they will live to be 90. This means their life expectancies after retirement at age 65 are another 25 years. Continuing to assume inflation of 4%, the table gives us a factor of 43.31.

Step by Step:

7. From page 233.

8. Using the life-expectancy table from page 229 as a guide, <u>enter the number of years of life after retirement</u> that you have decided to use for financial planning purposes.

9. <u>Enter the inflation assumption</u> that you are making for planning purposes. It can be the same assumption you used in Item 4, or you can raise or lower it if you have a different outlook for the more distant years.

10. Using the table at left, <u>enter the inflation adjustment factor</u> that reflects your inflation assumption as well as the years of life expectancy after retirement.

11. Multiply Item 7 by Item 10. This is the approximate total <u>spending you anticipate during all of your retirement years.</u> <u>Let's call it your "prime-time wealth."</u> In the Millers' case, this would be the total expected spending for the 25 years following retirement.

Millers:
- 7. $175,122
- 8. 25 years
- 9. 4% inflation
- 10. x 43.31
- 11. $7,584,534

RATES OF INFLATION / TABLE TWO

LIFE EXPECTANCY AFTER RETIREMENT

Years	3.0%	3.5%	4.0%	4.5%	5.0%	5.5%	6.0%
1	1.03	1.04	1.04	1.05	1.05	1.06	1.06
2	2.09	2.11	2.12	2.14	2.15	2.17	2.18
3	3.18	3.21	3.25	3.28	3.31	3.34	3.37
4	4.31	4.36	4.42	4.47	4.53	4.58	4.64
5	5.47	5.55	5.63	5.72	5.80	5.89	5.98
6	6.66	6.78	6.90	7.02	7.14	7.27	7.39
7	7.89	8.05	8.21	8.38	8.55	8.72	8.90
8	9.16	9.37	9.58	9.80	10.03	10.26	10.49
9	10.46	10.73	11.01	11.29	11.58	11.88	12.18
10	11.81	12.14	12.49	12.84	13.21	13.58	13.97
11	13.19	13.60	14.03	14.46	14.92	15.39	15.87
12	14.62	15.11	15.63	16.16	16.71	17.29	17.88
13	16.09	16.68	17.29	17.93	18.60	19.29	20.02
14	17.60	18.30	19.02	19.78	20.58	21.41	22.28
15	19.16	19.97	20.82	21.72	22.66	23.64	24.67
16	20.76	21.71	22.70	23.74	24.84	26.00	27.21
17	22.41	23.50	24.65	25.86	27.13	28.48	29.91
18	24.12	25.36	26.67	28.06	29.54	31.10	32.76
19	25.87	27.28	28.78	30.37	32.07	33.87	35.79
20	27.68	29.27	30.97	32.78	34.72	36.79	38.99
21	29.54	31.33	33.25	35.30	37.51	39.86	42.39
22	31.45	33.46	35.62	37.94	40.43	43.11	46.00
23	33.43	35.67	38.08	40.69	43.50	46.54	49.82
24	35.46	37.95	40.65	43.57	46.73	50.15	53.86
25	37.55	40.31	43.31	46.57	50.11	53.97	58.16
26	39.71	42.76	46.08	49.71	53.67	57.99	62.71
27	41.93	45.29	48.97	52.99	57.40	62.23	67.53
28	44.22	47.91	51.97	56.42	61.32	66.71	72.64
29	46.58	50.62	55.08	60.01	65.44	71.44	78.06
30	49.00	53.43	58.33	63.75	69.76	76.42	83.80

| RETIREMENT PLANNING WORKSHEET: SECTION 4 ||||
| **How much of your "prime-time wealth" will Social Security provide?** ||||
Overview	Step by Step	Millers	Yourself
For years, workers have been paying much more in Social Security taxes than was needed to fund the current level of benefits. That's because a surplus was needed to take care of the baby-boomers when they began retiring around 2010. Projections made at the time of the 1983 Social Security "reforms" predicted the surplus would peak at a huge $16 trillion before the baby-boomer drawdown began.	12. Enter the amount of <u>your combined</u> annual Social Security benefits as projected in your Social Security Statement (<u>in today's dollars</u>).	His: $15,696 + Hers: $7,848 = $23,544	
	13. Enter the <u>inflation adjustment factor</u> used in Item 6.	x 3.243	
Eleven years later the projected surplus had almost vanished. Critics of the 1983 changes said at the time that the surplus was based on several unrealistic assumptions having to do with birth rates, life expectancies, and economic growth. They were proven correct, and the reality is that the benefits will have to be substantially scaled back.	14. Multiply Item 12 by Item 13. This is the approximate amount of <u>your Social Security benefit during your first year of retirement</u>.	$76,353	
Once a year, an updated Social Security Statement is mailed automatically to workers age 25 or older who are not yet getting Social Security benefits. Your Statement provides you with a record of the contributions credited to your account (be sure to check it for accuracy) and an estimate of what your retirement benefit will be. If you will be retiring in the next 8-10 years, it will likely be fairly accurate. The further you go beyond 8-10 years, however, the more you may want to adjust the estimate downward to allow for economic and political realities.	15. Enter Social Security's annual cost-of-living increase. You might assume an increase less than the inflation assumption (made in Item 9) in order to reflect the possibility of benefit cutbacks.	3% annual increases	
You should get your Statement a few months before your birthday. If you'd rather not wait, you can request a Statement at any time. Call (800) 772-1213 or visit www.ssa.gov to get the ball rolling. While you're there, you can check out the "Retirement Estimator" at www.socialsecurity.gov/estimator/ which will give you an immediate online estimate of what your Statement will show.	16. Using Table Two on the opposite page, <u>enter the inflation adjustment factor</u> that reflects the inflation assumption in Item 15 as well as the years of life expectancy shown in Item 8.	x 37.55	
	17. Multiply Item 14 by Item 16. This is the approximate total amount of <u>Social Security you can anticipate receiving during all of your retirement years</u>.	$2,867,062	

RETIREMENT PLANNING WORKSHEET: SECTION 5			
How much of your prime-time wealth will your company's pension provide?			
Overview	Step by Step	Millers	Yourself

There are two different varieties of pension plans (which we'll review in chapter 20). One kind is called a "defined-benefit" plan because the focus is on the lifetime benefit you'll ultimately receive. These plans promise to pay you, when you retire, a certain dollar amount every month for as long as you live. If you participate in a defined-benefit plan, your employer is required by law to offer you a summary of the plan that's written in layman's terms. This is called a "summary plan description," and it should be readily available from your personnel department. Many companies also provide a personalized employee benefit statement once a year that provides an estimate of how much your monthly retirement check will be.
 	
    (Plans in the other major category of employer-sponsored retirement benefits are called "defined-contribution" plans because they place their emphasis on how much the employer will put into the plan for you each year. They should not be included in the worksheet at this point—we'll get to those on the next page.)
 	
    When you reach retirement and the time comes for your monthly pension benefit to be paid, you have several choices as to how you wish it to be calculated. See pages 250-251. If you are currently a participant in a defined-benefit plan, make an appointment with the appropriate person at your company to get your specific questions answered.
 	
    If you have participated in such a plan in the past at another company, you may have earned vested benefits there as well. Be sure to include them here also unless you have already moved them into a rollover IRA. In that case, enter the value of that account in Step 31.
	18. Enter the <u>amount of your annual pension benefit</u>. See your most recent employee benefit statement.
	
	19. If your benefit is "<u>indexed for inflation</u>," enter the factor used in Item 16. Or, if your benefit is <u>not</u> "indexed for inflation," enter the factor used in Item 8.
	
	20. Multiply Item 18 by Item 19. This is the approximate <u>total amount of pension income you can anticipate receiving during all of your retirement years</u>.
	
	21. Enter the <u>amount of your spouse's annual pension benefit</u> from his or her employee benefit statement.
	
	22. If your <u>spouse's benefit</u> is "<u>indexed for inflation</u>," enter the factor used in Item 16. Or, if your spouse's benefit is <u>not</u> "indexed for inflation," enter the factor used in Item 8.
	
	23. Multiply Item 21 by Item 22. This is the approximate <u>total amount of pension income your spouse can anticipate receiving during all of his or her retirement years</u>.
		$3,312
		
		25
		
		$82,800
		
		none
		
		N/A
		
		none	

RETIREMENT PLANNING WORKSHEET: SECTION 6
How much of your prime-time wealth must you provide?

Overview	Step by Step	Millers	Yourself

Overview

In step 27, we learn the amount that you must supply from your own retirement investment strategy. Of course, you don't need to have all your prime-time wealth available on your first day of retirement. After all, it's going to take the rest of your life to spend it all. The question is: How much of your prime-time wealth do you need to have <u>at the outset</u> (knowing that your investments will continue to earn a respectable rate of return after you retire)?

Table Three, shown below, will help you ascertain that amount. It assumes not only that your retirement capital earns a return (see headings which range from 6% to 10%), but also that withdrawals are made from your investment accounts each month to meet current spending needs. The withdrawals are designed to exhaust the investment account by the end of your life expectancy. For example, when you have a remaining life expectancy of 25 years, you can withdraw 4.00% of the account value during that year (1 divided by 25). The next year, when you have 24 years of life expectancy, you can withdraw 4.17% of the account value (1 divided by 24). And so on. In the Millers' example, I assumed a 7% long-term return during retirement. This is lower than the 10% expected return prior to retirement because they should be taking less risk at this stage of life.

You should understand that this provides only a rough blueprint of what each year's cash flow will be like. The 7% return is an average over a 25-year period. You might start off with a 15% return the first year, or a loss. If a given year's scheduled withdrawal is insufficient to cover that year's needs, you might have to "borrow" from next year and wait for your investment returns to catch up.

**RATES OF RETURN DURING RETIREMENT
TABLE THREE**

Years	6%	7%	8%	9%	10%
5	0.8368	0.8126	0.7891	0.7665	0.7445
10	0.7157	0.6764	0.6392	0.6039	0.5704
15	0.6080	0.5579	0.5115	0.4687	0.4292
20	0.5129	0.4559	0.4047	0.3587	0.3175
25	0.4299	0.3694	0.3166	0.2708	0.2311
30	0.3580	0.2968	0.2452	0.2019	0.1658
35	0.2963	0.2366	0.1881	0.1489	0.1174
40	0.2438	0.1873	0.1430	0.1086	0.0822

(LIFE EXPECTANCY labels the left column of Years)

Step by Step

24. Enter the amount from Item 11. I've been calling this <u>your prime-time wealth</u>. — **Millers: $7,584,534**

25. Enter the amount from Item 17. This is the approximate total amount of <u>Social Security</u> you anticipate receiving during all of your retirement years. — **Millers: $2,867,062**

26. Enter the sum of Items 20 and 23. This is the approximate total amount of <u>pension income</u> you anticipate receiving during all of your retirement years. — **Millers: $82,800**

27. Subtract Items 25 and 26 from Item 24. This is the total <u>amount of your prime-time wealth that you must provide</u>. — **Millers: $4,634,672**

28. Enter the average annual rate of return you are assuming your investments will earn <u>during</u> retirement. — **Millers: 7% rate of return**

29. Enter the factor from Table Three that reflects the life expectancy during retirement (Item 8) and the expected return on investments (Item 28). — **Millers: × .3694**

30. Multiply Item 27 by Item 29. This is the amount of capital you should have on hand as you enter retirement. — **Millers: $1,712,048**

RETIREMENT PLANNING WORKSHEET: SECTION 7
How much will your current tax-deferred portfolio be worth when you retire?

Overview	Step by Step	Millers	Yourself

Overview

Now that we know your prime-time wealth goal, let's see how far along you are toward achieving it. In this section, we project the current values in any tax-deferred accounts you may have into the future. For the Millers, I'm assuming a 10% average annual rate of return. If you'd like to use a different assumption, see the table below. Using a lower percentage assumption implies a more cautious view, and may require a higher level of savings between now and retirement.

RATES OF RETURN / TABLE FOUR

YEARS UNTIL RETIREMENT

Years	6%	7%	8%	9%	10%	11%	12%
5	1.34	1.40	1.47	1.54	1.61	1.69	1.76
6	1.42	1.50	1.59	1.68	1.77	1.87	1.97
7	1.50	1.61	1.71	1.83	1.95	2.08	2.21
8	1.59	1.72	1.85	1.99	2.14	2.30	2.48
9	1.69	1.84	2.00	2.17	2.36	2.56	2.77
10	1.79	1.97	2.16	2.37	2.59	2.84	3.11
11	1.90	2.10	2.33	2.58	2.85	3.15	3.48
12	2.01	2.25	2.52	2.81	3.14	3.50	3.90
13	2.13	2.41	2.72	3.07	3.45	3.88	4.36
14	2.26	2.58	2.94	3.34	3.80	4.31	4.89
15	2.40	2.76	3.17	3.64	4.18	4.78	5.47
16	2.54	2.95	3.43	3.97	4.59	5.31	6.13
17	2.69	3.16	3.70	4.33	5.05	5.90	6.87
18	2.85	3.38	4.00	4.72	5.56	6.54	7.69
19	3.03	3.62	4.32	5.14	6.12	7.26	8.61
20	3.21	3.87	4.66	5.60	6.73	8.06	9.65
21	3.40	4.14	5.03	6.11	7.40	8.95	10.80
22	3.60	4.43	5.44	6.66	8.14	9.93	12.10
23	3.82	4.74	5.87	7.26	8.95	11.03	13.55
24	4.05	5.07	6.34	7.91	9.85	12.24	15.18
25	4.29	5.43	6.85	8.62	10.83	13.59	17.00
26	4.55	5.81	7.40	9.40	11.92	15.08	19.04
27	4.82	6.21	7.99	10.25	13.11	16.74	21.32
28	5.11	6.65	8.63	11.17	14.42	18.58	23.88
29	5.42	7.11	9.32	12.17	15.86	20.62	26.75
30	5.74	7.61	10.06	13.27	(17.45)	22.89	29.96
31	6.09	8.15	10.87	14.46	19.19	25.41	33.56
32	6.45	8.72	11.74	15.76	21.11	28.21	37.58
33	6.84	9.33	12.68	17.18	23.23	31.31	42.09
34	7.25	9.98	13.69	18.73	25.55	34.75	47.14
35	7.69	10.68	14.79	20.41	28.10	38.57	52.80
36	8.15	11.42	15.97	22.25	30.91	42.82	59.14
37	8.64	12.22	17.25	24.25	34.00	47.53	66.23
38	9.15	13.08	18.63	26.44	37.40	52.76	74.18
39	9.70	13.99	20.12	28.82	41.14	58.56	83.08
40	10.29	14.97	21.72	31.41	45.26	65.00	93.05

Step by Step

31. Enter the current values of any tax-deferred investment accounts you/spouse have:
   a. Traditional IRAs — $24,552
   b. Roth IRAs (These will be withdrawn tax-free, a fact that is not reflected in this analysis. This simplifies the analysis as well as builds a more conservative picture.
   c. 401(k)/403(b) — $42,460
   d. Variable annuity
   e. Other

32. Enter the sum of all the accounts listed in Item 31. This is the total amount of tax-deferred capital that you and your spouse currently have working for you. — $67,012

33. Enter the average rate of return you assume your investments will earn between now and retirement. — 10% rate of return

34. Enter the rate of return factor (see table) that reflects your assumption about the annual rate of growth of your capital (Item 33) over the years between now and retirement (Item 5). — x 17.45

35. Multiply Item 32 by Item 34. This is an estimate of the value of your current tax-deferred capital when you reach retirement. — $1,169,359

RETIREMENT PLANNING WORKSHEET: SECTION 8			
How much will your current taxable holdings be worth when you retire?			
Overview	Step by Step	Millers	Yourself

Now, we calculate the current value in your taxable holdings and estimate their value at the time of your retirement. We will take into account the taxes due on your gains under the assumption they will be paid with funds from these accounts. For the Millers, I'll use the same estimated rate of return of 10% as before. You can use the table below to select another one if you wish. This table differs from the one on page 238 in that it assumes a 34% combined state/federal income tax rate.

RATES OF RETURN / TABLE FIVE

Years	6%	7%	8%	9%	10%	11%	12%
5	1.21	1.25	1.29	1.33	1.38	1.42	1.46
6	1.26	1.31	1.36	1.41	1.47	1.52	1.58
7	1.31	1.37	1.43	1.50	1.56	1.63	1.70
8	1.36	1.44	1.51	1.59	1.67	1.75	1.84
9	1.42	1.50	1.59	1.68	1.78	1.88	1.99
10	1.47	1.57	1.67	1.78	1.89	2.02	2.14
11	1.53	1.64	1.76	1.89	2.02	2.16	2.31
12	1.59	1.72	1.85	2.00	2.15	2.32	2.50
13	1.66	1.80	1.95	2.12	2.30	2.49	2.69
14	1.72	1.88	2.06	2.24	2.45	2.67	2.91
15	1.79	1.97	2.16	2.38	2.61	2.86	3.14
16	1.86	2.06	2.28	2.52	2.78	3.07	3.39
17	1.94	2.16	2.40	2.67	2.96	3.29	3.65
18	2.01	2.25	2.52	2.83	3.16	3.53	3.94
19	2.09	2.36	2.66	2.99	3.37	3.79	4.26
20	2.17	2.47	2.80	3.17	3.59	4.06	4.59
21	2.26	2.58	2.95	3.36	3.83	4.36	4.96
22	2.35	2.70	3.10	3.56	4.08	4.67	5.35
23	2.44	2.83	3.27	3.77	4.35	5.01	5.77
24	2.54	2.96	3.44	3.99	4.64	5.38	6.23
25	2.64	3.09	3.62	4.23	4.94	5.77	6.72
26	2.74	3.24	3.81	4.48	5.27	6.19	7.26
27	2.85	3.39	4.01	4.75	5.62	6.63	7.83
28	2.97	3.54	4.22	5.03	5.99	7.12	8.45
29	3.08	3.71	4.45	5.33	6.38	7.63	9.12
30	3.21	3.88	4.68	5.65	(6.80)	8.19	9.84
31	3.33	4.06	4.93	5.98	7.25	8.78	10.62
32	3.47	4.24	5.19	6.34	7.73	9.42	11.46
33	3.60	4.44	5.46	6.71	8.24	10.10	12.37
34	3.75	4.64	5.75	7.11	8.79	10.84	13.35
35	3.89	4.86	6.05	7.54	9.36	11.62	14.41
36	4.05	5.08	6.37	7.98	9.98	12.47	15.55
37	4.21	5.32	6.71	8.46	10.64	13.37	16.78
38	4.37	5.56	7.07	8.96	11.34	14.34	18.11
39	4.55	5.82	7.44	9.49	12.09	15.38	19.54
40	4.73	6.09	7.83	10.06	12.89	16.50	21.09

YEARS UNTIL RETIREMENT (vertical label at left)

Step by Step / Millers

36. Enter the current values of any <u>taxable investment</u> accounts that you/spouse may have that are not part of your contingency fund or set aside for a special purpose such as college or a house purchase:
   a. Bank savings/CDs — $ 3,188
   b. Money market funds
   c. Mutual funds — $ 8,524
   d. Brokerage accounts
   e. Other
   f. Other

37. Enter the <u>sum of all the accounts listed in Item 36</u>. This is the total amount of taxable investments that you and your spouse currently have working for you. — $ 11,712

38. Using the table at left, <u>enter the rate of return factor</u> that reflects your assumption concerning the future annual rate of growth of your long-term capital (Item 33) over the period of time between now and retirement (Item 5). — × 6.80

39. Multiply Item 37 by Item 38. This is an estimate of the <u>value of your current taxable holdings when you reach retirement.</u> — $79,642

RETIREMENT PLANNING WORKSHEET: SECTION 9		
How much should you save each year to meet your retirement goal?		

Overview	Step by Step	Millers	Yourself
Your final step is to calculate how much you need to save in the future to arrive at retirement day with the amount of capital needed. If the amount computed in step 43 is a positive number, you're already in great shape. Unfortunately, most of us need to continue adding to our retirement savings. Table Six will help you determine the annual amount which you need to add each year to a tax-deferred account (it assumes no taxes are paid on the returns earned).	40. Enter the amount from Item 35. This is the estimated value of your current tax-deferred investments when you reach retirement.	$1,169,359	
	41. Enter the amount from Item 39. This is the estimated value of your current taxable investments when you reach retirement.	$79,642	
	42. Enter the amount from Item 30. This is the amount of your prime-time wealth that you must provide from your retirement investment strategy.	$1,712,048	
	43. Add Items 40 and 41 and subtract Item 42. This is your estimated shortfall if you do not continue adding to your retirement savings in future years.	− $463,047	
	44. Using the table at left, enter the annual savings growth factor that reflects your assumption concerning the future rate of growth of your capital (Item 33) over the period of time between now and retirement (Item 5).	× .0058	
	45. Multiply Item 43 by Item 44. This is an estimate of the amount of new savings you need to add to your tax-deferred accounts each year.	$2,686	

RATES OF RETURN / TABLE SIX

YEARS UNTIL RETIREMENT

Years	6%	7%	8%	9%	10%	11%	12%
5	17.22%	16.80%	16.39%	15.99%	15.60%	15.22%	14.85%
6	13.92%	13.51%	13.11%	12.72%	12.34%	11.98%	11.63%
7	11.57%	11.16%	10.78%	10.40%	10.04%	9.69%	9.35%
8	9.81%	9.42%	9.04%	8.68%	8.33%	7.99%	7.67%
9	8.45%	8.07%	7.70%	7.35%	7.01%	6.69%	6.38%
10	7.37%	6.99%	6.64%	6.30%	5.98%	5.67%	5.38%
11	6.48%	6.12%	5.78%	5.45%	5.14%	4.85%	4.57%
12	5.76%	5.40%	5.07%	4.75%	4.45%	4.17%	3.91%
13	5.14%	4.80%	4.47%	4.17%	3.88%	3.62%	3.37%
14	4.62%	4.28%	3.97%	3.68%	3.40%	3.15%	2.91%
15	4.17%	3.84%	3.54%	3.26%	3.00%	2.75%	2.53%
16	3.78%	3.46%	3.17%	2.90%	2.65%	2.42%	2.21%
17	3.44%	3.13%	2.85%	2.59%	2.35%	2.13%	1.93%
18	3.14%	2.84%	2.57%	2.32%	2.09%	1.88%	1.69%
19	2.88%	2.58%	2.32%	2.08%	1.86%	1.66%	1.49%
20	2.64%	2.36%	2.10%	1.87%	1.66%	1.48%	1.31%
21	2.43%	2.15%	1.91%	1.69%	1.49%	1.31%	1.15%
22	2.24%	1.97%	1.73%	1.52%	1.33%	1.17%	1.02%
23	2.07%	1.81%	1.58%	1.38%	1.20%	1.04%	0.90%
24	1.91%	1.66%	1.44%	1.25%	1.08%	0.93%	0.80%
25	1.77%	1.53%	1.32%	1.13%	0.97%	0.83%	0.71%
26	1.64%	1.41%	1.20%	1.03%	0.87%	0.74%	0.63%
27	1.52%	1.30%	1.10%	0.93%	0.79%	0.66%	0.56%
28	1.42%	1.20%	1.01%	0.85%	0.71%	0.59%	0.49%
29	1.32%	1.11%	0.92%	0.77%	0.64%	0.53%	0.44%
30	1.23%	1.02%	0.85%	0.70%	(0.58%)	0.48%	0.39%
31	1.14%	0.95%	0.78%	0.64%	0.52%	0.43%	0.35%
32	1.07%	0.88%	0.72%	0.58%	0.47%	0.38%	0.31%
33	1.00%	0.81%	0.66%	0.53%	0.43%	0.34%	0.28%
34	0.93%	0.75%	0.61%	0.49%	0.39%	0.31%	0.25%
35	0.87%	0.70%	0.56%	0.44%	0.35%	0.28%	0.22%
36	0.82%	0.65%	0.51%	0.41%	0.32%	0.25%	0.19%
37	0.76%	0.60%	0.47%	0.37%	0.29%	0.22%	0.17%
38	0.71%	0.56%	0.44%	0.34%	0.26%	0.20%	0.15%
39	0.67%	0.52%	0.40%	0.31%	0.24%	0.18%	0.14%
40	0.63%	0.48%	0.37%	0.28%	0.22%	0.16%	0.12%

Numerous reforms are being floated as ways to remedy the system.

• **Increase payroll taxes again.** A former chief actuary for the Social Security Administration estimated that individual payroll taxes would have to be raised from their present 12.4% rate to more than 40% just to pay all the benefits currently being promised. Is it realistic to think that the next generation will tolerate increases of that magnitude? Should they? Not a chance.

• **Slowing benefit growth.** Social Security is already a terrible investment for today's workers under age 50. Reducing benefits would make it even worse. According to a 2001 report from the *President's Commission to Strenghten Social Security*, eliminating the Social Security deficit without increasing taxes would require that a retired couple's annual benefit be reduced by 12% (compared with what is currently promised) by 2020 and by 24% by 2030.

• **Means testing.** This involves requiring individuals to pass a test concerning their annual income before granting them full benefits. One such proposal suggests that benefits should start being reduced for anyone who enjoys an annual retirement income of $40,000, and eliminated entirely if the income exceeds $120,000. This is a truly terrible idea because it would: (1) undermine public support for the Social Security program by making it clear that it is just another welfare program where only the "needy" would receive full benefits; (2) discourage hard work, saving, and an attitude of self-reliance because your other retirement accounts would be used against you to deprive you of benefits that would be available only to those who weren't as frugal or farsighted; and (3) summarily break the promises of the past 70 years, further undermining respect for the law. Surely it's an evil thing to force people to pay all their working lives into such a system, continually reassuring them that their benefits will be there when they retire, and then defrauding them at the last minute.

• **Privatization.** There have been several proposals, such as one made by the Bush Administration in 2005, that would have allowed workers to divert part of their Social Security taxes to an account similar to an IRA where they would have control over how it is invested. In return, they would've surrendered part of their future Social Security benefits. Chile pioneered this approach years ago when faced with a similar dilemma, and it has worked well there. Other countries have since copied aspects of Chile's approach in privatizing their own plans. There are many variations on this theme, but none has received significant public support in the U.S. Nevertheless, it's difficult to envision a long-term solution without some form of privatization. I encourage you to read carefully any articles you see on this topic in order to stay informed.

Today's workers carry the triple burden of (1) paying far more in Social Security taxes than any previous generation, (2) waiting longer to collect than any previous generation, and (3) retiring with lower after-tax benefits than

Recommended Resource

Social Security, Medicare, & Government Pensions: Get the Most Out of Your Retirement & Medical Benefits

by Joseph L. Matthews & Dorothy Matthews Berman

This helpful book guides you through the maze of federal income and benefit programs. In plain language, it explains how to keep from missing out on income and coverage and how to collect all benefits due.

Pastors and Social Security

"The decision to withdraw from the Social Security system must be made solely on the basis of a pastor's conscientious objection to Social Security as a form of government welfare or assistance, and is not allowed under any other circumstances. There are also financial ramifications from that decision, and although they cannot be part of the decision, must be dealt with as a result of withdrawing. If a pastor elects to withdraw from Social Security, he needs to discipline himself and save and invest in an alternate retirement plan, as well as provide disability insurance in case he becomes unable to perform his duties for medical reasons."

— Larry Burkett

any previous generation. As unfair as this is, tomorrow's workers, our children, might have to pay even more, wait even longer, and receive even less. And that's why the truth about Social Security is indeed outrageous.

In light of uncertainties surrounding the level of Social Security benefits, especially after 2021 (see page 231), receiving significant support from the private retirement plans sponsored by your employer is all the more critical. A basic understanding of their strengths and weaknesses is essential if you are to plan realistically. We begin our look at such plans in the next chapter.

Bear in mind that the projections in the worksheet . . .

. . . are based on the assumption that you will live to a specific age. If the end of your (earthly) life comes earlier than you had assumed, there will be money on hand that you won't need. It can be left to your heirs and the Lord's work. If you die "on schedule," you and your money will run out at the same time. If you live longer than you had expected, you'll have a problem. There are two ways to deal with this "risk." One is to pick a very long life expectancy (e.g., 95 or 100). That way, you would be less likely to outlive your money. A second way, assuming you own your house, is to sell it or take out a "reverse mortgage" to create additional cash flow.

If all this seems a bit overwhelming, don't despair.

Inflation can be harnessed to work for you as well as against you. Before Section Five is completed, you'll have been given enough information to enable you to overcome three of the four most common elements of financial failure:

• **A failure to inquire.** Many are ignorant of the serious financial implications of our changing society and how they will be affected.

• **A failure to learn.** Once made aware, they may still lack the know-how needed to begin putting their financial house in order.

• **A failure to plan.** Even informed, knowledgeable people can let years go by without formulating goals and a strategy for achieving them.

But after I inform you of the seriousness of the situation, teach you the basics of survival, and lead you through the planning process, there's still one element that only you can overcome:

• **A failure to act.** Procrastination can be the greatest deterrent to reaching your financial goals. If you're like I was as a child, acting as if you'll never grow old, you've been losing valuable time. Commit yourself now to making the sacrifices needed to put your family's finances on a solid foundation. ◆

For Updated Information
For more on retirement investing and planning, check the links in the "Retirement" section of the SMI web site at www.soundmindinvesting.com. We have a regular monthly column for those nearing or currently in retirement.

Your Pension at Work

I. **Employer-sponsored pension plans that promise to pay you** *a specific dollar amount when you retire* **are called "defined-benefit" plans.**

   A. Usually, you are required to have worked for the company a certain length of time before you can participate in the plan.

   B. The amount of your retirement benefit is computed according to a formula that takes many variables into account. Among them are your salary, age at retirement, years with the company, Social Security benefits, and the survivors' benefit you select.

   C. You should fully understand the circumstances under which you will receive a retirement benefit and how the benefit will be computed.

II. **Employer-sponsored pension plans that pay** *specific dollar amounts into your retirement account each year* **are called "defined-contribution" plans.**

   A. These plans make no promises as to how much your benefit will be when you retire. Your retirement benefit will ultimately be determined by the amount and frequency of annual contributions and the investment performance experienced in your account.

   B. Under such plans the risk of poor investment returns rests with the employee rather than the employer. That's why employees generally have significant control over the investment portfolios.

   C. There are a variety of these plans with differing contribution requirements, limitations, and employer matching features. The 401(k) plan is by far the most common. In this chapter, we'll discuss the key features of the major kinds of plans.

   D. When you are ready to withdraw your benefits, these plans provide three alternative methods. Each has its own advantages, depending on your personal income and tax situation at that time.

**Although the *government* can change its rules anytime it
wants and arbitrarily reduce . . .**

. . . the Social Security benefits you've been "contributing" to for a working lifetime, it won't let *your employer* do that to you. After all, that wouldn't be fair. So let's look at employer-sponsored pension plans to see what help you can expect from your company. First, you should understand that there are two different kinds of pension plans. One kind promises only to put a certain amount aside for you each year and makes no projections as to the amount of your ultimate monthly benefit. This kind is called a "defined-contribution" plan, and it comes in a bewildering array of alphabet-like names such as SEP-IRA, 401(k), and 403(b). We'll look at these plans later in the chapter.

For now, let's concentrate on the *other* type of pension plan, the kind that has historically covered the greatest number of employees. According to U.S. government numbers, they cover about 44 million American workers and retirees.

**These plans promise to pay you, when you retire,
a certain dollar amount every month for as long as you live . . .**

. . . however, they promise nothing about how much money your company will put aside each year to accomplish this (other than to observe certain minimum federal requirements). These plans are called "defined-benefit" plans because the focus is on the *lifetime monthly benefit* you'll ultimately receive. Under this arrangement, the employer carries the burden of where the money for the contributions comes from as well as how well the investments do between now and your retirement.

The first barrier standing between you and your monthly pension check is meeting the eligibility requirements. Just because you've been hired doesn't mean you immediately qualify for a company's retirement plan. Usually they require (1) that you've reached a certain age, and (2) that you have been with the company for a certain period of time before you qualify to join the plan. It is customary that an employee must be at least 21 years old and have been with the company at least one year.

Once you're eligible, what you really want to know is . . .

. . . how much is my monthly benefit going to be when I retire? That depends on several factors. Each is fairly simple; let's take them one at a time.

• **Salary formula.** The goal of a monthly pension check is to help replace the earnings lost when you retire. That means your benefit is based primarily on the amount of your annual earnings while you were still working. Some formulas take an average of your earnings from all the years you worked for the company. Presumably, the earlier years were not as well paying, so this is not as favorable to you as a plan that uses a formula based on your final year(s) of service.

• **Years of service.** People who spend their entire career with the same company receive more than those who come along later. Your benefit is affected by the number of "years" you work for your employer. But how many hours are needed to constitute a "year of service"? Some plans may require 500 hours in a twelve-consecutive-month period, whereas others require 1,000 hours. Or what if you worked for 20 years, left for two years, and returned for another 18 years? Do you get credit for 38 years or just the last 18 years? And does it matter why you left for those two years? There are countless variations on this theme that can affect your benefit.

• **Vesting requirements.** When can you know for sure that you're guaranteed to receive at least some pension benefit from your employer? The day you start to work? The year you qualify to join the plan? After three years with the company? That's where the concept of "vesting" comes in. It means you have an absolute right to receive some money from a retirement plan, even if you resign or are fired. You're entitled to it no matter what.

Some plans call for "graded vesting," where you receive a right to a pension gradually (for example, 20% after three years, 40% after four years, and so on). Others provide for what is called "cliff vesting," an all-or-nothing approach where, for example, you could become 100% vested after five years but be entitled to nothing if you leave before then. The most favorable is "vesting upon entry" where you must wait for two years before qualifying to participate in the plan, but are immediately 100% vested upon entry. This is especially helpful to working women who, on average, change jobs more frequently than men.

• **Normal retirement age.** Most plans use formulas that consider 65 as the normal retirement age. If you choose to work past 65 (federal law prohibits age discrimination rules that would *require* you to retire before age 70), will your plan give you credit for the additional years worked? Or what if you wanted to take early retirement—how much will that decision reduce your monthly pension check? The rules governing these matters vary from plan to plan.

GOOD QUESTIONS TO ASK YOUR COMPANY ABOUT YOUR BENEFITS

❑ What do I have to do to participate in the plan?

❑ Do I contribute money, and if so, does the company match my contributions?

❑ What is the vesting schedule? That is, when will I be partially versus fully vested?

❑ What are the investments in the plan?

❑ Do I get to decide how the investments in my account are allocated among the various options?

❑ How do I make changes to the allocations?

❑ How quickly is my contribution deposited in my account?

❑ If a defined-benefit plan, is it federally insured?

❑ Can I borrow or withdraw money before I retire?

❑ Does the plan include death or disability benefits?

❑ What happens if I take early retirement?

❑ What happens if I work past the normal retirement age?

• **Social Security considerations.** So-called "integrated plans" deduct a portion of your monthly Social Security check from your monthly benefit check. Remember that your em-

Employee Stock Ownership Plans

ESOPs are similar to profit-sharing plans except you receive shares in your company's stock rather than a portion of company profits. The number of shares you receive is based on your salary, typically ranging in value from 5% to 25% of your annual compensation. Taxes usually aren't due until you leave the company or sell the shares.

403(b) Plans

A 403(b) plan is a retirement plan for employees of non-profit or tax-exempt organizations such as schools, hospitals, churches, charities, and ministries. They are sufficiently similar to 401(k) plans that eligible participants in these plans can learn much about how best to use them by reading the information in this chapter. Before investing money, however, it would be best to read the plan description for your 403(b). Both plans take their names from the section in the tax code in which they are regulated.

401(k) Web Resources

For more on invesitng in your 401(k) plan, visit SMI at www.soundmindinvesting.com. While you're there, read about our Personal Portfolio Tracker. It's specificallly designed to help you select the best funds in your 401(k) plan.

ployer has already paid hefty Social Security taxes. From his point of view, it seems reasonable that the company retirement plan formula recognize that you are receiving Social Security benefits to which the company has already contributed.

• **Survivors' benefits.** As an alternative to the basic "monthly check for life" benefit, federal law requires most plans to offer you another approach: a joint and survivor annuity. If this is selected, the monthly benefit check doesn't stop coming when you die; it goes instead to your spouse (or whoever you have named in the annuity). The trade-off is that your pension will be 10%–20% lower than it otherwise would be—after all, it has to last for two lifetimes now instead of just one—and the amount of the monthly check is cut in half when you pass on. Even so, it's good to know that your spouse will still be provided for at some level.

Armed with this information, you might now be wondering how the plan at your company . . .

. . . measures up in these various areas. If you aren't sure, it's time to find out! And don't worry about how you'll ever get your thoughts together in order to ask the right questions. Your employer is required by law to offer every participant a summary of the plan that's written in layman's terms. This is called a "summary plan description" and should be readily available from your personnel department. Ask for one. It will explain all of the above and lots more.

Many companies also provide a personalized "employee benefit statement" once a year that explains the amount of benefits you've earned to date and provides an estimate of how much your monthly retirement check will be. Other items that you're entitled to receive upon request include: the "summary annual report" (your plan's balance sheet), the Form 5500 (your plan's tax return and an excellent source of information concerning its financial health), and the retirement plan document itself (in case you happen to enjoy digging through page after page of mind-numbing legalese).

So far, we've been talking about retirement plans that promise to pay, upon retirement, a certain dollar amount every month for as long as you live. Under that arrangement, the employer makes all the contributions into the plan plus carries the burden of how well the investments perform until your retirement.

There is another major category of employer-sponsored retirement plans. They are called "defined-contribution" plans because . . .

. . . they place their emphasis on how much (if any) the employer will put into the plan for you each year. No promises are made with respect to how much your account will be worth when you retire. In this respect, they are like IRAs.

The advantage to employers of this approach is that *you* bear the investment risk between now and retirement rather than your company. If the investments do great, you'll have a healthy amount in the plan at retirement; if they perform poorly, you must make do with a lesser amount. This shift of the investment risk from the employer to you is significant; you no longer can "count on" having a specific monthly income. You should look at it as an opportunity! Here is another area that is now under your control where your Sound Mind strategy can help shape a balanced long-term portfolio that will be personalized to your specific goals and risk tolerance.

Over the years, Congress has created several varieties of defined-contribution plans. I've listed them in a table on the next page to give you an overview of the possibilities. Many companies have more than one of these plans in place in order to help you take the fullest advantage of the tax-sheltering possibilities. Though I cannot review all the complexities, the table will provide a general idea of the kinds of plans your employer may offer. Make an appointment with the appropriate person at your company to get your specific questions answered.

By far the most popular of these is the 401(k) plan.

About 70% of companies with 100 or more employees sponsor a 401(k) plan. In such a plan an employee elects to contribute (via payroll withholding) a portion of his or her paycheck to a tax-deferred investment account set up in the employee's name. Here are the primary features of traditional 401(k) plans (see sidebar for a brief introduction to the Roth 401(k) option):

• Contributions are tax-deductible in the year they're made.

However, there are limits imposed that affect the maximum amount you can contribute. According to IRS guidelines for 2013, the most a 401(k) plan can permit you to contribute is $17,500 plus an extra $5,500 "catch up" contribution if you're at least 50 years old. Your employer can elect to apply even more stringent limitations.

• Employees control how their money is invested.

However, they usually must choose from among a lineup of stock, bond, and money market funds selected by the employer. This limits the flexibility of the employee to invest in the funds or securities of his or her choice. To offset this drawback, some plans offer a "self-directed" or "fund window" option that allows you to enter buying and selling instructions through a broker, thus opening up a vast range of investment choices.

• All investment income and capital gains in the account grow tax-deferred.

The Roth 401(k)

The tax benefit of investing in a "traditional" 401(k) is immediate. You're allowed to reduce your taxable income by an amount equal to what you invest. (You'll pay the income tax when you withdraw money from your account in retirement.)

In contrast, the Roth 401(k), a retirement-plan option introduced in 2006, works the other way around. There's no tax break up front, but later you can withdraw your contributions, *plus all the earnings accumulated over the years*, tax-free. This makes the Roth 401(k) an especially attractive option for young investors who have many years to accumulate earnings.

As with traditional 401(k)s, employers may offer to match worker contributions. But with the Roth 401(k), matching money is treated differently under tax law than employee contributions. Employer-matching amounts are made with pre-tax dollars, which means any matching contributions will be subject to income tax when withdrawals are made (in other words, not all distributions from a Roth account may actually be tax-free).

Roth 401(k) withdrawals can begin at age 59½ (earlier if you become disabled), as long as the account has been active for at least five years. Withdrawals must begin by age 70½. However, mandatory distributions can be avoided by rolling a Roth 401(k) into a Roth IRA (see chapter 21). Because employee contributions and employer contributions face different tax treatment, consult a tax adviser before making this kind of rollover.

AN OVERVIEW OF THE MAJOR KINDS
OF DEFINED-CONTRIBUTION PLANS

Your company may offer one or more of the following defined-contribution pension plans. These are the most common types; however, there are many variations depending on the way your company's plan was initially structured. This is a highly technical area, and this table is merely intended to provide an overview. For more information on your specific rights and benefits, contact your company's Human Resources department.

Type of Plan	Profit Sharing	SEP IRA	401(k) Plan	403(b) Plan	Roth 401(k) or 403(b)
Brief summary	Your company annually contributes a portion of its profits, if any, into a fund for employees. Can be either a corporate plan or, if employer is not incorporated, can be a Keogh plan.	Simplified Employee Pensions use a form of employee IRAs rather than set up a separate company plan. Primarily funded by your employer, these accounts are highly portable if you change jobs.	A salary reduction plan where you decide how much of your salary to put in (up to a maximum level that is raised annually for inflation).The amount you contribute is not counted as taxable income.	Similar to the 401(k) plan, but limited to employees of public schools, government agencies, hospitals, religious organizations, and other nonprofit institutions.	Similar to traditional 401(k) and 403(b) plans, except you receive no tax deduction on the money you put in. No taxes are assessed upon withdrawal if you're over 59½ and have had the Roth for at least five years.
What is the most you can put in each year? *	You don't contribute.	You don't contribute.	$17,500 + $5,500 "catch-up" contribution if 50+ years old.	$17,500 + $5,500 "catch-up" contribution if 50+ years old.	Same as traditional 401(k) and 403(b) plans.
What is the most your employer can put in each year? *	25% of employee's W-2 compensation. Your contribution plus employer's can't exceed $51,000 or 25% of your salary (this limit includes your contribution), whichever is less.	25% of employee's W-2 compensation or $51,000. See sidebar on page 249 for mention of a second kind of IRA that has salary reduction features similar to a 401(k).	Can match a percentage of your salary deferral. Your contribution plus employer's can't exceed $51,000 or 25% of your salary (after deducting your contribution), whichever is less.	Can match a percentage of your salary deferral up to 100%. Your contribution plus employer's can't exceed $51,000 or 25% of your salary (after deducting your contribution), whichever is less.	Same as traditional 401(k) and 403(b) plans. Note: Matching contributions are on a *pre* tax basis; they will be taxed when you begin taking money out.
Are annual contributions fixed at a certain amount?	No. The amount contributed can change from year to year.	No. The amount contributed can change from year to year.	No. The amount contributed can change from year to year.	No. The amount contributed can change from year to year.	No. The amount contributed can change from year to year.
When do you receive ownership rights to your pension?	Typically 3-6 years.	Immediately.	Immediately on your contributions, but at the employer's discretion on any matching amounts.	Immediately on your contributions, but at the employer's discretion on any matching amounts.	Same as traditional 401(k) and 403(b) plans.
Can you borrow from your account?	Some plans allow borrowing at the employer's discretion.	No.	At the employer's discretion, but generally yes.	At the employer's discretion.	At the employer's discretion.

* Note: The amounts reflect year 2013 limits.

However, withdrawals are taxed at ordinary income tax rates in the year they're made. Thus, capital gains ultimately lose their potentially advantageous tax status when occurring within a 401(k) account.

• Payroll deduction provides a disciplined, consistent approach to saving for retirement.

However, once you put the money in, you normally can't get it out before age 59½ without paying a 10% early withdrawal penalty (plus the customary income taxes due on plan withdrawals as mentioned above). Most plans, however, do allow employees to borrow from their 401(k) accounts.

• Most employers with 401(k) plans match their employees' contributions to some degree. For example, a company might contribute 50 cents for every $1 the employee puts in. This is the feature that makes 401(k)s so attractive; the employer match provides an automatic and immediate profit on your contribution.

However, employers who offer matching programs put a ceiling on the amount they will match, say up to 6% of the employee's income. Thus, money contributed above the ceiling will not be matched. Furthermore, many plans require employees to remain with the employer for a certain number of years before the matching contributions *vest*, that is, become the property of the employee. They do this to discourage employee turnover.

The 401(k) has become the bedrock of our private pension system.

In 2011, an estimated 51 million American workers had investments worth $3.2 trillion in their 401(k) accounts. Based on those numbers, the average 401(k) account was worth about $63,000. According to a study by the Plan Sponsor Council of America, nearly 80% of those eligible to participate in a 401(k) do so. Yet, it's been estimated that 95% of those who participate in a 401(k) plan contribute less than they are allowed.

If possible, I encourage you to participate in your company's 401(k) plan at least to the point where you take full advantage of any employer-matching funds. If you're still working on getting your consumer debt paid off or building your emergency fund, that may not be possible immediately, but it should be one of your intermediate-term financial goals. If your 401(k) plan doesn't offer a matching feature, or if you can afford to contribute beyond the maximum matching percentage, then you will want to weigh the remaining advantages of 401(k)s versus the pros and cons of IRAs (see next chapter) before deciding which should have the priority in your retirement planning.

What happens to your 401(k) account should you change jobs?

Your first priority should be to repay any money you may have borrowed from your 401(k) account. Otherwise, it will be considered a distribution and applicable taxes and penalties will be assessed. Check with your current employer immediately to see how much time you have to repay the loan and avoid this.

SIMPLE–IRAs

Firms with fewer than 100 employees that do not otherwise offer a retirement plan can establish a Savings Incentive Match Plan for Employees IRA. These are not to be confused with the regular SEP IRAs described in the table on page 248. As of 2013, employees may make tax- deductible contributions in a SIMPLE-IRA up to a maximum of $12,000 annually, plus an extra $2,500 if age 50 or older. The employer must agree to one of two matching formulas: (1) matches 100% of the employee's contribution (up to 3% of their total compensation), or (2) contributes 2% of employee's compensation, whether they contribute or not (up to $5,100 maximum per year). Other than the higher contributions allowed, SIMPLE-IRAs are governed by the same rules as a traditional IRA. Furthermore, employees who participate in a SIMPLE-IRA can also contribute to a traditional or Roth IRA, subject to the income limitation tests.

Separation From Service

While most withdrawals from a 401(k) prior to age 59½ result in a 10% penalty, there is one important exception. If you are 55 or older and leave your employer (voluntarily or otherwise), you can withdraw part or all of your 401(k) money penalty-free. However, if you roll the money into an IRA, you lose the ability to make these earlier-than-usual withdrawals. This is an important and often overlooked difference between 401(k)s and IRAs, so plan carefully before rolling the money over to an IRA if you're 55 or older.

As for the longer-term considerations, you have several options and they can vary dramatically in terms of the investment and tax consequences. Two of them should be *avoided* if at all possible because they immediately bring the tax man into the picture:

• **Cash it out in a lump sum.** You'll have to pay income taxes on the entire amount, plus a 10% penalty for premature withdrawal if you're not at least 59½. (There's an exception—see bottom sidebar on previous page.) As a down payment on your tax bill, 20% of the account will be withheld and forwarded to the government.

• **Annuitize it.** This means to sign up for a series of regular withdrawals, usually monthly, based on your life expectancy using IRS tables. The withdrawals are designed to last through retirement, but if you change your mind and prefer to leave the money in your retirement account for further tax-deferred compounding, they can be discontinued after five years or upon reaching age 59 ½, whichever is later. You'll still owe income taxes, but you'll avoid the 10% penalty even if you're younger than 55. For more on annuitizing, see page 268.

The remaining options avoid any immediate tax liability. They leave the money in a tax-deferred account where it can continue to be invested and grow tax-deferred. The primary difference is where the account is.

• **Move it to an IRA.** This is usually your best option. It gives you the most flexibility in terms of investment choices and tax planning. You can transfer it to either an existing IRA into which you've been making contributions, or to a Rollover IRA. Moving to an IRA preserves the option of converting to a Roth IRA should that be advisable in years to come. A Rollover IRA also preserves the right to later move the funds back into a future employer's 401(k). Why might you want to do that? Two possibilities: (1) You can borrow from a 401(k) account (not that I encourage *that*!), and (2) Creditors cannot come after assets in a 401(k) account. None of the above applies to IRAs (although some states do extend creditor protection to IRAs).

If you choose this route, it's best if you carry out a trustee-to-trustee transfer where the money goes straight from the old plan to the IRA without passing through your hands. This avoids the possibility that you might end up with an unexpected tax bill by running afoul of the rules governing transfers where the employee temporarily takes possession of the money (see page 256).

• **Leave it in your former employer's 401(k) plan.** If your account is worth $5,000 or more, you have this option. You wouldn't elect this, of course, if you've been unhappy with the investment choices available. Nor if you contemplate borrowing from the plan in the future, because borrowing by former employees is typically not permitted. The advantage of this approach is its simplicity.

• **Move it to your new employer's 401(k) plan.** The biggest consideration is whether you find the investment choices in the plan to be attractive. If so, check to see if there's a waiting period before new employees are allowed to transfer in. Again, use the trustee-to-trustee transfer approach rather than personally taking possession of the money.

Federal workers participate in a retirement plan . . .

. . . similar to a 401(k) arrangement—the Thrift Savings Plan. Those hired after 1983 are covered by the Federal Employees Retirement System (FERS), which means, among other things, that the government matches employee contributions to the Thrift Plan in a very generous way. First, the government automatically contributes an amount equal to 1% of salary. Second, for every dollar employees contribute up to 3% of their salary, the government matches it with a dollar. Third, for every dollar employees contribute above 3% of salary (up to 5%), the government puts in 50 cents. By contributing 5%, therefore, employees have doubled their money just by virtue of the government's matching funds. Finally, employees can contribute beyond the 5% — up to a dollar limit of $17,500, or $23,000 for those age 50 or older (2013 limits). Although amounts beyond 5% of salary are not matched by the government, they do provide additional immediate tax benefits plus long-term tax-deferred compounding of investment returns.

According to government figures, 7% of FERS participants don't contribute to the Thrift Plan. In light of the generous matching provisions, this is surprisingly shortsighted behavior. Their goal should be to contribute 3% of their salary at a minimum, and 5% if at all possible. Federal workers hired in 1983 and earlier fall under the Civil Service Retirement System (CSRS). While CSRS workers are not eligible for matching funds, they can make contributions to the Thrift Plan and enjoy tax-deferred compounding.

One recent change to the Thrift Plan is the addition of a Roth TSP option. Just as with a Roth IRA or a Roth 401(k), money is contributed to the Roth TSP after the employee has paid tax on it. When the contributions and earnings are taken out in retirement, no tax is due. TSP-eligible employees may choose the traditional TSP, the Roth TSP, or a combination — in which case they would spread their contributions across the two plans while ad-

---

MANAGING THRIFT PLAN ALLOCATIONS

For Federal Workers	For Purposes of Assessing Risk When Rebalancing SMI Portfolio
The I Fund Invests in foreign stocks of 21 developed countries. Similar in performance to: Morgan Stanley EAFE Index.	Treat as Stock Category 5.
The S Fund Invests in stocks of small and mid-size U.S. companies. Similar in performance to: Vanguard Extended Market Index Fund.	Treat as Stock Category 4. *
The C Fund Invests in stocks of larger U.S. companies. Similar in performance to: Vanguard 500 Index Fund.	Treat as Stock Category 1. *
The F Fund Invests in corporate and government-backed securities. Similar in performance to: Vanguard Total Bond Market Index Fund.	Treat as Bond Category 2.
The G Fund Invests in non-marketable U.S. Treasury securities. Similar in performance to: Government-only money market funds.	Treat as Bond Category 1.

The L Funds: These funds invest in the five funds listed above. The percentage of holdings from each of the I, S, C, F, and G fund varies based on target date.

* U.S. stock-risk categories are explained on pages 147 - 150, bond categories on pages 133 - 136

hering to the previously described contribution limits.(A calculator found at www.tsp.gov can help you determine which one may be best for you.)

Changes in the way contributions to your TSP account are allocated can be made at any time. You can also transfer money from one TSP fund to another. Two such "interfund transfers" may be made each month into or out of any TSP fund. Changes in allocations and fund transfers may be made online at www.tsp.gov or by calling (877) 968-3778.

Other points of interest concerning the Thrift Plan: You can borrow from your account for purposes of buying a house, paying education or medical expenses, or alleviating a temporary financial hardship. When you leave your job with the government, you can roll your Thrift account assets into your personal IRA.

To make sure you're getting the most from your Thrift Plan opportunities, you may want to purchase a copy of *Your Thrift Savings Plan*, a privately published guide (i.e., not an official government publication) that's available via PDF download, as well as in print. You can order a copy at www.federaldaily.com.

For purposes of controlling risk, it's important to include your retirement plan investments as part of your overall portfolio.

This requires that you understand where the various choices in your retirement plan fit in terms of SMI's risk categories—see table below. (It might also be good to review the basics on pages 133-136, 147-150, and 174-176.) The SMI philosophy is that all of your long-term investments go into the same "pot," and it is the portfolio mix *of the entire pot* that matters. That means you should consider all of the investments over which you have decision-making authority,

MANAGING 401(K) OR 403(B) ALLOCATIONS

Investment Choices	For Purposes of Assessing Risk When Rebalancing Portfolio
International Stock Fund Invests primarily in foreign stocks, but many also allow some U.S.	Treat as Stock Category 5.
Growth Fund Invests primarily in stocks chosen for their potential to rise in price.	Treat as Stock Category 2 or 4.
Stock Index Fund Usually designed to give results identical to S&P 500 stock index.	Treat as Stock Category 2.
Equity Income Fund Invests primarily in stocks chosen for their dividend-paying potential.	Treat as Stock Category 1.
Balanced Fund Invests in a fixed combination of stocks and bonds.	Treat as Stock Category 1.
Government Bond Fund Invests primarily in long-term IOUs of U.S. Treasury.	Treat as Bond Category 3.
Money Market Fund and Guaranteed Investment Contracts Short-term IOUs of businesses, banks, government, insurance companies.	Treat as Bond Category 1.

including those in your retirement accounts, as you analyze how best to diversify your holdings to achieve the portfolio allocation you desire. By shifting some of your retirement plan holdings from stocks to bonds or vice versa, you can achieve the right balance between equity and interest-earning investments. (See an example with sample worksheets on pages 201-208).

Much has been said concerning the tendency of investors to be too conservative in their retirement plan investments. The SMI philosophy is that you should be guided by the mix appropriate to your season of life and investing temperament (see risk matrix on page 159). However, many others recommend using a common rule of thumb: subtract your age from 100 and allocate at least that percentage to your holdings in stocks. This formula gives younger workers, who can afford to take more risk, a greater opportunity for long-term capital growth.

A warning: Don't overcommit to your company's stock.

A 2002 study by the Institute of Management and Administration, publisher of a newsletter that monitors the investments in retirement plans, contained some startling findings. It was based on a survey of the retirement plan holdings of workers at 318 of the nation's largest companies. The study revealed that workers had more than a fourth (28%) of their 401(k) assets invested in the stock of just one company—their employer. (Employees at a dozen large companies had more than 75% (!) of their 401(k) assets invested in employer stock.) While these figures have moderated somewhat in recent years (in part due to the Pension Protection Act of 2006), a 2012 study found that employees in large companies still had nearly 16% of their holdings in employer stock.

You may recall that if a mutual fund wishes to meet the diversification standards of the Securities and Exchange Commission, it can invest no more than 5% of its holdings in the stock of any one company. Therefore, if workers are investing 16% of their money in a single stock, they are about three times more concentrated than the government's standard of prudence would suggest. Is this higher level of commitment to one security appropriate? The answer depends on another question: How much of your total retirement holdings are contained in your retirement plan at work?

For example, assume that all of your retirement plan assets are worth $100,000, but only $25,000 of that is in your 401(k). If you invested 16% of that $25,000 in your company stock, your holdings would amount to $4,000. This is a reasonable amount in a $100,000 portfolio. On the other hand, if $80,000 of your $100,000 was in your 401(k), then a 16% allocation would mean that $12,800 was invested in your employer's stock. This is, in my opinion, too high.

How is it that employees are building such a significant stake in their company's future? The four most common ways this happens are: stock-purchase plans that let employees buy shares at a discount, stock-options being given to employees, company stock offered as an option in 401(k) retirement savings plans,

Getting Your Money Out Early

Withdrawing funds from your tax-deferred plans prior to turning 59½ should be a last resort.

The tax consequences are severe—a 10% premature withdrawal penalty plus income taxes on any pre-tax contributions or earnings you take out. There are other ways to meet a temporary cash squeeze:

• Stop contributing to the plan. This may sound obvious, but many workers become so accustomed to having their contribution automatically deducted from each paycheck that they forget it's their choice.

• Borrow from your account. Most profit-sharing and 401(k) plans permit employees to borrow against their retirement account, often up to 50% of its value. Repayments typically must begin immediately and be completed within three to five years.

• If you have made after-tax contributions, withdraw them first. You'll have to pay the 10% penalty and income tax only on the interest earned while your money was in the plan. Or you may be able to avoid the taxes and penalty entirely by rolling the qualified plan balance to an IRA while taking out only your after-tax contributions.

and using company stock to match employee contributions into 401(k) plans. All of these avenues have one thing in common—the employee gets a "good deal" on the company stock, either receiving a discount from current market value or, in the case of 401(k) matching programs, getting shares "for free."

Obviously, there are pitfalls that arise from being dependent on a single company for one's income, health and life insurance, *and* retirement investments. Consider the risk of those in companies hit especially hard by the financial crisis that began unfolding in 2007-2008. Not only did many lose their jobs and health benefits, but they also watched the value of their retirement assets fall as the stock market value of their company's stock dropped. Even in good times, there are no guarantees that an employer's stock will do well. Look at the plight of Bank of America's employees for example. In 2011, BOA employees held an average of 13% of their 401(k) assests in the company's. That year, the bank's stock plunged 58 percent, and the company announced plans to lay off 30,000 workers.

The reasons that many fail to prudently limit their investments in their company stock are primarily emotional. They include the fear of being considered disloyal, fear of "missing out" if the company stock does well, peer pressure from co-workers, greed in wanting to accumulate stock at discount prices, and blind optimism concerning the company's future. From a strictly financial view, diversification is the more prudent strategy.

How much company stock is too much? There is no hard and fast rule concerning this because individual situations can vary widely. However, a general range that is useful is to limit your investing in any one stock (whether it's your company or not) to 5%-15% of your total investable assets. The smaller the value of your total portfolio, the more you should gravitate to the lower end of the range.

If you find yourself in a situation where you need to diversify, read the sidebar on page 256 first, and make sure you understand the implications of giving up employer securities in your plan. If you decide to sell, consider spreading out the selling over several years. This minimizes both the tax impact (for shares held outside your retirement plan) as well as the risk of selling too much during a period of market weakness. If your company uses its stock to match your 401(k) contribution, make sure you don't compound the lack-of-diversification problem by investing your contributions the same way.

All retirement plans have one thing in common: at some point, you're going to want to take your money out!

Your decision as to how to do this will be one of the most important and far-reaching ones of your financial life. You shouldn't make it hurriedly; in fact, you should begin thinking about it years ahead of time. Make sure you understand the laws (which Congress has succeeded in making complicated and confusing by changing them from time to time) and how they affect your range of options.

With defined-*contribution* plans, your options are clear cut. Most people choose to roll the money into an IRA, although some of the other options listed on page 250 may also be available. With defined-*benefit* plans however, the choices become more complex. Some of the factors that will influence your decision include your age at retirement, birth year, health and life expectancy, income tax bracket, other sources of retirement income, inflationary expectations, desire for certainty versus desire for greater potential future income, and the list goes on.

Basically, you have three choices: take all your money out in one large payment; transfer your account value to an IRA Rollover where you can continue to invest it on a tax-deferred basis; or take it in the form of monthly payments spread over the remainder of your life. Here are some guidelines to consider as you go about making your decision. After finding out from your employer the amounts of both your lump-sum benefit and your monthly income benefit, ask yourself these questions:

• **How long do I expect to live?** Obviously, you can only make a guess based on your health at the time and your family history. The reason this comes into play is that the monthly payment option is usually computed based on a life expectancy of age 80. The longer you live past 80, the greater the value of your total monthly pension and the better off you are versus taking the lump-sum.

• **How dependent are my spouse or heirs on my estate?** If your spouse is dependent on you, you might prefer the "joint and survivor" pension. It provides a monthly payment to you for life (about 10%–20% lower than it would otherwise be), with an ongoing monthly payment (reduced by half) to your spouse after your death. If *providing for your spouse* is a primary consideration,

THE THREE PRIMARY CHOICES FOR RECEIVING YOUR RETIREMENT BENEFITS FROM A DEFINED-BENEFIT PLAN

	Take your money in one large payment	Transfer your money to an IRA rollover account	Take your money in monthly payments
How do you receive your money?	Your employer pays your retirement benefit to you all at one time.	Your employer sends your entire retirement benefit directly to your new IRA account.	You choose the combination of amount and duration of guaranteed monthly payments.
What taxes will you pay?	The entire amount is taxed at ordinary income rates in the year it is received.	None until you begin making withdrawals (which will be taxed as income the year they are received).	The money you receive will be taxed as income the year it is received.
What other factors come into play?	A special tax formula that can reduce your taxes may apply. Depending on your birth year, income averaging over ten-year periods may be permitted. Early withdrawal penalty could apply if you are under age 59½.	You lose the option of reducing your tax burden by income averaging over a ten-year period. Your investments continue to grow tax-deferred and are under your direct supervision.	Early withdrawal penalty could apply if you are under age 59½ and do not choose the lifetime income option. If your employer provides your monthly payments by buying an annuity for you, a financially strong insurance company is of great importance.

these and other options should be explored fully with your pension administrator. If *providing for heirs* is the most important consideration, then the lump-sum option is the way to go.

• **How do I feel about inflation?** Unless your monthly benefit provides for adequate cost-of-living increases, you may find it difficult keeping up with inflation over the longer

Sometimes It Pays to Take Your Company Stock Out When Leaving a Retirement Plan

Employer stock can be an exception to the wisdom of rolling retirement plan assets into an IRA.

If you have appreciated company stock, you may be better off walking away with some or all of the actual stock certificates instead. You'll owe taxes on the value of the shares at the time you purchased them (or they were added to your account), and, if you're under age 55, you'll have to pay the additional 10% early withdrawal penalty as well.

But here's the advantage: if the shares have gone up a lot in value since you acquired them, you'll be taxed on those gains at the more-favorable long-term capital gains rate when you later sell the stock. Otherwise, if you roll the shares into an IRA, all of your gains on the stock will eventually be taxed as ordinary income at your regular marginal tax rate.

It takes some number crunching to figure out which route will be more profitable in the long run, but it's worth the effort.

term. The lump-sum approach burdens you with the responsibility and risk of investing, but following our Sound Mind portfolio recommendations should keep you ahead of inflation.

• **What other sources of income will I have?** Both options have their risks: the lump-sum carries the risk that comes with doing your own investing, and the monthly payment has the risk of not keeping ahead of inflation. You should also consider what additional help you can expect from Social Security and your investments.

The table on page 255 summarizes the tax implications and other important features of each of the three alternatives. For additional help, I encourage you to contact some of the leading no-load fund organizations. Just tell them you are facing this very important decision of whether to take your retirement in a lump-sum or roll it into an IRA. They've developed user-friendly explanatory material (Schwab, Fidelity, Price, and Vanguard have done especially good jobs) which will walk you through the technical aspects. No-load fund organizations offer their help free of charge because they're hoping to win you over as a long-term customer during your retirement years.

Be careful when "rolling out" of your company's retirement plan.

Prior to 1993, you were given 60 days to deposit your lump-sum benefit check into a Rollover IRA in order to avoid any tax bite and preserve your tax-deferred program. Under current law, though, your benefit check will be hit with a 20% withholding rate *if it's made out to you*. This is a form of withholding similar to what your employer takes out of your paycheck. So, even if it's your intention to deposit it into a Rollover IRA, you're going to be 20% short!

Say you have $50,000 in your employer's plan. They're going to withhold $10,000 (which they'll turn over to the IRS where it will be applied as a credit against your total tax liability for the year) and give you $40,000. But in order to avoid any penalty, you've got to deposit $50,000 in the Rollover IRA. See the problem? Unless you've got an extra $10,000 you can spare to make up for what was withheld, you're going to get hit with a 10% penalty (if you're under 59½) *and* taxes.

You can avoid this potential problem by removing yourself from the transfer process. Arrange in advance for your employer to send your money directly to your new IRA rollover account. This is called a trustee-to-trustee transfer (see page 264-265).

Why did Congress change the old way, which was working fine? Perhaps to discourage workers from electing the lump-sum option (where they might spend it rather than save it). According to one survey, nearly half (46%) of the people who change jobs cash out their 401(k) holdings. So, then again, maybe the government was simply hoping to raise new revenues from those unsuspecting citizens who were unaware that the rules had, once again, been changed. ◆

CHAPTER PREVIEW

Your Personal Pension: The Ins and Outs of IRAs

I. **Individual Retirement Accounts can play a key role in your retirement investing strategy. Their are two primary kinds you should know about:**

   A. The traditional IRA—or "tax-deductible IRA"—offers a potential tax deduction if you meet certain tests. All the investment earnings in it compound tax-*deferred* until you begin taking them out at retirement. At that point, you pay taxes at ordinary income rates on the money as it's withdrawn.

   B. The newer "Roth IRA" offers no current tax deduction; however, all the investment earnings in it compound tax-*free*. In order to qualify for contributing to a Roth in a given year, your income must be below certain levels for that year.

   C. We look at the factors to consider in deciding whether a Deductible or Roth IRA is best for you.

II. **The control you have over your IRA makes it very flexible.**

   A. You select the financial organization with which you do business and control how your IRA assets are invested.

   B. You decide whether to contribute each year, and if so, how much.

   C. You select the timing and amount of your withdrawals.

III. **In this chapter, I answer several general questions concerning the use of IRAs.**

   A. What are some of the drawbacks of investing through an IRA?

   B. If you have access to a 401(k) plan, what priority should it be given?

   C. What rules govern the conversion of a traditional IRA to a Roth IRA?

   D. What is an IRA rollover?

   E. What is the best way to move your IRA?

   F. What are the rules for taking money out of an IRA?

   G. Which financial firms offer the most attractive terms for opening an IRA?

IV. **A variable annuity is another way to build a personal pension. We look at its pros and cons as well as some guidelines for when to invest in one.**

Your retirement income rests on what has been referred to as a three-legged stool.

Social Security has traditionally been regarded as the first of the three legs; however, the problems with Social Security make it impossible to project with confidence the level of monthly benefits 20 years and more into the future. Historically, the program has provided 35%-45% of retirees' monthly income; to be on the conservative side, investors under age 50 should use a lower assumption to reflect the uncertainty.

Private employer-sponsored retirement plans are the second leg (see chapter 22) and provide about 15%-20% of retirees' monthly income on average, according to the Social Security Administration. But there's a lot of room for variation here. For workers who spend most of their careers with the same company, it would not be unusual to receive a pension equal to 30%-40% of what they were making at the time of retirement. On the other hand, corporate America has been strongly moving away from defined-benefit plans in recent years, so your employer might not even offer a plan that pays a guaranteed monthly pension.

In any event, it is obvious that the third leg of personal savings and retirement funds will continue to play a very important role in providing adequate retirement incomes. And one of the best ways to go about building your personal retirement funds is by using an Individual Retirement Account (IRA).

What is now called the "traditional" or "deductible" IRA first appeared . . .

. . . on the financial scene in 1974 when Congress voted to allow certain working persons — those not covered by a pension plan at work — to put away up to $2,000 a year for retirement *and deduct it* on their federal income tax return. Not only did they enjoy *immediate* tax-savings, they also were excused from paying any income taxes on the *investment profits* they made. Until they began withdrawing the money upon retirement, they had the pleasure of watching their money grow tax-deferred. After the deductibility of home mortgage interest, IRAs offered the best tax break available to the middle class.

Not many were able to take advantage of it, however, because only a relatively small percentage of the work force lacked a work-related pension benefit of some kind. In 1980, six years after IRAs were first introduced, only 2.6 million federal tax returns included deductions for IRA contributions.

In 1981, Congress liberalized the law, making deductible IRAs available to *all* wage earners, regardless of whether they participated in a retirement plan at work. This is when the IRA concept really took off. By 1985, the number of tax returns claiming an IRA deduction had soared to 16.2 million. Congress soon decided it had been too generous in allowing taxpayers to keep so much of their income. In passing the Tax Reform Act of 1986, the law was changed to eliminate the tax deduction on contributions to deductible IRAs for wealthier taxpayers — namely, those whose adjusted gross incomes exceeded the levels specified in the so-called "phase-out range" (more on this shortly). There was one exception to this change: Taxpayers who were not active participants in an employer-sponsored retirement plan could still make fully deductible contributions to their IRAs regardless of their level of income.

The new complexity left taxpayers confused concerning the deductibility of their contributions. The result was predictable — the use of IRAs plummeted. In 1987, the first year under the new law, the number of tax returns claiming IRA deductions fell by more than half. By 1994, only 4.3 million returns reflected IRA contributions.

The IRA landscape grew even more complicated in 1997 when Congress gave us the "Roth IRA."

Named for Sen. William Roth, a consistent supporter of IRAs, this new option was an effort to reinvigorate the IRA concept and encourage middle-income folks to save more for their retirement. The Roth IRA differs from the traditional IRA primarily in the way taxes are handled — do you want to pay them now or pay them later? In a traditional IRA, you receive a tax deduction for the amount you contribute (save on taxes now) and eventually pay income tax on all contributions and gains when money is taken out down the road (pay taxes later). With a Roth IRA, your current contributions are not deductible at all (no tax savings now) but all of your future withdrawals, even your investment gains, are tax-free (no taxes to pay later, ever).

Along with the Roth came regulations that govern who qualifies for one — not everyone does. But if you qualify, is a Roth a better bet than a traditional IRA? Either way, *your total IRA contributions are still limited to $5,500 in 2013.* (IRA contribution limits are indexed to inflation, so the limits typically rise from year to year. Also, see sidebar on page 262.) The big question is which kind will give you the best long-term result. It can be a confusing analysis, and the outcome will vary depending on the assumptions you make.

Let's pretend we're in IRA school . . .

. . . and, as teacher, I'm going to lead you through some general principles that will help guide your decision as to the best place to invest your retirement money. The first is this: If you participate in a 401(k) where your contributions are matched, and you're currently not contributing up to the full amount that would be matched by your employer, you don't even need to consider IRAs at this point. If this describes you, your homework assignment is to channel your efforts into taking full advantage of the employer matching opportunity in your 401(k). Meanwhile, you're dismissed for the rest of the chapter. You can stay if

---

IRA Phase Out Ranges

In recent years, those at higher income levels have increasingly become eligible for tax deductions on contributions to traditional IRAs. The first number shown is the highest "Modified AGI" permitted in order to receive a full deduction. Above those levels, the phase-out kicks in. The second number is the limit above which you receive no tax deduction.

If covered by a retirement plan at work:

Single Taxpayers

2013	$59,000-$69,000

Married, Filing Jointly

2013	$95,000-$115,000

If <u>not</u> covered by a retirement plan at work:

There is no limit on earnings for single taxpayers, or for married, filing jointly, if the spouse also is not covered at work. For those married, filing jointly, where one spouse <u>is</u> covered at work, a full deduction is permitted at incomes of $178,000 or less. The deduction begins phasing out from $178,000-$188,000, and there is no deduction for those with incomes greater than $188,000. All numbers refer to 2013 rules.

What Is Modified Adjusted Gross Income?

Modified AGI is your "adjusted gross income" as shown on your 1040 tax return with certain modifications. The calculation is explained in IRS Publication 590, available at www.irs.gov.

you want, but I'm going to be giving all my attention to the other students.

Now, I want to divide the rest of you into five groups according to your annual income. But not your gross income. Instead, Congress has complicated the task by making us use what they call "modified adjusted gross income" (MAGI). *Groan!* I know, but don't blame me. I'm just trying to help you sort through your options. So, with MAGI in mind (see sidebar on previous page), look on the blackboard below to see which of the five groups you belong to. Be sure to read the small print, especially Footnote 2. Now consider the following general guidelines:

• Group 1: You have the greatest flexibility. You can choose to make either a fully deductible contribution to a traditional IRA or a non-deductible contribution to a Roth IRA. Later we'll have a "Traditional versus Roth" discussion that will be helpful in making your decision.

YOUR INCOME LEVEL DETERMINES YOUR BEST IRA OPTION

Your Income Group	Modified Adjusted Gross Income for Single Taxpayers	Modified Adjusted Gross Income for Married Taxpayers[1]	Deduction for Contribution to Traditional IRA?[2]	Eligible for Contribution to Roth IRA?
Group 1	$59,000 or less	$95,000 or less	Yes	Yes
Group 2	$59,000 to $69,000	$95,000 to $115,000	Partial	Yes
Group 3	$69,000 to $112,000	$115,000 to $178,000	No	Yes
Group 4	$112,000 to $127,000	$178,000 to $188,000	No	Partial
Group 5	More than $127,000	More than $188,000	No	No

These income levels are adjusted each year. [1]When filing jointly. [2]If you are not covered by a work-related retirement plan, contributions to traditional IRAs are fully deductible regardless of your income level.

• Group 2: You're in the "phase-out range" where the government begins taking away your tax deduction for contributing to a traditional IRA. Because your family income is more than $95,000 but less than $115,000, only a portion of your contribution is tax-deductible. (Single taxpayers have a lower threshold at each step along the way as can be seen on the board.) As a rough rule of thumb, you lose $200 in tax deductions for every $1,000 in income above the $95,000 threshold. You'll also want to pay attention during the "Traditional versus Roth" discussion.

One quick note — mixing deductible and non-deductible contributions in the same IRA can *greatly* complicate your tax situation when you finally withdraw the money. If possible, set up separate IRAs to keep these different types of contributions separate.

• Group 3: You're over the limit. Because your MAGI is $115,000 or more, you receive no deduction ☹ unless you're a Footnote 2 person. You could make a non-deductible contribution to a traditional IRA, but why do that with the Roth option available? You're Roth material all the way.

• Group 4: Like Group 3, Roths are your best option. But you're in the "phase-out range" where the government begins taking away your right to make a full Roth contribution (it falls about $200 for every $1,000 in income above the threshold). Still, take what you can get.

• Group 5: What can I say? You've been too successful and Congress figures you don't need any tax incentives to save for retirement.

Now, all you Footnote 2 folks who aren't covered by a retirement plan at work, pay attention. You're the exception to the rule. No matter what group you're in and no matter what I just said, you are entitled to a full tax deduction for any contributions you make to a traditional IRA. And unless you're in Group 5, a Roth IRA is also an option.

Okay, that covers the basic "who qualifies for what?" question.

Now let's look at three questions that will help you decide what's best when choosing between a Roth and a Traditional IRA.

The first question to consider is: Do you expect to be in a lower tax bracket when you retire than you are now? If so, choose a traditional IRA. You get a tax benefit now while your rates are higher, and pay tax later when they're lower. Conversely, if you anticipate a higher bracket in retirement, take your tax lumps now and put the money in a Roth. It'll sure feel good coming out tax-free in the future.

Having said that, this question is probably useful only if you anticipate retiring and beginning IRA withdrawals within 10-15 years. Beyond that it's too hard to predict what might happen to tax rates, not to mention personal circumstances. Plus, the longer your time horizon, the greater the tax-free advantages of the Roth become. So, throw the first question out of the equation if your time horizon is longer than 15 years.

The second question is: Would you like to postpone withdrawals beyond age 70½, or possibly leave the IRA intact for your beneficiaries? If so, opt for the Roth, which has no mandatory withdrawal requirements.

The final question is: Can you afford to contribute the maximum allowable amount into a Roth? Remember, those are after-tax dollars. Assuming you're in the 25% tax bracket, you'd have to actually set aside $7,334 — $5,500 for your Roth and $1,834 for federal taxes. If you can do that, you'll get a better deal with the Roth (see the sidebar at right).

To sum up, unless retirement will be arriving shortly and with it the expectation that you'll be in a lower tax bracket, the Roth IRA is the superior choice for most retirement savers.

If you're still considering a Traditional IRA, be sure you take these drawbacks into consideration.

It's easy to become so impressed with the power of tax-deferred compounding that we can overlook a few of the disadvantages of the

---

Going Head to Head: Comparing a Roth to a Traditional IRA

Assume Ben and Caleb have $7,334 pretax dollars to invest each year in an IRA strategy, that they earn 8% a year, and that they're in the 25% tax bracket, both before and during retirement.

Ben chooses a Roth IRA. He pays $1,834 in taxes and puts the remaining $5,500 in his Roth each year. After 20 years, he has $271,826 which he can withdraw tax-free.

$7,334 pre-tax dollars
−$1,834 tax going in @ 25%
$5,500 net into Roth
@ 8% annual compounding
$271,826 net after-tax dollars

Caleb chooses a traditional IRA. He puts $5,500 in his IRA and has $1,834 remaining. To obtain tax-deferred growth on that portion, he invests it in a variable annuity (see page 269). However, only $1,375 would be available to invest because taxes of $459 (25% of $1,834) would have to be paid first.

After 20 years, Caleb has a combined accumulation of $339,783 but has to pay taxes as the money is withdrawn. After tax, he receives $254,837. This is $16,989 less than Ben's $271,826 (which equals the tax Caleb had to pay on his annuity profits).

$5,500 into Traditional IRA
@ 8% annual compounding
$271,826 gross accumulation
−$67,956 tax coming out @ 25%
$203,870 net after-tax dollars

$1,834 pre-tax dollars
−$459 tax going in @ 25%
$1,375 net into variable annuity
@ 8% annual compounding
$67,956 gross accumulation
−$16,989 tax on gain
$50,967 net after-tax dollars

So the Roth has an advantage—while the $5,500 limit appears to be the same for both the Roth and traditional IRAs, the Roth actually maximizes the use of $7,334 pre-tax dollars whereas the traditional represents only $5,000 pre-tax dollars.

traditional IRA. One is that it turns lower-taxed capital gains into higher-taxed ordinary income. That's because, under current tax law, when you begin taking your money back out, it *all* gets taxed the same way — as ordinary income — even though a sizable portion of your growth came in the form of capital gains.

Another drawback are the rules governing how much you must take out each year. If you run afoul of them, the penalties are unbelievable (see page 279).

And third are the estate-tax implications. These are the taxes we Americans pay for the privilege of dying and leaving what wealth we may have attained to our loved ones. (The first $5.25 million is exempt in 2013 and, unless Congress changes the law yet again, the exempted amount should rise with inflation.) This tax has always struck me as outrageous because the estate that we leave behind is comprised of wealth that, by and large, has already been taxed at the local, state, and federal level. It seems criminal for the government to come back for more. Thankfully, the federal estate tax hits fewer taxpayers than it did just a few years ago, but for those who do get hit, Uncle Sam will claim 40% of everything above the exemption amount.

The question is: How does the traditional IRA fit into all this? It suffers the same fate as most other tax-deferred retirement accounts. According to the *Wall Street Journal*:

> *Death is brutal for retirement accounts, because the government still insists on collecting all the income taxes owed. Sure, your heirs may be able to delay the impact, but eventually a combination of income taxes and estate taxes will wreak their havoc. With larger estates, you can get 60% or 70% of the retirement plan going to taxes. . . . By contrast, if you die with your money in a regular taxable account, only estate taxes get levied.*

Roth IRAs are better in regard to all three of the above concerns: (1) all monies taken out of a Roth are tax-free; (2) there are no mandatory distribution requirements; and (3) estate taxes still apply but no income taxes or penalties come into play.

What about converting my traditional IRA to a Roth?

When it comes to deciding if converting a regular IRA to a Roth makes financial sense, you need to ask some of the same questions we looked at on page 261: How does your current tax bracket compare with your anticipated tax bracket in retirement? Is postponing withdrawals and/or being able to pass the account to your heirs important to you?

There are also two other factors that come into play. If you convert your IRA, you will have to pay income tax on any gains in the account, plus any deductible contributions you've made over the years. It all comes due on this year's tax return, which can add a sizeable sum to your tax bill. If you have the resources to pay those extra taxes without having to raid any of your retire-

Catch-Up Contributions

If you're in your 50s, the government wants to encourage you to save even more for retirement. Thus, the recent concept of "catch-up" contributions where you can put even more in your retirement account than the regular limits would lead you to believe.

For 2013, 401(k), 403(b) or 457 plan participants who are 50 or older by the end of the taxable year may make maximum catch-up contributions of $5,500. Since this is in addition to the regular $17,500 limit, that means your true maximum is $23,000. The catch-up amount will be indexed for inflation in future years.

Catch-up contributions to IRAs are also allowed. The maximum catch-up contribution to an IRA is $1,000. Again, these amounts are in addition to the new limits. Example: 2013 IRA limit of $5,500 per person plus $1,000 catch-up contribution equals total contribution of $6,500 for those 50 or older by the end of 2013. The catch-up limit for IRAs is currently not indexed for inflation in the future, although the standard IRA contribution amount is.

ment accounts for cash, then you might want to consider converting. If you will have to pull money out of the account just to pay the tax bill, chances are converting is not a good move for you. Not only will you lose out on future appreciation on these funds, but you'll pay a stiff early withdrawal penalty if you're under age 59½.

If you have the cash on hand to pay the tax bill, and converting looks good to you, a final question to consider is how far off is your retirement? At a bare minimum, you should have at least five years before you'll need to tap the converted IRA. That's because you'll face early withdrawal penalties if the Roth is not established for five years before withdrawals begin. A five-year horizon is a minimum, not an automatic signal to proceed. The Roth's advantages build with time, so the longer the Roth will be intact, the better your chances that the conversion will be worthwhile.

How should you invest the money you put into your IRA?

An IRA is not, in and of itself, an investment. It's merely a tax shelter that can contain a wide variety of investments of your choosing. To gain the most from the tax-deferred advantage, put fixed-income investments in your IRA (because a large part of their total return is interest income. When withdrawn at retirement, income from IRA will be taxed at your highest marginal tax rate). The tax deferral is less helpful for investments in which a large part of the total return is from *growth.*

WHEN YOU HAVE A CHOICE, SHOULD YOU CONTRIBUTE TO A 401(K) OR AN IRA?

	401(k) Plan	Deductible IRA	Roth IRA
Are you eligible?	❑ Your company offers a 401(k) plan. ❑ You meet the customary eligibility requirements.	❑ You're not a participant in a retirement plan at work, OR ❑ You have Modified AGI of less than $115,000.[1] Also, you must be under 70½ and have earned income during the year.	❑ You have Modified AGI of less than $188,000.[3] ❑ You have earned income during the year.
What is the most you can put in each year?[2]	$17,500 in 2013.	$5,500 per spouse in all IRAs combined in 2013.	$5,500 per spouse in all IRAs combined in 2013.
Will you receive matching funds from your employer?	Generally yes. See page 260.	No.	No.
Are contributions tax-deductible?	Yes.	Yes, but reduced for those with income in the phase-out range.	No.
Can you borrow from your account?	At the employer's discretion, but generally yes.	No.	No, but principal contributions may be taken out penalty free.
Investment options?	Generally limited.	Vast.	Vast.
How are withdrawals taxed once you reach age 59½?	Contributions and gains are taxed as ordinary income.	Contributions and gains are taxed as ordinary income.	Contributions are tax-free. Gains are tax-free assuming the plan has been in place 5 years.
When do you have to begin taking distributions?	No later than age 70½ unless still working.	No later than age 70½.	No mandatory distribution age.

[1] A sliding scale comes into play to determine how much of your contribution is deductible. See page 260. [2] The amounts shown do not include the "catch-up" contributions permitted to people 50 years or older— see sidebar on opposite page. [3] For those with income between $178,000 and $188,000, a sliding scale comes into play to determine the amount that can be contributed. See page 260.

This is because, compared to fixed-income investments, growth returns (i.e., capital gains) are treated less harshly from a tax standpoint. For most taxpayers, the tax on long-term capital gains is limited to 15% (higher-income taxpayers pay a top capital-gains rate of 20%).

Don't invest in tax-exempt securities like municipal bonds and annuities in your IRA. There's no point in putting investments that are already tax-exempt into an IRA; there's no additional tax savings. With municipal bonds, you're lowering your investment potential as well as because they yield significantly less than corporate or government bonds.

What is an IRA rollover?

A rollover is a tax-free distribution of cash or other assets from one retirement program that you then contribute to another retirement program. The amount you roll over tax-free is generally taxable later when the new retirement program makes distributions to you (or your beneficiary).

There are two kinds of IRA rollovers. In one, the money you're putting into your new IRA comes from a qualified employer plan (such as those discussed in chapter 20). In the other, the money you're putting into your new IRA comes from another IRA. In this second kind of rollover, you must complete the transaction within 60 days of receiving the check (although completing it within 60 days of the *date* on the check is safer because you can prove you complied with the time limit). If you miss the 60-day deadline, you may be assessed income tax and early withdrawal penalties on the full amount of the check.

Also, such a change can be done only once in any one-year period (the period begins on the date you receive your money from the old IRA, not on the date you roll it over into your new one). You may, however, roll over assets from separate IRAs during a one-year period. In other words, each "old" IRA has its own one-year period, and if you have several IRA accounts, it's OK if they overlap. You must roll over into your new IRA the same amount (the same "property") you received from your old one.

What is an IRA asset transfer
(sometimes called a trustee-to-trustee transfer)?

There's another way to move your IRA—have the trustee/custodian of your new IRA do it for you. A transfer of funds at your request from your old IRA *directly* to your new one is not only simpler but it avoids any potential problems associated with missing the 60-day deadline. Also, it is not affected by the one-year waiting period mentioned above.

I recommend using either a no-load fund organization or a discount broker that also offers no-load mutual funds. Once you sign the authorization forms provided, they will take care of the paperwork in what is called a trustee-to-trustee transfer. It couldn't be easier!

If you have more than one IRA account, you might consider combining them into one. It's not unusual for people to have many different IRAs spread around various places that were offering the "best deal" at the time their contribution was made. By combining them into one account at a no-load mutual fund organization, you'll save on annual account fees and cut your paperwork. More important, you'll have a much easier time managing your investments and tracking their performance.

As always, there's an exception: be sure to keep IRAs of different types separate. Putting an IRA with non-deductible contributions together with one containing deductible contributions is not only confusing, it can cost you down the road if you can't distinguish which withdrawals should and should not be taxed.

It's worth moving your IRA where it can get better returns even if they amount to only 2%-3% a year. For example, someone with $10,000 in an IRA earning 8% a year will have $68,485 in 25 years. But if that same person could earn 10% instead, the total would rise to $108,347. That extra $40,000 provides additional months of income once the person retires.

The longer you wait before withdrawing money from your IRA, the longer it can continue to grow tax-deferred.

Since it's your money, you might think that it's up to you to decide when to start tapping your IRA account and how much to withdraw each year. Naturally, because the federal government is involved, it's not that simple.

The IRS imposes very strict rules that dictate how long you can postpone making withdrawals from your IRA, as well as the minimum amount you must withdraw each year. (They want you to start taking your money out so you will begin paying some of those long deferred income taxes.) The minimum withdrawal amounts are called "required minimum distributions," and the latest you can wait to begin making them is April 1 of the year after you reach age 70½. If you violate the IRS guidelines, there are some horrendous penalties awaiting you. Here are the basics.

• Up to age 59½ — Take it and pay a penalty. The general rule is that IRA withdrawals are taxed as ordinary income in the year you receive them. If you withdraw money before reaching age 59½, you are also hit with a 10% penalty that is in addition to any income tax you owe. The penalty does not apply if you have a disability, or if you begin a series of scheduled annuity payments based on your life expectancy (see page 266).

Things get slightly more complicated if you've made nondeductible contributions, because they've already been taxed. In that case, only part of your

Concerning IRA Fees
Many advisers suggest that you pay any fees associated with your IRA account out-of-pocket rather than allowing them to be deducted from the account. This preserves the capital in the IRA for futher tax-deferred growth.

For More on the Technical Aspects of IRAs
Request IRS Publication 590. It's free. You can download it at www.irs.gov, or call the IRS Forms Distribution Center at 800-TAX-FORM (800-829-3676).

withdrawal is taxed and part of it is treated simply as a return of your nondeductible contribution. The 10% penalty is applied to the taxable amount of your withdrawal. This is true of both traditional and Roth IRAs.

LIFE EXPECTANCIES FROM IRS TABLES	
Age	Expectancy
70	27.4
71	26.5
72	25.6
73	24.7
74	23.8
75	22.9
76	22.0
77	21.2
78	20.3
79	19.5
80	18.7
81	17.9
82	17.1
83	16.3
84	15.5
85	14.8
86	14.1
87	13.4
88	12.7
89	12.0
90	11.4
91	10.8
92	10.2
93	9.6
94	9.1
95	8.6
96	8.1
97	7.6
98	7.1
99	6.7

• **Age 59½ to age 70½—Take it or leave it.** You have the greatest flexibility in your 60s. You can take out as much as you like, or nothing at all. The amounts you withdraw are no longer subject to the 10% penalty tax. Of course, normal income taxes apply. If they can afford it, most people are inclined to make no withdrawals during this period in order to make the most of the benefits of tax-deferred growth.

• **Age 70½ and over—Leave it and pay a penalty, unless you've got a Roth.** You've gotten the most from the tax deferral, and the IRS now insists you make a withdrawal whether you need the money or not. Listen carefully: The law says that you must take your first minimum annual distribution no later than April 1 of the year *after the year* you reach 70½. The IRS calls this your "required beginning date." Furthermore, you must take additional minimum annual distributions no later than December 31 of each year after you attain age 70½.

For example, if you were born on March 15, 1950, you'll turn 70½ on September 15, 2020. You must make your first minimum withdrawal on or before April 1, 2021. Then you must make your second minimum withdrawal by December 31, 2021. These deadlines are for people who have resisted taking their distributions. You don't have to wait this long. In fact, most people would benefit from taking their first required distribution three months early to avoid having their first two distributions occur in the same tax year.

If you wish, you can begin making penalty-free withdrawals as soon as you turn 59½. Remember that when you begin withdrawing IRA funds, you'll pay taxes at that time. *Being tax-deferred is not the same as being tax-free.* Don't think of a traditional IRA in the same category as a truly tax-free investment such as municipal bonds or a Roth IRA.

How is the minimum annual withdrawal calculated?

We've been discussing the concept of "required minimum distributions," but don't let that give you the impression that you are restricted to taking small amounts out of your IRA. You're free to empty the entire account anytime you want (of course, the penalty tax applies before age 59½, and the income tax applies regardless of your age). But assuming you *want* to minimize your withdrawals, how is the required minimum calculated?

Regulations issued by the IRS in 2002 have greatly simplified this task. Now, IRA owners and retirement plan participants will generally all use the same new uniform life expectancy table. Only taxpayers with a spousal beneficiary more than 10 years younger can use a different method; they have the option to use their actual joint life expectancy.

The minimum amount that must be withdrawn annually is calculated by dividing your account balance (as of December 31 of the previous year) by the applicable life expectancy. The table at far left shows the value to use if the calculation is based on the life expectancy of the owner of the IRA. For example, a 70-year-old person with a year-end IRA value of $250,000 would be required to withdraw at least $9,124 the following year (250,000 divided by 27.4).

What if you fail to withdraw the minimum? That's where the "horrendous" penalty I referred to previously comes in—a 50% nondeductible excise tax is assessed on the shortfall, that is, on the difference between what you should have withdrawn and what you actually withdrew. If the 70-year-old retiree in the above example withdrew $6,000 the following year, the excise tax would amount to $1,562 (50% of the difference between $9,124 and $6,000). And the excise tax would not be deductible on that year's income tax return.

The moral of this is that it's really important to pay close attention to the details when you're planning how you want to use your IRA during retirement. The rules can be complicated, especially those that relate to what's best in terms of naming a beneficiary. In this regard, make sure you have adequate tax planning counsel and plenty of time to make your decisions. The 2002 regulations made some of the old conventional wisdom regarding estate-tax planning obsolete, so review your beneficiary choices if you haven't looked at them in the past decade or so.

Roth's offer more flexibility than traditional IRAs if you face a cash crunch.

In a Roth, you always have access to the principal you've contributed without income taxes or penalties. In addition, earnings can generally be withdrawn early without penalty if the distributions are for death or disability, high medical expenses, qualified higher education expenses for you, a spouse, child or grandchild, or first-time-home-buyer expenses. Naturally there are many details to each of these exceptions, so you'll have to do some research to find out more specifics, but generally you can get away with just paying income taxes and no penalties in these cases. With traditional IRAs, if you touch any of it early, you pay dearly.

If you need to tap your traditional IRA before reaching age 59½, there is a way around the 10% early withdrawal penalty. It involves invoking the annuity option.

You don't read much about the strategy I'm about to describe. Possibly it's because financial advisers don't want to encourage the investing public to spend their IRA funds prematurely. I certainly can understand that. On the other hand, on those occasions where the need for cash is so great that a decision to withdraw it from an IRA has already been made, wouldn't it be good to know there's a way to do it without paying the 10% penalty? Here's the key as explained in IRS Publication 590:

"Generally, if you are under age 59½, you must pay a 10% additional tax on the distribution of any assets (money or other property) from your traditional IRA.... [But y]ou can receive distributions from your traditional IRA that are part of a series of substantially equal payments over your life (or your life expectancy), or over the lives (or the joint life expectancies) of you and your beneficiary, without having to pay the 10% additional tax, even if you receive such distributions before you are age 59½. You must use an IRS-approved distribution method and you must take at least one distribution annually for this exception to apply.... You may have to pay [a] recapture tax if you do not receive the payments for at least 5 years under a method that qualifies for the exception."

In essence, you can decide to temporarily treat your IRA as an annuity. The amount of your annual withdrawal depends on your life expectancy at the time, and all withdrawals are taxable as income in the year you receive them. Once you begin your withdrawals, you must continue taking them for at least five years, or until you reach 59½ if that period is longer. The table at left illustrates how this could work for a 52-year-old who is temporarily unemployed, but has a $300,000 IRA that resulted from a rollover out of his previous employer's retirement plan.

Age	Value of IRA	IRS factor	Annuity withdrawal	IRA after withdrawal	Assume 7% return	IRA at end of year
52	$300,000	32.3	$9,288	$290,712	$20,350	$311,062
53	311,062	31.4	9,906	301,155	21,081	322,236
54	322,236	30.5	10,565	311,671	21,817	333,488
55	333,488	29.6	11,266	322,222	22,556	344,777
56	344,777	28.7	12,013	332,764	23,293	356,058
57	356,058	27.9	12,762	343,296	24,031	367,326
58	367,326	27.0	13,605	353,722	24,761	378,482
59	378,482	26.1	14,501	363,981	25,479	389,460
60	389,460	25.2	15,455	374,005	26,180	400,185

His withdrawal schedule is designed so that, even though his payments increase each year as he ages, they are calculated based on his life expectancy so as to last the remainder of his lifetime. Upon reaching age 59½, he has the option of stopping the payments and once again working to rebuild his IRA account with additional tax-deductible contributions.

There are other IRS-approved distribution methods that result in higher yearly withdrawals for a fixed number of years, at the end of which his IRA would have been completely emptied. Consult a professional for guidance and a discussion of your options.

Even after you know which kind of IRA you want, the question still remains: Where should you open your account?

All the major banking, brokerage, and mutual fund institutions offer IRAs. I've provided the list below as a starting point as you look for a home for your IRA. The competition for your IRA business is fierce, as can be seen by the will-

A SOUND MIND BRIEFING

Look Before You Leap: A Primer on Variable Annuities

Variable annuities (VAs) are mutual funds wrapped up in a tax-sheltered package. Unlike a fixed annuity, where you are essentially lending money to the insurance company and, in return, agree upon a rate of return up front, the returns in a variable annuity aren't locked in ahead of time. They vary depending on how well the investments perform—that's why they're called "variable."

The VA has one major advantage over the fixed kind—<u>you</u> have control over the investments. Insurance companies typically offer a range of investment choices in their variable annuities, and let you decide how much of the money you give them goes into each category. Your eventual return is affected by three things.

• <u>Your allocation decisions</u>. If you decide to put all your money into the stock market just before a major sell-off, you'll get off to a slow start. On the other hand, if you play it safe in a money market fund, you're giving up the reason for choosing a VA in the first place—greater profit potential.

• <u>Investment fund performance</u>. It could be that even though you make excellent allocation decisions, the funds offered by your particular insurer just don't perform well. Just like mutual funds, some finish in the top ranks year after year, whereas others are perennial also-rans. Check out the track records of the funds in the variable annuity being offered to you. How do they compare with other variable annuity funds over the same period?

• <u>Fees, fees, and fees</u>. There are three kinds of fees you have to pay with most VA products. First, sales fees, usually disguised as "surrender charges." In the most common arrangement, there are no up-front sales charges; instead, the cost of commissions paid to the brokers and insurance agents is recovered by penalties paid if investors take money out of the annuity in the first seven years.

Next come the "contract fees," which include annual administrative and insurance fees. Among their other purposes, these fees guarantee that your beneficiaries won't get back less than you put in, regardless of how poorly your investment choices perform. According to Morningstar, these fees average about 1.3% per year. You pay these every year you own the annuity.

Finally there are the fees paid to the investment managers who make the portfolio decisions in the funds. These are similar to the management fees paid by shareholders of regular mutual funds and typically run about 1.0% per year. These also are ongoing.

So, you can see how the overhead expenses cut into your returns by about 2.3% each and every year, even assuming you hold your annuity longer than seven years and avoid the surrender charges. Another drawback is the loss of liquidity. Annuities are designed for retirement planning and are intended as long-term investments. Once you put your money into one, you're supposed to leave it there until at least age 59$\frac{1}{2}$. If you take it out sooner, you get hit with a 10% penalty from the government, just as with IRAs.

Are variable annuities worth the cost, red tape, and possible tax headaches down the road? Usually not. Because of the high costs and the possible tax disadvantages, many financial planners recommend VAs only as a last resort after all the other options have been explored and exhausted.

Their unique characteristics create a situation where it's difficult to decide which kinds of investments would be appropriate within a variable annuity. On the one hand, if you invest in equities with growth potential, you're going to end up paying ordinary income tax rates on what would otherwise qualify for long-term capital-gains tax treatment. With the capital-gains rate at 15% for most taxpayers (20% for some), it makes little

sense to put growth investments in an annuity.

On the other hand, if you put your VA money in fixed-income investments, then the high fees become particularly burdensome. Do you really want to pay 2.3% a year or more just to invest in bonds (which have historically returned about 5% a year)? The same investment in a low-cost, no-load mutual fund (such as those at Vanguard) would cost only about 0.2% per year.

In my view, a VA is appropriate <u>only</u> if you can pass all eight of the following tests:

❑ You're already making the maximum allowable contribution to your IRA (whether tax-deductible or not).

❑ You're already paying the maximum permitted into an employer-sponsored 401(k) plan.

❑ You have investment money you're willing to lock away for at least 20 years, which is the time needed to make up for the higher fees.

❑ You're in one of the higher tax brackets now (31% and up) *and* have a reasonable expectation that your tax bracket will be lower after you retire.

❑ You've set aside an amount of cash that's sufficient to cover your major expenses and emergency needs so that you're sure you'll have no need to withdraw your money before age 59$\frac{1}{2}$.

❑ You expect to make withdrawals in regular, systematic payments to supplement your other retirement income rather than withdraw your assets all at once.

❑ You anticipate that your regular monthly withdrawals will exhaust the assets in your annuity in your lifetime. (Due to tax laws, an annuity is not a good vehicle for accumulating capital to leave to your heirs.)

❑ You got a late start contributing to other retirement accounts and are using an annuity as a means for making up lost ground.

From the <u>Sound Mind Investing</u> newsletter. To learn more about the monthly SMI newsletter, use the postage-paid tear-out card in this book, or visit our website at <u>www.soundmindinvesting.com</u>.

ingness of the firms to waive their annual fees for IRA accounts. Many discount brokers (such as Firstrade) charge no annual fees for IRA accounts. They often offer huge numbers of mutual funds, many as no-transaction-fee options. As long as you aren't tempted by the easy access to trade more within your account, they can be a good deal worth investigating. The "deals" being offered change frequently, so these could be outdated by the time you read this. Check with these and other no-load fund organizations for their current policies.

Investors are fee-sensitive, as evidenced by the fact that financial organizations give such great emphasis to their low (or no) fees in their advertising. However, when selecting a home for your IRA, I would suggest you give greater weight to having a large number of investment alternatives from which you can choose. That's why I feel the fund supermarkets are usually a better option than opening your account directly with a particular fund organization. The exceptions to this rule are Vanguard and the Sound Mind Investing Funds, which offer convenient one-stop-solutions for indexing (chapter 14), Upgrading (chapter 17), and Dynamic Asset Allocation (chapter 18) strategies respectively. And keep in mind you can't go simply by how many funds an organization offers because many of them aren't suitable for an IRA. For example, as noted earlier, you wouldn't want to invest in tax-exempt securities such as municipal bonds in your IRA because there would be no additional tax savings. ◆

WHO'S OFFERING THE MOST FAVORABLE TERMS ON IRAs?

Fund Organization	Annual Fee Each Fund Held	Minimum To Avoid Annual Fees	Minimum To Open IRA Account	Minimum Automatic Deposit[1]	Toll Free Phone	For More Information
SMI Funds	None	None	$2,500	$100	877-764-3863	smifund.com
Vanguard	$20[2]	$10,000 per fund[3]	$3,000	$50	800-551-8631	vanguard.com
Firstrade	None	None	None	$100	800-869-8800	firstrade.com
Scottrade	None	None	None	$1	800-619-7283	scottrade.com
TD Ameritrade	None	None	None[4]	None	800-454-9272	tdameritrade.com
Schwab	None	None	$1,000[6]	$100	877-673-7970	schwab.com
Fidelity	None	None[5]	$2,500[6]	$200[7]	800-343-3548	fidelity.com

FOOTNOTES: The above data was valid as of mid-2013. [1]Monthly automatic investments can be made directly from your checking or savings account, a good way to be sure you save as well as benefit from dollar-cost-averaging. [2]Fee can be avoided by signing up for electronic delivery of statements. [3]If your total assets exceed $50,000, the $20 annual fee is waived regardless of individual account balances. [4]$500 minimum if funded by electronic transaction. [5]Fidelity reserves the right to assess low-balance fees in some situations. [6]The minimum is waived if you establish a monthly automatic deposit. [7]Monthly minimum is $100 for most Fidelity funds.

CHAPTER PREVIEW

Lowering Your Investment Risk as You Approach Retirement

I. **Because no one knows what the future holds for the investment markets, we can never know in advance which combination of investments will minimize risk while maximizing gains.**

  A. This uncertainty makes it difficult to decide with confidence how much to cut back your investment risk as you near retirement. To a large extent, your decision will reflect your personal investing temperament.

  B. The "risk matrix" contains my suggestions as to what is an appropriate allocation between stocks (higher risk) and bonds (lower risk) given your age and temperament. Other professionals may offer different suggestions. There is no universally agreed upon "right" allocation for a retired person.

II. **A study of historical returns since 1926 shows how various combinations of stocks and bonds have performed in the past.**

  A. In this chapter, I present a table that is useful for gaining an understanding of the potential risks and rewards from holding six different stock/bond allocations over various time periods ranging from one year to 30 years.

  B. A similar table is presented that is useful for gaining an understanding of the potential risks and rewards from holding shares in large companies versus those of small companies.

  C. There are no "sure things." It is inevitable that you must make decisions that involve trade-offs between the risks you're willing to take and the rewards you hope to reap.

**Like my sons, I wanted to see *Jurassic Park* when it came out
in the summer of 1993.**

As I expected, it turned out to be an action-packed, nerve-wracking tale over-flowing with amazing special effects. Having read the book, I enjoyed the intellectual stimulation and the way the story got me to thinking about the critical importance of boundaries.

Boundaries exist for safety reasons; breaking through them can be dangerous. The film is scary because the prehistoric creatures break through *physical boundaries* and attack the people. And it provokes us to weigh the risks before breaking through *scientific boundaries* and playing with the building blocks of life. It may even have something to say to societies that are breaking through *moral boundaries* and removing the reasonable limits on personal freedoms that have characterized civilized societies for thousands of years.

Because I'm a person who thinks a lot about how to help people invest more successfully, the film caused me to also reflect on the risks taken by those who willfully ignore *time boundaries*. We are quite limited as to what we can know of the future with certainty.

My favorite character in *Jurassic Park* is Malcolm, the "chaos theory" scientist. In the book, I particularly liked the passage in which he is describing to a co-worker why many events are inherently, inescapably unpredictable:

"Computers were built because mathematicians thought that if you had a machine to handle a lot of variables simultaneously, you would be able to predict the weather. Weather would finally fall to human understanding. And men believed that dream for the next forty years. They believed that prediction was just a function of keeping track of things. If you knew enough, you could predict anything.

"Chaos theory throws it right out the window. It says that you can never predict certain phenomena at all. You can never predict the weather more than a few days away. All the money that has been spent on long-range forecasting is money wasted. It's a fool's errand. It's as pointless as trying to turn lead into gold. We've tried the impossible — and spent a lot of money doing it. Because in fact there are great categories of phenomena that are inherently unpredictable."

"Chaos says that?"

"Yes, and it is astonishing how few people care to hear it."

Consider that last line: *". . . it is astonishing how few people care to hear it."* How well that applies to people when they're making investment decisions! We refuse to believe that the markets, like the weather, cannot be accurately predicted. Throughout my advisory career I've seen people suffer financially because they look to the forecasts and opinions of gurus and experts to guide their decisions.

I was slow in accepting this limitation myself. But it's important we learn to admit, "I don't know what the future holds. The financial commentators in the media don't know. Investment experts don't know. Nobody knows. So, I must face the fact that I can never know in advance which investment alternatives will make the most money, lose the most money, or do little at all."

This uncertainty makes it difficult to know how much to cut back our investment risk — and the potential gains we're hoping for — as we near retirement.

In chapter 13, I explained how this might be done. The "risk matrix" (see page 159) balances the two competing influences in your investment planning — your fear of loss and your need for growth. On the one hand, I believe that you should "be yourself" as you make investing decisions. The quiz I designed (see pages 160-161) helps you select the investing temperament best suited to your personality by probing the intensity of your fear of losing money (an ever-present possibility in the markets). It's important that you be emotionally comfortable with your strategy. Otherwise, it's questionable if you'll develop the confidence and discipline needed to hang in there when the periodic storms of market turbulence blow through.

On the other hand, your investing strategy must face the realities of your present stage of life — how much time remains before you reach retirement, and what financial goals do you hope to achieve by that time? If you structure your portfolio too conservatively, your investment capital may not grow by the needed amount. But if you take too great a risk, you could suffer a large loss just before you need to withdraw capital for living expenses.

In the matrix, I offer suggestions on how much to invest-by-owning (typically in stocks and stock funds) versus how much to invest-by-lending (in savings accounts, bonds and bond funds, and other fixed income holdings). As I pointed out at the time, however, "The matrix reflects my personal sense of risk. Some investment advisers might encourage you to take more risk than I suggest, others might recommend less."

After reviewing several of the books in my library on the subject of how to adjust your stock-to-bond mix as you grow older . . .

. . . it's clear that the guidelines I offer as you approach and enter retirement are somewhat conservative. For example, if you're 65 years old (in what I call the "early retirement years" of your financial life), the matrix indicates that the stock portion of your holdings not exceed 60% in stocks. The recommendations of other advisers called for portfolios with stock allocations ranging from 40% to as high as 75%. Their argument for higher stock holdings is that, although stocks are subject to occasional major setbacks, they are needed to keep ahead of inflation. The response to that argument is that, while it's true that stocks have always recovered from previous bear markets, older investors may have a need to withdraw their money before stocks

HISTORICAL INVESTMENT RETURNS
OF VARIOUS PORTFOLIO COMBINATIONS

Portfolio Consists Of >>>	Stocks: 100% Bonds: 0%	Stocks: 80% Bonds: 20%	Stocks: 60% Bonds: 40%	Stocks: 40% Bonds: 60%	Stocks: 20% Bonds: 80%	Stocks: 0% Bonds: 100%
Average of 745 1-Year Periods	12.3%	11.1%	9.9%	8.7%	7.6%	6.4%
Best 1-Year Period	① 61.0%	② 54.2%	③ 47.3%	④ 40.4%	⑤ 33.6%	⑥ 32.7%
Worst 1-Year Period	−43.3%	−33.6%	−24.0%	−14.5%	−6.3%	−5.6%
Result ²/₃ Of The Time	−4.7% to 29.3%	−2.6% to 24.8%	-0.7% to 20.5%	0.9% to 16.6%	1.5% to 13.6%	0.3% to 12.4%
Average of 721 3-Year Periods	11.1%	10.3%	9.5%	8.5%	7.5%	6.4%
Best 3-Year Period	⑦ 33.4%	⑧ 29.9%	⑨ 26.3%	⑩ 22.7%	⑪ 20.2%	⑫ 18.4%
Worst 3-Year Period	−16.1%	−10.5%	−5.1%	−0.7%	1.5%	−0.4%
Result ²/₃ Of The Time	1.6% to 20.6%	2.7% to 17.9%	3.6% to 15.3%	4.0% to 13.0%	3.8% to 11.2%	2.4% to 10.3%
Average of 697 5-Year Periods	10.9%	10.2%	9.4%	8.5%	7.5%	6.5%
Best 5-Year Period	⑬ 29.7%	⑭ 26.9%	⑮ 24.0%	⑯ 21.0%	⑰ 20.0%	⑱ 19.5%
Worst 5-Year Period	−6.6%	−3.7%	-1.1%	1.2%	2.3%	0.7%
Result ²/₃ Of The Time	3.3% to 18.4%	4.1% to 16.3%	4.6% to 14.2%	4.7% to 12.3%	4.3% to 10.8%	3.0% to 9.9%
Average of 637 10-Year Periods	10.7%	10.1%	9.4%	8.6%	7.7%	6.7%
Best 10-Year Period	⑲ 19.5%	⑳ 18.1%	㉑ 16.8%	㉒ 15.7%	㉓ 14.8%	㉔ 13.7%
Worst 10-Year Period	-3.4%	-0.9%	1.2%	3.1%	4.0%	1.3%
Result ²/₃ Of The Time	5.5% to 16.0%	5.7% to 14.5%	5.8% to 13.1%	5.5% to 11.7%	4.9% to 10.5%	3.9% to 9.5%
Average of 577 15-Year Periods	11.0%	10.4%	9.7%	8.8%	7.9%	6.9%
Best 15-Year Period	㉕ 19.7%	㉖ 18.0%	㉗ 16.2%	㉘ 14.4%	㉙ 12.7%	㉚ 11.4%
Worst 15-Year Period	4.1%	4.5%	4.8%	4.8%	4.1%	2.4%
Result ²/₃ Of The Time	7.1% to 14.9%	7.0% to 13.7%	6.7% to 12.6%	6.2% to 11.5%	5.4% to 10.4%	4.4% to 9.5%
Average of 517 20-Year Periods	11.0%	10.4%	9.7%	9.0%	8.1%	7.2%
Best 20-Year Period	㉛ 18.3%	㉜ 16.7%	㉝ 15.1%	㉞ 13.5%	㉟ 11.8%	㊱ 10.5%
Worst 20-Year Period	6.4%	6.3%	6.0%	5.5%	4.6%	2.4%
Result ²/₃ Of The Time	7.9% to 14.0%	7.7% to 13.1%	7.3% to 12.2%	6.7% to 11.2%	6.0% to 10.3%	5.0% to 9.4%
Average of 457 25-Year Periods	11.0%	10.5%	9.9%	9.1%	8.3%	7.4%
Best 25-Year Period	㊲ 17.2%	㊳ 15.7%	㊴ 14.1%	㊵ 12.5%	㊶ 10.8%	㊷ 9.4%
Worst 25-Year Period	7.3%	7.1%	6.7%	5.9%	5.1%	3.5%
Result ²/₃ Of The Time	8.9% to 13.2%	8.5% to 12.5%	8.0% to 11.7%	7.4% to 10.9%	6.6% to 10.1%	5.6% to 9.2%
Average of 397 30-Year Periods	11.2%	10.7%	10.0%	9.3%	8.4%	7.5%
Best 30-Year Period	㊸ 14.5%	㊹ 13.5%	㊺ 12.4%	㊻ 11.2%	㊼ 10.0%	㊽ 8.9%
Worst 30-Year Period	9.1%	8.5%	7.7%	6.6%	5.2%	3.6%
Result ²/₃ Of The Time	10.0% to 12.4%	9.5% to 11.8%	8.9% to 11.1%	8.1% to 10.5%	7.2% to 9.7%	6.1% to 8.9%

Notes: The source for performance data was the Ibbotson SBBI 2013 Classic Yearbook published by Morningstar in Chicago. The data for stocks are based upon total returns (capital appreciation and dividend income) of the Standard & Poor's 500, a "blue-chip" stock index. The data for bonds are based on Ibbotson's "intermediate-term government bonds" total return (capital appreciation and coupon interest income) index which uses bonds of approximately five-years maturity. The period covered runs from 1950 (after the atypical events of the Depression and WWII) through 2012. Portfolios were rebalanced to their original allocations every 12 months.

have time to rebound. Interest income from bonds is certain; good returns from stocks in the short run are not. A guiding principle should be that you take as little risk as possible in attaining your income goals. For example, if a 20% stocks, 80% bonds mix will generate adequate investment income, then a 65-year old should move in that direction even if he or she has a temperament that would suggest a higher stocks allocation.

So, it's a matter of balance. You need stocks for growth and bonds for income, but, putting your emotions aside, how much of each would be best given your current age and the amount of time before you'll need to begin cashing in your portfolio?

To help put that question into historical perspective, I've prepared the table on the left. The six columns correspond to the different approaches for organizing your investments that are found in the risk matrix. They range from a very aggressive strategy of investing all your money in blue chip stocks to a more conservative strategy of investing only in government bonds. For each of the six portfolio combinations, the historical results over the past half-century are shown.

Let's start at the top (scenarios one through six) with a look at "rolling" one-year periods. Market results are usually stated in terms of calendar years. For instance, an analyst might claim that a search of the historical data since 1950 revealed that the single worst 12-month performance for a portfolio of large-company stocks was a loss of 36.9%. What the analyst has done is to look at the year-by-year results and picked 2008 as the 12 months with the worst performance. But investors don't invest only on January 1, so that report is somewhat misleading as to the potential risk. That's where the use of "rolling" periods can be helpful. Here's how I ran the calculations.

After looking at the results from buying on January 1, 1950, and holding for 12 months, I then "rolled" to the next month to see what happened if the stocks had been purchased on February 1 and held for 12 months. Then I moved to March 1 and did the same thing. And so on. Continuing in this way, I computed the results for all of the 745 12-month holding periods from 1950 through 2012. This is in contrast to only 62 periods when calendar years alone are considered. Using this more exhaustive process provides a more accurate picture of the degree of volatility and level of returns that can be expected from different blends of stocks and bonds. In our example, I found that the worst-case one-year performance for the large-company stocks in the S&P 500 index was actually a loss of 43.3% (March 2008–February 2009) as shown in scenario 1.

The 48 different scenarios shown in the table reflect the basic risk-reward relationships we have discussed in previous chapters.

If you study the numbers you'll see once again that:

• **The shorter your holding period, the higher the risks and potential rewards.** Over a 30-year holding period (scenarios 43-48), the range of *likely* results is relatively narrow. They are shown on the line where it says, "Result ⅔ of the time." Even in an all-stock portfolio (such as scenario 43), this range of likely results is less than three percentage points a year from low to high. As you move up the table to shorter holding periods, the range broadens, that is, it becomes more volatile. By the time you get to a one-year holding period in the all-stock portfolio (scenario 1), there is a 34 percentage-point difference from low to high in the range of likely results.

• **The more you allocate to stocks, the higher the risks and potential rewards.** The table illustrates the extent to which blue chip stocks carry greater risks than intermediate-term government bonds. As you move from right to left across the table, from all bonds to all stocks, the "best" and "worst" results become more exaggerated. These extremes don't come along very often, so you shouldn't weigh them too heavily in your decisions, but it's good to keep in mind the full range of possibilities. During 2007-2009, stocks experienced the worst bear market since the Great Depression. This was immediately followed by unusually high returns from 2009-2013. It's important to not extrapolate such periods as being "normal." They're not, and the table can help you take the emotion out of deciding on the appropriate stock allocation for your situation.

• **There's no sure thing.** Pretend you watched the companies in the S&P 500 index return an average of 21.7% per year, every year, for five years. This is what happened from March 1993–February 1998. You say to yourself, "I want to get in on this!" and in March 1998 you invest your retirement money in those very same stocks. Imagine your disappointment as the next five-year period unfolds and you actually *lose* money—an average of 3.0% each year. Not only did you fail to earn the 10.9% "average" double-digit gain typical of a five-year holding period (scenario 13), but your returns didn't even fall within the range of results that investors who held on for five years received two-thirds of the time. You, unfortunately, were invested during one of the five-year periods that was an uncharacteristic underachiever. You knew it could happen; scenario 13 shows that stocks actually have lost money during some five-year periods, the worst being a decline of 6.6% annually. You were hoping it wouldn't happen to you. But it can, and it did. That's why Wall Street is always reminding you that "past performance is not a guarantee of future results."

Let me show how you might apply the data in the table to come up with an allocation strategy for your personal retirement investing.

Let's assume you're 55 years old. Based on normal life expectancies, an argument could be made for assuming a retirement age of 70 or even 75, but in keeping with tradition, let's assume you plan to retire at age 65. This means your current time horizon is 10 years. You have two goals: (1) to earn average returns of 10% per year, and (2) to do it with as little risk as possible. The risk matrix suggests that a Daredevil (like you) consider an 80% stocks, 20% bonds allocation. With a time frame of 10 years, that leads you to reflect on scenario 20.

An 80/20 mix returned 10.1% per year during the *average* 10-year holding period over the past 60+ years. That's only slightly higher than your goal of 10% per year (nice to have a little cushion), but not so far off that you feel a need to move down to a lower-risk 60/40 allocation (scenario 21). The 80/20 allocation shows a range of 5.7% to 14.5% represents what actually happened in two-thirds of the 10-year periods observed. The remaining one-third of the time, the result was outside this "likely" range. This means that roughly 17 times out of 100 the result was less than 5.7% per year (that's the scary part), and 17 times out of 100 it was better than 14.5% per year (a much more encouraging possibility).

Emotionally, the difficult part of this will be to stay with your 80% stock allocation as you get closer to age 65, especially if you've "fallen behind" the pace you need to maintain. As you consider the probable results for the final three years, you will need to remind yourself that those negative one- and three-year numbers (scenarios 2 and 8) are *already reflected* in the 10-year calculations that you based your asset allocation strategy on initially. So, hopefully your overall 10-year results will still fall within the likely range.

There's one wrinkle I can suggest that would minimize the risk that poor results in the final few years will sabotage your strategy. If at any point along the way, you find that you could likely reach your 10-year target with a dramatically lower stock allocation, I would suggest you make the change. For instance, investing $193,000 on a tax-deferred basis for 10 years at 10% gets you to $500,000. Assume this is your plan. But if you averaged 15% annually during the first six years, your portfolio would already be up to $446,000. At that point, you would need to average only 2.9% during the final four years to reach your goal. So why not move everything into a bank savings account or CD, virtually guaranteeing your success? Some would hesitate, saying you could make more by staying with your 80/20 allocation. Perhaps. Perhaps not. Nobody knows. The important thing is to reach your goal, not "make more money."

One way to continue using a relatively high stock allocation as you enter retirement (if that's your wish) is to extend your time horizon. You can do this by investing a portion of your capital in a money-market account. Pick an amount that, along with your Social Security and any pension you receive, will absolutely ensure you can live comfortably over the next five years. Then, knowing your liquidity needs are met, you can commit to a five-year holding period and the higher stock allocations that such a time frame permits. Short-term fluctuations won't be a concern.

How much should you invest in small company stocks versus those in larger companies?

Because the table on page 274 uses the Standard & Poor's 500 index to represent stock-market returns, it implicitly assumes that all of your stock investing is done in larger companies. But shares in smaller companies also offer significant profit opportunities. They have the potential to grow to 10, 20, or 50 times their present size. Of course, they also carry higher risk because they are more easily devastated by economic setbacks. Let's look at the historical risks and rewards of investing in small companies versus large ones.

The first data column in the table below shows the historical results from the S&P 500 index, and the column on the far right shows similar data for a portfolio consisting solely of small company stocks. These are the kinds of stocks that "micro-cap" funds invest in—by today's standards, they're not just small, they're *very* small, typically having market values of $1 billion or less. (To put that into perspective, Apple is worth more than $400 billion.) The middle column shows the results from having your stock allocation split evenly between large and small companies. You can observe that:

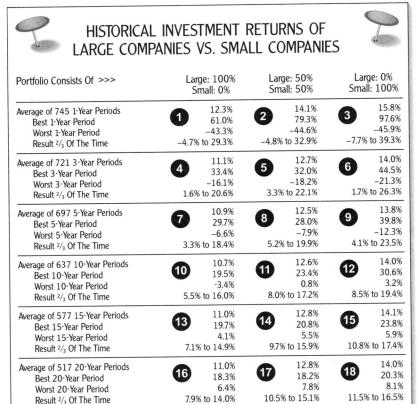

HISTORICAL INVESTMENT RETURNS OF LARGE COMPANIES VS. SMALL COMPANIES

Portfolio Consists Of >>>	Large: 100% Small: 0%		Large: 50% Small: 50%		Large: 0% Small: 100%	
Average of 745 1-Year Periods	❶	12.3%	❷	14.1%	❸	15.8%
Best 1-Year Period		61.0%		79.3%		97.6%
Worst 1-Year Period		−43.3%		−44.6%		−45.9%
Result ⅔ Of The Time		−4.7% to 29.3%		−4.8% to 32.9%		−7.7% to 39.3%
Average of 721 3-Year Periods	❹	11.1%	❺	12.7%	❻	14.0%
Best 3-Year Period		33.4%		32.0%		44.5%
Worst 3-Year Period		−16.1%		−18.2%		−21.3%
Result ⅔ Of The Time		1.6% to 20.6%		3.3% to 22.1%		1.7% to 26.3%
Average of 697 5-Year Periods	❼	10.9%	❽	12.5%	❾	13.8%
Best 5-Year Period		29.7%		28.0%		39.8%
Worst 5-Year Period		−6.6%		−7.9%		−12.3%
Result ⅔ Of The Time		3.3% to 18.4%		5.2% to 19.9%		4.1% to 23.5%
Average of 637 10-Year Periods	❿	10.7%	⓫	12.6%	⓬	14.0%
Best 10-Year Period		19.5%		23.4%		30.6%
Worst 10-Year Period		-3.4%		0.8%		3.2%
Result ⅔ Of The Time		5.5% to 16.0%		8.0% to 17.2%		8.5% to 19.4%
Average of 577 15-Year Periods	⓭	11.0%	⓮	12.8%	⓯	14.1%
Best 15-Year Period		19.7%		20.8%		23.8%
Worst 15-Year Period		4.1%		5.5%		5.9%
Result ⅔ Of The Time		7.1% to 14.9%		9.7% to 15.9%		10.8% to 17.4%
Average of 517 20-Year Periods	⓰	11.0%	⓱	12.8%	⓲	14.0%
Best 20-Year Period		18.3%		18.2%		20.3%
Worst 20-Year Period		6.4%		7.8%		8.1%
Result ⅔ Of The Time		7.9% to 14.0%		10.5% to 15.1%		11.5% to 16.5%

Notes: The source for performance data was the Ibbotson SBBI 2013 Classic Yearbook published by Morningstar in Chicago. The data for stocks are based upon total returns (capital appreciation and dividend income) of the Standard & Poor's 500, a "blue-chip" stock index. The criteria for measuring small-company stock performance has changed over the years, but tends to be based on the total returns of those publicly-traded companies that fall in the bottom 5% in terms of size (market value). The period covered runs from 1950 (after the atypical events of the Depression and WWII) through 2012. Portfolios were rebalanced to their original allocations every twelve months.

• The *average* returns from small companies are higher than those of large companies over every time period measured.

• For holding periods of less than 10 years, the risk of loss from investing in smaller companies is greater. This is seen in the worst-case scenarios.

• For holding periods of 10 years and more, the historical results clearly favor smaller companies over large ones.

• A reasonable case is made for having a significant portion of your stock allocation, perhaps as much as 50%, diversified among micro-cap stocks or mutual funds that specialize in them.

One group is not "better" than another. They offer different strengths that are suitable for different investing needs. Large companies typically offer higher dividends and greater price stability; smaller companies offer higher long-term growth potential.

A SOUND MIND BRIEFING

Once You Reach Retirement, Which Assets Should You Draw From First?

by Eric J. Reinhold, CFP, MBA, RFC, CPhD

Once you reach retirement and begin drawing from that storehouse of wealth you've worked so hard to accumulate, the question naturally arises: Which asset accounts should you withdraw from first? This is an often overlooked question, since most banks, mutual fund companies and brokers are focused on how to solicit and where to invest your money.

Let's look at four of the most common retirement vehicles: traditional tax-deductible IRAs, Roth IRAs, tax-deferred annuities and taxable investments. For purposes of this discussion, I'll assume that any pension plan assets from your place of employment have been rolled over into a traditional IRA at retirement. The starting point is to answer this question: "Are my intentions to pass a significant portion of these assets to my family, or will I be utilizing them for myself?"

• To favor your heirs, withdraw from your annuity and traditional IRAs first. Let's suppose that your desire is to maximize what you can pass along to your family at the time of your death. This means you want to minimize the tax consequences to your heirs even though it would cost you a little more in income taxes in the meanwhile. With this in mind, you'll not want to generate income by selling assets that receive a "step-up in basis" at your death. For example, if you purchased Micro Inc. at $5.00 a share (your "basis"), and Micro is priced at $50.00 a share on the date of your death, $50.00 a share becomes the new tax basis enjoyed by your heirs (and the capital gains tax on the $45.00 per share profits is completely avoided).

Even better than the "stepped-up basis" deal is the treatment of Roth IRAs. These are passed to your children with their tax-free advantages intact, meaning the account can continue to grow tax-free over the beneficiary's life expectancy if they elect to make only the minimum-required withdrawals each year. Over time, this can be an incredible benefit.

For passing on wealth, it is to your advantage, then, to initially draw from your annuities or traditional IRAs where there is no step-up in basis at your death. In the case of an annuity, a portion will be taxable upon withdrawal (the amount above what you invested), and in the case of a traditional IRA, all of the withdrawal will be taxable. If left to your heirs, however, these assets would be subject to income tax on *your* basis. And, depending on your heirs' tax situation, the rate of taxation could be as high as almost 40%. In addition, estate taxes can take as much as 40% of what's left. When all is said and done, your children may only be inheriting 36 cents on the dollar from your tax-deferred retirement accounts.

• To increase your giving. If your tax bracket situation is such that your heirs might receive only 36 cents on the dollar from your annuity and IRA retirement accounts, you may want to consider leaving a portion of the resources to charity. One of the simplest ways to do this is by making your spouse the first beneficiary and a church and/or charities your secondary beneficiary. Your spouse is taken care of, but upon his/her death, the charity would get 100% of the remainder. The government would not receive its customary 64%, and your children's inheritance would only be reduced by 36% of that value. Since annuities and IRAs pass outside of probate, you do not have to change your will or trusts. You simply have to ask for a "change of beneficiary form" from the company at which you have your investment and update it to reflect your desires. Over the course of time, if the Lord leads you to pass this money along to different organizations, you can easily update your beneficiary form again.

• To maximize your lifetime income, withdraw from your taxable investments first. If your priority is not maximizing inheritance but rather maximizing your retirement income, then you would want to first withdraw from your taxable investments in order to prolong the tax-deferral aspects of your annuity and IRAs for as long as possible. The compounding of tax-deferred dollars is hard to beat. For a traditional IRA, you can postpone making withdrawals until age 70$\frac{1}{2}$; in the case of an annuity, it will vary from company to company. To postpone your withdrawals even further, you may want to consider a Roth IRA which requires no minimum distributions ever. Upon your death, the assets provide tax-free income to your children when annuitized over their lifetimes, as mentioned previously.

Depending upon your desires, an ideal strategy may be to combine both concepts. Let your tax-deferred investments continue to grow and designate your spouse as the first beneficiary and church/charities as the secondary beneficiary while utilizing your taxable investments as a source of income. Meanwhile, you could make annual gifts to family members so they are able to enjoy the benefit in their younger years when it is most often needed.

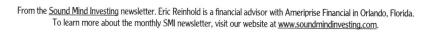

From the Sound Mind Investing newsletter. Eric Reinhold is a financial advisor with Ameriprise Financial in Orlando, Florida.
To learn more about the monthly SMI newsletter, visit our website at www.soundmindinvesting.com.

How you react to the data in this chapter depends largely on your temperament.

Preservers will tend to focus on the worst-case scenarios, thinking if it has happened before, it might happen again. Daredevils will look at the best-case numbers, ignoring the downside risks. Nothing in this chapter is meant to sway you toward a certain class of investments. Rather, it was written to help you better understand that there is no single "right" way to arrange your portfolio when nearing retirement, and that you must make trade-offs between the risks you're willing to take and the rewards you hope to reap.

Let's return to the opening theme of this chapter—nobody knows what the future holds or which investments will do best in the coming year. That's why our Sound Mind portfolios are based on a strategy of diversification—spreading out your money into several different areas so that you won't be overinvested in any single hard-hit area *and* you'll have at least some investments in the more rewarding areas.

As you consider your investing strategy, let me encourage you to:

• **Acknowledge your limited vision.** *"Now listen, you who say, 'Today or tomorrow we will go to this or that city, spend a year there, carry on business and make money.' Why, you do not even know what will happen tomorrow. . . . As it is, you boast and brag. All such boasting is evil"* (James 4:13-14, 16).

• **Look to God, not man, for wisdom.** *"If any of you lacks wisdom, he should ask God, who gives generously to all without finding fault, and it will be given to him"* (James 1:5).

• **Diversify your risks and stay flexible.** *"Give portions to seven, yes to eight, for you do not know what disaster may come upon the land"* (Ecclesiastes 11:2).

• **And above all, let the Lord be your treasure.** *"Delight yourself in the LORD, and he will give you the desires of your heart"* (Psalm 37:4).

This counsel from Scripture is a guide for all of us, not just during these uncertain economic times but as a way of life. It is my belief that it's ultimately impossible to self-destruct financially if our decision-making is pointed in the direction of God's glory. It's to that theme we turn in the next section. ◆

Investing That Glorifies God

A Biblical Blueprint for Building Your Financial House on Solid Rock

The awesome beauty of nature. The innocence of childhood. The security of a world at peace. The exuberance of romantic love. The joy of living life freely and fully.

All are noble themes. Great literature, art, and music have been inspired by them. They capture our emotions and imaginations. They challenge our values and influence our priorities. They reflect universal longings of the human spirit. But although uplifting, they fall short of the noblest and greatest theme of all.

A grander theme runs through all of human history, from the beginning of recorded time to this very moment. It explains why we're here, why things happen as they do, where history is headed, and why the world, as we know it, must eventually end. It underlies everything that is, and is the reason for everything that is not.

This theme is the incomparable glory of our God, surely the greatest theme in all the universe! In his book *Keys to Spiritual Growth*, John MacArthur describes it this way:

> *God possesses intrinsic glory by virtue of who He is. This is not given to Him. If man had never been created, if the angels had never been created, would God still be a God of glory? Certainly! If no one ever gave Him any glory, any honor, or any praise, would He still be the glorious God that He is? Of course! That is intrinsic glory — the glory of God's nature. It is the manifestation and combination of all His attributes. . . . It is His being, as basic as His grace, His mercy, His power, and His knowledge. All we do is recognize them. So we say, "Yes, it's true; God is glorious!"*

The theme of God's glory is a continuous golden thread which is woven throughout Scripture. We see it operative from the opening story of creation through the triumphal establishment of Christ's kingdom. The infinite worth of God's glory is emphasized again and again. We should, therefore, be mindful that in all of our daily decision-making, including that small part that has to do with our financial and investing decisions, our primary goal must always be kept uppermost in mind — that of glorifying our wonderful God. In this section, we will explore what investing "for the glory of God" might involve.

CHAPTER PREVIEW

Investing That Glorifies God Acknowledges His Sovereignty

David praised the LORD in the presence of the whole assembly, saying, "Praise be to you, O LORD, God of our father Israel, from everlasting to everlasting. Yours, O LORD, is the greatness and the power and the glory and the majesty and the splendor, for everything in heaven and earth is yours. Yours, O LORD, is the kingdom; you are exalted as head over all. Wealth and honor come from you; you are the ruler of all things. In your hands are strength and power to exalt and give strength to all. Now, our God, we give you thanks, and praise your glorious name."

(1 Chronicles 29:10-13)

"Who has known the mind of the Lord? Or who has been his counselor? Who has ever given to God, that God should repay him?" For from him and through him and to him are all things. To him be the glory forever! Amen. Therefore, I urge you, brothers, in view of God's mercy, to offer your bodies as living sacrifices, holy and pleasing to God—this is your spiritual act of worship. Do not conform any longer to the pattern of this world, but be transformed by the renewing of your mind. Then you will be able to test and approve what God's will is—his good, pleasing and perfect will.

(Romans 11:34-12:2)

Shortly after my 25th birthday, my father passed away and I inherited my share in a million-dollar restaurant business. Think about it . . .

. . . only 25 and already having just about everything you could reasonably hope for in life. I was financially secure and young enough to enjoy it! I was married to my college sweetheart, the girl of my dreams, and we had two healthy boys. In a world that values position, I was the head of six businesses employing two hundred people. In a world that values freedom, I could go places I wanted to go, pursue interests I wanted to pursue, be any kind of person I wanted to be. And yet, in some way, something was missing. In spite of it all, I wasn't really fulfilled.

Well, why not? If you had asked me, I couldn't have told you. Instead of feeling peace, I felt pressure to achieve further success in a business I didn't really enjoy. Instead of feeling happy, I felt guilt over my undeserved financial security. In looking back, I can identify two major areas of stress.

First, there was my time. Eighty-hour weeks are common in the restaurant business. When I was carrying management duties, I awoke at 4:30 A.M., arrived at the store by 5:30, and worked through breakfast, lunch, and dinner, leaving around 8:00 P.M. after taking the evening inventory. I would do this six days a week and take Tuesday off. When my friends with regular jobs would call on weekends to see if I could play, I'd say "No, I've gotta work. Would you like to do something on Tuesday?" No one ever did.

So, when I had two weeks off, I really appreciated it. But before I could really catch my breath, the two weeks were up and it was time to go back. What if you're 25 with a life expectancy of 75 and you've got 50 years to fill? Did I want to spend them running restaurants? For the first time, I began thinking about not only what I would do with my life, but also about what was *worth* doing.

I started really wondering about such things as . . .

. . . What's life all about? Where did I come from and where am I going? Where do I fit in now that I'm here? Mortimer Adler, the famous educator, said that the driving force behind human behavior is a search for significance. I could relate to that. Don't we all want it to somehow matter that we were born, that we worked and played, that we laughed and cried, that we visited this place? I wanted a purpose that had credibility, that would be adequate to take me all the way in life. Though a Christian, I did not realize my key purpose in work and play was to glorify God.

Then, there was my inheritance. I really hadn't made peace with it. My pride said I should make it on my own! Have you ever read the life story of a real financial achiever — someone who started out with nothing much, but who through force of will and intellect and creativity and courage established a business empire? When you finished reading, your response probably was respect, perhaps inspiration. That's how I felt.

I wanted to feel adequate in my own right — not just as the caretaker of my father's business. Years earlier, I had graduated in the upper tenth of my class with a major in banking and finance. Now I found myself attracted to the investment world. I thought that if I could set meaningful goals, and achieve them, in an area where my father had not been very proficient, at least I'd feel better about myself and maybe some of the other pieces would fall into place.

So I'll tell you what I did. I decided to try to make my fortune in the stock market.

(You can see what an original thinker I was.) But, hey—this was 1970, one of the exciting "go-go" times on Wall Street. Everyone seemed to be making money, even amateur upstarts like me. Well, I threw myself into it all the way. I subscribed to all the leading investment-industry publications and began reading. Although I was working hard running the family business, I made time to teach myself the various trading and charting techniques. I began trading, and I kept meticulous records of my successes and failures. At one point, I had four brokers—simultaneously! They loved me because I churned my accounts continuously. A few more like me and they would have been the office superstars. Eventually I had a ticker installed right in my office so I could get instant quotes from the New York and American Stock Exchanges. (Before the Internet came along, this was a big deal.) It was great! I was trading, making a little money in spite of myself, and having fun at it.

Then, one of my brokers introduced me to . . . (imagine the ominous soundtrack to *Jaws* playing in the background) . . . commodities futures. Given my propensity for trading, this was probably a criminal act on his part. In those volatile and emotional markets, I was soon swimming with the sharks. Surveys have indicated that nine out of ten commodities speculators lose money. It was said that you needed ice water in your veins to stay calm under the daily pressures. The leverage, the risks, and the rewards are great.

Think of the attraction this held for me as I sought to prove myself: I could make more money, make it faster, and make it *under greater stress*. What an arena! If you're up for playing Russian roulette with your self-esteem and your bank account, you should check it out. Personally, I loved it!

For a time, commodities became my driving purpose. You know, everyone has a driving purpose.

Everyone is driven by something. What drives you? I'll tell you how to find out. Ask yourself these questions. How do you spend your most precious resource, your time? What successes excite and exhilarate you the most? What defeats irritate and frustrate you the most? The ones tied to your driving purpose.

Well, for a time, commodities was it for me. I remember making and losing $10,000 (in 1970 dollars!) in a single day of trading. I remember driving along the Pennsylvania Turnpike on a summer getaway with Susie and ruining the whole effect by stopping every 75 miles to call my broker back in Louisville. Every hour I stopped. Can you believe it? Susie couldn't: "You mean we're stopping again?!" She just didn't understand. I had left town still holding a heavy short position in frozen pork bellies and I had to be careful. (For you laymen, that means that I had sold 200 tons of bacon I didn't own to a buyer I had never met for a price one of us would soon regret. Obviously, I was hoping it wouldn't be me.)

I remember that I made more money in commodities than I ever made in stocks.

But to my surprise, in spite of this success, I was not any deep-down happier. The up and down emotions . . .

. . . from running a restaurant chain and speculating in the markets was no foundation upon which to build a fulfilling life or a healthy marriage. I was searching, trying to fill the emptiness but not really knowing how. It's been said: "There's a God-shaped vacuum in the heart of every man placed there by God that only He can fill."

But I didn't know that. To be sure, Susie and I had Christian upbringings. I have a loving mom who took me to church when I was a boy, and I learned about God: how He had visited earth in the person of Jesus Christ, had died on a cross and in so doing had somehow accepted the penalty for my own personal sins, and had come back to life again and was seen by more than 500 people. At least that's what they taught me, and I accepted those teachings. But somehow, in the process, I never developed a full picture of a *personal* God.

In the Sunday school where I grew up, there were all these colored drawings of Jesus and His disciples. They were walking through the desert, and He was teaching and healing people and feeding the multitudes. Miraculous things! And I used to think: "Boy, I wish I could have been there and seen *that*! To see an honest-to-goodness miracle!" Did you ever wish that? To see something undeniably supernatural? Well, I did. But Jesus lived 2,000 years ago—a long, long, *long* time ago. So remote, so far away, that it almost wasn't even real. And it made God seem far away, because I never heard of those kinds of miracles anymore.

So I had gradually gotten the impression that you couldn't really know God now. He was there, but . . .

. . . seemed too far away. I didn't see any way to relate to Him in any meaningful, practical, relevant way. When I got to heaven, whatever and wherever that is, I could learn more about God. But until then, in this life, I assumed it was completely up to me to find my own way, to make my life count.

About this time, one of my very best friends came to town for a visit. We'd gone through high school together and were as close as brothers. He went to Ohio State to study engineering and had become involved with one of those Christian student organizations. He married a girl he met there, and they became really enthusiastic about spiritual things.

They came home about once a year and, when we would get together, always wanted to talk about the Bible and the Christian life. Now you know, when you're not into that, a little bit goes a long way—so once a year was just about right for them!

Well, sure enough, Bob and Carole called to ask if they could stop by. I really wasn't up for it. I asked Susie, and she wasn't up for it. But he was a dear friend, so what can you do? After reluctantly concluding there was no gracious way out of it, I returned to the phone and said, "Great, we'd love to see you! How soon can you get over here? How about staying for dinner?"

After dinner, it wasn't long before Bob shifted the conversation to spiritual matters.

He saw us living the comfortable life and asked Susie at one point: "Susie, are you happy?" And she answered, "We've really got a lot to be thankful for." He said: "I can see that. But are you happy?" And she paused, then simply said, "No."

Well, I was surprised! I didn't know she was unhappy. And I was embarrassed. You just don't want your wife . . .

. . . to go around admitting she's unhappy. Before I could jump in and try to salvage the situation ("What Susie really meant by that was . . ."), Bob asked one of the most surprising questions I'd ever heard. He asked: "Have you ever considered asking Jesus Christ to take control of your life?"

That really took me off guard, because no one had ever suggested to me that Jesus was even remotely interested in assisting in the everyday management of my life, let alone asked if I would be willing to let Him. Anyway, Susie responded: "This may sound egotistical, but I don't think I want anyone running my life or telling me what to do."

The question scared her because, in our limited understanding of what it meant to give God "control" of our lives, it might mean that we had to go to the mission fields of Africa or something else equally traumatic. As for me, I certainly wasn't attracted to the idea of God telling me what to do. I suppose I imagined that He would rob my life of any fun, or joy, or excitement.

Besides, as a man I felt it would be a sign of weakness to depend on anyone else. Is there a higher, more masculine ethic . . .

. . . than absolute self-sufficiency? Remember William Henley's words from "Invictus"?

It matters not how strait the gate, How charged with punishments the scroll, I am the master of my fate: I am the captain of my soul.

Isn't that why James Bond and Indiana Jones are so appealing—they're overwhelmingly adequate for any conceivable situation. As a man, I especially wanted to be completely in control of my own destiny.

But even so, Bob and Carole shared some things that night that shed new light on the basics of the Christian faith that we had learned as children. The first point they made was that God is, after all, a personal God, that He loves us as individuals, and that He offers a wonderful plan for our lives. Christ said, "*I have come that they may have life, and have it to the full [that it would be abundant and meaningful]*" (John 10:10). I said this was hard to understand because it was obvious that the world is terribly messed up and that everyone is not experiencing an abundant life.

They responded with words something like: "The reason for that is we're the ones who choose to go our own independent ways and separate ourselves from God. Generally we don't give Him much thought. He's irrelevant to the important decisions we make everyday. So, with that attitude, how *can* we know or experience God's love and plan for our lives?

"Although we were created to have fellowship with God, we have chosen to pretty much do our own thing, and fellowship with God has been broken off. Our independence, which may be characterized by either active rebellion or just passive indifference, is evidence of what the Bible calls sin. The consequences of our living independently from God is that we have been spiritually separated from Him.

"It's obvious that we sense this and try to bridge the separation and reach God. But we usually want to return to Him on our own terms of reference: a relatively moral life, some charitable work here and there, going to church regularly, perhaps even giving some money to charity. But these things aren't enough."

Bob continued: "The truth is, we must approach God on *His* terms of reference. That's fair, isn't it? After all, He *is* God. But what exactly. . .

. . . are God's terms of reference as to how we should bridge this gulf of separation? That's where Jesus comes in. God has made a special provision for our rebellion against Him. It's through Jesus that we're reconciled to God. The Scriptures say, 'God demonstrates his own love toward us in this: while we were still sinners, Christ died for us.'

"There's nothing we can add to this—we can only accept it as one would accept a gift. Ironically, that's the hardest part. Our pride says we should contribute our fair share to this arrangement. Unfortunately, in this case, we have nothing to negotiate with. God looks at our meager efforts at righteousness, compares them to His holiness, and says in His book, 'All have sinned and fall short of the glory of God.'

"Since we're helpless to save ourselves, God took the initiative and provided the way back in Jesus Christ, who died in our place to pay the penalty for our rebellion and gives us right standing with God once more."

As I was listening, I was thinking, "Bob, I've heard most of this since we were kids. We used to go to church together all the time. This isn't what I really want to know. What I *really* am curious about is why do you and I believe pretty much these same things about who Christ was, but you're so excited about it, so fired up, and I'm not? What has happened to make you so different now?"

After they left, Susie and I continued to talk. I can still remember lying on our bed with arms outstretched . . .

. . . reading a little blue booklet they had left us, and sharing how we felt about what they had said. We eventually came to a prayer at the end of the booklet, which read:

> *Dear Father, I need You. I acknowledge that I have been directing my own life and that, as a result, I have sinned against You. I thank You that You have forgiven my sins through Christ's death on the cross for me. I now invite Christ to again take His place on the throne of my life. Fill me with the Holy Spirit as You commanded me to be filled, and as you promised in Your word that You would do if I asked in faith. I pray this in the name of Jesus.*

Then, right under the prayer was the suggestion that, if the prayer expressed the desire of our hearts, why didn't we pray "right now." I started to turn the page, but Susie said to wait, and asked, "What do you think of this prayer?" I said it was a nice prayer. She said, "Why don't we pray it right now?" I was surprised that she was so eager.

But as we talked, my mind returned to Bob and how, to him, Christ was so real and so personal. It was obvious to me that his relationship with Christ was on a much more intimate level than mine. I recognized that if the claims Jesus made about Himself were true, He offered a significance and purpose to life that the world could never match; that, as God, He was truly worthy of first place in my life.

After all, when you think it through to its logical conclusion, if the claims of Jesus are true, knowing Him is worth everything. Think about it . . .

. . . If He's worth anything, He's worth everything. What I mean by this is that if Jesus *was* who He claimed to be, then He's worthy of our complete devotion. If He *was not* who He claimed to be, then Christianity is a hoax and illusion.

There's no doubt that 2000 years ago, there appeared a Jew who went about talking as if he were divine. His claims sound like the ravings of a madman. After all, He claimed to be without sin, to be the judge of the world, to be able to give eternal life, to be the only way to salvation, and to be able to satisfy the deepest needs and longings of the human heart.

These are not comments that can easily be written off as minor boasts. Those who saw and heard him were said to be astonished and amazed. One of the strangest aspects of Jesus' story is that even non-Christians, when they read his teachings, don't come away with the impression that he was deranged or a megalomaniac. Even they admit that he was perhaps the greatest teacher on love and human relationships that the human race has yet produced. And when he said he was "humble and meek," they find it easy to believe him. How can his astonishing claims of divinity be reconciled with the fact that he is held in high regard by non-believers the world over? They can't. C.S. Lewis put it well:

> "I am trying here to prevent anyone from saying the really foolish thing that people often say about Him: 'I'm ready to accept Jesus as a great moral teacher, but I don't accept His claim to be God.' That is the one thing we must not say. A man who was merely a man and said the sort of things Jesus said would not be a great moral teacher. He would either be a lunatic — on a level with the man who says he is a poached egg — or else he would be the Devil of Hell. You must make your choice. Either this man was, and is, the Son of God; or else a madman or something worse. You can shut Him up for a fool, you can spit at Him and kill Him as a demon; or you can fall at His feet and call him Lord and God. But let us not come with any patronizing nonsense about His being a great human teacher. He has not left that open to us. He did not intend to."

That's why if Jesus is worthy of any obedience, He's worthy of total obedience. If Jesus is worthy of any of our worship, He's worthy of all of our worship. In other words, if Jesus is worth anything, He's worth everything.

And I decided, lying there on the bed next to my wife, that I wanted to know Christ the way my friend did.

I wanted to share in his excitement of knowing God personally if that were possible.

If it required me to make Him sovereign in my life, so be it.

So, I confessed my sins to God. There were many of them. Maybe the greatest sin of all was being indifferent to God—being what you might call a casual Christian—professing some sort of belief in God but really not treating it seriously. So Susie and I prayed together that night. Not because we were in church, not because everyone else was praying, but because we wanted to know God as never before.

God is sovereign. Being sovereign means "possessed of supreme power that is unlimited in extent, enjoying autonomy, having undisputed ascendancy." We see this aspect of God portrayed in Scripture repeatedly.

> *I am God, your God. . . . I have no need of a bull from your stall or of goats from your pens, for every animal of the forest is mine, and the cattle on a thousand hills. I know every bird in the mountains, and the creatures of the field are mine. If I were hungry I would not tell you, for the world is mine, and all that is in it.* (Psalm 50:8-12)

> *Remember the former things, those of long ago; I am God, and there is no other; I am God, and there is none like me. I make known the end from the beginning, from ancient times, what is still to come. I say: My purpose will stand, and I will do all that I please.* (Isaiah 46:9-10)

> *His dominion is an eternal dominion; his kingdom endures from generation to generation. All the peoples of the earth are regarded as nothing. He does as he pleases with the powers of heaven and the peoples of the earth. No one can hold back his hand or say to him: "What have you done?"* (Daniel 4:34-35)

Amazingly, although God is sovereign over all He has made and could dictate our every thought and movement, He tolerates pockets of resistance to His reign. He allows us to make a decision of monumental importance: whether to willingly embrace Christ's rule in our lives and affections or to continue exercising our own self-rule and independence. We are allowed the audacity of challenging His "undisputed ascendancy" in our own lives.

What makes the choice so difficult is that the results are counterintuitive.

If we should abdicate control of our lives and invite His Spirit to guide us according to His purposes, we would expect a loss of freedom, power, and happiness. *The actual result is just the opposite.* We are never more free, never have more strength to reach our potential, and never experience more fulfillment than when we acknowledge His sovereignty over our lives. The reason for this is that only when we place our faith in Christ does He come to live within us, and it is His actual presence—the personal presence of the omnipotent Creator God of the universe—that raises our daily existence to a higher, entirely new level of existence.

On the other hand, we can choose to continue living independently, doing as we think best. We expect that way of living to give us the best chance of building a future that will be the most satisfying. But again, the result is just the opposite of what we expect. We find that achieving our goals provides only short-lived fulfillment. The thrill of acquiring material possessions wears off. Fame has a short shelf life, and perversely it creates greater anxiety than emotional security. A famous Hollywood producer, when asked how fame, fortune, and immense popularity had changed his life, gave this startling reply: "Success means never having to admit you're unhappy." His success did not end his unhappiness; it just allowed him to deny it.

Investing that glorifies God has a requisite first step: first we must invest ourselves. We do this by . . .

. . . willingly trusting His sovereignty — not only over the physical universe, but over our very lives as well. That night, Susie and I asked Christ to take our lives and make us the kind of people He wanted us to be. We gave Him our lives. God says: "If you'll give Me your life, I'll give you My life." It has been called "The Great Exchange." In light of who He is and all that He offers, what could be more reasonable?

> "Who has known the mind of the Lord? Or who has been his counselor? Who has ever given to God, that God should repay him?" For from him and through him and to him are all things. To him be the glory forever! Amen. Therefore, I urge you, brothers, in view of God's mercy, to offer your bodies as living sacrifices, holy and pleasing to God – this is your spiritual act of worship. Do not conform any longer to the pattern of this world, but be transformed by the renewing of your mind. Then you will be able to test and approve what God's will is – his good, pleasing and perfect will. (Romans 11:34–12:2)

It should go without saying that when we present ourselves to God as "living sacrifices," our material possessions are included. After surrendering all that we are and ever hope to be to His eternal sovereignty, the idea that we're also acknowledging God's ownership of the world's wealth (including ours) shouldn't be surprising. When we made The Great Exchange, part of the transaction involved exchanging ownership privileges for management responsibilities. It's called stewardship.

God owns it all. He doesn't need our help or our money. The fact is we have nothing He needs . . .

. . . and He has everything that we need. Bob Benson, one of my favorite writers, had a way of telling humorous stories in simple ways that revealed great truths. I'm grateful to him for putting things into perspective for us:

> Do you remember when they had old-fashioned Sunday School picnics? I do. As I recall, it was back in the "olden days," as my kids would say, back before they had air conditioning.

> They said, "We'll all meet at Sycamore Lodge in Shelby Park at 4:30 on Saturday. You bring your supper and we'll furnish the iced tea."

> But if you were like me, you came home at the last minute. When you got ready to pack your picnic, all you could find in the refrigerator was one dried up piece of baloney and just enough mustard in the bottom of the jar so that you got it all over your knuckles trying to get to it. And just two slices of stale bread to go with it. So you made your baloney sandwich and wrapped it in an old brown bag and went to the picnic.

> When it came time to eat, you sat at the end of a table and spread out your sandwich. But the

Recommended Resource

The Journey Home: A Walk with Bob Benson

Selected & Edited by R. Benson and others

God gifted Bob Benson with a skill for communicating great truths in simple and humorous ways. This book is a collection of stories from among his several books, gathered by his son after his father went to be with the Lord. You'll laugh, and perhaps shed a tear, and learn a few new ways to think about our God.

The Journey Home: A Walk with Bob Benson, R. Benson, Copyright 1997, Beacon Hill Press, pp. 108-110. Used by permission.

folks who sat next to you brought a feast. The lady was a good cook and she had worked hard all day to get ready for the picnic. And she had fried chicken and baked beans and potato salad and homemade rolls and sliced tomatoes and pickles and olives and celery. And two big homemade chocolate pies to top it off. That's what they spread out there next to you while you sat with your baloney sandwich.

But they said to you, "Why don't we just put it all together?"

"No, I couldn't do that. I couldn't even think of it," you murmured in embarrassment, with one eye on the chicken.

"Oh, come on, there's plenty of chicken and plenty of pie and plenty of everything. And we just love baloney sandwiches. Let's just put it all together."

And so you did and there you sat, eating like a king when you came like a pauper.

One day, it dawned on me that God had been saying just that sort of thing to me. "Why don't you take what you have and what you are, and I will take what I have and what I am, and we'll share it together." I began to see that when I put what I had and was and am and hope to be with what he is, I had stumbled upon the bargain of a lifetime.

I get to thinking sometimes, thinking of me sharing with God. When I think of how little I bring, and how much he brings and invites me to share, I know that I should be shouting to the housetops, but I am so filled with awe and wonder that I can hardly speak. I know that I don't have enough love or faith or grace or mercy or wisdom, but he does. He has all of those things in abundance and he says, "Let's just put it all together."

Consecration, denial, sacrifice, commitment, crosses were all kind of hard words to me, until I saw them in the light of sharing. It isn't just a case of me kicking in what I have because God is the biggest kid in the neighborhood and he wants it all for himself. He is saying, "Everything that I possess is available to you. Everything that I am and can be to a person, I will be to you."

When I think about it like that, it really amuses me to see somebody running along through life hanging on to their dumb bag with that stale baloney sandwich in it saying, "God's not going to get my sandwich! No, sirree, this is mine!" Did you ever see anybody like that — so needy — just about half-starved to death yet hanging on for dear life. It's not that God needs your sandwich. The fact is, you need his chicken.

Well, go ahead — eat your baloney sandwich, as long as you can. But when you can't stand its tastelessness or drabness any longer; when you get so tired of running your own life by yourself and doing it your way and figuring out all the answers with no one to help; when trying to accumulate, hold, grasp, and keep everything together in your own strength gets to be too big a load; when you begin to realize that by yourself you're never going to be able to fulfill your dreams, I hope you'll remember that it doesn't have to be that way.

You have been invited to something better, you know. You have been invited to share in the very being of God. ◆

Investing That Glorifies God Values His Majesty

O God, you are my God, earnestly I seek you; my soul thirsts for you,
my body longs for you, in a dry and weary land where there is no
water. I have seen you in the sanctuary and beheld your power and
your glory. Because your love is better than life, my lips will glorify
you. I will praise you as long as I live, and in your name I will lift up
my hands. My soul will be satisfied as with the richest of foods; with
singing lips my mouth will praise you. On my bed I remember you;
I think of you through the watches of the night. Because
you are my help, I sing in the shadow of your wings.
I cling to you; your right hand upholds me.

(Psalm 63:1-8)

The God who made the world and everything in it is the Lord of
heaven and earth and does not live in temples built by hands. And he
is not served by human hands, as if he needed anything, because he
himself gives all men life and breath and everything else. From one man
he made every nation of men, that they should inhabit the whole earth;
and he determined the times set for them and the exact places where they
should live. God did this so that men would seek him and perhaps reach
out for him and find him, though he is not far from each one of us.

(Acts 17:24-27)

**I can remember only one time during my childhood when
I was asked "the" question that all kids face . . .**

. . . "What do you want to be when you grow up?" I was probably around
10 years old and was out with my mom doing some routine shopping. We were
riding along when suddenly she popped the big question. She was visibly
amused when I immediately replied, "A disc jockey!" In my formative radio-
listening, rock-and-roll years, being a disc jockey must have seemed like it would
be all the fun in the world. Mom's reaction, however, communicated that while
being a disc jockey might be fun, it didn't reflect a highly developed sense of
ambition. Neither of my parents ever asked me the question again, and to play
it safe, I never brought the subject up.

So as I moved through my teen years, an only child and obvious "heir apparent," it became the accepted wisdom that I would someday run the family business. In many respects, this greatly simplified things. I always knew that I had a
summer job and what it would be — learning some new facet of restaurant operations (from the ground up). When I enrolled in college, I didn't agonize over a
major — I went to business school and majored in finance. When I graduated, I
didn't worry about job interviews — I simply returned home and went to work.

There was only one problem with all of this. I hated the restaurant business!
I had no interest in food or cooking. I had poor people skills and felt inadequate
as a leader. Rare was the morning I didn't dread getting up and going to work.
But get up I must, and that's exactly what I did the morning after Bob and Carole's
visit. I went off to work without giving the events of the night before — the talking
with Susie, the soul-searching, the prayer of surrender — much thought at all. We
had a special evening, sure, but now it was Monday morning and my life in what
I thought of as "the real world" had resumed.

For Susie, it was an entirely different story. The little booklet our friends had
left with us said that *faith* was the "engine" of the Christian life and that *feelings*
were the "caboose." We should not be controlled by our feelings, but as we exercise
faith and obedience, feelings would follow. So she had whispered her prayer of surrender on that basis, and we went to sleep not "feeling" any different.

**The next morning, however, she awoke with great joy.
She now understood — truly "knew" — for the first time . . .**

. . . that her forgiveness was based on placing her faith in Christ alone. It was
not a matter of her trying to be good and holy for God, but rather just giving every
area of her life over to Him *so He could be holy through her*. He would supply the
strength. She felt totally accepted by God and had peace beyond question that
she would be with Him in heaven for eternity. This was the way to relate to God
that she had been looking for her whole life! She was so joyous over this that she
began calling her friends and family to tell them this incredibly great news.

You can imagine my surprise at coming home from another routine day at the office to find this exuberant evangelist in our house. I don't recall exactly what was said that evening; I only remember that Susie "took off" in her spiritual growth and that it took a long time for me to catch up.

(Perhaps if the truth be known, I never have. The Lord has blessed me with many wonderful friends and teachers who have guided, corrected, and encouraged me in my Christian growth—I am indebted to them all. But there is also a secret life of the believer where our fears and hopes, joys and sorrows are rarely made known to others. It is only in the intimacy of the daily life in Christ between husband and wife where these matters can be shared or exposed. The "outside world" has little grasp of how married partners refresh each other and provide a desperately needed source of balance, wisdom, role modeling, inspiration, and challenge. Susie has been all these things and more to me. Without question, she has been the greatest single influence in my Christian life. We've been married for more than 40 years, and I've never appreciated her more, respected her more, or loved her more than I do today. That's the kind of marriage God has built in us as we have trusted daily in His plans and in His power to live the Christ-centered life.)

Through the years, I had put my work and other family-related demands ahead of her needs, yet she remained committed to me and the sacred aspects of our marriage. As I gradually developed a new awareness of God in my life, I began to learn how to love Susie in a deeper, purer, and more protective kind of way. I finally began to see that my wife and children have a higher call on my time and attentions than my bread-winning activities. Let me tell you—there's nothing finer that can happen to a man, a husband, a father, than to be able to sit and listen to his wife and children pray to a God whom they know in a personal way.

As we sought to know our God better, our interest in spiritual matters grew. We were introduced to Christian ministries that were devising creative new ways for taking the message of God's love and forgiveness to people in all walks of life. One of them was Campus Crusade for Christ (now called Cru). Through a series of events too lengthy to detail here, we received an invitation from Crusade's president, Dr. Bill Bright, to join his staff at the ministry's headquarters. It required a move to southern California, one that was made possible when the Lord answered our heartfelt prayers to send someone to run the family business in my absence. We loaded up the station wagon, our two boys, Tre and Andrew, the cat and bird, and headed west for a "mission trip" that was to last almost two years.

I can still remember what it was like "reporting for work" that first week in California. I was thrilled . . .

. . . that for the first time in my life I would be doing work that *I* had picked out, that I would enjoy, and that had a challenge and purpose that I found ful-

Recommended Resource

The Secret: How to Live with Purpose and Power

by Bill Bright, founder of Cru

This book contains much of Cru's excellent teaching concepts, including the essence of the material that Bob and Carole left with us that night. In chapter four, "What Does It Mean to Be Filled with the Spirit?" you will find a simple way of understanding how God wants to work through the life of every one of His children. It will be a life-changing truth if you take God at His word and apply it. It was for us.

Cru has made a great deal of material available for free on their web site. Check it out at www.cru.org.

filling. It was an unforgettable, incredibly stimulating experience. We formed friendships that are warmly treasured to this day. We joined expository Bible studies that opened up Scripture in new and personally relevant ways. We saw answers to prayers that radically changed our views of God's willingness—no, make that eagerness—to meet the needs of His children. We went to give, yet received more back than we could have ever imagined.

In the summer of 1974, Susie and I traveled to Fort Collins, Colorado, for an annual staff event within Cru. The staff had gathered together for a week of vision-building workshops and seminars. We heard many inspirational speakers, but one in particular quickly captured everyone's attention. To say that Ronald Dunn's messages were well received would be to greatly understate his impact. I have talked with Cru staff who, 25 and 30 years later, still recall with great appreciation (as I do) how his words were so encouraging to them that summer.

It was one of those rare times in life when "you just had to be there" to understand why it was special. His messages were really quite basic, just reminders of some of the "old truths" that we might have forgotten along the way, yet they were so meaningful to his audience. I still remember, vividly, the question he posed as he set the stage for one of his primary points:

"What is it, do you believe, that God wants from you more than anything else?" It was a sobering question.

I knew God wanted my obedience, my service, my thanksgiving, and much more. But what did He want *the most?* I really didn't know how to answer. What would you have said? From my notes, Ron's answer went something like this:

> *I believe it is the testimony of the word of God, in both the Old and New Testaments, that the primary thing, the ultimate thing, that God wants from us is not our service. He wants our searching! That we would seek the Lord. That we would seek the Lord.*

In Acts 17, Paul leaves no doubt that *the* primary purpose behind all of God's creative work is that we would seek Him.

> *The God who made the world and everything in it is the Lord of heaven and earth and does not live in temples built by hands. And he is not served by human hands, as if he needed anything, because he himself gives all men life and breath and everything else. From one man he made every nation of men, that they should inhabit the whole earth; and he determined the times set for them and the exact places where they should live. God did this so that men would seek him and perhaps reach out for him and find him, though he is not far from each one of us.*

More than anything else, the Lord wants us to seek Him. He wants to be the object of our affection and the focus of our attention. He wants to draw us to seek Him. If this is the case, then it shouldn't be surprising to think that God will negotiate circumstances or engineer certain events in order to bring us to the place where we come to the end of ourselves and are compelled to seek Him.

Now some may ask how the idea of "seeking the Lord" applies to Christians who have already sought Him out and placed their faith in Him. Ron's response was tremendous:

> When the apostle Paul wrote to the church at Philippi, he recounted his conversion experience, saying: "But whatever was to my profit, I now consider loss for the sake of Christ. What is more, I consider everything a loss compared to the surpassing greatness of knowing Christ."
>
> If I'd been writing that I might have said "the surpassing greatness of serving Christ." You know, he's had about every experience a fellow could have. There's not been anybody that has been able to serve in the magnificent magnitude that the apostle Paul has. Yet he comes to the end of this life and he says "I am continually giving up everything and counting everything but loss that I may . . . know Him."
>
> Well, now Paul, I thought you already knew Him. You met Him on the road to Damascus thirty or forty years ago. What do you mean you're counting everything but loss that you may know Him?
>
> Paul would say: "Well, you can know Him, and then you can know Him some more." You can know Him, and you can know Him, and you can know Him, and you can know Him some more. You see, my friends, the Christian life is not starting with Jesus, and then graduating to something better. It is starting with Jesus, staying with Jesus, and ending up with Jesus.
>
> I tell you I get excited when I realize that the Bible over and over again makes it clear that Jesus Christ is God's "everything." In Colossians, we read that all the fulness of the Godhead dwells in Him bodily, and we are complete in Him. All the fullness of the Godhead dwells in Jesus bodily, and I like the way Williams translates it "And you are filled with it too through union with Him." I mean, Jesus is everything.
>
> He's the Means to the end, and He's the End. He's the Door, and He's what you find on the other side of the door. He's the Light of the world, and He's what you see when that light shines. He's the Fountain, and He's also the Living Water that comes out of the fountain. He's the Alpha and the Omega. He's all that you need.
>
> And so to seek the Lord means that we seek for nothing else. We find in Jesus Christ our all in all. And so Paul is saying that the quest of the Christian life is not "How can I trust Him more? or How can I serve Him more?" but "How can I know Him better?"
>
> The goal of the Christian life is not service. The goal of the Christian life is Jesus. And our service is the overflow of our fellowship with the Lord Jesus Christ. So it means we need seek for nothing else, but it also means that we should settle for nothing less.
>
> I'll tell you what I think is happening in evangelical circles today: that we are settling for something less than the Lord Jesus Christ. We were on our way with Jesus, and we met something else along the way that caught our attention, and we settled for that. I started out with the Lord. My heart was filled with the joy of the Lord. I just wanted Him, that's all! I was seeking the Lord, but in my seeking the

Recommended Resource
<u>Don't Just Stand There, Pray Something!</u>
by Ronald Dunn

This is the most helpful and practical book about prayer that I've had the pleasure to read. Ron Dunn, who is with the Lord now, was a gifted teacher who was great at communicating through the use of stories about everyday life. Much of the material that I found so life-changing in the summer of 1974 is here. I enthusiastically recommend this book!

For information about Ron's ministry or to order his books and tapes, visit www.rondunn.com.

Lord, along the way I found service. And I find that often I end up settling for that.

Let me encourage you in something. As you seek the Lord, if you meet service, or a gift, or a doctrine along the way, don't stop and settle for that. Please, you must keep on going and seek the Lord. Constantly seek the Lord. Don't settle for anything less than Jesus, and the fullness of fellowship with Him day by day.

As I listened to Ron, it was immediately clear to me that I had taken a wrong turn somewhere. My serving God was a well-intentioned "living sacrifice," which I desired would please Him, but it also represented a kind of detour. I so desired to *serve* Him, to "invest" my life for Him, that I no longer made time to *seek* Him. I resembled the workaholic husband who had little time for his wife, and when she pointed this out he claimed he was "doing it all for her." This error can be quite a subtle thing; it seems to happen in the smallest of increments. You are not even aware of it until one day God works through your circumstances to get your undivided attention, and you "awaken" to find yourself miles off course.

If not consciously resisted, the spirit-sustaining pleasure of spending time alone with Him each day is easily lost to the "tyranny of the urgent." And this tendency to get caught up in the physical and visible world around us often surfaces in an even more compelling way in the area of our stewardship. If we don't guard against it, our financial goals, projects, and ambitions inevitably capture an ever-increasing share of our thought life and physical energies.

In addition to acknowleding His sovereignty, investing that glorifies God has a second indispensable precondition—it never loses sight of the fact . . .

. . . that He is the pearl of great price, causing us to joyfully set aside all that we have (and all that competes for our time) so that we may experience the priceless treasure of fellowship with God in Christ Jesus. We value His majesty and our communion with Him above all earthly ambitions and wealth. There is no greater thrill, no greater joy than to walk away from a time of prayer and meditation having met God.

It is as Jonathan Edwards has written:

The enjoyment of God is the only happiness with which our souls can be satisfied. To go to heaven, fully to enjoy God, is infinitely better than the most pleasant accommodations here. . . . [These] are but shadows; but God is the substance. These are but scattered beams; but God is the sun. These are but streams; but God is the ocean.

Jonathan Edwards, The Works of Jonathan Edwards [Edinburgh: Banner of Truth Trust, 1974], p. 244.

To glorify God, we must see Him as our great treasure. Our hearts and lives must be kept centered in Him. Christian service, although done in His name, is no substitute. Obtaining, securing, and increasing our store of wealth, although used for family support and kingdom purposes, is no substitute.

To invest more time, thought, energy, research, and emotional energy in these areas than we invest in enjoying His presence is to grieve His Father's heart. There are at least three reasons this must be true.

• It reveals that our pleasures are misplaced.

To delight more in the companionship of the creation around us than in the Creator who made us is idolatry. Even to delight more in the gifts we offer Him than in the gift His presence offers us is to elevate our glory above His. Our pleasure is to be in Him.

> *O God, you are my God, earnestly I seek you; my soul thirsts for you, my body longs for you, in a dry and weary land where there is no water. I have seen you in the sanctuary and beheld your power and your glory. Because your love is better than life, my lips will glorify you. I will praise you as long as I live, and in your name I will lift up my hands. My soul will be satisfied as with the richest of foods; with singing lips my mouth will praise you. On my bed I remember you; I think of you through the watches of the night. Because you are my help, I sing in the shadow of your wings. My soul clings to you; your right hand upholds me.* (Psalm 63:1-8)

• It reveals that our confidence is misplaced.

Isn't our security, whether spiritual, physical, emotional, or material, to be found in His loving promises rather than our human efforts and disciplines? Our confidence is to be in Him.

> *One thing I ask of the LORD, this is what I seek: that I may dwell in the house of the LORD all the days of my life, to gaze upon the beauty of the LORD and to seek him in his temple. For in the day of trouble he will keep me safe in his dwelling; he will hide me in the shelter of his tabernacle and set me high upon a rock.* (Psalm 27:4-5)

> *Keep your lives free from the love of money and be content with what you have, because God has said, "Never will I leave you; never will I forsake you." So we say with confidence, "The Lord is my helper; I will not be afraid. What can man do to me?"* (Hebrews 13:5-6)

• It reveals that our gratitude is misplaced.

To whom or what do we owe our successes? The free-enterprise system that rewards hard work? The company we labor for? The government programs that provided needed assistance? Our investment counselor or broker who helped us have a good year? No, God is the source of our blessings and "the giver of every good gift." Our gratitude should be toward Him.

> *David praised the LORD in the presence of the whole assembly, saying, "Praise be to you, O LORD, God of our father Israel, from everlasting to everlasting. Yours, O LORD, is the greatness and the power and the glory and the majesty and the splendor, for everything in heaven and earth is yours. Yours, O LORD, is the kingdom; you are exalted as head over all. Wealth and honor come from you; you are the ruler of all things. In your hands are strength and power to exalt and give strength to all. Now, our God, we give you thanks, and praise your glorious name."* (1 Chronicles 29:10-13)

The kingdom of heaven, and the King who reigns over it, are *"like treasure hidden in a field. When a man found it, he hid it again, and then in his joy went and sold all he had and bought that field"* (Matthew 13:44).

Do our daily lives—the decisions we make and the dreams we pursue—reflect that Christ is our treasure?

It's in this very area that Sam Storms' words lift my spirit. In *Pleasures Evermore: The Life-Changing Power of Enjoying God,* he put it this way:

> *Falling in love with the Son of God is the key to holiness. I want to be attuned to God's heart, to be of one mind, one spirit, one disposition with Him. If this occurs, it will only occur as the fruit of fascination with all that God is in Himself and all that He is for me in Jesus. The inability to walk with consistency in the things you know please God ultimately will only be overcome when your heart, soul, mind, spirit, and will are captivated by the majesty, mercy, splendor, beauty, and magnificence of who God is and what He has and will do for you in Jesus.*

> *I must confess that I have ransacked the dictionary for words to describe what I have in mind. Here is what I mean by falling in love with Jesus. I, you, we were made to be* enchanted, enamored, *and* engrossed *with God;* enthralled, enraptured, *and* entranced *with God;* enravished, excited, *and* enticed *by God,* astonished, amazed, *and* awed *by God;* astounded, absorbed, *and* agog *with God;* beguiled *and* bedazzled; startled *and* staggered; smitten *and* stunned; stupefied *and* spellbound; charmed *and* consumed; thrilled *and* thunderstruck; obsessed *and* preoccupied; intrigued *and* impassioned; overwhelmed *and* overwrought; gripped *and* rapt; enthused *and* electrified; tantalized, mesmerized, *and* monopolized; fascinated, captivated, *and* exhilarated *by God;* intoxicated *and* infatuated *with God!*

> *Does that sound like your life? Do you want it to? This is what God made you for. There is an ineradicable, inescapable impulse in your spirit to experience the fullness of God in precisely this way—and God put it there!*

It is my earnest hope and prayer that I would faithfully seek the majesty of His companionship daily. My practice is, however, that too often I settle for too little. Perhaps you can identify with me in this. If so, may God grant us that we increasingly glorify Him in our seeking. ◆

Recommended Resource
Pleasures Evermore:
The Life-Changing Power of
Enjoying God

by Sam Storms

This compelling and highly readable book presents a fresh and liberating perspective on why a relationship with God is not only possible but irresistibly pleasurable. Storms explains that a life devoted to God should also be a life devoted to the pleasure of reveling in Him and all He has done.

25

Investing That Glorifies God Advances His Kingdom

Remember this: Whoever sows sparingly will also reap sparingly, and whoever sows generously will also reap generously. Each man should give what he has decided in his heart to give, not reluctantly or under compulsion, for God loves a cheerful giver. And God is able to make all grace abound to you, so that in all things at all times, having all that you need, you will abound in every good work. As it is written: "He has scattered abroad his gifts to the poor; his righteousness endures forever." Now he who supplies seed to the sower and bread for food will also supply and increase your store of seed and will enlarge the harvest of your righteousness. You will be made rich in every way so that you can be generous on every occasion, and through us your generosity will result in thanksgiving to God.

(2 Corinthians 9:6-11)

Command those who are rich in this present world not to be arrogant nor to put their hope in wealth, which is so uncertain, but to put their hope in God, who richly provides us with everything for our enjoyment. Command them to do good, to be rich in good deeds, and to be generous and willing to share. In this way they will lay up treasure for themselves as a firm foundation for the coming age, so that they may take hold of the life that is truly life.

(1 Timothy 6:17-19)

Frankly, I was completely unqualified for the task . . .

. . . I was asked to undertake for Cru (see page 295). I had no previous hands-on experience. I lacked the innate personal temperament that it seemed to call for. I had no sphere of influence that could be tapped for guidance or assistance. In short, I was in over my head.

What was my job? I was to bring all of Cru's fund-raising efforts under one umbrella. The goal was to make staff members more sensitive to the feelings and interests of the ministry's supporters, which would (hopefully) also make the process of raising financial support more productive over the longer term. When I started, my department had one person in it—me! This indicated to me that, far from Cru spending too much time and attention on fund-raising (a charge made against many parachurch ministries), it spent very little.

So there I was in a job for which I was ill-equipped. As a businessman back home, I had experienced what it was like to be asked to make large contributions, but I had no experience in doing the asking. It required me to think through what biblical principles should guide me in formulating a strategy. Eventually, I saw the challenge primarily as one of evangelism and discipleship. Here's why.

It had been my experience that, as a donor, I would tend to make a token contribution to help others with "their" favorite causes while I thought nothing of making much larger gifts to *my* favorite causes. I was now volunteering time with Cru because the Great Commission had become one of my favorite causes. How had this happened? As I had grown in my faith, my desires to tell everyone about the abundance of the Christian life had greatly increased, as had my desires to be obedient to the Lord's commands. Both of these desires found consummation in the Great Commission. Therefore I reached this conclusion: lead others to Christ and help them grow, and in due course they will also want to see the Great Commission being fulfilled. To the extent they see that happening through the ministries of Cru, they will happily and generously give. The strategy also aligned our motivations properly (*How can we help these people grow?*) rather than as manipulators (*How can we get these people to give to us?*).

The primary strategy I proposed led to a series of Executive Seminars for business and professional couples. These events featured a heavy emphasis on knowing Christ, understanding the Spirit-filled life, and the importance of sharing your faith with others. Fully one-fourth of the program was devoted to building healthy marriage relationships. There was also free time for recreation, socializing, or just plain relaxing. In the entire four-day seminar, we presented the financial needs of the ministry in only one 45-minute session. We trusted the Lord to prompt people to give—only He knew who was spiritually ready and how large a gift was appropriate for them. It was an exceptionally low-key approach.

A Confession

While I'm on the subject of working with the late Bill Bright, it's probably time I make a confession. Part of the reason that I wanted to serve with Cru was the opportunity of working closely with Bill because, among other things, it would give me the opportunity to see if the private life and public persona were one and the same. I had often wondered about some of our best-known Christian leaders—are they truly the kind of people they appear to be? Would an honest "behind the scenes" look that caught their unguarded moments enhance or diminish my respect for them? Cynical of me, I know, but what can I say? It was something I wondered about. I discovered that Bill and Vonette Bright *were* authentic. When I think of them, the characteristic that comes to mind first is their love for our Savior and for His people. That is what motivated their passion for reaching the world for Him. Susie and I left our time of service with great affection for them personally and deep respect for their faithful role modeling of the life in Christ and their sincere commitment to bring glory to His name and to His name alone.

Was it successful? Absolutely! We saw hundreds of men and women give their lives to Christ. Marriages were healed; parents and children were reconciled. Christians were emboldened to share their faith as a way of life in their home communities. Thousands of participants looked back on the event as a meaningful stepping-stone in their spiritual growth.

The strategy also was successful in raising money, though in ways we did not anticipate. When Christians develop a conviction about relinquishing their lives for Christ and His gospel, they do give generously as never before. But large amounts did not stream into Cru. Most of the people who began giving more did so back where they lived—to their churches, mission boards, and local parachurch outreaches. It's to Bill Bright's credit that he continued to enthusiastically support the Executive Seminar ministry for many years, far beyond the time when it had become apparent that Cru was not the primary financial beneficiary. He had often said publicly that he wanted Cru, whenever possible, to be a servant to local churches and other Christian ministries. Privately, he was as good as his word.

I placed this chapter third in this section because you can't appreciate the wisdom of "laying up treasure in heaven" until . . .

. . . you've settled two other issues. We are made in God's image for God's glory, and our lives should be pointed in the direction of that foundational truth. The only way we can reflect His glory is by making The Great Exchange, giving Him our lives so that He can give us His life—so that it is His life in us that is shining forth (chapter 23). God is the treasure hidden in a field—we joyously go and surrender all that we have in order that we might know Him (chapter 24).

Now we move from discussing the treasure hidden in a field to treasure hidden in the heavenlies. Randy Alcorn, in his excellent book *Money, Possessions, and Eternity*, helps us make the transition.

In the greatest sermon ever preached, Jesus masterfully defined the believer's proper relationship to money and possessions: "Do not store up for yourselves treasures on earth, where moth and rust destroy, and where thieves break in and steal. But store up for yourselves treasures in heaven, where moth and rust do not destroy, and where thieves do not break in and steal. For where your treasure is, there your heart will be also" (Matthew 6:19-23).

We must understand that Christ's basic position on wealth is not that it should be rejected but that it should be pursued. According to Jesus, God has an investment mentality. Our Creator and Savior agrees wholeheartedly with us—"Wealth is worth seeking." There is just one difference—He is talking about seeking true wealth.

Jesus vividly described what it is like when we discover true wealth: "The kingdom of heaven is like treasure hidden in a field. When a man found it, he hid it again,

**Recommended
Resource**

The excerpt on the
right was taken from

Money, Possessions,
and Eternity

by Randy Alcorn

Copyright 2003
by Eternal Perspective
Ministries. Used by
permission.

I found this book
challenging on many
levels and have received
excellent comments back
from others to whom I
have recommended it.
Warren Wiersbe said
about it, "The Christian
who wants a balanced
survey of the Bible's
philosophy of wealth will
not be disappointed. The
pastor who wants to
teach his people and
parents who want to train
their children will get
great help from it."

and then in his joy went and sold all he had and bought that field" (Matthew 13:44).

Of course, the great Treasure is Christ himself. To gain Christ — this was what made everything else seem comparatively worthless to Paul (Philippians 3:7-11). But part of gaining Christ was the prospect of eternal reward, symbolizing Christ's stamp of approval on his faithful service while on earth.

What does it mean to lay up treasure in heaven instead of on earth? It means that Christ offers us the incredible opportunity to trade earthly goods and currency for eternal kingdom rewards. By putting our money and possessions in his treasury, we assure ourselves of eternal rewards beyond our comprehension.

Imagine for a moment that you are alive at the very end of the Civil War. You are living in the South, but your home is really in the North. While in the South, you have accumulated a good amount of Confederate currency. Suppose you also know for a fact that the North is going to win the war and that the end could come at any time. What will you do with all of your Confederate money?

If you were smart, there is only one answer to the question. You would cash in your Confederate currency for U.S. currency — the only money that will have value once the war is over. You would keep only enough Confederate currency to meet your basic needs for that short period until the war was over and the money would become worthless.

The believer has inside knowledge of an eventual major change in the worldwide social and economic situation. The currency of this world — its money, possessions, fashions, and whims — will be worthless at our death or Christ's return, both of which are imminent. This knowledge should radically affect our investment strategy. For us to accumulate vast earthly treasures in the face of the inevitable future is equivalent to stockpiling Confederate money despite our awareness of its eventual worthlessness. To do so is to betray a basic ignorance of or unbelief in the Scriptures.

Let me assume the role of "eternal financial counselor" and offer this advice: choose your investments carefully; compare their rates of interest; consider their ultimate trustworthiness; and especially compare how they will be working for you a few million years from now. If the nonbeliever sees with what Jesus called the "bad eye," the Christian's view of finances will be, must be, radically different than his. True, we may participate in some of the same earthly investments, our strategies may appear to overlap at times, and occasionally our short-term goals will be similar. But our long-term goals and purposes will be, must be, fundamentally different. As Christians we must not take our cue from the world but from the Word.

Although acting on the hope of future reward is a legitimate motivation, I believe that generous giving is essentially an affair of the heart.

In my *Sound Mind Investing* newsletter and this book, teaching financial management skills and investing strategies have never been ends in themselves. No, my friends, the truth is that stronger financial foundations mean little to me if they're not accompanied by increased generosity on your part. What motivates me is a driving desire to see our wonderful God glorified as the message of salvation in His Son is carried around the world to people He loves, people who are lost without Him. And that, more often than not, requires money. *That's* why I want you to have more—so you can *give* more.

However, to only help you increase the *amount* of your giving would be to miss the major emphasis of Scripture—that God looks at the *attitude* of the giver rather than the gift. That's why giving is an affair of the heart.

Have you ever really considered the depth of your heavenly Father's commitment to you?

When you placed your faith in Jesus Christ, it's as if God said:

"My child, I pledge to love you with an everlasting love. I'll constantly be watching over you, and will certainly be sure to provide for your needs. I'll guide your steps through life, and offer you my advice so you can make good decisions.

"As you depend on me, I'll give you strength to endure difficult times. I'll always be listening for you, so you can pray to me whenever you want and I'll hear you. I'll answer your prayers like a loving parent—granting what is good and helpful, and withholding when I have something better.

"I'm going to give you spiritually useful abilities so your life will be productive and purposeful and filled with beautiful moments. And I'm preparing a wonderful place for you in eternity—I have some great plans for our times together!

"You are precious to me, so you can trust my love for you is genuine, and deep, and permanent. I'll never grow tired of you, never abandon you, and never be unfaithful to my promises. Never. In this special relationship of ours, I'll always be true to you. And I want you to always be true to me."

That's reasonable, isn't it? That we would always be true to Him? As Paul asks in Romans 12:1, *"When you think of what he has done for you, is this too much to ask?"*(Living Bible). No, it's not too much to ask.

But we aren't always faithful, are we? To our regret, we have divided affections. We love the Lord, but we also—to varying degrees—love the world. Christians in America are among the top 1% of wealthy people in the history of the world, and we spend almost all of it on ourselves. Surely our self-centeredness and indifference to the people and purposes on God's heart must grieve Him.

We should, therefore, pray. And give God permission to do whatever is needed in our lives to work a change in our hearts so that, more than the things of this life, we want more of Him. The Westminster Catechism defines prayer as "an offering up of our desires unto God for things agreeable to His will..." What we pray for reveals our desires. If we desire for God to get all the glory possible from our lives, we should pray, among other things, that

He makes us cheerfully generous people.

As you give more generously, you more fully reflect God's life in you, for God is a giver.

• **You make God happy.** *"Each man should give what he has decided in his heart to give, not reluctantly or under compulsion, for God loves a cheerful giver..."* (2 Corinthians 9:7).

• **You testify to His sovereignty in your life and ownership of all that is yours to control.** *"David praised the LORD in the presence of the whole assembly, saying ...'Yours, O LORD, is the greatness and the power and the glory and the majesty and the splendor, for everything in heaven and earth is yours ... Wealth and honor come from you; you are the ruler of all things. In your hands are strength and power to exalt and give strength to all. Now, our God, we give you thanks, and praise your glorious name"* (1 Chronicles 29:10-13).

• **You reflect where your treasure is.** *"Do not gather and heap up and store up for yourselves treasures on earth, where moth and rust and worm consume and destroy, and where thieves break through and steal. But gather and heap up and store for yourselves treasures in heaven, where neither moth nor rust nor worm consume and destroy, and where thieves do not break through and steal; For where your treasure is, there will your heart be also"* (Matthew 6:19-21 Amplified).

• **You show your complete trust in Him to supply for your needs.** *"I am amply supplied, now that I have received from Epaphroditus the gifts you sent. They are a fragrant offering, an acceptable sacrifice, pleasing to God. And my God will meet all your needs according to his glorious riches in Christ Jesus"* (Philippians 4:18-19).

• **You ensure greater spiritual usefulness.** *"Whoever can be trusted with very little can also be trusted with much, and whoever is dishonest with very little will also be dishonest with much. So if you have not been trustworthy in handling worldly wealth, who will trust you with true riches?"* (Luke 16:10-11).

• **You reap eternal benefits.** *"Command them to do good, to be rich in good deeds, and to be generous and willing to share. In this way they will lay up treasure for themselves as a firm foundation for the coming age, so that they may take hold of the life that is truly life"* (1 Timothy 6:18-19).

• **And, most importantly, you magnify His glory.** *"This service that you perform is not only supplying the needs of God's people but is also overflowing in many expressions of thanks to God. Because of the service by which you have proved yourselves, men will praise God..."* (2 Corinthians 9:12-13).

Perhaps you feel that your financial circumstances are such that you can't tithe at this time.

I don't know your circumstances. It helps to have walked in others' shoes in understanding the challenges they face. Fortunately, God does this better than anybody. He knows the pressures you're under, the desires you have, and the temptations you face. And knowing all of that, He still wants you to be generous in your giving.

In my own life, I have used 2 Corinthians 8-9 as a guide when making lifestyle decisions that affect my ability to give. The people praised in these passages were not wealthy, but nevertheless *"their overflowing joy and their extreme poverty welled up in rich generosity. For I testify that they gave as much as they were able, and even beyond their ability"* (8:2-3).

Our giving to God is a tangible way of showing that He truly holds first place in our lives. Many families justify not giving by saying they first need to get debt-free, a second family car, a savings reserve for rainy days, or funding for their retirement plan. These are all good and worthwhile things . . . unless they crowd our wonderful God out of His rightful place.

Have you considered what would happen if your income suddenly dropped 10%? Would you make it through, albeit with some sacrifice needed? Of course. In all likelihood, you can tithe (even though you may think you can't).

We are not *commanded* to give generously. Rather, our giving is a test of the sincerity of our love (8:8) and our willingness to trust in God's utter faithfulness (9:8).

If you're already giving generously, you have my respect. If not . . .

. . . I'm trying to encourage you to move decisively in that direction. Under His Spirit's direction, you can increasingly become the kind of cheerful and grateful giver that delights His heart. He's always been faithful to you. By your generosity, you can be increasingly true to Him.

We should give *with a sense of urgency*. This should incline us to give what we can now rather than saving up in order to give more later. Later may be too late.

Once in our weekly staff devotions at my office, we prayed for two children whose mom died suddenly over the weekend. Brain aneurysm. No warning, just here one minute and in heaven the next. Only 42 years old. Ultimately, perfection for her but sorrow for the family. All her plans and good intentions for the future—for her children, her career, her service to the Lord—gone in a moment. Not going to happen.

When I heard the news, I immediately thought of a passage from a book I was reading only the day before (*Becoming Real* by Steven James). The author was talking about the uncertainty of life, and encouraging his readers to make the most of each day, each week. He wasn't trying to depress them or bring them down; he was trying to wake them up:

Everyone dies in the midst of something.

People die in the midst of going to the dentist's office or driving home from vacation or taking a shower or watching TV or mowing the lawn or barbequing ribs on the back deck or enjoying a good night's sleep. People die in the midst of arguments, grudges, dreams, plans, careers, headaches, heartaches, and courtships. People die in the midst of marriage and puberty and old age. Some die in the midst of being born. Or even before that.

We all die. And we don't die when we expect to die or after our dreams have all come true or when we've finally made it in the world. No, most of us die in the midst of pretending we'll never die. We die living as if tomorrow were guaranteed and this life will last forever.

When death stalks us or claims a close relative or friend, we weep in shock. How could this happen? It's so out of the blue! Death is never out of the blue. It's always there, right before our eyes. And soon after the tragedy, we go right back to living as if each moment didn't count for eternity.

Life is a gift. Death is a certainty. Dying is one thing we're all capable of, one thing we all ultimately succeed at.

I've often heard people say things like, "you've got your whole life in front of you!" That's simply not true. We don't have our whole lives ahead of us. We have our whole lives behind us. What we have in front of us is a mystery that could be over at any moment.

It's sobering to reflect on the brevity and frailty of our lives.

Yes, sobering, but also very beneficial for the Christian who wants the Lord to receive the greatest glory possible from his or her life. None of us wants to waste opportunities to make the most of the life and gifts God has given us. Facing up to the chance of dying unexpectedly — owning it as a real possibility — provides a much needed sense of urgency. Often we tend to postpone things, thinking, "There's always next year." No, there's not always next year. Not always. For millions every day, there's not even tomorrow.

How essential, then, to live with one eye on eternity, being fully awake to the knowledge that "just one life, will soon be past; only what's done for Christ will last." A familiar cliché perhaps, but not a truer line has been written.

Don't let the time slip by. You have opportunities to live and give boldly for God. I want to encourage you to give generously to your church and to missions — to share the gospel of Christ with the world, to disciple new believers in their faith, and to offer mercy and help with their physical needs. If you do this, your eternal satisfactions will be great.

"That is what the Scriptures are talking about when they say, 'How beautiful are the feet of those who preach the Gospel of peace with God and bring glad tidings of good things'" (Romans 10:15 Living).

Perhaps, on the day you meet the Bridegroom face to face, you will receive not only a hearty "Well done!" but also, as He grasps you by the shoulders and hugs you to Himself, you'll hear His whisper, "Beautiful! Your acts of worship were beautiful. You brought delight to my heart!"

And you'll be filled with the greatest joy you've ever known. ◆

Investing That Glorifies God Upholds His Righteousness

I will listen to what God the LORD will say; he promises peace to his people, his saints—but let them not return to folly. Surely his salvation is near those who fear him, that his glory may dwell in our land. Love and faithfulness meet together; righteousness and peace kiss each other. Faithfulness springs forth from the earth, and righteousness looks down from heaven. The LORD will indeed give what is good, and our land will yield its harvest. Righteousness goes before him and prepares the way for his steps.

(Psalm 85:8-13)

What man is wise enough to understand this? Who has been instructed by the LORD and can explain it? Why has the land been ruined and laid waste like a desert that no one can cross? The LORD said, "It is because they have forsaken my law, which I set before them; they have not obeyed me or followed my law." . . . This is what the LORD says: "Let not the wise man boast of his wisdom or the strong man boast of his strength or the rich man boast of his riches, but let him who boasts boast about this: that he understands and knows me, that I am the LORD, who exercises kindness, justice and righteousness on earth, for in these I delight," declares the LORD.

(Jeremiah 9:12-13, 23-24)

The commencement speaker at the University of California School of Business had these words of advice: *"Greed is all right. Greed is healthy.*

"You can be greedy and still feel good about yourself. Greed works." The comments reportedly were received with laughter and applause by the new graduates. The speaker was Ivan Boesky, a man of vast wealth. Not too many months later, he was sent to prison for violating securities laws in his relentless quest to acquire even more.

How much is enough, anyway? Obviously, for some, there's no such thing as ever having "enough." It's not because they have material wants that are left unmet; Ivan Boesky couldn't possibly have spent, no matter how extravagant his personal lifestyle, all the money he had. There are those for whom money represents success, status, superiority, and power. They are pursuing it in a doomed attempt to fill an inner emptiness. But that emptiness is like a black hole; no matter how much you put in, it never fills with light. Ironically, Boesky's very life gave the lie to his words. Greed, it turns out, doesn't work after all.

Fortunately, we Christians already understand this. Greed may be something to watch out for . . .

. . . when doing business with "the world," but followers of Christ are not like that. We *them*, we can relax. *They* would never take advantage of us, right? . . . Right? . . . Hello? . . .

Perhaps I imagine that my question is being received with less than thunderous agreement because I have received many letters from readers of my newsletter that contain horror stories of the various financial atrocities committed against them by people they trusted to have their best interests at heart. They met these people at church, in a couples' Bible study, through a Christian friend, or through some other association that would lead them to believe the person was trustworthy. Unfortunately, limiting your business transactions solely to Christians is no assurance that everything will work out happily ever after.

That reminds me, have I ever told you about my $100,000 tennis racket?

During my tenure with Cru, the idea struck me how great it would be if I found competent Christian people to invest with. They would perform the day-to-day work of the investment projects, and eventually Susie and I could live off the income and be free to continue devoting our time to ministry pursuits.

Well, it wasn't long (wouldn't you know it?) before I was approached about investing in a real-estate project. I was introduced by a co-worker to a friend of his (let's call him Dugan) who was a developer in the greater San Diego area. Dugan and his partner Roberts needed temporary financing on one of their projects until their permanent construction loan was approved. They were willing to pay a healthy rate of interest, personally guarantee the loan, plus pledge some stock Dugan owned as additional collateral. They had done other projects previously and had development experience. I verified with the lending institution that their loan request had, indeed, received approval, pending receipt of their pro forma financial statements.

Dugan and his wife were super people; you couldn't help but like them. They entertained us at their country club. They invited us over for friendly tennis (Dugan gave me one of his rackets so I could practice regularly). Since we were living away from Kentucky, they even included us in their plans for Thanksgiving dinner. We were practically family! So everything seemed to line up pretty well. And what seemed to confirm it was that the opportunity to invest with a Christian had come along just when it seemed the natural direction to go.

You know something went wrong, or I wouldn't own a tennis racket that cost me $100,000. Here's the sorry sequence of events.

• Through negligence, Dugan missed the deadline for submitting the financial statements to the lender, and they lost their construction loan.

• The economy was going through a downturn, and they could not get another loan commitment. The project never got off the ground. Fortunately, I still had the personal guarantees of the Dugans and the Robertses.

• Roberts died suddenly of a heart attack. Being a sensitive guy who doesn't want to invade a widow's grief, I let some time go by before asking for her share of my money. While I was being noble, her late husband's attorney was helping her hide her assets; she eventually produced a financial statement that made her appear penniless. Curiously, six months after the sudden departure of Mr. Roberts, the former Mrs. Roberts overcame her grief and married the helpful attorney.

• Dugan and his wife filed for protection under the bankruptcy laws and moved to northern California. I never heard from them again.

• The stock Dugan pledged was in a land development company that was operated and controlled by his brother. The brother later told me that things were going so well that my stock holdings would be worth $1 million within three years. This was a little optimistic; the company expanded too quickly, eventually lost its land holdings, and disappeared into bankruptcy never-never land. I never heard from the brother again.

What did I learn from this misadventure? I learned not to make certain unwarranted assumptions . . .

. . . when dealing with fellow Christians. First, I assumed that because Dugan had experience and seemed to know what he was doing, he was competent. I didn't really check him out. It turned out that his personable style made him competent only as a promoter. It was little help in the nitty-gritty of day-to-day details. Second, I assumed that these were people of integrity. They seemed so *sincere!* Yet

**PRYOR'S RULES
FOR EVALUATING
INVESTMENTS THAT
SEEK YOU OUT**

Rule #1
Assume the investment is being offered to you by a representative of Ivan Boesky. It's not that the person soliciting your investment is likely to be as greedy or dishonest as Boesky. I just want to help you to stay alert and not repeat the mistake of making unwarranted assumptions. All the remaining rules logically follow from this one.

Rule #2
Apply all decision-making guidelines for making the "right" decisions that I gave in chapter 16 (pages 176-178). All of them.

Rule #3
Ask the individual to put everything of importance (like representations of risk, how much money you're guaranteed to make, how long it's all going to take) in written form. Assume nothing; verify everything.

Rule #4
Check his facts out thoroughly. Ask someone you trust, who has nothing to do with the deal, to help you. Assume nothing; verify everything.

Rule #5
Investigate his track record. Contact other investors with whom he's done business. Assume nothing; verify everything.

Rule #6
Ask for personal character references, including one from his pastor. Then call the people and talk with them personally. Assume nothing; verify everything.

Rule #7
If you decide to go ahead, put the entire deal in writing, signed by all concerned, so that you have a legally enforceable position. Handshake deals are out.

Rule #8
Make absolutely, positively no exceptions to Rules #1 through #7. And, oh yes, assume nothing and verify everything.

they readily hid behind the bankruptcy laws to avoid repaying the money they had so earnestly besought me to lend them. Boy, had I learned an important lesson! I wouldn't make *those* mistakes again. I would make *new* ones.

This brings me to the story of my $50,000 Swiss army knife key ring.

Jack, a good Christian friend, brought it back as a souvenir from one of the frequent business trips to Europe he made for a business deal we were in together. I won't go into all the details here. I'll just skip to the new lessons I learned about *other* unwarranted assumptions you shouldn't make. First, I assumed that all the facts of the deal were exactly as Jack had represented them to me. (By the way, note that I no longer needed go-betweens to introduce me to people like Dugan—by this time I was going directly to my close personal friends to lose my money.) I know that Jack truly believed—evidently too optimistically—everything he was telling me. The point is that I would never have accepted the story just on the word of a stranger. I would have expected documented proof of all the facts. With Jack, my guard was completely down.

Second, I assumed that because I could trust my friend, the usual precautions didn't apply. In chapter 16, I gave you five guidelines for making investment decisions (see pages 196-198). In this one deal, I broke the first four of the guidelines without hesitation.

Guideline 1: The deal wasn't consistent with my long-term strategy because I didn't have one.

Guideline 2: I didn't take much time to pray about it or seek counsel from others.

Guideline 3: I never really understood the logistics of the deal or why it was supposed to work the way it was.

Guideline 4: The investment totally failed the common sense test of prudence.

In retrospect, it's so improbable that it could have worked that I'm too embarrassed to even tell you what it was about.

In short, my trust was totally in the knowledge and experience of my friend. The reason I didn't give the guidelines a thought is that I hadn't learned to apply biblical principles to financial decision-making at that point. (Larry Burkett was just getting his financial-teaching ministry started in those days.) This happened in 1976, and I was still flying on gut instinct.

I hope you appreciate the "school" I went to in learning these lessons that I'm passing on to you for the unbelievably low price of only $24.99. The tuition for this one cost me $50,000 (or just $49,990 if you want to count the $10 value of my Swiss army knife key ring).

Well, enough about the importance of ethics (or lack thereof) as they apply to investment opportunities that come seeking *you* out. Let's look at the flip side—ethical considerations when you are the one taking the initiative.

Let's begin by looking at the two major approaches to "ethical" investing.

According to an April 2013 article in *Forbes*: "Over the last two years, [socially responsible] investing has grown by more than 22% to $3.74 trillion in total managed assets, suggesting that investors are investing with their heart, as well as their head. In fact, about $1 of every $9 under professional management in the U.S. can be classified as an SRI investment."

• **Socially responsible investing (SRI)** is the *traditional secular* term used to describe the process of taking certain ethical considerations into account when investing one's portfolio.

SRI proponents have generally been in favor of race-based affirmative action, animal rights, ramped-up environmental protection, affirmation of homosexuality, gun control, low-income housing, and so-called women's issues. They have generally opposed air pollution, alcohol sales, defense and weapons contractors, gambling, nuclear power, and tobacco products. This list of concerns shows that SRI activists hold, for the most part, politically liberal views concerning the way society, business, and government should be organized and operated.

• **Biblically responsible investing (BRI)** is the *conservative evangelicals' answer* to SRI. This approach uses biblically based screening criteria rather than secular ones. BRI has yet to gain the following that SRI enjoys, but it's growing.

The Timothy Plan (www.timothyplan.com, 800-TIM-PLAN) was one of the early entrants into the BRI field. It's a fund family that avoids not only alcohol, tobacco, and gambling companies, but also screens out companies involved in abortion, pornography, immoral entertainment, and other business activities that undermine traditional sexual values.

Obviously, what constitutes social responsibility is in the eye of the beholder. Many news sources have examined key differences among SRI mutual funds in how they define "responsible" behavior. Even among secular SRI funds, it's common for there to be disagreement as to how certain companies should be treated. The lesson is clear: If you're interested in an "ethical" fund, be sure the fund you select reflects *your* moral values.

All practitioners of SRI/BRI create a set of portfolio guidelines . . .

. . . called "screens," which reflect the ethical values they wish to see represented in their investments. It's generally agreed that SRI/BRI falls into three main camps:

• **Avoidance investing or "negative screening" (penalize the bad guys).** Investors in this category develop guidelines designed to weed out companies engaged in activities or practices that they find objectionable. This is probably the most common approach, and is what most individual investors mean when they say they are interested in "ethical" investing.

• **Advocacy investing or "activist screening" (convert/replace the bad guys).** This is the opposite of avoidance investing because it is quite willing to invest in companies with the intention of changing objectionable corporate behavior by exercising one's ownership privileges via shareholder resolutions. This strategy calls for an ongoing effort after the investment is made.

• **Affirmative investing or "positive screening" (reward the good guys).** This is a proactive strategy where investment opportunities are sought in companies that are working to achieve those societal goals that the investor believes are important. Companies that underwrite community housing projects, search for alternative energy sources, manufacture pollution-control products, or have "nondiscriminatory" employment and promotion practices are examples of areas targeted for proactive investing.

Is it advisable to buy mutual funds that invest in companies without paying heed to the moral issues . . .

. . . surrounding those companies' products, services, or policies? In almost every financial decision we make—whether it be spending for consumer goods, spending on housing, spending on entertainment, spending on education for our children, or spending on investments—we run the risk of putting money into the hands of those whose activities are in opposition to our values. Even using skills and talents to help one's employer grow and prosper takes on an ethical dimension when looked at through the lens of stewardship. When legitimate ethical questions arise about a company's activities, where does each individual draw the line as to what constitutes an acceptable level of involvement with that company?

This is a difficult question, one on which Christians of good will can, and do, have differing views. The position I have taken in my *Sound Mind Investing* newsletter is not as activist as some would like. Still, I have cordial relationships with proponents of BRI such as Art Ally (founder of the Timothy Plan funds) and Rusty Leonard (founder of Stewardship Partners) that are built on mutual respect.

I believe that those seeking to be more ethical in their investments sincerely strive to be faithful stewards. They want to be sure they do not lend economic support to those worldly forces in opposition to what they see as biblical values. I respect their concerns. I offer my perspective on BRI merely as one among many ways the matter can be approached. I have never attempted to impose it on others, nor have I insisted it is the only correct approach. But I do believe it is a reasonable one. It seems to me to be both biblical and practical.

Faith-Based Investing Mutual Funds

Unlike many SRI funds, this BRI fund has screens that eliminate investments in abortion and pornography-related products and services:

The Timothy Plan
(800) 846-7526
www.timothyplan.com

I believe we would all agree that the Christian view of stewardship is centered in our relationship with Jesus Christ and recognizes that He is Lord over all aspects of our lives, not just our investment portfolios. Thus, it seems to me that decisions as to (1) where and for whom we will *work*, (2) how and for what we will *spend* our money, (3) how and in what we *invest* our money, and (4) where and how much we *give* of our money must all be kept in view. None of these is exempt from the scope of our stewardship responsibilities — and none is inherently more important than the other. It is this view of the "interconnectedness" of these four areas that, ultimately, leads me to the conclusions I reach. I think this will become clear shortly.

There's a difference between choosing a direct relationship and having accidental contact.

In my *Sound Mind Investing* newsletter, I have brought BRI options to the attention of our readers many times over the years. Still, it's fair to say that the *Sound Mind Investing* newsletter has not placed an emphasis on the use of BRI mutual funds There is a straightforward reason for that: In my view, regular mutual funds are acceptable investment vehicles, even though they may, on occasion, hold objectionable companies in their portfolios. The important stewardship issue for me is that I don't *directly* involve myself with morally questionable enterprises in the four areas mentioned above — my work, my spending, my investing, and my giving.

Let's say we're talking about the tobacco industry. Philip Morris (now part of the Altria Group) is the nation's largest cigarette manufacturer. It is on just about every SRI investor's "bad" list. Until about six years ago, it also happened to own Kraft Foods, the largest food and beverage company in the U.S. While this ownership situation has changed, it was a great example of the difficulty one faces if trying to avoid any contact with objectionable companies. Here's how I would have applied my "direct involvement" criteria when Kraft was still owned by Philip Morris (Altria):

• **My work**: Our work matters to God. He works, and He created us to be co-workers with Him. It's not something we do apart from Him. As authors Doug Sherman and William D. Hendricks point out in *Your Work Matters to God*: "All legitimate work is an extension of God's work. By legitimate work, we mean work that somehow contributes to what God wants done in the world, and does not actively contribute to what He does not want done." Because I want to avoid actively contributing to the production and sale of harmful products, I wouldn't take a job at Philip Morris. But because the products of Kraft Foods are generally useful, I would be willing to work there.

Don't misunderstand me here. If you work at a company engaged in questionable activities, I'm not suggesting you need to quit your job tomorrow.

Hopefully, you can use your position to effect positive change within your company. We're called to be salt and light, and that includes in the workplace. But I do think this is an area that deserves more thought than many Christians appear to give it.

• **My spending:** I don't buy Marlboros (an Altria/Philip Morris product), but even when Altria owned Kraft, I saw nothing wrong with buying Kraft cheese and salad dressings, or other Kraft products such as A-1 steak sauce, Grey Poupon mustard, Planters nuts, Fig Newtons, Jell-O desserts, Tang or Kool-Aid juice drinks, Cool Whip frozen topping, or Maxwell House coffee.

How could I buy the products of a subsidiary company such as Kraft knowing that my money will eventually find its way to a parent company of whom I disapprove? Because the complexity and interconnectedness of corporate America make it almost impossible to avoid this. Even assuming you could do the necessary research, it's unrealistic to think that Christians should go to the grocery or mall with a catalog in their hand listing the thousands of products that shouldn't be bought.

I do agree, however, that it's possible to effectively focus attention on just one or two companies via consumer boycotts (see sidebar at right). If a substantial segment of the Christian community was engaged in a united effort to bring about a change of behavior at Kraft (or any other company), I would certainly be willing to join in, even if it meant avoiding a long list of products.

• **My investing**: I won't buy Altria Group (Philip Morris) stock, but I'll buy a mutual fund that might own some Altria stock. To me, there's a difference between making a direct conscious attempt to profit from the sale of tobacco products versus the indirect incidental contact I might have with Altria when I'm only trying to invest in a diversified portfolio of stocks that span the spectrum of American economic life. The Vanguard S&P 500 ETF used in our Just-the-Basics strategy owns shares in Altria. Let's assume I invest $10,000 in this fund that has roughly $133 billion in assets; how much ownership in Altria would this give me? I would own .000000075 of a fund that owns less than one percent of Altria. That means if Altria were divided into more than 1.4 *billion* pieces, I would own *one* piece. Such a microscopic ownership interest is, in my view, meaningless.

Furthermore, we should bear in mind that *when mutual funds buy shares of stock, that money doesn't go to the company in which they're investing*. Many investors are under the false impression that companies cash in when you buy their stock (or invest in mutual funds that own their stock). This is not the case because such transactions take place in what's called the "secondary market." Investors are buying shares from *other investors*, not from the companies directly. It's the same as if you purchased a used Chevrolet. Your money would *not* go to General Motors, which got its money a long time ago and could care less whether you buy the Chevrolet or not. SRI funds are no different from "regular" funds in this regard.

• **My giving**: It could be that a job with Altria Group would pay more than others available to me, or that a direct investment in Altria stock would have earned more than diversifying in a mutual fund. In either event, my giving could be increased. But that's not a sufficient inducement—greater giving potential doesn't necessarily "trump" my direct involvement ethic. My giving must flow from morally responsible decisions I make in the other three stewardship areas.

Now, perhaps you believe my "direct involvement" criteria is *not* morally responsible.

You believe that even *indirect* involvement is wrong. I respect your right to believe that, but I don't believe the Bible requires it. Nor is it likely you can live up to such a standard across the full stewardship spectrum. Consider:

• **Your work**: You can work only for companies that have no questionable activities, either at the parent company or in any of their subsidiaries. Not AT&T, Disney, Johnson & Johnson, Viacom, General Electric, Bayer, Sony, Bank of America, Aetna, Wells Fargo, Time Warner, CBS, Merck... well, you get the idea. All of these well-known companies (and many, *many* more) fail screening tests used by Christian groups. If it's wrong to invest in them, even indirectly, surely it's wrong to work for them.

• **Your spending**: Unlike the indirect support given when buying a company's stock, buying its products puts money straight into their pockets. With some companies, such as Anheuser-Busch InBev, it's relatively easy to know what to avoid. But would you be able to avoid the thousands of consumer products offered by others on the list of offenders? Not

The Case for "Socially Responsible <u>Spending</u>"

To do an effective job of withholding support from objectionable companies, we must be ready to boycott—not merely their securities, but more importantly, their products and services.

Consider this excerpt from a story in *Mutual Funds* magazine:

"Will simply avoiding a company's stock affect its behavior? The short answer is that there's no proof that it will, nor even a rigorously articulated theory as to why it should. One argument is that steering clear of corporate bad guys lowers those companies' share prices, ultimately raising their cost of capital. That may be technically possible, but unrealistic: Even if boycotting shares lowered the price, that might serve mostly to open the door for management to take the company private at a bargain price. *Companies need customers more than they need any particular group of investors*" [emphasis added].

Companies primarily profit from our spending, not our investing. Targeting our routine daily spending can be a potent force for change. I encourage you to spend strategically to reward those companies that enhance the quality of life from a Judeo-Christian perspective and avoid rewarding those whose activities undermine the health of the family and children. If a company's behavior is offensive to your deeply held convictions, why reward it with your patronage?

Consider the potential effectiveness of a boycott:

• <u>Everyone can participate</u>. All of us are consumers; not all of us have investment portfolios. Even if we do, we might not hold shares in the offending companies we are trying to influence. If you believe the value of your involvement is directly tied to the size and makeup of your investment portfolio, what do you do if your investments are modest in size and/or include no holdings, directly or indirectly, in the company in question? You may conclude that there's no role for you to play.

• <u>Ease of recruitment</u>. There are millions of Christian families who would be quite upset with various companies if they knew the facts concerning those companies' activities and sponsorships. But in our society, it can be quite awkward to talk to your friends about personal money matters concerning their investments and how they can/should use them to stand for biblical values. On the other hand, it's relatively easy to hand someone an article on a boycott and ask that he or she take this information into account before doing any further business with that company.

• <u>Ease of implementation</u>. Working for change through your investing requires adding an activity to already busy schedules, namely researching who holds the shares and communicating your requests that they divest their holdings. But to work for change through your spending adds no new time demands. It merely requires a change in spending patterns. This makes it easier for each of us to get involved as well as making it easier to ask others.

• <u>Concentration of forces</u>. We can more readily join together and make our influence felt when we are all directing our efforts at a single decision-maker—the top officer of a particular company. In contrast, consider the challenge of influencing hundreds of fund managers and institutional investors (who may not share the same concerns) to sell a significant amount of their stock.

Businesses need our spending, not our investing, for their continued existence. Even if a million like-minded families decided to sell their mutual fund shares in protest, most companies would have only a public-relations problem. But if a million families who previously purchased a company's goods and services took their spending elsewhere, that business would notice a decline in sales and profits. That would be a far more serious problem.

likely, because such a list probably would include companies such as Johnson & Johnson (maker of Aveeno, Band-Aids, Carefree, Johnson's Baby products, Lactaid, Motrin, Mylanta, Neutrogena, and Tylenol to name a few) and General Electric (appliances, housewares, lighting, consumer electronics)?

• **Your investing**: Avoiding even indirect involvement with certain companies would mean that your ability to follow the biblical admonition to diversify your risk would be severely limited. Let's start with the stock market. Aside from the handful of Christian-screened stock funds available (assuming they meet your purity tests, which some may not—for example, not all screen out companies offering benefits to homosexual couples), no other funds qualify.

If you decided to buy individual stocks rather than use a stock fund, how many of the Fortune 500 companies do you believe are operated according to Christian principles from top to bottom? That would mean the application of a biblical moral ethic in *all* of the following: their hiring and firing decisions, employee pay and benefits, environmental impact policies, the way they price their products or services, their borrowing and lending decisions, and the whole of their advertising and marketing strategies. I doubt you can find even one.

U. S. government bonds, notes, and Treasury bills are also out. Whether promoting abortion or undermining traditional family values through humanistic arts, education, and welfare programs, there is much for Christians to be concerned about in the way our government spends money.

Well, then, you can always just leave your money in the bank, can't you? Yes, but not with any assurance that your bank isn't using your deposits to make loans to help build such businesses as the local newspaper that aggressively attacks Christian home-schooling in its editorials. Or the bookstore that has several racks of pornographic magazines right by the front door where even young children can see them. Or the abortion clinic that has become the largest in your state. Or the music store in the local mall that promotes music and videos that glamorize sexually destructive and drug-addicting lifestyles. The possibilities are almost limitless. The question is not *if* your bank has made loans to businesses engaged in practices abhorrent to you, but rather *how many and for how much*. And where do the banks get the money to make these loans? From the savings put on deposit by trusting folks like you and me.

• **Your giving**: It's sometimes suggested that even if a strict SRI strategy results in a much lower return on investments, it's a worthwhile tradeoff. My question is: *how much lower*, and in return for *how great an increase* in "purity"? If a set of SRI funds is 95% free of objectionable holdings and returns 7% annually over five years, while a set of "regular" funds is 85% free of objectionable holdings and returns 12% annually during the same period, was the tradeoff worth it? You may say yes, because it was a matter of conscience, and I won't object. But others in good conscience might say no, it wasn't worth it.

Having one's gains significantly lowered in return for a marginal improvement in the moral content of a fund portfolio can strike some as poor stewardship. After all, in the Parable of the Talents (Matthew 25), the emphasis was on the return on investment, not how the bankers might have improperly used the deposits. While greater profit potential doesn't automatically overshadow moral concerns, neither should moral concerns—especially when the involvement is indirect and incidental—automatically be exalted above the return we get on our investments. A reasonable balance between the two—as well as with the "work" and "spending" categories—is needed.

There has been an ongoing debate within investing circles as to whether an SRI/BRI strategy hurts performance.

Obviously, when you add ethical screening criteria to the list of factors that investors normally consider when selecting stocks (such as revenue and earnings growth, valuation, competitive position, and industry fundamentals), you reduce your investment options. All things being equal, this should make it more difficult to get better results than your neighbor who has hundreds more companies to choose from.

Aaah, but all things *aren't* equal claim the SRI proponents. They would say that it pays to be a good corporate citizen. Perhaps, but studies have yet to prove a beneficial link between stock performance and any of the most commonly applied social screening criteria. In fact, the majority of SRI funds were notorious underperformers during most of the 1990s. A study by Morningstar, however, did seem to indicate things were slowing improving in certain asset classes:

> *SRI investors still face a shortage of good supplemental choices. The SRI universe is still heavily skewed toward types of funds that are designed to be used as core holdings. 60% of the strict secular screened funds are domestic large-cap or allocation funds, in fact, whereas only 25% of these funds are mid-cap, small-cap, or overseas offerings. And although several of the large-cap-oriented funds are solid offerings—and a few are rather good ones—most of the smaller-cap and international offerings are unattractive for one reason or another. Thus, while it's not hard to find an attractive SRI core holding, it continues to be difficult to build a good all-SRI portfolio.*

Using the Morningstar database, I examined the track records of the 51 SRI U.S. stock funds that had at least a 10-year performance history. As a group, they trailed the average U.S. stock fund, 7.34% annually versus 8.22% for the 10 years ending June 30, 2013. Furthermore, when I broke them down by peer group and compared apples to apples, I found that 73% of the funds underperformed the average fund in their risk category while only 27% did better.

Some may say that any difference in mutual fund performance results is worth the sacrifice in order to have all of one's investments line up with one's sense of values. And I would agree that, if it's a matter of personal conviction, one should certainly investigate the BRI fund options.

In sum, our options are limited by the fact that we are "in the world" and must function in it.

Paul writes in 1 Corinthians 5:9-10, *"I have written you in my letter not to associate with sexually immoral people—not at all meaning the people of this world who are immoral, or the greedy and swindlers, or idolaters. In that case you would have to leave this world."* Paul recognizes the impossibility of completely avoiding all contact with disagreeable associations in the course of living our daily lives.

Some people believe that it's wrong to have *any* money invested in objectionable companies. Even if such a standard was attainable, there is still the question of whether the incremental gain in the purity of the portfolio is worth the likely decrease in investment return. For example, I want to breathe clean air, yet I don't feel the need to walk around wearing a gas mask—at a certain point, the marginal improvement in purity isn't worth the increased restriction. Likewise, I avoid investing directly in companies whose products or policies run counter to my values, but I also don't fret that minuscule holdings of objectionable companies may temporarily pass through my fund portfolio as I enjoy the higher returns and ease of use that my newsletter's mutual-fund-based investing strategies have historically provided.

Am I saying that "if you can't do it perfectly, then don't even make an attempt"? Of course not. I'm saying that it is helpful to make a distinction between the things you *can* do perfectly (or almost perfectly) and the things you cannot. I believe that it's possible to almost completely avoid having *direct involvement* or lending *direct support* to objectionable companies. So, make it a priority to do so all across the stewardship spectrum.

Ultimately, I want us to become more *effective* by extending our ethical concerns to all areas of stewardship—our work, our spending, our investing, and our giving. Far be it from us as Christians, who are responsible for handling God's wealth for God's glory, that we should provide *direct* financial support to the very people and institutions whose activities are undermining the biblical values we hold dear. And with respect to the things that you cannot do perfectly, such as avoiding all *indirect* involvement in your spending and investing, do what you reasonably can *while keeping your stewardship responsibilities in balance.*

As Christians continue to explore the issues involved in deciding where to "draw the line" concerning our financial associations, may our discussions be governed by Ephesians 4:2-3: *"Be completely humble and gentle; be patient, bearing with one another in love. Make every effort to keep the unity of the Spirit through the bond of peace."*

Another Perspective:
The Case for Biblically Responsible Investing

My friends at the Biblically Responsible Investing Institute take issue, as you might imagine, with some of the observations I make in this chapter. Their leader, Rusty Leonard, asked for an opportunity to present his side, and being the fair-minded guy that I am, I readily agreed. — Austin

Biblically Responsible Investing (BRI) is an approach used by Christians seeking to be the best possible stewards of the wealth the Lord has given them. Here is how BRI investors respond to common questions about this approach:

There are no pure companies. Aren't they all involved in something objectionable?

This is true. We are all sinners and all companies are also impacted by sin at some level. Still, some companies actively profit from sinful behavior or encourage it directly though the type of business they are engaged in. It is not reasonable to believe that Jesus would approve of us investing His money (we are simply his stewards) in companies that actively promote sin. BRI seeks to eliminate such companies from your portfolio. While no company is entirely free from sin, most actually operate in ways that are consistent with Christian beliefs.

There are too many gray areas. Isn't it impossible to draw a line between moral and immoral activities?

Actually, everyone does draw the line somewhere with regard to how their beliefs will affect their investments. Some do this with intentionality but most, sadly, draw that line without giving much thought to it. BRI investors, however, take their stewardship responsibilities seriously and actively seek to prevent the Lord's money, over which they have been given temporary stewardship, from being used in a manner that would clearly harm other human beings or undermine the Lord's efforts to sanctify our world. Moreover, such an investor now has the resources to do just that with a variety of worthwhile BRI mutual funds and separate accounts available. In the end, individuals should consider how they would explain to Jesus Himself where they decided to draw the line.

The stake I have in a company via outright ownership of its stock or through shares of a mutual fund is too small to be of significance. How can that matter?

Does not God call His people to be holy? Does He qualify this directive? Does He tell us to be holy only in the big things of life or only in the areas where it will make a perceivable difference? No, it is an all-encompassing charge with no qualifying statements attached that might lessen or nullify the requirement under certain conditions. This is because He is more interested in the condition of our heart than of anything else. He is pleased when we take steps of faith that honor Him and bless His kingdom. BRI allows us to do this and we hope that we will positively impact our world as well.

Won't my financial returns suffer?

Studies have shown that screened portfolios, on average, perform no different from unscreened portfolios. The key to beating indices and other fund managers appears to be more reliant on manager skill rather than what stocks are excluded from consideration due to moral concerns.

Performance is a key question in considering an investment, but investors should also be aware of how those returns were produced. Investments should be chosen according to their performance, but it is not necessary to compromise your faith in investing. Resources are available to help you align your investments with your values.

The Biblically Responsible Investing Institute is part of Stewardship Partners, a North Carolina-based investment firm committed to helping investors align their faith with their investments using a BRI strategy. For information, call 800-930-6949, or visit www.stewardshippartners.com.

Investing that glorifies God upholds His righteousness.

So far in this section, we have discussed why investing that glorifies God acknowledges His sovereignty (God owns it all), values His majesty (He is the treasure), and advances His kingdom (we are to manage His wealth for achieving God-given goals). If you are committed to making money-management decisions that reflect your firm convictions about those first three truths, you will have no problem understanding why our investing should also uphold His righteousness.

> *This, then, is how you should pray: "Our Father in heaven, hallowed be your name, your kingdom come, your will be done on earth as it is in heaven." (Matthew 6:9-10)*

It naturally follows that you will feel a solemn obligation to use your financial leverage to the maximum in order that His righteousness is revealed and upheld. No one will need to persuade you that it is a good thing. You will be grieved to think it would be otherwise.

> *Righteous are you, O LORD, and your laws are right. The statutes you have laid down are righteous; they are fully trustworthy. My zeal wears me out, for my enemies ignore your words. Your promises have been thoroughly tested, and your servant loves them. (Psalm 119:137-140)*

Our God is righteous. He does not need to conform to a righteous standard; He is the standard. Because He is righteous, we must regard what belongs to Him—our time, talents, and treasure—as consecrated for righteous purposes. The thought of turning God's wealth over to His enemies, to use against His glorious name and His church, should be abhorrent to the faithful steward. We must take care to avoid financing activities that lead others into temptation and sin.

> *Whoever welcomes a little child like this in my name welcomes me. But if anyone causes one of these little ones who believe in me to sin, it would be better for him to have a large millstone hung around his neck and to be drowned in the depths of the sea. Woe to the world because of the things that cause people to sin! Such things must come, but woe to the man through whom they come! (Matthew 18:5-7)*

Because the Lord is righteous, we have an obligation to withhold direct support, insofar as possible, from those businesses whose corporate activities either actively mock or passively undermine the biblical values that God has given as the basis for righteousness in society. I believe this can be done most effectively by boycotting their products and services (see sidebar, page 317). Withholding investment support from their stocks and bonds can also be helpful if done in a united fashion at the national level. Both of these strategies can play a role in the spending and investing decisions of every follower of Christ. ◆

CHAPTER PREVIEW

Investing That Glorifies God Seeks His Wisdom

The heavens declare the glory of God; the skies proclaim the work of his hands. Day after day they pour forth speech; night after night they display knowledge. There is no speech or language where their voice is not heard. Their voice goes out into all the earth, their words to the ends of the world. In the heavens he has pitched a tent for the sun, which is like a bridegroom coming forth from his pavilion, like a champion rejoicing to run his course. It rises at one end of the heavens and makes its circuit to the other; nothing is hidden from its heat.

The law of the LORD is perfect, reviving the soul.
The statutes of the LORD are trustworthy, making wise the simple.
The precepts of the LORD are right, giving joy to the heart.
The commands of the LORD are radiant, giving light to the eyes.
The fear of the LORD is pure, enduring forever.
The ordinances of the LORD are sure and altogether righteous.

They are more precious than gold, than much pure gold; they are sweeter than honey, than honey from the comb. By them is your servant warned; in keeping them there is great reward. Who can discern his errors? Forgive my hidden faults. Keep your servant also from willful sins; may they not rule over me. Then will I be blameless, innocent of great transgression. May the words of my mouth and the meditation of my heart be pleasing in your sight, O LORD, my Rock and my Redeemer.

(Psalm 19:1-14)

The last out. The eighteenth hole. The final buzzer. The checkered flag. The runner's tape. Match point.

In sports, all the players know where the "finish line" is. They can then train themselves and compete accordingly. But in the world of investing, very few clear rules are acknowledged by all the players. It's a kind of come-as-you-are, no-holds-barred event. You're free to participate without any preparation, training, or study of any kind. You don't need a doctor's certificate showing you're "financially fit" and able to afford the risk. Nor do you need a diploma as proof you've studied the disciplines involved and may actually know what you're doing. If you show up with a few dollars, you're almost invariably invited in.

This ease of entry usually makes people feel qualified to play. The financial media assure you that other everyday-folks with investment training similar to yours (that is, little or none) are making large sums with only minutes a day of effort. Surely, it can't be all that difficult. So you begin your playing days. That's what I was drawn to in the late 1960s, and it's what I returned to in the late 1970s.

Susie and I returned home to Kentucky just in time for Christmas 1974. We had reached a point in the growth and staffing of the new department I had helped build at Cru . . .

. . . that one of my assistants could now take over. The ministry-wide fundraising activities, such as direct mail, had been brought together under one coordinated strategy, and the Executive Seminars were going very well. Meanwhile, we were getting a little homesick for family and friends, not to mention Kentucky's cold winters and green summers. I wasn't eager to return to the restaurant business, but industry trends and cultural changes were beginning to threaten our long-term profitability—a hard look at our future plans and prospects was in order. Bill and Vonette Bright graciously gave us a "going away" party at their home. The pictures we still have of that evening always generate warm memories of the many friends we made on Cru staff during our time there.

The next few years of my life were primarily devoted to selling the family business. In one sense, it was a difficult decision to make. I was the third generation of our family to operate restaurants in Louisville; my grandfather had opened the first one in 1922. A family tradition that spans more than half a century is not easily abandoned. Yet, it was increasingly obvious that smaller "chains" like ours (we operated six restaurants) could not survive for long against the money and marketing muscle of the large national companies. It was quickly becoming an uphill battle to maintain our market share. Add to the equation that my heart wasn't really in it, and it seemed the most prudent course was to sell the business while it was still performing well. With the consent of my mother (who owned one-half of the stock), we began a process that took almost three years to complete.

On the day in 1977 when I walked away from closing the final sale of the last of the restaurants . . .

. . . I was a happy man. I was deeply in love with my wife and three boys (God gave us Matthew while we were living in California). I still had a fair amount of money in the bank (despite my past errors of judgment). I was healthy. And I was unemployed.

I took advantage of my free time to pursue my ministry interests. I enjoyed serving on the founding board of directors of Cru's Christian Embassy project in Washington, D.C. I was invited to be part of a group of businessmen and professional athletes who were starting a new training ministry—Pro Athletes Outreach—which was designed to "win, build, and send" pro players from the major sports. I started a Christian Business Men's Committee in Louisville. I had a lot of fun, and seeing the results from these efforts has been extremely satisfying. But our financial resources weren't so great that we could simply live off our investment income; I knew that I soon needed to make a career decision.

Initially, I didn't know what new direction my business life should take, but I did have a few thoughts as to the general framework. First, I recognized that my innate personality (according to the widely used Performax personal profile test) had a "perfectionist" bent. I'm the kind of person who gives attention to detail, has high quality standards, and likes to have an orderly working environment. Second, I considered my entrepreneurial background—I had always worked for my family or myself. Once I make a decision, I like to see it implemented quickly and efficiently. I didn't relish the thought of working within a slow-moving bureaucracy. Third, I determined that I would never again participate in any project where my success or failure primarily resided with someone else. I would never forget my $100,000 tennis racket and other souvenirs. If I was going to fail, it would be entirely due to my own shortcomings. Finally, I still had an interest in finance and the investment markets. *Is that appropriate?* I wondered. *Last time I had gotten involved, it had almost taken over my life. Would I be like an alcoholic opening a tavern?*

As Susie and I prayed about these matters, our thoughts eventually came together in a decision that I should form an investment advisory firm . . .

. . . with one of my closest friends, Doug Van Meter, as my partner. We had become fascinated with a style of investing known as "market timing." The idea is to sell all of your stock holdings and move to the safety of money-

Why do you call me "Lord, Lord," and do not do what I say? I will show you what he is like who comes to me and hears my words and puts them into practice. He is like a man building a house, who dug down deep and <u>laid the foundation on rock</u>. When a flood came, the torrent struck that house but could not shake it, because it was well built. But the one who hears my words and does not put them into practice is like a man who built a house on the ground without a foundation. The moment the torrent struck that house, it collapsed and its destruction was complete.
Luke 6:46–49

<u>All Scripture is God-breathed</u> and is useful for teaching, rebuking, correcting and training in righteousness, so that the man of God may be thoroughly equipped for every good work.
2 Timothy 3:16–17

For <u>the Lord gives wisdom</u>, and from his mouth come knowledge and understanding.
Proverbs 2:6

market funds when significant market weakness is anticipated. If you're correct, you not only pocket the interest earned while waiting out the downturn, but you get to buy back in at lower prices. In theory, it sounds great. In practice, it's very tough to do consistently well. (For more on market timing, see pages 151-153.)

Our company had a modest beginning. Doug moved into my existing office, bringing a few small accounts with him. We worked hard, traveling far and wide to sell our services to anyone willing to listen. Just as importantly, the market was kind to us. Our timing system worked very well—our average client account gained more than 32% *annually* during our first three years (compared to about 18% for the S&P 500 index). On the strength of that performance, we were able to move into deluxe quarters in the downtown financial district. We were on our way.

That was more than 30 years ago. Since that time, my understanding of the investing process has been shaped by the books and financial periodicals I have read, the up and down markets I have experienced, and the mistakes I have made (will they never end?). Most of this book has been devoted to laying down for you a foundational understanding of how investments and the various markets work. Unavoidably, the emphasis has been on the technical and logistical basics. In this chapter, I want to focus almost exclusively on what is needed in terms of *attitude* and *practice* to be successful. It has been fascinating for me to discover that these principles, many of which I learned the hard way, were to be found in God's Word all along if only I had known where to look! Wisdom for investments, and all of life, can be found in the Bible.

Perhaps the most difficult aspect of applying what follows is trying to erase from your mind the preconceived ideas you have about what it means to be a "savvy" investor. If you're like most people . . .

. . . you have accumulated years of impressions concerning financial wizardry from the secular world. Most of them, however, are nothing more than a collection of contradictions, misconceptions, and false assumptions. You must try to forget what you *think you know* so you can learn what you *need to know.*

As you read this chapter, I am hoping to change more than your opinions; I am hoping to begin changing your convictions. An opinion is merely your preference when choosing among several alternatives. It's when you prefer one type of vacation over another or prefer one music style over another music style. An opinion is merely a personal preference. But a conviction is rooted in your core values. Your convictions will not change without your values changing also. And the values you hold are what you draw from when setting personal boundaries. In *Changes That Heal*, psychologist Henry Cloud describes boundaries this way:

> *Boundaries, in a broad sense, are lines or things that mark a limit, bound, or border. In a psychological sense, boundaries are the realization of our own person apart from others. This sense of separateness forms the basis of personal identity. It says what we are and what we are not, what we will choose and what we will not choose, what we will endure and what we will not, what we*

feel and what we will not feel, what we like and what we do not like, and what we want and what we do not want. Boundaries, in short, define us. In the same way that a physical boundary defines where a property line begins and ends, a psychological and spiritual boundary defines who we are and who we are not.

So when I say I want to help change your convictions, I'm talking about a foundational part of your identity—how you see yourself spiritually and your moral responsibilities. It all follows from the earlier chapters in this section: because God is the glorious Creator/Sovereign and we are the creature/stewards, we see knowing Him as the true treasure, and because we cherish Him, it is our heart's desire to advance His kingdom and uphold His righteousness.

What convictions do I hope to change? The ones that have crept in from worldly "wisdom." Convictions that say it's OK . . .

. . . or merely a matter of personal preference whether you borrow to invest, invest in limited partnerships that involve cosigning for debt, frequently adjust your portfolio in response to changing world events, always seek the maximum return, or invest for short-term results. Such tactics may occasionally be profitable, but more often they are self-destructive. In any event, they go against God's wisdom as given to us in His Word. We need to learn to think with new minds in order to understand His will.

> *I urge you, brothers, in view of God's mercy, to offer your bodies as living sacrifices, holy and pleasing to God — this is your spiritual act of worship. Do not conform any longer to the pattern of this world, but be transformed by the renewing of your mind. Then you will be able to test and approve what God's will is — his good, pleasing and perfect will.* (Romans 12:1-2)

As we renew our minds, we not only see more clearly who God is; we also gain insight into our own natures.

As investors, we are our own worst enemies. This observation stems not only from my many years of practical experience, but also is confirmed by God's Word. Given our fallen natures, it would be surprising if we *weren't* the primary problem we face when investing. Consider for a moment the kind of people we are. The failings of our wisdom, our motives, our emotions, and our clarity of vision are well documented in the Scriptures.

- **Our wisdom is flawed.**

> *Let no person deceive himself. If any one among you supposes that he is wise in this age, let him become a fool [let him discard his worldly discernment and recognize himself as dull, stupid and foolish, without true learning and scholarship], that he may become [really] wise. For this world's wisdom is foolishness (absurdity and stupidity) with God.* (1 Corinthians 3:18-19, Amplified)

- **Our motivations are impure.**

> *The heart is deceitful above all things, and it is exceedingly perverse and corrupt and severely, mortally sick! Who can know it [perceive, understand, be acquainted with his own heart and mind]?* (Jeremiah 17:9, Amplified)

• **Our emotions are powerful.**

For I know that nothing good dwells within me, that is, in my flesh. I can will what is right, but I cannot perform it. I have the intention and urge to do what is right, but no power to carry it out. (Romans 7:18, Amplified)

• **Our vision is limited.**

Come now, you who say, "Today or tomorrow we will go into such and such a city and spend a year there to carry on our business and make money." Yet you do not know [the least thing] about what may happen tomorrow. . . . You boast [falsely] in your presumption and your self-conceit. (James 4:13-14, 16, Amplified)

As we renew our minds, we can begin to put proper boundaries in place that not only define our Christian priorities and values but *will also serve to protect us from the markets and ourselves.* The reason for having an individualized investment strategy is to provide these needed boundaries.

You begin by acknowledging that you need help. Your financial life has no central focus. You make decisions as situations arise based on what you've read is best, what a friend says is best, or just by throwing a dart and hoping for the best. You find yourself tugged in all directions, looking something like this:

Having a specific strategy in place helps *contain and focus* your impulses by providing boundaries. It boxes you in and takes away your freedom to do what you might want. But it offers a new kind of freedom—the freedom to do what you should. It gives you a sense of perspective and a new way of knowing what's "right" for you. The illustration on the next page shows four biblically based boundaries to a focused investment strategy: objective, mechanical criteria for decision making; a portfolio that is broadly diversified; a long-term, get-rich-slow perspective; and a manager's (rather than owner's) mentality. Let's now look at how these boundaries come into play in practical ways in everyday situations.

Boundary One:

Using mechanical guidelines rather than your own intuition and judgment.

He who trusts in himself is a fool, but he who walks in wisdom is kept safe. (Proverbs 28:26)

But the fruit of the Spirit is . . . self-control. (Galatians 5:22-23)

Mechanical guidelines require that you develop objective criteria to follow for your buying and selling decisions. One example would be to use the risk matrix (page 159) to select a specific mix of stocks and fixed-income investments. The allocations that are laid out for you provide explicit, objective boundaries to help you diversify according to your risk tolerance and age. They help make your investment shopping *purposeful*. Such boundaries protect you from giving in to sales presentations on some "really attractive" investment that you don't need at present.

Another example would be setting value criteria for timing your stock buying and selling. Using the price/earnings benchmark explained on page 153, you might decide to take profits in any stock once its P/E ratio reaches a certain predetermined level. Or you might look to buy underpriced stocks when the P/E is near the low end of its historical range.

Guidelines can help you control your losses. When you buy a stock or fund that doesn't perform as you hope, it can be difficult emotionally to admit it didn't work out. People often hold onto weak companies for years hoping to sell when they can "get even." This is a form of denial; the loss has already taken place. This emotional trap can be avoided by a mechanical guideline that says, "I'll sell if it drops x% from where I bought it because if it gets that low, there's a probability I misjudged the situation."

The dollar-cost-averaging strategy (see chapter 15) uses mechanical guidelines to help you know how much to invest and when. The discipline imposed by these programs is helpful because our judgment tends to be unduly influenced by news events of the moment. There will always be bad news, but news is rarely as bad or good as it might first appear. These guidelines protect you from overreacting (along with everyone else) to the crisis or euphoria of the moment.

The markets go to extremes because they are driven by emotions, not reason. Also, professional money managers are afraid of getting left behind and looking bad (they want job security too, you know), so they go along with the crowd and panic like everyone else. Mechanical guidelines help you harness the powerful emotions that often cause investors to do precisely the wrong thing at precisely the wrong time. Mechanical rules may appear dull, but that's actually a virtue—the most successful market strategies tend to be dull because they are measured, not spontaneous.

Before leaving the subject of emotions, may I suggest another idea about how to remain objective? Don't give investment advice to friends and family, and don't tell them what your investment holdings are. It's not a question of secrecy; it's the tendency you'll have to lose your objectivity about the investments in question. It's important to remain flexible and follow your guidelines, right? But how can you take a loss in this great stock or fund that you've told everybody about? You might find yourself thinking, *This is humiliating. Everybody will think I'm an idiot. Better to at least wait until I can get out at "break-even" so I can save face.* Oops, that's exactly the kind of emotional decision-making you want to avoid.

Boundary Two:
Building a broadly diversified portfolio to protect against the uncertainties of the future.

> *Give portions to seven, yes to eight, for you do not know what disaster may come upon the land.* (Ecclesiastes 11:2)

> *But the fruit of the Spirit is . . . peace.* (Galatians 5:22)

Acknowledging our limited vision is to remember the reality check from *Jurassic Park* (page 272). Be honest with yourself and say, "Not only do I not know what the future holds, none of the experts do, either." Since we don't (and can't) know the future, we can never know in advance with certainty which investments will turn out most profitably. That is the rationale for diversifying—spreading out your portfolio into various areas so that you won't be overinvested in any hard-hit areas and you'll have at least some investments in the most rewarding areas.

Once you accept that "nobody knows," it makes a lot of sense to diversify and relax. Then you're free to:

• **Ask hard questions of anyone trying to sell you an investment.** Make them support and document every assertion, promise, or guarantee. You don't need to let them intimidate you anymore, because you know the truth: nobody knows for sure, no matter how confident they sound, whether what they're recommending will truly turn out to be the best for you. Then, before you act, review the decision-making guidelines I suggested on page 312.

• **Ignore all forecasts by the "experts." They're guessing.** There's a kind of Newton's Law of Motion for economics: For every forecast by a group of experts with impressive credentials, there's an equal and opposite forecast by another group of experts with equally impressive credentials. Besides, if you've ever noticed, most forecasts seem to assume that the current trends (whatever they are) will continue. If they *were* to have any value, we'd need to know when the current trends will be reversed.

• **Ignore the media's explanations for why the markets are acting as they are. They're rationalizing.** Almost every item of economic news has both positive and negative implications, depending on what you want. For example, lower interest rates are good news if you're a borrower, bad news if you're a saver; a strong dollar is good news for importers, bad news for exporters. When the news is released, the media watch the markets' reactions. The next day, they merely emphasize *that aspect of the news* that the markets paid most attention to. If lower rates cause the stock market to go up, the media say it's because low rates are good for the economy; if the market goes down, the media say it's because low rates encourage renewed inflation. You should recognize that the media's explanations of market behavior are merely after-the-fact rationalizations.

• **Ignore most of the direct mail that you receive promoting an investment advisory letter. They're grossly exaggerating.** I'm talking primarily about the ones with the bold-letter "hype" that promise easy or guaranteed profits due to their consistent accuracy in making predictions about the markets. Such claims are deceptive—every newsletter writer is correct in some of his expectations and wrong about others. Some are right more than they're wrong, but nobody is consistently right. There's always a possibility that you can lose your money in the markets—it's irresponsible to imply otherwise. Such claims by any newsletter writer (or broker or anyone else) should immediately raise a red flag in your mind and call his credibility into question.

Boundary Three:
Developing a long-term, get-rich-slow perspective.

Dishonest money dwindles away, but he who gathers money little by little makes it grow. (Proverbs 13:11)

But the fruit of the Spirit is . . . patience. (Galatians 5:22)

Fewer things cause investors more losses than a short-term, get-rich-quick orientation to decision making. Patience, a fruit of the Spirit, is in short supply among investors today. Many have the attention span of a strobe light. A long-term view is extremely productive when investing; such a perspective has three major benefits:

❶ **It allows you time to do first things first.** I've already discussed the importance of being debt-free and having an emergency fund before proceeding into stocks, bonds, and other investments (other than those in your retirement plans). Once that foundation is laid, you can handle market risk with greater confidence. In the face of market setbacks, a long-term view says, "I'm investing with my surplus funds. This sell-off is no threat to my immediate well-being. I've got time to be patient and wait for the recovery."

❷ **It allows you to let those "once-in-a-lifetime, you-don't-want-to-miss-this-one-but-you-must-act-now" deals go by.** You've got plenty of time, and you don't want to invest in anything you haven't had time to carefully investigate and pray about. Trust me—there's always another day and another "great deal."

❸ **It allows you to be more relaxed when your judgment turns out less than perfect (surprise!).** For example, those times when the stock you just bought goes lower (which it always will) or the one you just sold goes even higher (which it always will). Why let that frustrate you? In your saner moments, you know it's extremely unlikely you're going to buy at the exact low or sell at the exact high. Taking the long view says, "It doesn't matter whether I bought at $14 when I could have bought at $12. The important thing is that I followed my plan. Over time, I know my plan will get me where I want to go."

Boundary Four:
Accepting management responsibility for your decisions, which leads you to study the basics and seek counsel when making important decisions.

> *Every prudent man acts out of knowledge, but a fool exposes his folly.* (Proverbs 13:16)
>
> *But the fruit of the Spirit is . . . faithfulness.* (Galatians 5:22)

Ultimately, you are accountable for what happens. You have been given a steward-ship responsibility that you cannot delegate away. You can delegate *authority* to someone else to make certain investment decisions, but you cannot delegate your *responsibility* for the results that come from those decisions.

Once you "own" this fact, you will take your management obligations even more seriously. Many Christians do not see themselves as "investors" simply because they don't have large stock portfolios. I believe they have a misconception as to what invest-ing involves. As I pointed out earlier, *investing decisions involve deciding what you will do without today in order that you might have more of something later.*

Cutting back on your spending (sacrifice convenience/luxury) in order to get debt-free (gain peace of mind and freedom) is an investing decision. Buying a used car rather than a new one (sacrifice status and ego) in order to start saving for a house someday (gain shelter and security) is an investing decision. Keeping your savings in money-market funds instead of bond funds (sacrifice yield) in order to have your principal safe (gain stability and flexibility) is an investing decision.

Knowing that managing this part of your life responsibly is a God-given task will help you to become more realistic about your needs in these key areas:

• **More realistic about your need for additional knowledge.** You accept that you must learn certain financial and investing basics. You can't just say, "Oh, I don't have the time (or interest or intellect) for that." You understand that some study will be necessary.

• **More realistic about the limitations of what investing can accomplish for you.** As you study, you learn that rates of return over the long haul tend to be in the 8%-10% range, not 15%-20% as many imagine. The idea that you will readily make large returns to bail you out of your problems is a dream. And mixed in that 8%-10% average will be good years (gains of 20% to 40%) and bad years (losses of 20% to 40%). It's not a smooth road.

• **More realistic about the strengths and weaknesses of the investment industry.** The industry does not have your best interests, first and foremost, at heart. It is awash in conflicts of interest (brokers get paid for selling securities, publishers get paid for selling magazines, financial networks get paid for attracting viewers). Your naïveté will dimin-ish as you develop a healthy skepticism. On the plus side, America is still a land of great economic opportunity for those who are willing to diligently apply themselves and who do not easily give up.

• **More realistic about the markets themselves.** You'll no longer believe that "the pros" know something you don't, and you'll see the widely erratic swings as being evidence of emotionalism rather than calm reason. You'll discover there are few absolutes, other than preservation of your capital and survival, to guide you as you navigate the tumultuous storms and cross-currents.

These doses of realism will be very, very good for you.

We can't avoid taking risks.

Life is filled with uncertainties. Even getting out of bed in the morning and driving to work is not without its risks. But we can manage our financial affairs so that when the unexpected comes along, we can isolate the damage it does. The blueprint for planning in this manner is given to us in the Scripture, and it is incorporated into the strategies taught in this book. Know where you're going. Avoid debt. Spend less than you earn. Save for the future. Diversify your investments. Exercise self-control and stay with your plan.

In his book *Storm Shelter*, financial planner Ron Blue points out that while economic uncertainty is certain, God's principles are adequate for our protection. They've been tested through the centuries and never found wanting.

The picture is as clear in my mind as it was nearly thirteen years ago. As I pulled off the interstate en route to my office, I did not see the road markers; instead my eyes swam with the signs of the times.

The year was 1982. Interest and inflation rates had soared to all-time highs, investors faced crushing 70 percent tax brackets, and the price of gold leapfrogged daily. Taking stock of the situation, most analysts warned of a devastating financial explosion within the next few years.

As I drove to work that day, the economic consequences seemed both crippling and inevitable. I had just launched our investment and financial counseling firm. How, I wondered, were we supposed to respond to the clients who came to us for advice? Could anyone afford to purchase a home with 15 to 20 percent interest rates? Which kinds of investments and tax plans could stand up to double-digit inflation? And if the predicted monetary collapse did occur, would the resulting political turmoil uproot even the best-laid financial plans?

One of my fears as I navigated the interstate highway that day was that we faced a "worst-ever" economic climate. Yet economic uncertainty — and its accompanying effects on our sense of security and well-being — are nothing new.

Ten years earlier, in 1972, we had been saddled with Watergate and an oil crisis that threatened to throttle the world's economy. Who can forget the lines at the gas stations or the rationing of fuel oil that winter? Then, too, I remember being hit with wage and price controls for the first time since World War II. And for the first time in my memory, the prime rate hit ten percent. Economic security seemed an elusive, if not impossible, dream.

Ten years before that, in 1962, the specter of economic and political uncertainty had hovered in every corner of the world. Our amazement at seeing a shoe-pounding Nikita Khrushchev vow to "bury" us turned to horror as the Cuban missile crisis unfolded. At that point a nuclear holocaust seemed at least possible, if not imminent. And Vietnam lay just around the corner . . .

In 1952, in the shadow of the spread of Communism, amid the mud and blood of the Korean War, bomb shelters were among the best-selling items in the United States. In 1942, we faced Pearl

Harbor and felt the full force of our entry into World War II. In 1932 we awoke to the nightmare of the Great Depression.

And on and on and on. The point is that we will always face uncertainty. Suddenly, I felt the subconscious click of the proverbial light bulb: The biblical principles of money management I had been teaching and using for years would work under any economic scenario. Armed with these concepts, I knew exactly how to help our clients weather the coming storm, no matter how hard the financial winds blew.

The predicted financial blowout never did occur. Yet as our business grew in the years that followed, we faced a thousand different financial situations that seemed specially tailored to test the worth and endurance of the money-management concepts our firm espoused. But in each and every case the biblical principles held fast, strengthening our clients' economic positions — and bringing them peace and security in the bargain.

Investing that glorifies God seeks His wisdom.

The wisdom found in God's Word is there for our protection and His glory. In financial matters, it points to God Himself as our true treasure and helps us see that *we* are the ones who suffer when we seek our treasure elsewhere.

Let's not settle for the creation when we can have the Creator.

Let's not settle for the temporal when we can have the eternal.

Let's not settle for knowing man's wisdom when we can know God's wisdom — Christ Himself.

Where is the wise man? Where is the scholar? Where is the philosopher of this age? Has not God made foolish the wisdom of the world? For since in the wisdom of God the world through its wisdom did not know him, God was pleased through the foolishness of what was preached to save those who believe. Jews demand miraculous signs and Greeks look for wisdom, but we preach Christ crucified: a stumbling block to Jews and foolishness to Gentiles, but to those whom God has called, both Jews and Greeks, Christ the power of God and the wisdom of God. For the foolishness of God is wiser than man's wisdom, and the weakness of God is stronger than man's strength.

Brothers, think of what you were when you were called. Not many of you were wise by human standards; not many were influential; not many were of noble birth. But God chose the foolish things of the world to shame the wise; God chose the weak things of the world to shame the strong. He chose the lowly things of this world and the despised things — and the things that are not — to nullify the things that are, so that no one may boast before him. It is because of him that you are in Christ Jesus, who has become for us wisdom from God — that is, our righteousness, holiness and redemption. Therefore, as it is written: "Let him who boasts boast in the Lord." (1 Corinthians 1:20-31)

May God grant us the grace to know Him. To seek for nothing else, and to settle for nothing less. ◆

CHAPTER PREVIEW

Investing That Glorifies God Enjoys His Blessings

Delight yourself in the LORD and he will give you the
desires of your heart. Commit your way to the LORD; trust
in him and he will do this: He will make your righteousness
shine like the dawn, the justice of your cause like the noonday sun.

(Psalm 37:4-6)

As the Scripture says, "Anyone who trusts in him will never
be put to shame." For there is no difference between Jew and Gentile—
the same Lord is Lord of all and richly blesses all who call on him.

(Romans 10:11-12)

[The gifts you sent] are a fragrant offering, an acceptable sacrifice,
pleasing to God. And my God will meet all your needs
according to his glorious riches in Christ Jesus.
To our God and Father be glory forever and ever. Amen.

(Philippians 4:18-20)

I have concluded that I have very little ability to discern what is valuable in life and what isn't.

I don't always see clearly which experiences are blessings and which ones do me harm. In fact, it's probably safe to say that I really don't even know—with complete certainty—what I truly want.

That being the case, one of the most exciting steps I can take is to pray and ask God for things. I neither know which requests He'll grant nor have the slightest insight into how He'll work through circumstances in granting those requests He does. But I'm learning it's usually in the most improbable and unexpected ways.

After about five years of hard work, Doug and I had built our advisory business to what could fairly be called a "successful" level. Our investment performance results had frequently placed in the top 5% among advisers nationwide. Money goes where it's treated best, and we had attracted enough clients to the point that we were both taking home six-figure incomes. Plus, I still had time for my ministry interests. All in all, things were working out pretty well.

Then, starting around 1985, I entered a period where I seemed to have the reverse Midas touch. In about a three-year span, my financial roof fell in thanks to a variety of unrelated events: a home that took three years to sell, unprecedented losses in my personal futures trading account, and a costly business venture in South Carolina, to name a few.

The summer of 1987 was the worst period of my business life. In April, with the Dow around 2,300, we had sold all stock funds and placed our clients 100% into money market funds. We did this because we felt the market had risen too far, too fast. The environment had become one of high risk. As the Dow continued to make new highs over the summer months (and everybody "knew" it was going to 3,000), we began losing clients to other firms who had no such reservations about risk. Our warnings to our departing clients fell on deaf ears. I'm sure many felt we were out of touch with the realities of the market. In truth, they and their new money managers were the ones out of touch, as the October crash violently demonstrated. In a single day, the Dow Jones dropped 23%, and it did not recover to its former level for two years. The crash vindicated our caution, but it was too late to stabilize our client base. The defections dealt a major blow to our company and required Doug and me to take drastic salary cuts and make other expense-related adjustments.

So there I was facing substantial business and personal financial pressures that I would never have dreamed of a few years earlier. And I was asking . . .

. . . "Lord, why is this happening to me? I travel and speak in Your name. I work and give diligently for Your causes. How come You're treating me like this? Please get me out of this mess. Please reassure me that everything's going to be all right. Please let me know that You're still here with me."

You know what the Lord said to me?

Nothing. I've never heard from the Lord *directly* in all my life. I know some people who have, but I never have. However, the Lord does speak to me by giving me ideas and impressions as I read and meditate in His Word. And, over time, the answer to my pleading questions came. It was as if He said:

"You prayed that you could become mature, didn't you? I'm teaching you how to depend on Me more."

"You prayed for more faith, didn't you? I'm giving you a chance to trust Me more."

"You prayed that you could be used to minister to others, didn't you? I'm training you so you can serve Me more."

"You prayed that you might know Me better, didn't you? I'm helping you to seek Me more."

"You prayed that you might glorify Me with your life, didn't you? I'm refining you more."

When we pray prayers that contain such "spiritual" requests, we can have confidence we're praying according to God's will. We expect Him to grant us, in His own timing, these qualities of the Christian life we're seeking. But I think that subconsciously we must believe that God answers them with a kind of supernatural lightning bolt. Something like, "Well, bless your heart, child, here's all the faith, love, and Christlikeness you'll ever need." Zap!

Well, unfortunately, it usually doesn't work that way.

Do you want to mature in your Christian walk? Then expect some suffering.

Not only so, but we also rejoice in our sufferings, because we know that suffering produces perseverance; perseverance, character; and character, hope. And hope does not disappoint us, because God has poured out his love into our hearts by the Holy Spirit, whom he has given us. (Romans 5:3-5)

Do you want your to be faith strengthened? Then expect it to be tested.

Consider it pure joy, my brothers, whenever you face trials of many kinds, because you know that the testing of your faith develops perseverance. Perseverance must finish its work so that you may be mature and complete, not lacking anything. (James 1:2-4)

Do you want God to use you to minister to others? Then expect God to first comfort you during your own pain.

Praise be to the God and Father of our Lord Jesus Christ, the Father of compassion and the God of all comfort, who comforts us in all our troubles, so that we can comfort those in any trouble with the comfort we ourselves have received from God. (2 Corinthians 1:3-4)

Do you want to know God better? Then expect to give up the things of this world that are holding you back.

But whatever was to my profit I now consider loss for the sake of Christ. What is more, I consider everything a loss compared to the surpassing greatness of knowing Christ Jesus my Lord, for whose sake I have lost all things. I consider them rubbish, that I may gain Christ and be found in him. . . . I want to know Christ and the power of his resurrection and the fellowship of sharing in his sufferings. (Philippians 3:7-10)

Do you want to glorify Him with your life? Then expect to go through trials.

In this you greatly rejoice, though now for a little while you may have had to suffer grief in all kinds of trials. These have come so that your faith — of greater worth than gold, which perishes even though refined by fire — may be proved genuine and may result in praise, glory and honor when Jesus Christ is revealed. (1 Peter 1:6-7)

Most Christians, at one time or another, will ask God why He allows pain, suffering, and disappointment . . .

. . . to touch His children (in general) and touch *us* (in particular). When we meet the Lord face-to-face, we'll have an opportunity to ask Him in person (although seeing His glory may be all the answer we need). I wouldn't be surprised if part of the answer turns out to be: "Those things happened *because I was answering your prayers, in order to give you what you asked for.*"

As I began to gain an insight into this, I found myself uplifted. Trials are all the more difficult if they seem to be needless or a waste. Once you begin to see that they are purposeful, it's a great thing because then you know that (1) they will come to an end when the purpose is accomplished, (2) you will somehow, in some way, have gained something of great value, and (3) you will have glorified God by trusting Him and giving Him time to work.

A passage that encouraged me during this time was Jeremiah 29:10-14. God was revealing to the Israelites why they were having the excruciating experience of being taken as slaves into the Babylonian captivity.

¹⁰This is what the LORD says: "When seventy years are completed for Babylon, I will come to you and fulfill my gracious promise to bring you back to this place. ¹¹For I know the plans I have for you," declares the LORD, "plans to prosper you and not to harm you, plans to give you hope and a future. ¹²Then you will call upon me and come and pray to me, and I will listen to you. ¹³You will seek me and find me when you seek me with all your heart. ¹⁴I will be found by you," declares the LORD, "and will bring you back from captivity."

Here are the encouraging truths I found in these verses:

• Trials eventually come to an end, and God can be absolutely counted upon to fulfill His promises (verse 10).

• God is still thinking about us, even when we're feeling lonely in our trials (verse 11). He is listening to our heartfelt prayers (verse 12).

• The only thoughts that God has toward us are thoughts of peace that include a future that is hopeful and good (verse 11).

• God allows our trials to come because they are necessary to accomplish His purpose in our lives (verse 11).

• God's purpose is that we would seek Him (verse 13).

• God allows Himself to be found when we search for Him with all our heart. He purposes to ultimately bring about our restoration (verses 13-14).

In this passage, the Israelites have been removed from their land and torn from their possessions, yet God does not tell them to seek the restoration of their land. He does not tell them to seek their possessions. He does not tell them to seek their freedom. He tells them to seek but one thing—Himself. And one way that God has of causing us to seek Him wholeheartedly is by allowing us to lose those other things that we highly prize.

So I knew I needed to seek God, be patient, and wait. I *wanted* to please God; I wanted to trust God. But the circumstances . . .

. . . around me were so utterly discouraging. It's not always easy to expect the best and believe that everything will work out for our good. To the Israelites in exile, 70 years must have seemed like an eternity, and three years can seem like 70 when you're badly hurting.

I concentrated my devotional times in books that gave me hope. I repeatedly read Job and the Psalms. In addition to Scripture, I read *The God of All Comfort* by Hannah Whitall Smith. I read Amy Carmichael. I read *Disappointment With God* by Philip Yancey. I read *Desiring God* by John Piper. They were all very encouraging.

During this time, I discovered what it means to give to God out of my poverty rather than out of my surplus. In the 1970s, Susie and I had volunteered two years of our lives to a form of missionary service. But the gift of those two years in the 1970s paled in comparison to the effort of even one week of walking with God during the tough times in the 1980s and saying to Him, "I still love You. I still trust You. I am not offended. I am doing the very best I can to believe You are working everything out together for my good." The two years were given when I was on top and life was good; each week was given when I was on the bottom and circumstances were bleak. In a fashion similar to the widow and her mite, I believe a single week of "hoping against hope" can be more pleasing and glorifying to God than a two-year missionary journey.

Perhaps you have had occasion to survey the landscape of your life and found very little evidence that God has "plans to prosper you and not to harm you, plans to give you a hope and a future."

May I encourage you to immerse your mind daily in words that will help you to know God more intimately and that will remind you that your God is always present, invariably loving, inevitably faithful, and absolutely worthy of

Recommended Resource

The Pleasures of God: Meditations on God's Delight in Being God

by John Piper

Published by Multnomah Books, Copyright 2000.

This is one of my very favorite books! Starting with Scriptures that show our God is a happy God, John Piper goes on to look at various aspects of God's happiness. Chapters include:

• The Pleasure of God in His Son,

• The Pleasure of God in His Creation,

• The Pleasure of God in the Prayers of the Upright,

and the one I quote from on this page,

• The Pleasures of God in Doing Good to All Who Hope in Him.

Understanding what gives God pleasure may enable you to know our glorious God better than you have ever known Him before.

Visit John Piper's Desiring God Ministries web site at www.desiringgod.org.

all your confidence. Consider the promises of God found later in Jeremiah: God is revealing in greater detail what it will be like when the trial His people are going through in Babylon has served its purpose. God declares in Jeremiah 32:

> They will be my people, and I will be their God. I will give them singleness of heart and action, so that they will always fear me for their own good and the good of their children after them. I will make an everlasting covenant with them: I will never stop doing good to them, and I will inspire them to fear me, so that they will never turn away from me. I will rejoice in doing them good and will assuredly plant them in this land with all my heart and soul. (Jeremiah 32:38-41)

Those are tremendous promises. In sharing His father's heart, God promises He will "never stop doing good" to you. In *The Pleasures of God*, John Piper looks at the passage this way:

> He will keep on doing good. He doesn't do good to his children sometimes and bad to them other times. He keeps on doing good and he never will stop doing good for ten thousand ages of ages. When things are going "bad" that does not mean God has stopped doing good. It means he is shifting things around to get them in place for more good, if you will go on loving him. He works all things together for good "for those who love him" (Romans 8:28). "No good thing does he withhold from those who walk uprightly" (Psalm 84:11). "Lo, it was for my welfare that I had great bitterness" (Isaiah 38:17). "It is good for me that I was afflicted, that I might learn your statutes" (Psalm 119:71). . . .
>
> But the promise is greater yet. Not only does God promise not to turn away from doing good to us, he says, "I will rejoice in doing them good" (Jeremiah 32:41). "The LORD will again take delight in prospering you" (Deuteronomy 30:9). He does not bless us begrudgingly. There is a kind of eagerness about the beneficence of God. He does not wait for us to come to him. He seeks us out, because it is his pleasure to do us good. "The eyes of the LORD run to and fro throughout the whole earth, to show his might in behalf of those whose heart is whole toward him" (2 Chronicles 16:9). God is not waiting for us, he is pursuing us. That, in fact, is the literal translation of Psalm 23:6, "Surely goodness and mercy shall pursue me all the days of my life." God loves to show mercy. He is not hesitant or indecisive or tentative in his desires to do good to his people. His anger must be released by a stiff safety lock, but his mercy has a hair trigger. . . .
>
> But still the promise is greater. First, God promises not to turn away from doing us good. Then he promises that he will do this good with rejoicing. Finally, he promises that this rejoicing over the good of his people will be with all his heart and with all his soul. . . . When God does good to his people it is not so much like a reluctant judge showing kindness to a criminal whom he finds despicable; it is like a bridegroom showing affection to his bride. And add to this, that with God the honeymoon never ends. He is infinite in power and wisdom and creativity and love. And so he has no trouble sustaining a honeymoon level of intensity; he can foresee all the future quirks of our personality and has decided he will keep what's good for us and change what isn't; he will always be as handsome as he ever was, and will see to it that we get more and more beautiful forever; and he is infinitely creative to think

of new things to do together so that there will be no boredom for the next trillion ages of millenniums. . . .

When we say that God exults over his people with loud singing, we mean that he exults over those who hope in his love. In this way God maintains his rightful place — the place we love for him to have — at the center of the gospel. There is a condition we must meet in order to know him as our God and be a part of the wonderful covenant in which he never turns away from doing us good but rejoices over us with all his heart and all his soul. That condition is to put our hope in him as the all-satisfying Refuge and Treasure. God takes pleasure in this response with all his heart, because it magnifies the glory of his grace and satisfies the longing of our soul.

As I sought the Lord during those days, I opened my heart to whatever He had purposed for me. I had previously assumed I would continue in the investment advisory profession for the remainder of my career; now I wasn't so sure. Perhaps the Lord was using these difficult circumstances to change the direction of my working life. As long as I was financially comfortable and had a large client base, why would I consider anything else?

So, just in case a career change was part of His agenda, I surrendered to the Lord all aspects of my professional life. If He wanted to rebuild my company, that would be fine. If He wanted me to take a job working for someone else, that would be fine. If He wanted me to leave the business world and go back into full-time ministry work, that would be fine. I was finally in the best place for a child of God to be: "Whatever You want, Lord, before You even reveal it, the answer is yes." I added a brief P.S. "But what I'm really hoping for is work that's mentally challenging, emotionally satisfying, and that somehow involves a ministry to people."

The answer came unexpectedly (and unrecognized by me at the time) in October of 1989. I was having lunch with longtime friend Larry Burkett . . .

. . . and his ministry associate in charge of their counseling activities, Steve Humphrey. As we discussed the financial challenges facing the average Christian family, they felt what was lacking was a monthly investment newsletter with a truly Christian perspective. Larry said there was a great need for a reliable source of information, written with easy-to-understand, "user-friendly" wording, which would guide readers through the investment process step-by-step with instruction and counsel from a biblical perspective. It would help Christians make the varied and often complex investment decisions they face, as well as continually attempt to help its readers "renew their minds" with God's principles.

My initial response was, "You're right. Sounds great — too bad nobody's doing anything like that." It didn't occur to me that *I* should undertake the task — after all, I was an investment manager, not a writer or publisher. But as the weeks passed, the Lord seemed to keep bringing me back to Larry's comments. The number of investment services and products being offered today is mind-numbing in their variety.

The tendency is to feel overwhelmed. The need was obvious. So I began to pray. Though I agreed he had a great idea, I wondered whether I should be the one to do it.

I began to pray for wisdom: "Lord, do You want *me* to try to do this? Well, it would certainly be mentally challenging—I don't have much experience as a writer and none as a publisher. If I could succeed in encouraging my readers, it would be emotionally satisfying because I know from my own experience how important encouragement is in sustaining our hope during the tough times. And to the extent Christians get their finances and investments straightened out and give more to Your work, it would certainly have a ministry component. But Lord, I don't have the experience or the start-up money or the wisdom to pull this off—*I'd have to depend totally on You.*" Hmm. . . .

After many other closed doors and much prayer, Susie and I felt the Lord was indeed orchestrating events so that I would begin moving in that direction. At a time when I was wondering if I should go into publishing, it "just happened" that Doug and Gena Cobb, two of our best friends, had built a successful publishing business centered on a lineup of monthly computer software journals. Their company was the national leader in its field. Their counsel and prayers were invaluable. The first *Sound Mind Investing* newsletter was issued in July 1990.

SUMMARY OF SECTION SIX

God's wondrous and breathtaking glory
is the greatest theme in all the universe.

God is the sovereign/owner of all His creation, including us.
When we acknowledge His lordship in our lives, as is only reasonable, we
can begin to be transformed into His likeness by the renewing of our minds.

Renewed minds lead to new values.
We see Him as our great Treasure and seek Him as the source of our sufficiency.

Renewed minds lead to new motivations.
We want to invest our lives to see His kingdom built rather than
our own, to see Him receive the glory rather than ourselves.

Renewed minds lead to new ambitions.
We want to live a life worthy of the Lord and to uphold
His righteousness before an unbelieving world.

Renewed minds lead to new sources of wisdom.
We have a new commitment to His written Word and a
new passion for knowing Christ—the Wisdom of God.

Renewed minds lead us to new blessings.
We see Him as the giver of every good gift and learn to be
content with His purposes, which are always
for our good "to give us a future and a hope."

People are often curious as to how a "biblically-based" investment newsletter . . .

. . . differs from a "regular" one. I explain it this way. Society's perspective is that we came into existence strictly by chance. Accordingly, we are just animals seeking to fulfill our needs. Furthermore:

• The goal of work is to do whatever is necessary to achieve success. Indicators of success are the acquisition of money, possessions, and influence.

• Because life is short, lifestyles are geared to immediate gratification — gaining as much pleasure as possible as quickly as possible. This leads to higher consumption now and less saving for the future. A high level of debt and continuous use of credit is considered an acceptable means to this end.

• Investing is geared to get-rich-quick strategies with a short-term time horizon. The recessionary phases of economic cycles are dreaded and pose a constant threat to economic survival.

• Because there is no ultimate purpose or morality, we are free to invent our own. Ethics are relative and personal. They generally play little, if any, role in making spending or investing decisions.

Contrast these views with a biblical perspective that maintains we came into existence through the creative hand of God. We are essentially spirit beings with an eternal purpose. It follows that:

• The goal of work is to use our God-given talents to serve others or fulfill a calling. Indicators of success are peace with God, showing love for others, contentment in life.

• Because eternal life is possible, a lifestyle of deferred gratification that is focused on eternal issues is appropriate. This leads to less consumption now and more saving for the future and for giving to Christian ministry. A high level of debt and continuous use of credit is discouraged as an unnatural and enslaving lifestyle.

• Investing can be geared to slow-but-sure strategies with a long-term time horizon. Economic cycles are prepared for through a strategy of saving and diversification.

• Because God has a moral purpose for His creation, a law of sowing and reaping prevails. Ethics are based on Biblical wisdom and play an important role in making spending and investing decisions.

Jesus is almost universally regarded as the wisest moral teacher of all time, even by millions who do not consider themselves Christians. After finishing what we call "The Sermon on the Mount," he said, *"Everyone who hears these words of mine and does not put them into practice is like a foolish man who built his house on sand. The rain came down, the streams rose, and the winds blew and beat against that house, and it fell with a great crash"* (Matthew 7:26-27).

Although our society may be building on sand, at the personal and family level we still have the choice of preparing for the inevitable storms of life by following biblical principles. Take a good look around you. Rarely has the truth of the old hymn been so obvious: "On Christ, the solid Rock, I stand. All other ground is sinking sand, all other ground is sinking sand."

Nearly 25 years have now come and gone . . .

. . . since the day I bravely had 500 copies of the first issue printed. The start-up phase was physically demanding, emotionally satisfying, financially unprofitable, and spiritually fulfilling. The way in which events have unfolded have reminded Susie and me on several occasions that our God *"is able to [carry out His purpose and] do superabundantly, far over and above all that we [dare] ask or think [infinitely beyond our highest prayers, desires, thoughts, hopes or dreams] — To Him be glory in the church and in Christ Jesus throughout all generations, for ever and ever"* (Ephesians 3:20-21, Amplified).

One of the biggest surprises of my new publishing career has been the number of warm and encouraging letters I receive from my readers. They express appreciation for the fact that they are understanding certain financial and investing matters for the first time, and the new hope they have that they can really take control of their investment lives rather than relying on others. Their enthusiasm, and the number of them that say the newsletter "is an answer to prayer," is quite humbling. I mention this only to point out how wonderfully God answered my prayer that He would give me a ministry as well as a business. He has, and I've never felt so gratified by anything I've done in my professional life.

God is a loving Father to His children. If you're facing challenges, financial or otherwise, He can help you just as He helped me. Trust Him.

The story is told of the young Christian student who was distraught because of an argument he had with his girlfriend. He made an appointment to see the youth minister of his church for advice. When he arrived, his wise friend began their meeting with this prayer:

"Dear God of creation, who created the universe from nothing, scattered billions of stars at a mere word, engineered every favorable condition necessary to support life on this blue planet, populated the oceans and the lands with creatures of unimaginable variety and complexity, orchestrated all of nature and made man its master . . .

"God of Moses, who turned the mighty Nile into a river of blood, sent hordes of frogs, swarms of lice and flies, a plague of disease and boils, devastating hail, locusts that covered the sky, and the death of Egypt's firstborn in order to answer the prayers of his people for freedom. . .

"God of David, who with a river stone dropped a warrior giant to his death and made a shepherd boy a king . . .

"God of the disciples, who on Pentecost received Your power, spoke in other languages so 3,000 were baptized on one day, and then turned the world upside down for Christ . . .

"Father of Jesus, who made the blind see, the lame walk, lepers whole and the dead to rise, and gave His life to rescue those who were hopelessly dead in sin and made them alive to righteousness and eternal life . . .

"God of creation, God of history, God of the Bible, God Almighty . . . could You possibly be of some help with this young man's girlfriend? Amen."

When I heard this story, I couldn't help but smile. How like that young student I can be! Stopping for a moment to reflect on God's sovereign power—and His promise to use it always for my good if I'll put my trust in Him—puts my daily concerns into a whole new perspective.

In truth, my problems are so small, so transitory. And God is so big, bigger than I can possibly imagine. Surely, I trust Him for too little. Perhaps you do, too. If the youth minister had been praying for your concerns, how would he have closed his prayer?

• ". . . could You possibly show this couple how to get out of debt and save for the future as Your word commends?

- "... could You possibly lead this man to a job that would be a better fit for the way You've made him and for the financial and family needs that he has?"

- "... could You possibly enable this child of Yours to have victory over temptations and live a life that's honoring to You?"

- "... could You possibly help this widow to make wise investing decisions as she seeks to be a good steward of Your wealth?"

- "... could You possibly show this family how they can give even more to take the saving message of Christ to those who have never heard?"

Could He possibly? We know the answer is, "Of course!" He is the One about whom Jesus said *"with God all things are possible"* (Matthew 19:26).

Our part is to trust Him. We have it on the highest authority that *"Everything is possible for him who believes"* (Mark 9:23). And again, *"If you have faith as small as a mustard seed . . . Nothing will be impossible for you"* (Matthew 17:20).

There is one exception, however, one thing that God *has* declared is impossible for us: *"And without faith it is impossible to please God, because anyone who comes to him must believe that he exists and that he rewards those who earnestly seek him"* (Hebrews 11:6).

So let us seek Him, trusting Him to deliver us through the difficulties of life, remembering that we pray to a God who is too strong to ever lose control of any situation, too wise to ever make a mistake, and too loving to ever abandon us. Just the kind of God we need.

Investing that glorifies God enjoys His blessings.

As I indicated at the beginning of this chapter, it's a tricky matter to accurately discern which experiences in life will ultimately work for our good. The reason for this is not that bad things are necessarily good things in disguise, but rather our God is so great that He can take the bad things and *transform* them into good things. He does this because He purposes to use everything in life that we might "be conformed to the likeness of his Son."

Knowing that what appears good (wealth and success) can actually be bad for us, and that what appears bad ("trials of many kinds") can actually be good for us, gives one a certain humility in praying. This truth is beautifully expressed in the *Prayer of an Unknown Civil War Soldier:*

> I asked God for strength that I might achieve. I was made weak, that I might learn humbly to obey.
>
> I asked for help, that I might do greater things. I was given infirmity, that I might do better things.
>
> I asked for riches, that I might be happy. I was given poverty, that I might be wise.
>
> I asked for power, that I might have the praise of men. I was given weakness, that I might feel the need of God.
>
> I asked for all things, that I might enjoy life. I was given life, that I might enjoy all things.
>
> I got nothing that I asked for but everything I hoped for. Almost despite myself, my unspoken prayers were answered.
>
> I am, among all men, most richly blessed. *(Source Unknown)*

We're all looking for peace in an uncertain world. We don't know what the future holds, but we know who holds the future. Our trust in Him is never misplaced. Paul wrote: "For to me, to live is Christ, and to die is gain." Paul could say that because dying brought him even more of what he was living for. But today, if for us "to live is business success," then to die is loss. If for us "to live is financial riches," then to die is loss. If for us "to live is the praise of men," then to die is loss. Because dying takes all of those things away. On the day that we die, what wealth we may have will be of zero value to us, of no help or comfort whatsoever. But knowing Him will mean everything. And that's why He is our peace.

If you'll aim your life in the direction of God's glory, you'll enjoy His blessings. They may or may not be material blessings. But in whatever form God sends them, you can be sure they will satisfy your deepest longings. *"Praise be to the God and Father of our Lord Jesus Christ, who has blessed us in the heavenly realms with every spiritual blessing in Christ"* (Ephesians 1:3).

To conclude this section and my book, I've collected a few of the hundreds of promises God has made to you in His Word. Consider who you are and what you have, and give thanks!

- You are *a child of God*.
- You are *protected* by the name of Jesus.
- You have *peace* with God.
- You are *free from condemnation*.
- You have been *cleansed* by Christ's blood.
- You are a *joint heir* with Jesus Christ.
- You are *confident* that all things work together for your good.
- You are *inseparable from the love of God*.
- You have *eternal life* in Christ Jesus.
- You are *abiding in Christ;* Christ is abiding in you.
- You are *free of the vicious cycle* of sin and death.
- You are *adequate* for anything because your adequacy comes from God.
- You are *chosen* by God to be holy and blameless.
- You have *wisdom* and insight to know His will.
- You are able to walk boldly *into Christ's presence*.
- You are *strengthened* with His power through His spirit in the inner man.
- You *don't have to be anxious* about anything.
- You are *able to do all things through Christ* who strengthens you.
- You are *indwelt by Him* in whom all fullness dwells.
- You've been presented to God, *holy, blameless, and beyond reproach*.
- You are able to come boldly before His throne of grace and find *mercy* every time.
- *He who is in you is greater* than he who is in the world.
- You have not been given a spirit of fear, but of *power* and of *love* and of *a sound mind*.
- *You are complete in Christ!* ◆

SPECIAL
THANKS!

"In your hearts set apart Christ as Lord. Always be prepared to give an answer
to everyone who asks you to give the reason for the hope that you have."
(1 Peter 3:15)

We would not be able to progress very far in our Christian faith apart from the many acts of kindness shown to us by God's people. I have been immeasurably helped, encouraged, and inspired along the way by others who have lived out 1 Peter 3:15 to my benefit, many of whom have gone to be with the Lord in recent years. I want you to know of the debt I owe:

To those who introduced Susie and me to the Spirit-controlled life . . .

Bob McConnell—for coming and sharing the wonderful discovery of the Spirit-filled
life with us 43 years ago, and being an intercessor for us for many years.

Bill and Vonette Bright—for modeling the Christian life so powerfully that we knew, beyond
ever questioning again, that the gospel must be true. It is the only explanation for your lives.

To those who helped me to grow in my faith . . .

Sim and Mimi Fulcher—for becoming our beloved extended family in Christ.
Susie joins me in praising our Father for your faithful and generous love to us for 35+ years.

Ron Dunn—for helping me realize I was settling for service and that I must continue to
seek Christ; that it was possible to know Him, and know Him, and know Him some more.

John Piper—for helping me through his writings to understand
that God is most glorified in me when I am most satisfied in Him.

To those who have been partners in ministry . . .

Larry Burkett—whose creative thinking, gracious support, and ongoing encouragement
not only led to the birth of the *Sound Mind Investing* newsletter but its early survival as well.

Catharine Gividen, Vicki Mosher, Mark Biller, Joseph Slife, Kevin Woo,
Jon Renner, and Matt Bell — a God-given staff who have labored with great
dedication and excellence to provide a growing number of readers with biblical counsel.

To my sons and their wives . . .

What wonderful gifts you are to us! To have three terrific sons who have given
their lives to the Lord Jesus, and for you to have married precious women who
love Him as well. Tre, Andrew, and Matthew—thanks for the work you each
have done at various times in contributing to this book and the work here
at SMI, furthering, we trust, the reach of the gospel of Christ.

And most of all to Susie . . .

Other than our Lord, no one knows you like I do. Others don't know of your tenacity
and faithfulness in prayer. Or of the steadfast trust you have in His goodness even in the
face of crushing disappointments. Or of the deep love you have for His Word and the price
you have paid when standing firm in upholding it. But I know all these things and much more. And
so it is with great insight that I thank the Lord for giving me a wife of noble character.

"A wife of noble character who can find? She is worth far more than rubies.
Her husband has full confidence in her and lacks nothing of value."
(Proverbs 31:10-11)

TOPICAL INDEX

SCRIPTURE REFERENCES

A Parting Word of Encouragement

In the Introduction, I said that to find peace of mind in your investing, you need to become *an initiator* rather than *a responder*. Initiators have made the effort to develop a strategy that specifically takes into account their current financial condition, long-term goals, and personal investing temperament.

I hope you will use the information I've provided in this *Handbook* to develop your personal financial plan, and that you will faithfully allow it to guide your investment decision-making. Like tens of thousands of my readers, you can do this! You don't need to look to the "experts" like our friend nearby. After all, *"God has not given [you] a spirit of fear, but of power and of love and of a sound mind"* (2 Timothy 1:7 NKJV).

You've been equipped with what you need to know. Now, go and begin the process of taking charge of your financial future.

Cordially in Christ,

"That's it? Buy low and sell high?"